THIRD EDITION

LET'S BEGIN READING RIGHT

Developmentally Appropriate Beginning Literacy

MARJORIE V. FIELDS
University of Alaska Southeast

KATHERINE L. SPANGLER
University of Alaska Southeast

MERRILL,
an imprint of PRENTICE HALL
Englewood Cliffs, New Jersey   Columbus, Ohio

LIBRARY OF CONGRESS CATALOGING-IN-PUBLICATION DATA

Fields, Marjorie Vannoy.
    Let's begin reading right : developmentally appropriate beginning literacy / Marjorie V.
    Fields, Katherine L. Spangler.—3rd ed.
       p. cm.
    Includes bibliographical references and index.
    ISBN 0-02-337283-4
       1. Reading (Primary) 2. Child development. 3. Child—Language. 4. Reading—Language
    experience approach.   I. Spangler, Katherine. II. Title.
    LB1525.F43   1995
    372.4'1—dc20

                                                        94-18915
                                                            CIP

Cover photo: Werner Bokelberg/The Image Bank
Editor: Linda James Scharp
Production Editors: Laura Messerly and Linda Bayma
Text Design Coordinator: Julia Zonneveld Van Hook
Cover Designer: Susan Frankenberry
Production Buyer: Pamela D. Bennett
Electronic Text Management: Marilyn Wilson Phelps, Matthew Williams,
    Jane Lopez, Karen L. Bretz

This book was set in Century 731 by Prentice Hall and was printed and bound by R.R. Donnelley
& Sons Company. The cover was printed by Phoenix Color Corp.

© 1995 by Prentice-Hall, Inc.
A Simon & Schuster Company
Englewood Cliffs, New Jersey 07632

Earlier editions © 1991 by Macmillan Publishing Company and © 1987 by Merrill Publishing
Company.

Photo credits: p. 13, 122, 192, 193, 238, 250 by Richard Crisci; p. 65 by Gail Fleming; p. 92, 116,
163, 209 by David Gelotte; p. 9 by Bruce Johnson/Prentice Hall and Merrill; p. 188, 231 by Mary
Kancewick; p. 5, 23, 52 by Jean-Claude LeJeune; p. 15 by Tom Priest Photography; p. 222, 225,
228, 235, 242, 248, 317 by Katherine L. Spangler; all other photos by Marjorie V. Fields.

Printed in the United States of America

10 9 8 7 6 5 4 3 2 1

ISBN: 0-02-337283-4

Prentice-Hall International (UK) Limited, *London*
Prentice-Hall of Australia Pty. Limited, *Sydney*
Prentice-Hall of Canada, Inc., *Toronto*
Prentice-Hall Hispanoamericana, S. A., *Mexico*
Prentice-Hall of India Private Limited, *New Delhi*
Prentice-Hall of Japan, Inc., *Tokyo*
Simon & Schuster Asia Pte. Ltd., *Singapore*
Editora Prentice-Hall do Brasil, Ltda., *Rio de Janeiro*

PREFACE

This book reflects our many years of teaching language arts courses for teachers, always working at better ways of helping pre-service and in-service teachers incorporate new views of literacy into their own classrooms. It is often difficult for them to visualize the kinds of teaching and learning we recommend because these approaches were not common in their own educational backgrounds. Therefore, we have used extensive examples from actual classrooms to assist readers in understanding the teaching ideas presented.

Our recommendations for teaching literacy combine developmentally appropriate early childhood practice with current views of emergent literacy and whole language instruction. In addition, we link the early childhood, emergent literacy, and whole language research recommendations with constructivist learning theory. *Let's Begin Reading Right* constantly reminds readers of how young children learn, challenging them to use that understanding as the basis for teaching decisions.

We start by briefly explaining how children construct knowledge. Then we give some detail on how that process works with oral language acquisition, and we build on that to explain how youngsters come to understand and use written language. This theory base provides the foundation for all subsequent teaching descriptions and recommendations. We include numerous examples of children's writing as evidence of children's thinking and hypotheses as they progress in their knowledge of written language. Children in preschool through the primary grades are our main focus, though we briefly address infant and toddler literacy development.

We designed this book also to help the teacher of young children to understand and validate the importance of play in the child's literacy development. Oral language proficiency, symbolic representation concepts, and meaningful interaction with print are linked to play. We have made a special point of describing print-rich play environments that encourage youngsters to explore functional writing. Recommendations for providing a variety of experiences and oral language opportunities as part of helping children learn to read and write also encourage developmentally appropriate early childhood education practices. Teaching examples demonstrate the importance of an authentically integrated curriculum for meaningful involvement in literacy events.

In an attempt to dispel the pervasive misconception that skills are not taught in whole language approaches, we carefully explain reading and writing skills development within an emergent literacy whole language context. Answers to the inevitable questions about teaching phonics and spelling assure the fearful that their children are being helped to learn phonics and spelling in the most effective ways. Reading skills discussions emphasize the necessity of helping youngsters balance their focus on graphophonemic, semantic, and syntactical information when reading. We try to show that this balance is essential for maintaining a focus on meaning while reading. We also explain how writing skills—from learning to form letters of the alphabet to using punctuation effectively—are best learned through authentic reading and writing activities. We also offer a chapter that focuses entirely on selecting instructional materials for authentic reading and writing.

We discuss assessment procedures that are congruent with holistic approaches to literacy, and we give detailed examples of how effective teaching and assessment occur simultaneously. Chapter 8 explains performance-based assessment, documenting acquisition of literacy skills during children's meaningful involvement with print. This chapter also explains current assessment recommendations in terms of developmentally appropriate practice. We tried to dispel some common confusions about performance-based assessment by describing the various components involved. Detailed reading and writing instructional conference scenarios, in chapters 6 and 7 as well as 8, help in visualizing assessment as part of a child-centered approach to teaching.

CHANGES IN THE THIRD EDITION

As we worked on this revision, we were again amazed at how much classrooms had changed in the four years since the previous edition. These changes include the materials teachers use to teach, the level of diversity in classrooms, and the current "hot" issues. *Whole language* is no longer considered a new idea and thus has been adapted and interpreted in various and even conflicting ways. *Developmentally appropriate practices* has also become a common term, with many interpretations of its meaning. The diversity among teachers, families, and children that contributes to the United States' strength also fosters disagreement and misconception. We end this edition with a series of issues for discussion, hoping to engage readers in continued dialogue during their professional development.

Though we didn't plan on it, we rewrote most of the book for this edition. Sometimes it was changes in our own understanding and awareness that prompted the changes, while other times it was changes in the schools or additions to emergent literacy research. Our continued study and increased understanding of constructivist learning theory suggested some of the revisions implemented in this edition. Continued dialogue in the whole language research led to other refinements in our recommendations. Often it was our own students and their struggle to understand our message that prompted changes for clarification. We believe that all of these influences contribute to making each edition stronger than the one before.

We added Ms. Montoya's multiage classroom not just because we see so many teachers preferring this grouping, but also because it allowed us to emphasize teaching to individuals rather than to grade levels. We added more about teaching children with various backgrounds, cultures, and languages because we see teachers needing to know more about this than ever before. Similarly, children with special needs are included as part of the regular classroom focus in our discussions. Our review of instructional materials from textbook companies has changed due to the significant changes made by those companies. We continued to expand our coverage of holistic assessment because there are so many more options than previously. We enjoy continuing to grow and change and are pleased to be able to offer a new edition that reflects that.

ACKNOWLEDGMENTS

Marjorie Fields

I wish to thank the many teachers who let me learn in their classrooms, especially Kathy Hanna, Chris Thomas, and Vivian Montoya in Juneau, Alaska; Deborah Hillstead and Lori Irons in Vancouver, Washington; the teachers at Arleta, Sabin, and Irvington Schools in Portland, Oregon; and Sally Harper at Punahou School in Honolulu. The graduate and undergraduate students who used the manuscript as a text have also made major contributions to its clarity, serving as the response group for the polishing phase. Sue Oliphant and Martha Scott were especially helpful with suggestions for revision. Susan Ogden provided an incredible quantity and quality of clerical and research support for this project, with Linda Squibb and Ruth Ryan assisting significantly with the reference citations. I also wish to express appreciation for the sabbatical leave granted by my university, which allowed me to do this writing. Of course I must also thank my husband for constant support and patience during this project and always.

Katy Spangler

I wish to thank the many colleagues, teachers, and friends who have made this project possible. Many friends and neighbors provided child care while I worked. Students have given me valuable feedback on the previous edition. Richard Crisci and Mary Kancewick took many of the wonderful pictures in this book; and the teachers and children at Fire Lake Preschool, and Eagle River, Muldoon, Ursa Major, and Oceanview Elementary Schools allowed us in their rooms with our cameras. My family was patient with me. Connie Chambers, Bonnie Herbert, and Janice Summers welcomed me into their classrooms under the guise of volunteer while what I was really doing was collecting data for this book.

The authors also wish to thank the reviewers of this text: Linda Anderson, Northwestern Michigan College; Joyce S. Choate, Northeast Louisiana University; Michael P. Ford, University of Wisconsin-Oshkosh; Linda Leonard Lamme, University of Florida; and Tim Wilson, Sul Ross State University.

CONTENTS

1

UNDERSTANDING EMERGENT READERS AND WRITERS

2

Encouraging Emergent Literacy Through Play and Experiences   42

3

Encouraging Emergent Literacy Through Oral Language and Story Time   70

4
ASSISTING EMERGENT READERS   100

5
ASSISTING EMERGENT WRITERS   138

6

SUPPORTING INDEPENDENT WRITERS   182

10
CONSTRUCTING YOUR UNDERSTANDING 336

LET'S BEGIN
READING RIGHT

wus uponu tim thr wusz

u ceng cobu snak that wusz

hrand gud and hznam wos

huk he hd ufrad that wus a ping win

UNDERSTANDING EMERGENT READERS AND WRITERS

If a child has a theory, no matter how primitive, that child will pay attention to instances which confirm or contradict that theory.

ELEANOR DUCKWORTH, 1987

The first step in exploring how to help young children to become literate is knowing about children themselves. This first chapter focuses on how children learn, how they learn language, and how they learn written language. We will describe children who are just beginning to read and write, from preschool through primary grades. This chapter explores how youngsters in these early childhood years learn and think differently from adults and older children. These children are not only physically smaller and less competent than older kids, but also different intellectually. They perceive the world, its people, and print in a unique fashion.

Examining these differences is helpful in tailoring learning experiences to the needs of young children. Unless we make this effort, we run the risk of school becoming a place where children are fitted into teacher-made tasks rather than a place where they are helped to refine their views of the world and come to greater understandings of it and themselves. Our goal as teachers is to foster those kinds of understandings, not merely to train children in giving correct answers.

Early childhood educators historically have emphasized all aspects of child development. Teachers of young children deal with the "whole child" rather than focus only on intellectual development. Even though we are discussing the language arts curriculum area, it is impossible to ignore the child's total development. We know that reading and writing involve the child's social and emotional self, and we know that physical development works together with intellectual development in all learning.

Because physical development is observable, adults accept and understand its nature more easily than intellectual or emotional development. No one questions that children sit before they stand, stand before they walk, or walk before they run. We see children's gradual progress in specific skills such as jumping and throwing. Our acceptance of immature efforts toward physical prowess can be our guide in acceptance of immature intellectual and emotional responses. Adults are less likely to expect youngsters to perform physical feats beyond their capacity than they are to expect youngsters to master advanced academic or social skills. For instance, a toddler throwing a ball isn't likely to be criticized for lack of good aim; yet that same toddler is apt to be scolded for not wanting to share a toy with another child. Both achievements take time. It is easy to accept that children don't look like adults, but apparently hard to understand that they don't think like adults.

How Children Learn

Understanding how children learn is essential to effective teaching, yet schooling practices have long been based on an incomplete and superficial view of the learner. Old teaching methods considered the student as a passive recipient of the teacher's knowledge. However, research has demonstrated that learning actually is an active process in which each learner must construct personal understanding (Ferreiro, 1986; Kamii, 1991; Piaget, 1964).

We reject the view of learning as merely memorizing and repeating. This book presents the view of learning as thinking, experimenting, and interpreting. Teachers around the world are changing to educational practices that encourage thought, support experimentation, and assist interpretation processes (Grossi, 1990; Holdaway, 1991; Landsmann, 1990; Teberosky, 1982). This requires teaching in ways very different from those you probably experienced as a child. It is a more demanding process both for teachers and students, but most people consider it worth the effort. The goal is not just to teach children what their teachers have learned, but rather to create learners and decision makers for an unknown future.

Reasoning

Children work hard at making sense of their world; they are constantly learning both in and out of school. Unfortunately, in the past, they had to do most of their learning outside of school because their school days were taken up with busywork to please the teachers. In the process of figuring out how things work, children come up with some amazing theories. These "wrong" answers are proof that children are producing their own knowledge, because no adult would have told them such things (Kamii, 1991).

Adult explanations tend to stop the thinking and learning process by making youngsters distrust their own reasoning.

Andrew explains that waves are sometimes made from wind and sometimes made from the ocean. This thinking sounds fairly reasonable to an adult until you get past the surface and find out what those words mean to the child. When pressed for further detail, Andrew reveals that the things that live in the ocean, "like fish and whales and seals," make waves when they swim. He says that fish make little waves, whales make big waves, and seals make middle-sized waves. This explanation demonstrates Andrew's reasoning ability and his active involvement in trying to understand his experiences and observations. He himself has made waves by splashing in a swimming pool and apparently is using that experience to explain the surf he plays in at the beach.

Questions vs. Information

Adults often have a hard time letting such false impressions go uncorrected. They want to give children their adult understanding, but end up giving them only their words. For instance, Andrew can give the "correct" explanation when asked where rain comes from, citing the clouds with water and the sea as the source. Hearing this answer, you would believe that Andrew has learned about rain. But if you delve deeper into Andrew's knowledge, you find that he has merely learned the right words; he really has no idea what they mean. This is evident from Andrew's answer when asked about where clouds come from; he apparently forgets what he just said about rain coming from clouds that came from the ocean. Instead, he uses his own observation of a local paper mill and says that clouds come from "the mill paper thing; it stinks. It makes clouds go higher and higher, and they stay there."

As long as Andrew keeps thinking, he will keep learning. Adult explanations tend to stop the thinking and learning by making youngsters mistrust their own reasoning. The best approach to teaching, then, is asking questions instead of giving information. Questions that cause a child to look at a situation differently or that create an intellectual conflict encourage deeper thought. We might point out that there are no paper mills where Grandpa lives, and ask why there are clouds there. Such questioning requires sensitivity to the child, however, so as not to be disrespectful or discouraging. We must accept children's thinking in order to help them to develop confidence in themselves as thinkers (Bredekamp & Rosegrant, 1992). It is all too easy to destroy that confidence by insisting on adult views of correct thinking. Without confidence in their own thinking, children cease their efforts to understand, and thus limit their intellectual development by merely repeating what they are told.

Experience

Youngsters can perceive flaws in their reasoning not only through adult questioning, but also as a result of their own questions about their observations.

Therefore, effective teaching provides ample opportunity for observation through firsthand experiences. Experiences provide essential fuel for thought.

In fact, experiences tend to be the bases for the initial explanations children create for themselves. Tanya's description of tidal action demonstrates the role of experience in a child's understandings. She surprised her teacher by talking about when the sea "drains." When Ms. Montoya asked Tanya what she meant, Tanya said, "When it goes away; like in the shower." As she pondered Tanya's words, Ms. Montoya realized that Tanya's perception was based on a limited view of tides. The community where they live is at the head of a huge bay and when the tide goes out, it leaves behind only mud flats. Indeed, it would be reasonable to consider that the water had "drained." Only different experiences of tides would alter Tanya's understanding. However, seeing a different result of tidal action won't alter her theory immediately. It is typical for youngsters (and adult learners) to try to keep their original ideas and to create a subsystem or additional explanation for the new phenomenon. Eventually, more encompassing theories are created as more and more variations are included. Learning seems to be driven by a search for coherence, or consistency (Siegrist & Sinclair, 1991).

The fact that she has an idea, or hypothesis, will help Tanya to continue learning the subject. As Eleanor Duckworth (1987) tells us, it is through the exploration of their own theories that children learn and become more aware of evidence that either fits their current views or that indicates the need for a different theory. Teachers who encourage children to formulate any ideas—right or wrong—generate thought and activate the learning process. Teachers who give children adult answers, by contrast, close thought.

Different Kinds of Learning

We don't mean to say that teachers should never tell children anything. Though children must construct their own understanding of complex ideas, there is much factual information that someone needs to tell them. Much of this information consists of names given to things in our language. Young children constantly ask to have things named for them as they learn to talk. The names we use for letters, numbers, shapes, and colors also are part of the information adults can and do give to children. However, the meaning behind the names and the relationships among items named cannot be given to anyone; everyone has to make sense of those in his or her own way. We sometimes see teachers who focus on teaching the names for things and who seem to forget that there is much more to know.

Piaget's theory that there are three kinds of knowledge, each learned in a different way, can guide teachers in selecting appropriate teaching approaches. These three kinds of knowledge are social knowledge (sometimes called conventional knowledge), physical knowledge, and logico-mathematical knowledge. Social knowledge is the language and customs of a given group and varies from culture to culture. Because this information is part of the culture, it is appropriate that it is passed on to children through cultural transmission processes of demonstrating and explaining. It doesn't exist apart from the culture and therefore a child can't figure it out alone.

Social (conventional) knowledge can be learned through direct instruction.

Physical knowledge is gained through exploration.

Physical knowledge, on the other hand, is not culture-bound and is the same the world over. No matter what language a child speaks, water flows and mud squishes in exactly the same ways. Children gain physical knowledge as a result of acting on objects or materials and observing the results.

Logico-mathematical knowledge is the most complex of the three kinds of knowledge. It involves processing all available information and experiences, creating relationships among them all. Thus, social knowledge and

Logico-mathematical knowledge comes from reflective, analytical thought, using all information and experiences and creating new understandings.

physical knowledge feed into the construction of logico-mathematical knowledge. As they construct their own unique understandings, children use information adults have told them and knowledge they have learned through their own experiences with objects. Logico-mathematical knowledge is created in the mind of the learner and is gained through analytical thinking. The teacher's role is to encourage thinking by providing experiences to think about, opportunities for reflection, and questions to get children to examine and improve their theories. Differences of opinion among peers is often the best impetus to get children to rethink their current ideas. Teams of youngsters working together are likely to learn much more than individuals working alone.

Children learn better when they can debate their ideas with other children. If Sukey disagrees with Chantel, they will each explain and defend their ideas. The argument will cause each girl to think more about what she believes. One may persuade the other or they may continue to disagree; either way, the debate process is part of the learning process. Therefore, effective learning environments include ample opportunity for children to interact and discuss their views (Vygotsky, 1978). The teacher's opinion is not the only one that counts, nor is the teacher's voice the only one that can be heard. Effective teaching encourages youngsters to exchange viewpoints.

HOW CHILDREN LEARN LANGUAGE

Though the language of a culture involves significant amounts of social knowledge learned from hearing that language, studies of language development show that children do much more than imitate others as they learn to talk (Halliday, 1982; Piaget & Inhelder, 1969). In fact, while learning to talk, children provide some of the best examples of how they construct knowledge. If you have been around young children, you have heard evidence that they do more than mimic adult language; rather, they create their own theories about language. They obviously use the ideas gained from adult models, but analyze them in an effort to understand how it all fits together. This is the logico-mathematical learning process applied to language. Youngsters construct their own understanding of language as they practice it, trying out their current theories about how it works.

Children have a lot to learn in the process of becoming verbal. Early in life, babies master the idea that speech is a means of communicating with other human beings—a way of expressing their desires, sharing their feelings, and explaining their experiences. Then they go on to master the complexities of accurate communication. When they are only about six months old, they imitate intonations, so that their speech sounds as if they are creating sentences. This has been called "pseudolanguage" (Pflaum, 1986). At this point they still have to work on the specific sounds involved. Before their first year is over, babies have narrowed their utterances from all the possible sounds to those significant in their environment. Babies in Mexico will trill the *r* sound, while babies in Germany will practice the guttural sounds they hear, and English-speaking babies will learn neither. Before long, they all begin to make the sounds of their language in combinations that mean something specific. As soon as they acquire this ability to communicate with words, they begin to string them together for even greater results.

As they begin to use words in combination, children try to put them together in ways matching the grammatical rules of their language. English-speaking children put the subject before the verb and, when they become more sophisticated, the object after the verb. Later, they clearly demonstrate their learning process as they reinvent grammar rules such as adding an *s* to make a plural in *foots* and *mouses* and adding *ed* for the past tense in *runned* and *digged*. They also are motivated to increase their vocabulary and incessantly ask the names of things.

By the time teachers see them in preschool, most children seem to be proficient with language. They generally are able to make themselves understood to others and are good at understanding what others say to them. How did they learn so much in such a short time? They did not learn it by being drilled in the sounds and grammar of their language.

The Child's Process

An old joke says if we taught children to talk the way we teach them to read, there would be a lot of nontalkers. Yet few people seem to turn the joke around and suggest that if we taught children to read the way we teach them to talk, we wouldn't have many nonreaders. Teaching children to read the way we teach them to talk is precisely what current research is suggesting that teachers do.

Therefore, let's look carefully at how a child learns to talk. Watch the neighbors' new baby, Betsy, as her parents bring her home from the hospital. Already there is communication between Betsy and her parents. Mostly, she makes random noises and cries to express her discomfort; however, her communications bring responses from her parents, sisters, and brothers. People babble to her in imitation of the sounds she makes, or someone feeds or changes her in response to her cries. She discovers the power of communication. Halliday (1975) said youngsters "learn to mean" before they learn the forms for expressing their meanings. We see this same sequence as children learn to write.

The social contexts of language give it meaning. When Betsy's dad bathes her, he talks to her about how warm the water is, how slippery the soap feels, and what cute little toes she has. When her mother dresses her, Betsy hears about her dry diaper, the snaps on her jumpsuit, and her sweet smile. When her big brother, Johnny, plays with Betsy, he shows her all his toys and tells her what is happening as he drives his toy trucks around her baby seat. Johnny makes her laugh.

Betsy hears language, both that directed to her and that surrounding her, as her family goes about its daily life. She likes to participate in the con-

An old joke says "If we taught children to talk the same way we teach them to read, we'd have a lot of nontalkers." Let's turn the joke around: Let's teach children to read the way we teach them to talk. Then there won't be so many nonreaders.

versation, and her progress with the forms of language is seen as she utters strings of sounds that make her family stop and listen. These sounds are much like "real" language, but close attention reveals that there are no words in Betsy's sentence. She has mastered some general sounds of language but not the specifics; she seems to have picked up the intonations, such as those of questioning or scolding, that go with different meanings. Betsy scolded her mom roundly when she saw her mom standing on the counter one day to reach something. She didn't need words to do it: Her tone of voice said it all.

More and more, the sounds Betsy makes are the sounds she hears. One day she makes a "da" sound, and her dad suddenly pays attention, and bends over her and repeats, "Da da." When Betsy is about a year old, she is able to make several sounds that get a specific response from her family. She may make the same sound to mean different things, which she indicates by her tone, facial expression, pointing gestures, or other nonverbal clues. Mostly, her family understands her intent due to the situation. For instance, "Ma ma" can mean "Where is Mama?" or "I want my Mama!" or "There is my Mama." Soon she begins to add action words to nouns and communicate in two-word sentences. Again, these two-word "telegraph" sentences can mean different things, depending on the context in which they occur. Already Betsy knows that the meaning is inherent not in the words alone, but also in the mutual understanding between speaker and listener. This interpersonal aspect of communication remains true even after Betsy has mastered adult-sounding sentences.

The Home Environment

As Betsy's knowledge of words and ability to create sentences increase, her previously "good" grammar seems to deteriorate. Her big sister, Mandy, is concerned because Betsy says, "I goed to the store." Mandy patiently corrects her and says, "No, you *went* to the store." "That's right," says Betsy happily as she wanders off. Their mother comforts Mandy by explaining that Betsy will talk correctly before long and that Betsy makes mistakes because she is trying to make sense of grammar right now. Obviously, Betsy is not imitating adult language here. Her errors are clear evidence of her active efforts at making sense of language. Betsy's mistake is an overgeneralization of the rule for the past tense form. Mandy's mom asks her not to correct Betsy for fear of discouraging Betsy from practicing language.

When she is three years old, Betsy still finds it hard to make all the sounds in her language. She still can't make *l, r,* or *s* sounds because they take more coordination than she has yet mastered. But, although she may say *tore* instead of *store*, she gets upset if someone else says the words incorrectly. Betsy's mother knows that the baby talk will disappear by itself if others talk to Betsy in adult language rather than imitate her baby talk. Correcting her actually can slow down the learning process because it can create fear of failure and reluctance to talk. Reluctance to talk gets in the way of practice important to learning.

As Betsy becomes more proficient with language, she has much she wants to say and speaks eagerly. Betsy sometimes trips over her words in her rush to speak. Her uncle thinks that she is stuttering so he says, "Slow down, Betsy. Start again and say it slowly." While this may appear to be sound advice, Betsy's mother asks him not to interrupt Betsy or call attention to the problem. Uncle John gets a valuable lecture on *normal nonfluency*—how it isn't stuttering but can become stuttering if a child is made nervous about it (Swan, 1993). Betsy's mother tells him that the best help he can give Betsy is his undivided attention so she won't feel rushed.

As Betsy's family helps her learn their language, they don't have to be told about most of the important things they do to help her learn. Talking to her and paying attention to her when she talks are the most helpful, especially given their serious efforts to understand her early communication attempts. Her brothers and sisters sometimes point to various things when they don't understand Betsy, saying "Is this what you mean?" People around her help her to communicate beyond what she can do on her own (Vygotsky, 1978).

Her family also naturally assist Betsy's language attempts by adjusting how they speak to her according to her changing ability to understand.

Families teach language to their children by being language models and by trying to understand when youngsters try to communicate.

Apparently, an unconscious accommodation to a child's emerging language ability guides the length and complexity of adult speech to children (Schachter & Strage, 1982). Therefore, adults automatically tend to simplify their grammar, limit their vocabulary, repeat words often, and enunciate slowly and clearly to young children.

Betsy's parents, like many other parents, respond to her speech by adding to what she said and extending her immature sentences. So at Betsy's first birthday, when she says, "Ma ma!" her mother might say, "You want Mama to come pick you up?" At two years, when she says, "Daddy gone," her mother would reply, "Yes, Daddy is gone to work now." And at three years, when she says, "See me riding," her dad says, "Look at Betsy riding fast on her red tricycle!" These expansions or elaborations of her speech help Betsy increase the complexity of her language. Such modeling is sometimes referred to as scaffolding.

Story time provides another important component of Betsy's language development. Storybooks offer a rich source for vocabulary development, for familiarity with a variety of sentence structures, and for understanding the unique forms of written language. Children who haven't been read to arrive at school unable to process the dialect of book-talk. They understand only context-laden language, which utilizes both the situation and nonverbal communication to add meaning to the words. When confronted with the decontextualized language found in books, these youngsters don't know how to make sense of it.

The amount and kinds of Betsy's experiences also influence her language complexity. When she plays outside, she feels the prickly softness of the grass as she rolls on it, she experiences the smooth hardness of the driveway where she rides her trike, and she squeals with delight at the flying sensation when she swings. What a great many things she has to talk about now, and what a great many words she can add to her vocabulary if someone listens and extends her speech as she tells about playing outside.

Not all children have such an ideal language environment (Cazden, 1988; Healy, 1990). Some are ignored when they make sounds or even when they cry. Some are spoken to only a little or do not have their questions answered. Some come from families in which adults simply do not talk a great deal or the adult sentences are short and lack complexity and specificity. Some children lack the coordination to create speech, some can't hear language to imitate it, and some are too fearful to speak. These children need more time and ample opportunity to experience the kinds of language stimulation that are a part of Betsy's everyday life.

More to Learn

Even children from optimal language environments have much to learn about language when they reach preschool. They may sound quite mature, but their vocabulary remains limited, as is their ability to deal with different grammatical structures. They can become confused about a new word or one with several meanings. They also can become confused by the difference between *ask* and *tell*. Have you ever told children they could ask questions after a guest speaker's presentation? They don't ask the speaker questions; they tell their personal experiences! They get confused by questions in general because questions turn around the natural order of a sentence. Passive forms also turn around the familiar sentence patterns and result in miscommunication. For instance, when we say, "Betsy was given a tricycle by her dad," children look at us quizzically and wonder why Betsy's dad would want a tricycle.

Generally, children do learn a great deal of language in a short time. When they get to school, they must be allowed to continue their oral language development in the way that has already proved successful for them. They also must be encouraged to learn written language in the same active and interactive ways they learned oral language. These include observing and experiencing communication as well as having their own attempts at the process encouraged. Adults who accept and value the errors children make as they construct their own understandings are also essential for both oral and written language development. In addition, books and real-life experiences assist children in bringing meaning to oral and written language. Subsequent chapters will include more detailed discussions about how teachers can promote these active and interactive experiences.

It used to be commonly accepted that oral language development preceded written language development and was the basis for learning to read and write. We now realize that oral and written language are even more

Adults who accept and value the errors children make as they construct their own understandings are essential for both oral and written language development.

closely intertwined. Children actually are learning about reading and writing at the same time they are learning to talk. Learning the language of literacy assists oral language learning, as much as the other way around.

HOW CHILDREN LEARN WRITTEN LANGUAGE

Ideas about how people learn to read and write have changed radically since you were in first grade. When researchers began watching youngsters closely, they began to question traditional assumptions about how children learn. As with other kinds of language learning, becoming literate is more than memorizing what an adult tells or shows a child. Children do use information and examples from adults, but they construct their own knowledge of literacy. They direct their own process of learning to read and write by actively generating and testing a series of personal hypotheses about written language.

Documentation of children's learning processes reveals that they do not learn much about reading from formal instruction. Most of what they learn is a result of their informal, everyday experiences with print in their everyday lives (Sulzby, 1986). These experiences include being read to, pretending to read and write, finding their favorite cereal labels at the store, or seeing how their own names are written. Obviously, adults play an important role in this process, but it is not a role of telling youngsters how reading works. That is something children themselves must make sense of in their own ways by analyzing pertinent information and experiences to construct their own understanding. Youngsters need social knowledge about the representational system for literacy in their language, but becoming literate involves complex analytical thought to make sense of the information available.

Another major change in our understanding of literacy development is that we no longer talk about learning just to read; we now know that learning to read and learning to write are inseparable. Reading exposes a child to models for writing, and writing involves a theory of how to create something readable. Thinking about one enhances understanding of the other, and both are learned simultaneously. Now we refer to both of these functions by the term *literacy*. Recognition that oral language and written language are interrelated also has generated further integration of curriculum. The whole language approach to literacy reflects these concepts of interrelatedness.

Learning Sequence

We used to think that children learned first to talk, then to read, and then to write. No one meddled much with learning to talk, but there were many prescriptions for what children had to learn before they could learn to read. The whole field of reading readiness, with its auditory discrimination exercises and visual discrimination workbooks, was based on ideas about what children had to know before they could read. It was assumed that proficiency in reading would provide a suitable prerequisite for learning to write. The idea of rigid sequences in learning has been thrown out and replaced with new understandings that make reading readiness activities ridiculous (Holdaway, 1991).

The term *emergent literacy* describes the current view of literacy development. There is not a point in a child's life when literacy begins; it is a continuous process of becoming (Teale & Sulzby, 1986). Children are working on all aspects of oral and written language at the same time. Even before Betsy

There is not a point in a child's life when literacy begins: It is a continuous process of becoming.

could talk, she liked to hear stories read and would play at reading. Certainly, before she could read she was trying to write like the other people in her family did. Scholars view these activities as legitimate reading and writing processes; we no longer talk about prereading or reading readiness experiences.

In the past, the forms of written language—the letters and the sounds they represent—were taught first. More recently, educators thought that children must know the functions of written language—the ways in which it is used—before details about letters are relevant. However, careful observation of children reveals that they pay no attention to adult ideas about these kinds of sequences, either. They do need to understand the purposes and uses of written language, but many youngsters are working hard at identifying letters at the same time that they are learning about the functions of print (Sulzby, 1986). To further confuse adults, youngsters go about this complex process in individually unique ways. Despite some commonalities, different children tune in to different aspects of written language and generate their own unique hypotheses (Dyson, 1985).

What this means is that schools, teachers, and workbook publishers cannot dictate how children will learn to read and write. Rather, teachers, parents, and other adults who know a child should support that child's individual efforts to learn. As Betsy grows up, her family answers her questions about print, provides her with paper and other writing materials, lets her see the family reading and writing, and generally offers a print-rich environment filled with books and other kinds of writing. When she goes to preschool, her teacher provides much the same kind of support for Betsy's emerging literacy. Rather than predetermining what Betsy must master at a given time, both her home and her school encourage her to learn in her own way. Both environments help her to see the usefulness of reading and writing; both offer experiences that further her understanding and excite her enthusiasm for learning. This is the developmentally appropriate approach to language and literacy (see Table 1–1).

Literacy and the Home Environment

Adults can act as models, advisors, resources, and cheerleaders to children when they learn to read just as they did when children learned to talk. Older children also can assist younger ones in becoming literate just as they helped them with other language acquisition. Betsy's four older brothers and sisters don't realize that they teach the younger ones, but they do a fine job. The younger children in the family always want to do whatever the older ones are doing. When they see their older siblings reading, they want to read, too. At first, they know only that reading involves looking at the book or newspaper or cereal box. Then they discover that there is a message contained in books even beyond the fascination of the pictures. When big brother Joey was in second grade, he would invite his three younger brothers and sisters to sit on his bunk bed and entertain them by reading library books.

When Joey was at school, two-year-old Amy would ask her four-year-old brother, John, to read to her. John couldn't read actual words, but he could tell a story, turn the pages, and admire the pictures with Amy. In these sessions, both Amy and John were learning a great deal about reading. Amy was learning that books were a source of information and pleasure; John was practicing the idea of getting meaning from a book. He was aware of the print and its relationship to the content but couldn't yet decipher it. At this point in his development, John tried to put together a prize toy from a cereal box. He was having trouble, so Grandma offered to help, saying, "Let me read the directions." John replied, "I already did." Grandma persisted, saying, "Let me see if you missed anything." John handed her the direction sheet, which contained both illustrations and printed instructions, and said matter-of-factly, "I missed the words." John's statement accurately described his current level of reading: He was able to make meaning from pictures but not from print.

You might ask, "Does this family have a television?" So often television is blamed for people not reading. The parents in this family enjoy books, but they also enjoy television and think that selected, limited viewing isn't necessarily bad. Like many parents, they know children learn new words and are exposed to a vast array of ideas and information through television. Also, like

TABLE 1–1
Developmentally Appropriate Literacy Education

APPROPRIATE Practice	INAPPROPRIATE Practice
The goals of the language and literacy program are for children to expand their ability to communicate orally and through reading and writing and to enjoy these activities. Technical skills or subskills are taught as needed to accomplish the larger goals, not as the goal itself. Teachers provide generous amounts of time and a variety of interesting activities for children to develop language, writing, spelling, and reading ability, such as: looking through, reading, or being read high quality children's literature and nonfiction for pleasure and information; drawing, dictating, and writing about their activities or fantasies; planning and implementing projects that involve research at suitable levels of difficulty.	The goal of the reading program is for each child to pass the standardized tests given throughout the year at or near grade level. Reading is taught as the acquisition of skills and subskills. Teachers teach reading only as a discrete subject. When teaching other subjects, they do not feel they are teaching reading. A sign of excellent teaching is considered to be silence in the classroom and so conversation is allowed infrequently during select times. Language, writing, and spelling instruction are focused on workbooks. Writing is taught as grammar and penmanship. The focus of the reading program is the basal reader, used only in reading groups, and accompanying workbooks and worksheets.

Bredekamp, S. (Ed.). (1987). *Developmentally appropriate practice in early childhood programs serving children birth through age 8.* Washington, DC: National Association for the Education of Young Children.

many parents, they are often uncomfortable with some of this new learning. They use what they believe is both the good and the bad on television for helping their children to grow intellectually and emotionally.

When adults make television viewing an active rather than passive experience, viewing can be a source of language, critical thinking, and a vehicle for values transmission. Television can provide a valuable background for literacy, but when families use it as a substitute for talking, thinking, and family interaction, it has negative consequences (Healy, 1990).

Oral Language and Written Language

Children learn written language in the same way they learn oral language because it is language (Goodman, K. S., 1986). This idea has become well accepted since Chomsky's early writing on the topic in 1972. Although the ways in which written language is different from oral language must be considered, understanding how youngsters learn to talk helps us to understand how they master reading and writing, too. Researchers who have studied written-language acquisition (Dyson, 1985; Ferreiro, 1986; Goodman, Y., 1986; Teale & Sulzby, 1989) have shown that young children learn written and oral language the way Piaget said they learn many other things. They learn by constructing their own rules and relationships rather than by being told about them.

Chomsky's research also demonstrated that children's drive to make sense of print is similar to their determination to utilize spoken language. Chomsky's recommendation was that children be allowed to direct their own process of learning to read, just as they directed their learning to talk. Does this mean that we simply leave children alone to learn to read? No, it means that adult assistance in the process should closely resemble the type of adult assistance given children as they learn to talk (Morrow, 1993).

When we help a baby learn to talk, do we conduct lessons on the sounds of words and then try to get the baby to blend those sounds together to make language? Did Betsy's family allow her to say only words that she could pronounce properly? Did they restrict her speech to vocabulary-controlled topics or to sentences that she could form properly? Did they group her with others who only could talk at her level? Of course not. They encouraged her to experiment with language in any way she chose, and they rejoiced with her at each discovery. They provided Betsy with models of rich language and helped her to learn through her own observation and experimentation as she tried to join in oral communication. In short, they included her in the oral interaction of the family at whatever level she was currently capable of participating.

MISCONCEPTIONS ABOUT BECOMING LITERATE

We have been discussing the processes of learning to read and learning to talk as overlapping procedures. It may seem strange to think of learning to read and learning to talk as happening at the same time. It is a new insight to realize that babies and toddlers are beginning the process of learning to read when books and print become part of their lives. Yes, babies are learning to read, but no one makes a child sit down for a lesson disguised as a game. Betsy and Amy's mother, Deborah, laughs at advertisements for materials for teaching babies and toddlers to read. She thinks the idea of trying to teach those little ones about reading with an artificial presentation of pictures and letters is silly.

She doesn't laugh, though, when Amy comes home from kindergarten feeling like a failure over her phonics workbook. Deborah is very upset to discover that the teacher was drilling children on isolated letters and sounds apart from any meaningful context. She has a right to be upset. The National Association for the Education of Young Children (NAEYC) published specific guidelines for developmentally appropriate education practices (Table 1–1) that clearly described such practices as inappropriate (Bredekamp, 1987). Constance Kamii, one of the scholars whose research was used for the NAEYC guidelines, stated that a phonics skills focus in kindergarten is based on an erroneous assumption of how children learn (Willert & Kamii, 1985). Carol Chomsky (1979) said that teaching reading by pronouncing the sounds of letters is a method that may be appropriate for teaching a foreigner who

Old approaches to teaching reading and writing ignore what children actually do to learn to read and write.

does not speak the language. Kenneth Goodman calls it teaching kids to "bark at print" (Goodman, 1986).

Inappropriate educational practices will persist as long as people remain ignorant of what is actually involved in becoming literate (Ferreiro, 1991). After they have figured out how to read and write, people tend to forget how they actually did it. They usually focus on some observable details of the process, and end up with a view of reading and writing as knowing letters and sounds. Many also believe that copying writing models is the way to learn about writing and that writing consists of transcribing sounds.

These erroneous beliefs ignore the complex intellectual activities that actually are required for becoming literate. These beliefs ignore the vast amount of understanding about the structure of written language that is essential to reading and writing. They ignore the essential role of social situations and meaningful contexts. They also ignore what children actually do when they learn to read and write.

Teaching practices must focus clearly on the desired goals. Most would agree that the goal of reading and writing instruction is literate human beings who can read to select the more rational argument among conflicting theories and who can express ideas effectively in writing. Knowing the sounds of letters and correct spelling of words obviously is useful, but becoming literate involves much, much more.

How Good Readers Read

Most people would just say they want children to be good readers. What is a good reader? Can we get some clues about how to create good readers by examining one?

Betsy's oldest sister, Mandy, is one such example. Her teachers describe her as an exceptional student and a fluent reader. Mandy likes to read and spends much time with library books. She often chooses reading over other activities. When she is reading, Mandy is oblivious to everything else around her. Her younger sisters and brothers get upset because they can't get her attention away from her books. Good readers freely choose to read and tend to concentrate as they read.

This year Mandy is reading horse stories. She got hooked on the *Black Stallion* (Farley) series, and when she finished those, she started reading every other horse story she could find. Although she doesn't have a horse and rarely has been on one, Mandy knows about horses from her reading. When she reads, Mandy can pretend that she owns a horse that carries her galloping over sand dunes or green meadows. Mandy's cousin, David, is reading another type of book—the *Choose Your Own Adventure* (Bantam Books) type of reading excitement. Both Mandy and David read mainly for pleasure, while David's brother, Michael, has always chosen to read for information. Michael became an expert on marine mammals through his reading in grade school, and then in junior high he switched to reading about hunting and camping. He uses the information he has gathered from reading for his week-end expeditions. Good readers find pleasure and purpose in their reading.

As we watch Mandy read, her eyes flash across and down the page. How can she possibly see every word, let alone every letter on the page? She doesn't. If she were to read slowly enough to see each letter, the process would be so laborious that she would not find pleasure in reading and would not often choose to read. If she had learned to read by thinking that she was supposed to sound out each letter and blend words together, she might have continued to look at each letter and never have become a good reader.

What about reading all the words? Mandy knows exactly what the story is about; she can tell you details and will speculate excitedly about what might happen next. But she does not labor over individual words. If she comes to a word that she doesn't know, she usually can skip over it and still get the meaning from the rest of the sentence. After a few times of skipping over the same word and getting meaning from the context in that manner, she has an idea of what the word means even if it isn't part of her general vocabulary. If the printed word is part of her spoken vocabulary, she eventually figures it out using strategies that combine graphophonemic clues with semantic clues related to the meaning of what she reads.

When Mandy reads something at an easier level where she knows all the words, she can really fly. She isn't aware of the physical process, but her eye often identifies the words merely from their general outline or configuration. These configuration clues serve as shortcuts to identifying sight words, thus increasing reading speed and fluency. An observer might describe Mandy as a youngster who doesn't see most of the letters or many of the words she reads and even reads books with words that she doesn't know. Is Mandy typical of good readers? Research tells us yes.

The Child's Process

Mandy shows us a model of where we're headed, but let's remember there is a complex journey from the starting point to where Mandy is. In fact, just getting to the point where letters are relevant involves a massive learning process (Edwards, 1994). Researchers around the world have carefully tracked this process among children in several countries. They have studied children's writing as evidence of their thinking and understanding. This research shows that the ways in which children construct their understanding of written language are much the same whether youngsters are reading and writing in Hebrew, Spanish, Italian, French, or English (Ferreiro, 1990; Landsmann, 1990; Pontecorvo & Zucchermaglio, 1990; Siegrist & Sinclair, 1991; Sulzby, 1986; Teberosky, 1990). The study of children's evolving theories of writing demonstrates another remarkable similarity: Children's literacy development parallels the development of literacy for the human race (Goodman, 1990; Temple, Nathan, Temple, & Burris, 1993). Children's writing demonstrates principles of representation found in ancient Chinese, Egyptian, and Greek writing. Children's progression from pictures and related symbols to the use of more abstract and arbitrary representation (see Table 1-2) occurs in the sequence of such progressions historically. Piaget found that individual children constructed knowledge of many topics in ways that reflect the historical development of understanding (Piaget & Garcia, 1989).

Children use all the information provided by their environment as they look for patterns that will make sense in reading, writing, and other topics of interest. At first, they do not distinguish between drawing and writing and will use the terms interchangeably. In fact, all their marks on paper at this point may consist of scribbles that look much the same. Some children still

TABLE 1–2
Writing Forms Chart

Form	Characteristics & Hypotheses
scribbles	random marks with no differentiation between drawing and writing
drawing	illustration tells a story
linear-repetitive	marks in a line, fairly uniform in size and shape (repetitive); looks like longhand
copying standard writing	may or may not be linear, but contains elements of actual words
memorized forms	frequently used and important words love, Mom, Dad, own name, etc.
letterlike forms	contains elements of actual letters, looks like letters; no more than two similar forms next to one another

quantitative principles	the number of letters is significant
	    reflects hypotheses about number of letters necessary for a word
	    big things have big names
	    progresses to reflect number of oral language syllables

qualitative principles beginning invented spelling	which letters used is significant
letter names as sounds	reflects hypothesis that letters make the sound of their names
simplified phonics	one letter per word or per syllable; only major sounds, few vowels
advanced invented spelling	attempts to regularize sound-symbol relationship; uses vowels; becomes readable
standard spelling	self-correction to match standard spelling models

will draw when asked to write after they are capable of some realism in their drawing (see Figure 1–1). A child may even ask you how to write something, while actually wanting help in drawing. The first big breakthrough comes when children arrive at the conclusion that writing, unlike drawing, does not reflect the shape of the objects represented.

FIGURE 1–1
Is this drawing or writing?

LINEAR-REPETITIVE FORMS

Once children have sorted out the differences between drawing and writing, their writing often becomes squiggly lines across the paper (see Figure 1–2). They proudly will fill up a page with this writing and may ask you to read it. These are emergent writers who have recognized the linear quality of print and are exploring that idea. This writing looks remarkably similar to the longhand, or cursive, writing commonly used by adults. Many youngsters are not concerned with the content of their writing yet, but are focused only on the form. When asked what they are writing, they may tell you "a letter" or else answer, "I'm just writing." Some youngsters obligingly will make up something for the writing to say; this rereading may change or it may stay the same each time the child repeats the reading. The latter response shows much more understanding about writing than the former.

LETTERLIKE FORMS

Children also notice the letters in the signs, books, posters, and all the hubbub of written advertising everywhere in their environment. Approximations of letters will appear in child writing as youngsters attempt to incorporate this information into their theory of writing (see Figure 1–3). Four-year-old Patricia combines linear squiggles, actual letters, and letterlike forms in her writing (see Figure 1–4). This combination is common as youngsters work on their understanding of print.

No matter how hard schools try to get all teachers to consistently use D'Nealian manuscript print (Graham, 1993–1994) or any other style of writing, children will see many conflicting styles as they ride down a busy street or page through a magazine. They often explore this data by copying print from signs or other writing around them (see Figure 1–5). Children eventually must not only figure out which characteristics transcend writing styles, but also face the chore of learning the uppercase and lowercase versions of each letter.

FIGURE 1–2
An example of the linear, repetitive writing form.

FIGURE 1–3
This writing uses letterlike forms.

LETTERS AS REPRESENTATIVE OBJECTS

Knowing that certain forms are involved in writing is still a long way from realizing that there is any connection between which letters are used and which words or meanings are intended. The challenge first is to recognize written marks as substitutes for objects rather than objects themselves (Ferreiro, 1990). Traditional teaching practices, which focus on the names and shapes of letters, emphasize letters as objects rather than the more complex understanding of letters in a representational system. Television shows such as *Sesame Street* that show animated letters dancing around further confuse the issue for youngsters.

Rich literacy environments that involve youngsters with actual reading and writing, on the other hand, help them to construct ideas of a representational system. Although the sequence in which children construct their theories about print is consistent, the speed at which they progress through the

FIGURE 1–4
Like most youngsters, Patricia combines various understandings in her writing. Here she has used linear squiggles and letterlike forms, as well as a few actual letters.

sequence is generally determined by environmental factors. These factors include the amount of reading and writing in the child's home, the level of support and safety for experimentation, and the type of schooling practices encountered.

As children begin to use letters or letterlike forms for writing, they are still puzzling out the written language system. The distinctions they have made between writing and drawing create a question of how each is used (see Figure 1–6). Youngsters commonly create the principle that pictures show what something looks like, while writing tells the name of the thing. Their next challenge has to do with how to make writing represent those names adequately (Ferreiro, 1990).

FIGURE 1–5
Children often explore the print in their environment by copying from signs or other writing around them.

How Many Letters Make a Word?

Most adults will assume that when youngsters focus on how to make writing represent certain words, they begin sorting out the sounds of letters. This may be what teachers are teaching, but what children are thinking about is something else. Those seemingly random strings of letters you see as part of their writing at this point are actually far from random. They reflect a child's serious thought and creation of theories about print. Typically, youngsters construct a theory about how many letters are needed for a word to say something. Most will decide on a minimum number and a maximum number of letters. They explore this quantitative principle by writing series of at least three letters and not too many more. At first, these may be repetitions of the same letter. However, youngsters will notice that words are made up of several *different* letters, never the same letter over and over. Thus, their strings of three to seven letters soon contain a variety of letters, and reflect construction of a qualitative principle as well as a quantitative principle (see Figure 1–7). At this point, some children use the same set of letters in the same order to represent any words they have in mind. As they explore and test their hypotheses, children continue to bring their writing creations to adults to read.

Big Things Have Big Names

Youngsters tend to be briefly content with having the same set of letters stand for different things. But soon they begin to look for differences in sets of letters that lead to different interpretations. As with all learning, solving

FIGURE 1–6
Brenton demonstrates his knowledge of writing, using both alphabetic and numeric symbols. He includes memorized forms of his name as well as three other words and has copied the date. His intent is that the writing tells about the volcano he drew.

one mystery opens the door to another. You might be thinking that now, finally, is the time when children learn about the sounds of letters. However, that is still not what children are thinking about even if someone is getting them to parrot information about letter sounds. Instead, their real learning

FIGURE 1–7
This child's writing shows a quantitative principle that words contain three to six letters. It also demonstrates a qualitative principle acknowledging that different letters must be used to make words.

focuses on further exploring their theory that the numbers of letters is the key. Common assumptions are that it takes more letters to write the name of a big person than a little one, and more letters to describe a group of objects than a single object. This means that children believe their mother's name must be long and their own short. Even after Andrew has made connections between the letters and their sounds, he writes his little sister Mary's name as *MR* and his mother's name, Katy, as *KDIO*. He obviously is adding extra letters to make his mom's name bigger than his sister's. Youngsters also assume that it takes more letters to write about a bunch of grapes than about one grape or about a flock of sheep than one sheep. Free exploration of writing in journals is important for encouraging children to try out these ideas.

REARRANGING LETTERS

Children also explore their theories about the need for different letters or different sequences of letters for different words in much more depth before venturing into the realm of phonics. Depending on how many letters a child knows, different patterns will emerge: Different letters might be used for different words, or only one or two different letters will be inserted for each, or else the same letters will be used but in different sequences. At first, children may focus only on those letters in their own name (see Figure 1.8). Thus, you see all words represented through various combinations of those few letters. This is an approximation of the actual system, but lacking important elements.

CHECKING AND DISCARDING THEORIES

As they continue to interact with print, children have opportunities to check their theories. They soon encounter problems such as the fact that Patricia's name is much longer than her dad's. They also may be perplexed by the fact that adults can't read what they have written. They know adults can read, so something must be wrong. A strong desire to become part of the literate society drives most youngsters to try again and again to make sense of the system. Well-meaning adults who give information that doesn't fit into the child's framework offer no help at all. Too often, adults are talking to a child about the sounds of letters while the child is focusing on how many marks it takes to make a word.

Finally, youngsters do begin to consider the sound of the word in relation to the letters used. However, they still may be focusing on the quantity of

FIGURE 1–8
Ian's writing explores the letter forms in his own name.

letters needed rather than on the phonics principles. This results in matching the number of symbols they write to the number of syllable sounds they hear (see Figure 1–9). This doesn't answer the question of why certain words are represented by certain letters, though, so youngsters must continue their work. Children's own names offer an important model as they try to answer their questions. At this point, Felicia's teacher's input might help Felicia notice other names and words that start with an *F.* Felicia knew "her letter" before any other and she could write her name when she was still scribble-writing other words. Name writing develops earliest and provides insights about other writing.

FIGURE 1–9
Syllable quantitative principle with emerging qualitative sound-symbol relationships. The child read this as "Better watch out, better not cry, better not pout, I'm telling you why, never get mad."

LETTER NAMES AS SOUNDS

Their own first initial is often the first letter sound children figure out. Then they are on their way with a new hypothesis that connects letters to sounds in words. This still doesn't mean that typical phonics lessons are relevant. Despite those lessons, children still go about their own business of making sense of things. They usually start with the theory that all letters represent a sound like the name of the letter. This is a logical deduction because it is true for most consonants and for long vowel sounds. The theory leads to some interesting results when applied to *y*, which then becomes the first sound in words spelled with a *w*. Thus Patrick writes *yot* and reads it *want*. The letter-name-as-sound theory also makes for difficult reading for adults when youngsters decide that *h* is the logical choice for the *ch* sound. Bryce combines his theories about *y* and *h* and logically writes *yh* for the word *witch*. As strange as this may seem to adults, the letter-name-as-sound theory reflects thoughtful consideration of the sound-symbol system and should be respected as such (see Figure 1–10). Simply telling children the socially accepted representation does not assist their learning at this point. Continued exposure to print eventually will lead to theories more in keeping with standard convention. This occurs in the same manner as exposure to adult speech helps children to progress from baby talk (Fields, 1988).

Letters that sound like their names
B, D, F, J, K, L, M, N, P, R, S, T, V

SIMPLIFIED PHONICS

English-speaking children tend to ignore the short vowel sounds in their writing and write at first mostly with consonants (see Figure 1–11). This reflects the fact that short vowels in English tend to have irregular, interchangeable, and indistinguishable sounds, shown in the dictionary as a schwa. In contrast, Spanish-speaking children's early writing is mostly with vowels, reflecting the dominant sounds in that language. Lessons in the

FIGURE 1–10

Can you figure out what the child knows about letter sounds?

I	YAH	I	YZ	POT	DA	ANT	POT	NT.
I	wish	it	was	part	day	and	part	night.

TABLE 1–3
Oral-Written Language Development Compared

Oral Language	Written Language	Understanding
babbling and cooing	scribbles	exploring the medium
language intonations	linear-repetitive forms	refining the form
native language sounds	letterlike forms	cultural relevance
first "words" (mama)	letter names as sounds	partial accuracy
"telegraph" sentences	simplified phonics	simplify for success
creative grammar	advanced invented spelling	overgeneralization of "rules"
adult speech	standard spelling	formal structure

sounds of vowels make much more sense in Spanish than in English because vowel sounds are consistent in Spanish.

When first exploring the sound-symbol connection (phonics) in writing, children tend to simplify the process to make it manageable. This simplification process also was demonstrated in their early speech when they spoke in one- or two-word sentences. Similarly, when youngsters begin to write by representing the sounds they hear, their early invented spelling may be limited to representing one or two main sounds from a word (see Figure 1–12). Despite the modifications typical of emergent writing, adults finally are able to begin reading the child's writing. Unfortunately, many adults only begin to value a child's efforts at this point, rushing and discrediting everything leading up to it. Too few teachers or parents understand the child's previous efforts, and they cannot see what they do not understand (Ferreiro, 1990). Thus, children's early writing is often dismissed as scribbling or playing around. Many adults do not understand the learning process even when it reaches the invented spelling level. Those who view learning as a memorization process are afraid that invented spelling means practicing errors (Tem-

FIGURE 1–11
This writing demonstrates the hypotheses that each letter makes the sound of its own name and that each letter represents one word. Translation: Bumble bee, can you sing you sing your name for me.

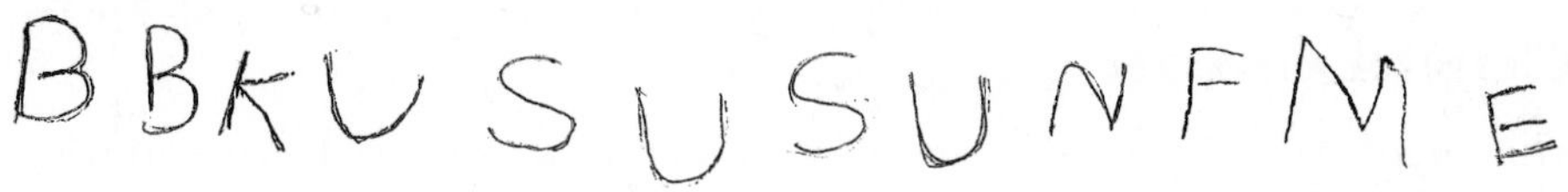

FIGURE 1-12

Invented spelling using a fairy tale format. To be read from bottom to top: Once upon a time. There lived a wolf. Who loved [to] eat little girls.

ple, Nathan, Temple, & Burris, 1993). Consideration of how errors in baby talk disappear should dispel these fears.

COMMUNICATING WITH ADULTS

When you understand the thinking behind children's various approaches to writing, you will be better able to match your teaching efforts to a child's current level. Though children's writing is valuable evidence of their learning, the product itself will not provide sufficient information until the final stages of the learning process. Even with knowledge of the process, you won't be able to figure out what hypothesis a child is using unless you also find out what the child is intending to do. You can't expect children to verbalize their hypotheses, but you usually can get them to tell you what they wrote. Then it is up to you to figure out the principles a child is using (see Figure 1–13). It is the teacher's job to provide opportunities for children to freely explore their current hypotheses. The teacher's role also is to provide support for thinking by encouraging peer debate, presenting challenging questions, and accepting children's efforts. These roles of the teacher will be discussed in subsequent chapters.

CONCLUSION

This chapter has presented information about how children learn as the basis for a discussion of how to teach. Literacy development was described in the

FIGURE 1–13
The child read his story as follows: A monster lived in outer space. He wanted to go down to Earth. He tried to get down to Earth but he couldn't. The gravity was too strong. But then he had an idea. He would take a space ship. The spaceship was not a spaceship— only wanted to go up.

THE MOSTR Bi Patrick mad octovr 12 1 993
a mostr lidi in otr sas he yuti to go dan to Earth
hetr trid togid ded to Earth bet he citit the gavd
wuz to sog bet then he hat e ider hwot tack a sas
sip the sassip waz no i sassip oln yot to go up

the ed

context of language development, emphasizing the integrated nature of language and literacy learning. Both oral and written language have been described as processes in which children actively construct knowledge rather than passively imitate or memorize.

DISCUSSION QUESTIONS

1. Many parents of preschoolers want to help their children learn to read. What are appropriate ways for parents to assist the beginning literacy process?
2. Many early childhood programs still try to teach the letters and sounds through memorization. How can you help other teachers change to more effective teaching approaches?
3. How is reading and writing instruction changed when teachers base their teaching on research about emergent literacy?
4. What do you remember about your own experiences in learning to read and write? Were you confused when adults just sat and looked at a book and said they were reading? Did you practice writing with lines of squiggles?

SUGGESTED FOLLOW-UP ACTIVITIES

1. Visit a preschool, kindergarten, or primary classroom. Analyze the materials available for children in terms of whether they are concrete or representational.

2.   Ask a four- or five-year-old to explain things such as where rain, clouds, or waves come from. Continue your conversation past the initial explanation to get the child's own perception rather than repetition of adult explanations.

3.   Spend a few minutes visiting with a two-year-old, a four-year-old, and a six-year-old on separate occasions. Document the rapid change in ability to communicate, in vocabulary, and in sentence constructions.

4.   Observe children of various ages as they write. Ask them about what they are writing, analyze the forms used, and try to determine their current theories about how writing works (see Table 1–2).

5.   Observe or talk to parents of young children to find out how they involve their youngsters in family reading and writing activities.

6.   Examine the National Association for the Education of Young Children's Developmentally Appropriate Practice Guidelines for recommendations regarding language and literacy learning.

7.   Practice explaining how children learn more by constructing their own knowledge instead of memorizing what someone tells them.

RECOMMENDED FURTHER READING

Books

Duckworth, E. (1987). *The having of wonderful ideas and other essays on teaching and learning.* New York: Teachers College Press.

Goodman, Y. (1990). *How children construct literacy.* Newark, DE: International Reading Association.

Halliday, M. A. K. (1982). Three aspects of children's language development: Learning language, learning through language, learning about language. In Y. Goodman, M. Haussler, & D. Strickland (Eds.), *Oral and written language development research: Impact on the schools.* Urbana, IL: National Council of Teachers of English.

Healy, J. M. (1990). *Endangered minds.* New York: Touchstone.

Kamii, C., Manning, M., & Manning, G. (1991). *Early literacy: A constructivist foundation for whole language.* Washington, DC: National Education Association.

Teale, W., and Sulzby, E. (1986). *Emergent literacy: Writing and reading.* Norwood, NJ: Ablex.

Teberosky, A. (1990). The language young children write: Reflections on a learning situation. In Y. M. Goodman, *How children construct literacy: Piagetian perspectives* (pp. 45–58). Newark, DE: International Reading Association.

ENCOURAGING EMERGENT LITERACY THROUGH PLAY AND EXPERIENCES

When a child creates with blocks, when he communicates with paint, when he uses his body freely as a means of expression, he is being taught to read.

J. HYMES, 1965

Curriculum guidelines for the early years include statements about teaching in the ways that children learn; about learning activities being relevant, interesting, and meaningful to children; about engaging children actively in learning; and about allowing them meaningful choices (Bredekamp & Rosegrant, 1992). These guidelines mandate early childhood programs that allow play and provide experiences with the world outside the classroom. This chapter describes authentic play and experiences and shows their link to literacy learning as well as to learning in general.

PLAY ENCOURAGES EMERGENT LITERACY

Play is prescribed for developmentally appropriate programs in the primary grades as well as in preschool and kindergarten (Bredekamp, 1987). Teachers and parents frequently quote the statement that "play is the work of children" and pay lip service to the value of play. Yet in practice, teachers often allow play only after other school work is completed or else assign the label "play" to teacher-directed activity. Many parents complain if their children report that what they did in school was play. These problems are symptoms of widespread misunderstanding of how children learn and the role of play in that learning.

Some educators have speculated that the term play has a bad reputation and should be abandoned. Some classrooms use terms such as "choosing time" instead of the P word. Whatever we call it, children's engagement in freely chosen activities of interest is vitally important to their learning. Play is the way in which children construct knowledge: It provides for exploration of the environment, experimentation with their ever-changing theories, practice in emerging skills, and peer interaction to stimulate thought about these activities. Those parents and educators who understand the value of these activities will defend play as basic to early childhood curriculum.

Play has a unique role in literacy development (Christie, 1991). Play provides a context for literacy development practice, content for reading and writing, and a mode of learning as well. We see play providing a context for practice when Caitlan writes a pretend phone message in the play house, we see play providing content for literacy when Demetrius writes about his block construction, and we see play as a mode of literacy learning when Anastasia pretends to read the book from yesterday's story time. Play as a mode of learning (Goodman, 1990) is particularly important because it represents an attitude valuable to all intellectual development. The playful attitude encourages intellectual risk taking in formulating new hypotheses and experimenting with them. The playful attitude sees this experimentation as pleasurable and encourages further learning.

Play provides a context for literacy development practice, content for reading and writing, and a mode of learning as well.

What do we mean by play? Sometimes what looks like work to an observer feels like play to the participant; sometimes what looks like play can feel like work. What is the distinction? Generally, work is what we must do to attain something of value or avoid something unpleasant, and play is what we choose to do because it is inherently interesting or pleasurable.

Usually, we would consider digging a ditch to be work, yet we see Dominic having a wonderful time digging a ditch to drain a big puddle on the playground. Because he chose to do this and is enjoying it, digging a ditch becomes play for him. On the other hand, we see a group of children in a kindergarten who appear to be playing with a set of blocks of various colors and shapes. A closer look reveals that this is not play, but rather a lesson in following directions for finding colors and shapes. Their teacher is directing the activity and now requests that they each find a red triangle and add it to their block structures. Several of the children appear restless and have to be reprimanded to pay attention. Because this block play is not self-selected or motivating to these children, it cannot be classified as play.

Exploratory Play

Dominic's ditch digging is a type of play in which children explore their environment and seek to understand it through manipulation. Sand and water play are in this category, as are other exploratory activities that cause youngsters to fiddle around with almost anything they can get their hands on. Obviously, teachers want to provide a variety of acceptable things with which young children can experiment. Children can then indulge their scientific curiosity yet not endanger themselves or damage their surroundings.

As he digs, Dominic encounters the properties of dirt. It seems hard and solid where packed, but he can loosen it into powder. Where water mixes with it, the dirt becomes soft and squishy. When the dirt turns into mud, it no longer brushes off his hands and clothes, but sticks to him. Dominic may find that dirt contains rocks or even something as interesting as worms. His discoveries become a foundation of knowledge that he draws upon as he goes on to create new theories about his world. Dominic's discoveries don't just enhance his science background; they will also provide new or added meaning to oral and written language that relates to his experience. He will extend his vocabulary as he shares his experiences with others and receives their responses. He will find personal meaning in books about digging in dirt or playing in the mud, such as *Muddigush* (Knudson, 1992). He may also use his experience as a topic for writing.

Dramatic Play

Now let's watch Kelly, who has a long scarf tied around her waist to simulate a skirt. Banging pots and pans around the playhouse, she admonishes two dolls propped at the table. "Hurry up and eat," she says. "We'll all be late. I have to get to work on time." When Scott wanders in, Kelly adds, "You be the dad, and then we'll get divorced." She hands him one of the dolls and tells him to get the baby dressed. But Scott wants to cook. He drops the doll and says, "I'll fix the dinner." Kelly gets visibly upset and yells, "No! I have to go to work now. It's morning." Scott continues to try to mesh his goals with Kelly's and suggests, "Let's pretend you came home now, and I fix your dinner." Reluctantly, Kelly agrees but insists that she has to leave first and then come back.

An observer of the dramatic play just described immediately notices the amount of language the children have used. We can tell at once that dramatic play enhances language development. The give-and-take involved in negotiating a script and playing cooperatively also provides children an excellent opportunity for practice in social skills, especially in becoming less egocentric. As children find out that others might not see things their way, their drive to play with other children causes them to compromise their initial positions. Realizing that theirs are not the only views of a situation represents intellectual as well as social growth.

Sometimes Ms. Montoya will notice a detailed plot emerge in dramatic play and she will encourage the children to make it into a written story. Because this is a multiage classroom spanning ages 5 through 8, youngsters who need help writing can consult with a more competent classmate. Ms. Montoya will take dictation if requested and will help children reconstruct their dramatic play into a written narrative theme. This assists the youngsters in exploring their topic more fully and also provides them with more literacy experience. Children get to see their play and their ideas take written form, and they will practice reading as they review what was written.

Dramatic play provides for literacy events in a variety of ways. Mrs. Hanna especially encourages her kindergartners to use reading and writing behaviors in real-life, functional ways during their play. Cookbooks by the play stove and storybooks by the doll crib encourage emergent reading. The scrap-paper notepads beside the phone in the playhouse offer a constant invitation to write. Youngsters use the notepad paper in many of the ways they see their families using writing. They not only take pretend phone messages, but also write notes to one another, notes as reminders to themselves, and grocery lists.

There are lots of grocery lists when the play store is set up. Mrs. Hanna reminds the children that it is important to have a list for going shopping. Each youngster writes a list using whatever form of writing that child chooses. Some can manage readable invented spelling, while others are drawing pictures; still others may be writing in squiggles, and some may choose to find the real words to copy. Most lists are a combination of

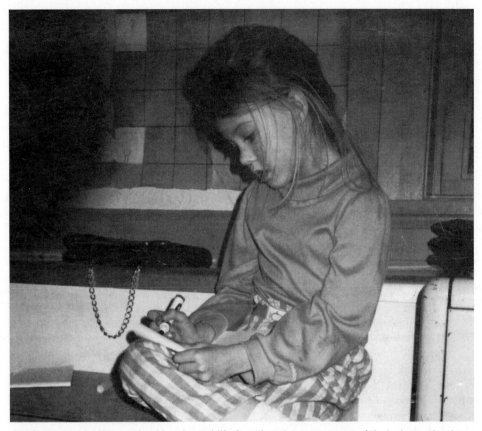

Children use reading and writing in real-life functional ways as part of their dramatic play.

approaches. Creating the grocery store involved many literacy events. After deciding on the name of the store, a committee of children made the store sign. Then the shelves needed to be labeled, and the food containers needed prices marked on them. One group of youngsters printed the money to be used in the store. Children learned much more from setting up the store themselves than if the teacher had done it for them.

Mrs. Thomas's first graders had a great time when they set up an airport ticket counter in the classroom. Like the kindergarten play store, this dramatic play center followed a relevant field trip. At the airport, the ticket agents had given the children a big box full of the throwaway parts of printed tickets. Everyone wanted to "write tickets" with these interesting scraps. In addition, some youngsters got involved painting artistic travel posters to decorate the area. Others made brochures about places to go. Mrs. Thomas allowed them to have a computer at the ticket counter to make things official. Several children worked together to plan and make the arrival and departure schedule chart. They brought suitcases from home to check in at the counter, and each suitcase had to be labeled with the proper destination.

Many children decided to write or dictate stories about their real or pretend trips. They expressed high interest in books about planes and stories about travel. The block area turned into a miniature airport for a while, with frequent toy plane takeoffs and landings. Playing airport turned into a theme for an integrated curriculum. It was an exciting time.

Dramatic play also fosters general intellectual development. Piaget (1962) tells us that play is a child's way of thinking through things. Because they cannot retain ideas in their heads to mull them over as an adult might, children play them out. If Kelly wants to understand her mother's impatience of that morning, Kelly is helped by reenacting it.

The scarf that Kelly has tied around her waist represents practice in another intellectual feat: She is using one thing to represent another (Nourot & Van Hoorn, 1991). Representation of this nature is the essence of our written language. Using a scarf to represent a skirt, a block for a telephone, or beads for pretend food helps Kelly understand that a set of squiggles can represent words, which in turn represent ideas.

Block Play

Let's look at what Mrs. Thomas's students, Matthew and Dustin, are building in the block area. When we come to watch, they begin to work even more diligently. They have created an elaborate set of roadways and are attempting to add bridges and ramps. They are testing the setup with small cars and trucks. When Dustin drives a truck under the bridge, his vehicle collides with Matthew's coming from the opposite direction. The boys decide to make traffic signs showing which way to go so they won't wreck again. They are so engrossed that they do not want to stop at lunch time. Finally, Mrs. Thomas says they must stop for lunch, but encourages them to leave their project where it is and make a sign asking that no one touch their highway. After lunch, Matthew and Dustin return to the block area.

The fine-quality wooden unit blocks are designed to assist children in making observations about relationships in size and quantity. Building bridges or spans of any sort with blocks provides practice in perceptual skills, such as determining size and distance. Blocks also naturally lead into practice with balancing and stabilizing. The various shapes and sizes of blocks make them excellent classification materials—especially when they are stored according to size and shape. Blocks are important educational materials and gain in value as children progress through the primary grades.

Block play enhances literacy development through practice with symbolic representation. The blocks can become whatever the child desires—bricks, houses, roadways, towers, or bridges. They can even be people, cars, or furniture. Children need frequent experience with symbols to represent other things as part of understanding that letters can represent language. Matthew and Dustin had sufficient understanding of written language to accept that traffic signs and a sign on their structure would communicate to others. They also had sufficient skill to be able to make the signs with some teacher assistance.

When children use blocks to represent other things, their play generally involves a theme from which dramatic play flows. Props such as miniature people, doll furniture, small animal figures, or small cars and trucks can extend block-play ideas as well as assist the dramatic play element. Block play can inspire themes for writing and art as well as for drama. Often a current theme being explored in all areas of the curriculum will find its way into the block area. The airport is one example; a block zoo or farm are others.

Continued Value of Blocks

Were you surprised to find a block area in a first-grade class? Many people expect such things in a preschool and even a kindergarten, but expect big changes as children enter first grade. However, the first-grade child usually is still in the preoperational stage of intellectual development and continues to require concrete materials for meaningful learning. Mrs. Thomas makes sure that her first graders have real experiences and concrete materials to help them in their thinking and understanding. She has several children in her class this year who are repeating first grade. They came to her "turned off" to reading but excited about opportunities to play. Mrs. Thomas believes that they were stopped short in their play and must have some of their needs met through play before they can go on. Most of all these youngsters need developmentally appropriate activities so that they can experience success and begin to feel good about themselves again.

She believes blocks are such important learning tools for six- and seven-year-olds that she managed to make room in her classroom for a fully equipped block area. Plenty of blocks are available so that children will not run out while in the middle of a project. Mrs. Thomas made sure there were shelves for storing the blocks; she knows that dumping them into a bin makes it impossible for children to find the block they need and that such storage may damage the blocks. She labeled the block shelves with the outline of the size and shape of the blocks that are to be stored in each section. This labeling assists children in cleanup and calls their attention to classification categories. Mrs. Thomas further enhances the block-play environment by frequently watching or admiring what is happening there. She gives her students the message that their block building is important. Mrs. Thomas's efforts are rewarded with wonderfully intricate and innovative block structures.

She considers it a shame that schools generally deprive children of this type of play just as they attain enough maturity to really create with raw materials. When she took her turn as a parent-helper in her children's preschool she saw that three- and four-year-old youngsters played with blocks more in an exploratory manner—messing around with what could be done with blocks. Frequently they got out the blocks and just spread them

Children are encouraged to build more intricate block structures when their teacher shows interest in their work.

around. When she taught kindergarten, she saw that with previous block-play experience and added maturity, her students were beginning to realize the potential of the blocks. Her first graders are becoming sophisticated in their block building.

Ms. Montoya agrees that blocks are important for her seven- and eight-year-old students as well as the five-year-olds. She used to consider blocks primarily as math and science materials, but has come to value them for language and literacy as well. She sees that block-play experience and the feelings of accomplishment that come from it provide interesting topics for discussion and writing. Of course, there is constant oral language involved in cooperative block play. As she encounters more and more students who speak little or no English, she discovers that they are drawn to the block area. Apparently, blocks speak all languages. As youngsters who speak little English coordinate their block-building efforts with native speakers of English, the block area becomes a language-learning area.

The Teacher's Role

Ms. Montoya sees ample evidence in her multiage primary class to convince her that the more experience they have with block building, the more youngsters benefit from blocks. Mrs. Thomas knows that six- and seven-year-olds need many opportunities to extend their language and thinking skills through dramatic play. She also knows that play provides great reasons to practice reading and writing skills, but she does not value that any more highly than she does the other benefits of play. Mrs. Hanna particularly welcomes the symbolic representation involved in this type of activity. She knows her kindergartners need this experience as they develop their understanding of the representational nature of language and literacy.

Mrs. Thomas attempts to provide as many play opportunities for her first graders as possible. She knows that they are still in the "golden age" of dramatic play and still emotionally and intellectually need that mode of dealing with ideas. Therefore, a play sink and stove are part of her room, as well as dress-up clothes and other props that can be used for various themes. Her students often use desk tops covered with a cloth to represent tables for playing house. Mrs. Thomas understands the continued need for water and sand play, too, so she never hurries children as they wash paint brushes or hands at the sink. Also, she never tells them not to play in the puddles or not to get dirty on the playground. She purchased a water-play table for the class, and sometimes she creates variety by filling it with rice or beans or sand. She provides further experiences with a variety of substances through frequent classroom cooking activities.

Mrs. Hanna provides a variety of props, multiethnic dress-up clothes, dolls with many shades of skin color, and a playhouse area in her kindergarten classroom. Because of limited space, she designed a structure that creates a cozy reading loft on top and a playhouse underneath. Some teachers sit at their desks during play time, thinking there is no role for them. Mrs. Hanna does just the opposite: She encourages dramatic play through her presence as an observer and sometimes as a participant when invited. Observing dramatic play not only encourages and assists play, but also allows the teacher to gather important diagnostic teaching information (Carter &

Jones, 1990). By watching her kindergartners in the playhouse or in the block area, Mrs. Hanna gains valuable information about children's interests, experiences, and levels of understanding about those experiences. She also can pick up clues about possible emotional problems if she sees a child who replays one theme over and over again or if she notices a child who seems unable to participate in this type of play. During her observations Mrs. Hanna finds out when children might have a narrative theme to put into writing. Occasionally, she takes notes on what they are saying and reads it back later to the children involved. These notes can become the core of a written version of their play.

As she observes play, Ms. Montoya notices interesting similarities between the ways in which individual children pursue play activities and how they approach literacy activities. Some are orderly, systematic, and cautious in how they get to the top of the climbing tower or in constructing the small structures they build. These same youngsters often are the ones concerned with correctness and neatness in their writing and who proceed with orderly caution in their reading attempts. Other youngsters proceed impetuously with seemingly little worry about the outcome whether they are climbing to new heights on the playground equipment, writing new words, or making meaning from a new book. They make glorious messes wherever they go—the art easels, the writing center, or the block area.

Play involving symbolic props, such as wooden beads used for pretend food or a doll used for a baby, gives children practice for understanding symbolic representation.

Mrs. Thomas, Mrs. Hanna, and Ms. Montoya value play as an integral part of their curriculum just as much as Ms. Reynolds does in her preschool. None of these fine teachers views play as a break from learning, but rather as an essential mode of learning. None of them relegates play to a time after the "real" work of school is done. They know that this is the real work of learning; therefore, they provide extended periods of time in their daily schedules to encourage this type of learning (Christie & Wardle, 1992). Furthermore, none of them tries to assign play topics, play areas, or playmates. They know that free choice is the essence of true play.

Active Play

Mrs. Thomas's classroom is not large but she makes provisions for large-muscle activity indoors and encourages active outdoor play at recess. Her first-grade classroom has space for a balance beam and a safe chinning bar. Students may use this equipment throughout the day. She never would consider keeping children from recess as punishment or as time to complete other work. Mrs. Thomas understands the importance of vigorous movement for proper development. Frequently, she will take youngsters outside at unscheduled times for special activities with large rubber balls or with a parachute.

In the preschool where she teaches, Ms. Reynolds has set aside an area for indoor large-muscle activity. There is plenty of space for running without getting hurt, a sturdy climbing tower, trikes, large blocks, a rocking boat, and a continually challenging variety of other interesting equipment. Ms. Reynolds provides time for outdoor play, too. When she taught in a child care center, Ms. Reynolds was even more careful about outdoor time because she had the children with her all day. She assumes that her half-day preschool students will have further chances to play outside in the afternoon.

When a child uses his whole body—two eyes, two hands, two arms, two legs and knees and feet—to pull himself up a scary slanted climbing board, he is being taught to read.

(J. Hymes, 1965)

Though unstructured running, climbing, and bike riding are the mainstay of outdoor play, organized games offer occasional alternatives for those who are interested. Chasing games such as the Chinese game, Dragon's Tail, contribute to understanding of language, number, music, and social studies as well as muscle control (McCracken, 1993). Ms. Montoya and her fellow teachers value the fact that there are no winners or losers in the Dragon's Tail game. They have learned many other excellent games from the group games book written by Kamii and DeVries (1980).

Games

Indoor games are an important part of their curriculum, too. Ms. Reynolds finds value in children making lotto games as well as playing them. Old magazines and catalogs are excellent sources of pictures for matching lotto. Mrs. Hanna helps her kindergartners to cut up pictures from magazines, their drawings, or snapshots to make puzzles. Ms. Montoya buys board games and puzzles for her class from yard sales. Mrs. Thomas bases her first-grade arithmetic curriculum on games suggested by Kamii (1985).

Whether the games are designed to teach arithmetic or are aimed more clearly at language arts skills, children practice language and thinking. Kamii and DeVries (1980) suggest the following criteria for choosing games: They should offer children the challenge of figuring out how to do something; children should be able to judge their own success; and all players should be able to participate actively throughout the game.

Manipulative Materials

Manipulative materials usually are located with the quiet games. The idea is to keep noisy, rambunctious work separate from that requiring closer concentration. Mrs. Hanna keeps beads, geoboards, puzzles, pegs, knitting supplies, play dough, small blocks, Legos®, Rigajigs®, and other small construction materials stored neatly on open shelves readily accessible to youngsters. These materials offer opportunities for children to problem solve and to construct knowledge about quantity, size, shape, patterns, and color. They also provide practice with visual discrimination, eye-hand coordination, and fine-muscle control that are helpful but not prerequisites for reading and writing. Mrs. Hanna makes sure there are materials representing various levels of difficulty. This way, each child will be able to find an appropriate challenge.

By the time children reach Mrs. Thomas's first grade, they have made progress in both large- and small-muscle coordination. However, Mrs. Thomas does not expect complete mastery and continues to provide opportunities to enhance coordination skills. Yes, this first grade has beads to string, play dough to squeeze, and puzzles to assemble. Mrs. Thomas knows that children in her class are now mature enough to experience greater success with these materials and to be creative rather than merely exploratory. She knows these activities assist all students in the process of learning to read and write, too. Mrs. Thomas also makes sure to figure out how Alice can participate in such activities from her wheelchair. Mrs. Thomas is helping Alice to develop perceptual abilities and be part of the class despite her inability to move her body as she desires.

Most people can understand that fine-motor coordination activities are related to literacy skills. These activities have been more welcomed into the school rooms of young children than gross-coordination activities—until first grade, that is. After that, it is less common to find the manipulative materials that we found in Mrs. Thomas's first-grade classroom, and even less common

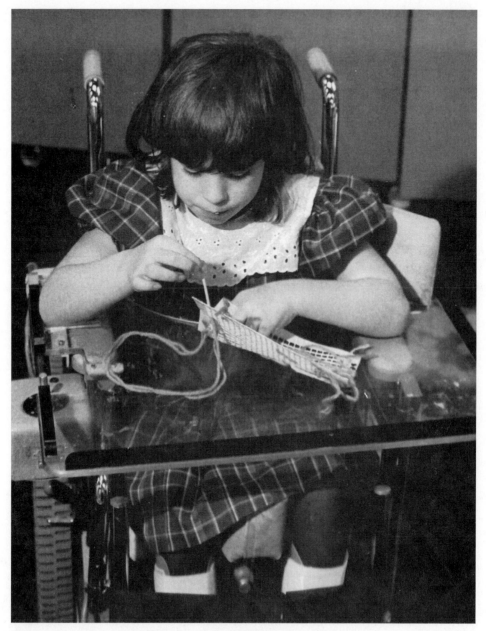

First graders still need activities to enhance coordination skills.

to find them used as a vital part of the program. Too often, schools relegate manipulative materials to be time fillers, after workbooks or work sheets are completed. This arrangement of priorities shows a lack of understanding of how young children develop and learn.

EXPERIENCES ENCOURAGE EMERGENT LITERACY

When a child looks ever so carefully at the scale in the store or at the life in his aquarium, he is being taught to read. When his year is a series of mind-stretching, eye-filling trips, helping him know more solidly his world, he is being taught to read.

(J. Hymes, 1965)

Children and adults need to bring meaning to the printed page in order to get meaning from that page (Lee & Rubin, 1979). Without some relevant experience or some personal meaning, much of the message that we read will be lost. Written words can extend our understandings, but they must build on an existing understanding. The common reaction of most adults who begin to read an article that is too technical—one that deals with unfamiliar facts and concepts—is to put the article aside. Adults and children tend to enjoy reading about the adventures of others that are similar to their own.

Writing also requires experiences so that the author will have something to write about. Even authors of fiction are told to write about what they know or their writing falls flat. Likewise, children are uninspired to write unless they have something of personal interest to share.

Even more than adults, children need to build on personal experience in their encounters with written and oral language. What we know about how young children think and learn, thanks to the work of Jean Piaget, tells us that children are much less able than adults to conceptualize ideas from mere words. Primary-grade students as well as preschool children, all in the preoperational stage, require concrete-level explorations to develop understandings. When youngsters interact with real objects, they begin to think about them and to develop their understandings (Forman & Kuschner, 1984).

Educators must make the distinction between constructing knowledge and learning facts. An adult can tell a child facts, and that child can memorize and repeat them. However, this performance does not imply understanding or necessarily involve thought. Although facts may be part of a complex understanding, they are not the same thing. Construction of knowledge involves higher-level thinking based on analysis of series of facts or events. Young children especially need firsthand experiences to encourage the hypothesis and experiment cycle of constructing knowledge (Piaget, 1973).

Sometimes adults are in a hurry for children to learn. Adults try to speed the learning process by substituting secondhand experiences for firsthand ones. They confuse passive exposure through pictures, films, or lectures with the active learning mode that Piaget's research told us is especially necessary for children under the age of eight. When these shortcut approaches

Experiences help children bring meaning to their reading and also give them something to write about.

result in a veneer of superficial knowledge, some adults think that the children have learned a great deal in a short time. However, knowing specific words and understanding what they represent are not necessarily the same thing. Just observe the results of youngsters' overexposure to television. These young children are able to talk about a number of things about which they understand little.

Firsthand experiences and observations take time. Betsy has to pour the water from one container to others over and over, on many different occasions, before she can understand that a short, wide container can hold the same amount as a tall, narrow one. Even then, the understandings she develops are only beginnings. Sometimes she will temporarily believe an incorrect idea due to her incomplete experience and her immature understandings. What a temptation it is to rush in and explain to her that she is wrong and to tell her the "right" answer. Knowledgeable teachers and parents resist that temptation; they know that Betsy can never discover what she has been told and that she understands best what she discovers for herself. As explained in Chapter 1, these adults know that if they tell Betsy that her perceptions of reality are wrong, Betsy only learns to distrust herself as a learner. When a child's immature view of the world tells her that the tall, narrow container holds more than the short, wide one, no amount of telling her otherwise will help her to understand. She will believe the wise adult and believe that she is wrong, but she will be confused and cease to trust and learn through her own thinking.

When teachers and parents have encouraged children to explore and experiment with their environment, the children build foundations of under-standing. They have experiences to think about, talk about, and write about; they expand their vocabulary with meaningful words related to their experiences; and they can relate personally to what others write about similar experiences. Children also gain practice in "reading"—or bringing meaning to a wide variety of experiences. They learn to "read" people's moods from their expressions or to "read" the weather from the color of the sky (Lee & Allen, 1963). Children learn to "read" symbols, such as the "golden arches," that relate to their experience. Additionally, they learn to read printed symbols with which they have had experience, such as the letters on the red sign that say STOP.

Home Experiences

Children have had a lot of experiences before preschool age, and once children enter school, much of their experience continues to occur outside of school. Some parents provide ample opportunity for their offspring to investigate pots and pans, plants and animals, and various textures, tastes, and smells. Other parents do little to encourage their children to explore, and some prevent children from investigating because of safety concerns. Some families take young children on walks and excursions, while others don't realize the importance of such trips.

Betsy's home is ideal for exploring. Her mother understands that babies need the intellectual stimulation of moving around and touching, tasting, and smelling. Betsy's mother uses the playpen to store dangerous or delicate objects, not babies. She keeps pins, needles, and other dangerous objects off the floor and covers electrical outlets so that little people can explore in safety. Though her children do have traditional toys, Betsy's mother knows that babies are interested in exploring more than toys. They don't learn much about the real world just from all that brightly colored plastic.

Older children in the family expand their learning experiences beyond toys by helping with chores. A two-year-old can put away canned food when

Children learn to read as a result of everyday experiences, such as reading the family shopping list.

groceries are unpacked, a four-year-old can sort and mate socks when laundry is folded, and a six-year-old can set the table. All the children get to help in cooking at some time, even though their help means more work for their mother.

Betsy and her brothers and sisters are fortunate to have a large yard for play. Their yard includes a paved area for riding tricycles, grass to run barefoot in, and dirt to dig in. Fruit trees, a vegetable garden, and pet rabbits in a cage also are in Betsy's backyard. The children in this family may choose from a variety of outdoor experiences. They are allowed to pick the fruit when it is ripe and eat it when it is washed; they can eat fresh peas out of the pod or pull up tender young carrots to see if they are mature; and they can gently pet the soft, furry bunnies. On warm days, the children add the delightful sensory experience of water play when they get to fill the plastic swimming pool.

Children who live in other places have other kinds of family experiences. Lucy, who lives at the mouth of the Kuskokwin River in southwest Alaska, helps with berry picking and enjoys eating the berries mixed with shortening, sugar, and sometimes fish. Lucy watches her mother skin seals when her father and brother go hunting, and learns about the value of dried seal gut that makes better raincoats than anything you can buy. She knows the feel of the soft fur from the animals her father traps, and she watches carefully as her mother prepares the skins to make warm winter clothing. She experiences the spring ice breakup in the river and knows that it means the family will travel by boat instead of their snowmobile for a while. Lucy is learning how to cut fish and looks forward to going with her family to fishcamp when school is out for the summer. There are so many interesting things for Lucy to do and to learn.

Betsy's family travels by van rather than boat or snowmachine, but family outings add to her learning, too. The family van has enough space, seat belts, and baby seats to take all five children safely and comfortably on errands or outings. These children go to the grocery store, the fabric store, and the hardware store. They get to ride along to pick up Aunt Marjie at the airport and to bring Mandy home from her ballet lesson. Along the way, they see bridges, trains, and construction work. Of course, they just don't stay in the van; they get out and explore the grocery store and learn to identify products on the shelves and vegetables on display. The get to watch the planes land at the airport and they get to pull the luggage off the baggage belt. These children are storing up many understandings to bring to oral and written language.

This family's everyday activities also provide the children meaningful experiences with written language. The younger ones watch as their mother writes the grocery list and they suggest items to include. Those who can write make notes of grocery items that they notice are running low, such as their favorite juice or lunch dessert. The schedule for various car pools is written and posted for daily reference. The children realize the importance of writing down the complicated plan for getting Joey to and from karate, getting Amy to and from swimming lessons, and getting Mandy to and from ballet. Another printed item posted prominently on the refrigerator door is the school lunch menu. The school-age children check it daily to decide whether to pack a lunch or buy one at school. Those who can't read the menu and don't yet need to nevertheless are aware of the significance of reading this notice.

School Experiences

A home environment rich in experience is the ideal model for early childhood education (Bredekamp, 1987). Schools traditionally have been organized on a factory model, but current recommendations are to use the home model instead. Elementary teachers have felt pressured to go along with the traditional approaches to education despite seeing how poorly they fit young children. Unfortunately, too many preschools try to emulate the inappropriate public school practices. Betsy's preschool teacher tries to create a school environment that provides many experiences similar to those Betsy has at home. Ms. Reynolds considers this especially important because not all children have these experiences available at their homes. Some of those children will be labeled "at risk for school failure" because of what they have missed. Ms. Reynolds tries to fill in the gaps.

Ms. Reynolds consciously plans experiences to help her young students find out some answers to their constant questions of *why*. She recognizes the intellectual curiosity of preschoolers and works at satisfying that curiosity in ways that will be meaningful to them. She knows that preschool students must learn through all their senses, not just through hearing. The preschool setting that she has prepared is a series of invitations to experiment. It includes sand and water, paint and paste, magnets and magnifying glasses, fish and guinea pigs, and props for trying out roles seen in the real world.

Ms. Montoya also makes sure that her students regularly have new, stimulating experiences, both in and out of the classroom. She changes the standard classroom offerings with new props or variations on a theme as she observes children becoming ready for new challenges. The water-play table might be set up for float-and-sink experiments for a while; at another time, it might contain funnels, hoses, and pumps for moving water in different ways; and at yet another time, it might have detergent added for blowing bubbles with straws. The sand area may contain toy trucks and road-building machinery; at other times, it may feature toy dinosaurs or zoo animals; and then later it may allow the combination of water and sand play for a different kind of sand experience. Props in the dramatic play area change to reflect the children's current interests based on the field trips they recently have taken.

Keeping in mind the ideal home environment as a model for her classroom, Ms. Montoya involves her students in frequent cooking projects. Sometimes these are related to literature or poetry enjoyed by the class. The book *Strega Nona: An Old Tale* (De Paola, 1975) led to a pasta festival. A parent brought a pasta machine to school and supervised a cooking center where youngsters made batches of pasta dough and fed it through the machine. The next day they cooked their pasta, and on the third day different small groups made different toppings. The end result was a variety of pasta dishes for a pasta feast. Other times, cooking is part of a social studies or science topic. Youngsters are amazed to find that they can actually crush peanuts and make peanut butter, that they can shake cream and make butter, and that they can squeeze oranges to make orange juice. Making different ethnic foods under the supervision of a parent expert is always considered a treat, too.

Cooking not only adds to children's knowledge base, but also involves reading recipes and cookbooks. Some children get inspired to write their own recipes or cookbooks, using their real and imaginary cooking experiences.

Planning Outings

Ms. Montoya knows that children also learn much outside the classroom, and she wants her students to be exposed to other environments. She plans excursions to visit the boat harbor, the fish-processing plant, and the neighborhood grocery store. She takes advantage of unplanned opportunities, such as when the house across the street was painted and when a nearby street was dug up so workers could replace some pipes. Instead of spending all her after-school time running errands buying, begging, and borrowing materials for class projects, she often saves the errands for school time. She asks an aide or parent helper to take three or four youngsters to the store for whatever is needed. The children prepare for the errand by making a list of items needed and checking to be sure they have enough money if they are buying something. These outings are valuable learning opportunities, especially for youngsters who don't have such opportunities with their parents.

For large groups, it is a good idea to plan excursions well in advance. Teachers find it worthwhile to visit the site ahead of time to decide how many children can be accommodated at one time, to acquaint themselves with possible hazards, and to analyze the potential for firsthand experiences. When she plans a field trip, Ms. Reynolds takes time to plan with hosts at the site. If a guide will lead the children on a tour, Ms. Reynolds makes certain that the guide will not spend much time talking, but will show children things and let them touch whatever they safely can. She emphasizes that these young children will not learn everything about the operation they are observing, but will learn a little now and more later. Experience has taught her that this caution is necessary as part of keeping well-meaning adults from trying to explain too much.

Mrs. Thomas thinks about the purpose of each field trip as she plans, and tries to vary the purposes as well as the places. Some outings help children to learn about processes, such as how houses are built or how bread is baked; others show behind-the-scenes activities, such as visiting a television or radio station, restaurant, or grocery store; other trips help children explore the community geographically in relation to their school and homes. Some are science excursions for studying nature (see Figure 2–1). Sometimes she

FIGURE 2–1
Dictated stories can provide a record of a science excursion that children can enjoy reading again and again.

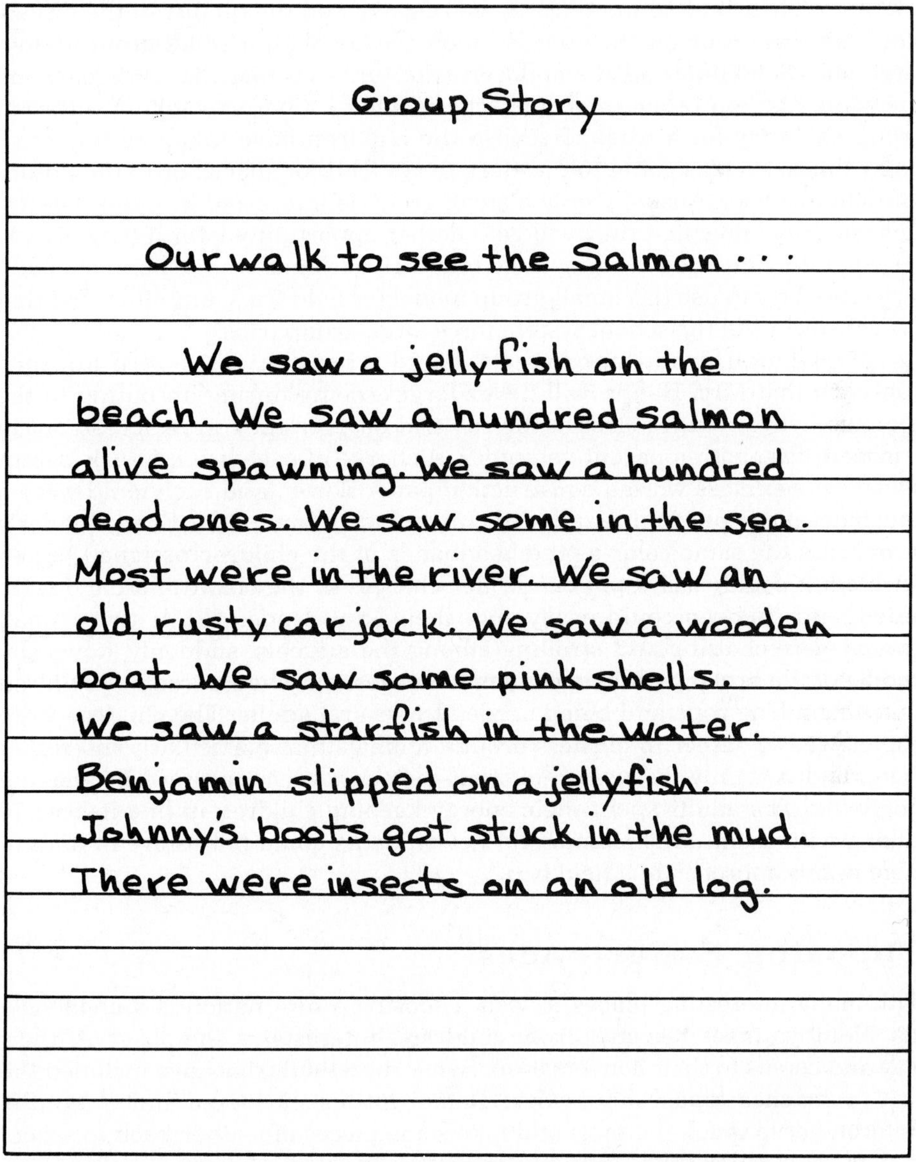

Group Story

Our walk to see the Salmon...

We saw a jellyfish on the beach. We saw a hundred salmon alive spawning. We saw a hundred dead ones. We saw some in the sea. Most were in the river. We saw an old, rusty car jack. We saw a wooden boat. We saw some pink shells. We saw a starfish in the water. Benjamin slipped on a jellyfish. Johnny's boots got stuck in the mud. There were insects on an old log.

and her first graders take a trip just for the enjoyment of having an adventure, smelling growing things, and feeling the breeze. All provide food for thought and ideas to draw or write about. Mrs. Thomas also tries to find books that relate to the field trips because she knows the children will be interested in them.

Ms. Reynolds is able to arrange for small groups to go on most of the outings she plans rather than take all twenty children at one time. With a group of five children and one adult, all children can get close enough to see and hear. Their interaction tends to be relaxed, and the quality of the discussion that can occur on the spot is much greater with a small group than a large one. Sometimes all the children take turns visiting the same place on the same day; on other occasions, the teacher or parents take a different group each day for a week. Because the children have taken certain trips many times, such as going to the store to get food for snacks or to the library to exchange books, usually only a small group is interested in those outings. The children know that they will get another opportunity later if they are too busy painting or woodworking to go today. Her friends who teach in elementary school try to use this small-group model for field trips, but often find that the constraints of the school system force large-group trips.

This small-group approach to field trips contrasts with another approach that Mrs. Hanna will never forget seeing during an outing to the zoo. She had her entire class at the zoo that day, but they were spread out in groups of five, with a parent volunteer in charge of each group. Each parent leader for her class wore a construction paper flower, and each child wore a construction paper headband with his or her name on it. Every leader's flower was the same color as the headbands of the children assigned to her. Each adult could easily spot one of her charges in the crowd if a child wandered, and children could easily spot their adult leader. While these small groups were chatting and strolling among the animals, suddenly, down the middle of the broad path between animal cages, marched a troop of children clutching a long rope and being herded by several adults. The children were not allowed to gather in clusters around animals that particularly interested them, and certainly discussion of what they saw wasn't easy while walking single-file. The adults spent their energy keeping children in line instead of talking with them. Mrs. Hanna and her students could only stare in amazement at this approach to a field trip.

Choosing Experiences

With many interesting places to visit, choosing a destination is a challenge. Ms. Montoya takes her cues from children's interests as she observes their play and listens to their conversation. Some successful trips have included the visit to the shoe repair shop, where Ramel got his shoe fixed and where the children got to touch the tools and take some pieces of leather back to school to play shoe repair; the pizza parlor, where they got to help put their own ingredients on a pizza and eat it; the animal shelter, where they got to pet the animals; and the dentist's office, where they sat in the examination chair, looked inside each other's mouths with the little mirror, and then received new toothbrushes. Each of these excursions resulted in pretend play to explore the ideas gained, and each stimulated significant drawing and writing.

Possibilities exist for brief field trips within the school building as well. A visit to the principal's office, a visit to see what the school secretary does, a visit to the nurse's office, or a peek inside the custodian's domain all inform and interest youngsters. Children also enjoy seeing other classrooms and meeting other teachers. Of course, children enjoy and benefit from frequent visits to the school library and the librarian.

Many preschool classes meet in church buildings. These settings offer the teachers and students the possibility of meeting the minister, seeing his or her office, and getting the minister to show youngsters the chapel and sanctuary. Churches often include a kitchen that could be useful for cooking experiences and have a recreation hall useful for large-muscle activities. Sunday school rooms that are unused by the kindergarten or preschool during the week also interest youngsters.

Every community and every part of the country has unique features and locations that contribute to the culture of that area. These can be the basis for fascinating field trips. For instance, children living in southeast Alaska should explore the harbors and fishing boats. They should be shown around a ferry, a hydrofoil, and a tourist cruise ship; they should get to examine a float plane and watch a helicopter transport machinery to a logging camp. For these children, no highways or railroads link communities, and their studies should reflect this reality. They do have knowledge of glaciers, icebergs, forests, beaches, eagles, and sea lions, however. And they have the rich cultural heritage of the Tlingits who lived there first and still thrive there. These influences will determine which fiction and nonfiction books will be most relevant for these children. These influences will also provide topics for writing.

Exploring an Alaskan fishing boat or an Arizona cactus are equally interesting adventures.

Children living in Phoenix, Arizona, would have a different set of relevant experiences. Instead of going to the woods to pick blueberries, they would visit the desert to examine the delicate cactus flowers in the spring and learn to avoid cactus needles. Instead of learning how to keep warm in winter, they would learn how to avoid overexposure in the summer. Instead of discovering the wonders of the beach at low tide, they would discover the difference between a riverbed when dry and then after a rainstorm. The animals, birds, and trees these children see, and then read and write about differ from those in Alaska, but certainly would be no less fascinating. The world of Arizona children would include black widow spiders, rattlesnakes, buzzing locusts, orange blossoms, and palm trees. The Papago, Hopi, and Navaho people native to that area weave blankets and make intricately painted pots instead of totem poles, and the relevant Native American literature and folklore is unique to this area. Both sets of experiences are equally valid for young children, and contribute equally to their development of literacy.

Children do not necessarily have to go someplace for an experience; sometimes that experience can come to them. Many people are flattered when a teacher asks them to come to school to share something about themselves or the work they do. A carpenter might come and demonstrate his tools, and maybe even spend time helping interested children in the woodworking center. A plumber or an electrician would be equally fascinating. Every year, Ms. Reynolds invites the mother of a new baby to bring the infant to school and let the children watch her bathe the baby in a plastic tub. This event always sparks bathing of dolls for several days as well as interest in writing and reading stories about babies. Persons from diverse cultures can bring artwork, clothing, or food samples to share with children. Painters, musicians, potters, and weavers can provide wonderful demonstrations for youngsters. Many of these interesting persons might be the parents of your students.

Art and Music Experiences

Visiting artists can inspire youngsters to try new art forms and techniques. Ms. Swedell's intricate weaving creates interest in learning to weave and she willingly assists those who want to try. Stefan's dad is a potter and he demonstrates how to make a simple pinch pot. Of course, young children cannot create beautifully finished products and often cannot even create recognizable objects. However, it is the process and not the product that is important to learning. Teachers who understand children and who care about art insist that all artwork must be the child's own work. Some teachers get sidetracked about the purpose of art activities and end up doing most of the work themselves in order to have something nice to display. Some classrooms even offer cut-and-paste work sheets in place of actual crafts or coloring sheets in place of actual art.

A good art area for young children provides a variety of paper, drawing materials, scissors, glue, easels, and paint always ready for use. This area should feature a changing variety of art-exploration challenges. Sometimes the challenge is to figure out how to use the materials provided to make something specific—what kind of bird could be made with these feathers and styrofoam? Other times, the challenge is to explore the potential of a new art medium—what does it feel like to finger paint with soap flakes? These opportunities for painting, sculpting, drawing, cutting, and pasting have a side benefit: They are directly related to fine-muscle and eye-hand coordination skills that children must use in reading and writing. In addition, children frequently wish to write or dictate a narrative to accompany their artwork. Though art is important in its own right, a discussion of literacy cannot overlook the link between representational art and writing.

Music events make important contributions to children's learning as well. Ms. Montoya's class really got excited when Jamaal's father demonstrated African drum playing. The children were allowed to play the drums under supervision and they got to make their own drums from a variety of materials. Drum playing became a major attraction in the classroom. Drum beats inspired dancing, and drum making inspired artistic efforts. Ms. Montoya related the study of patterns from math to the decorating and playing of drums. Some youngsters decorated their drums and tried to imitate an African decorative pattern Ms. Montoya found in a book, while others were interested in making patterns with the beat they created. Of course, some children just wanted to pound on the drums. A children's concert by famous violinist Linda Rosenthal offered another kind of live music experience.

Music is a constant part of life in Ms. Montoya's classroom, not just a special event. She uses a guitar to lead songs daily and her class soon has a large repertoire of songs memorized. She writes the words to the songs on chart paper so that the children who wish to can follow the print while they sing. Some youngsters make up their own songs and teach them to the class. The students in this multiage group class also have access to a variety of rhythm instruments and use them in many ways—for spontaneous parades, to lead dancing, to accompany singing, as part of pretend play, and just to mess around.

CONCLUSION

This chapter advocated blocks, games, manipulative materials, pretend play, exploratory play, and large-muscle play as integral parts of literacy development for children in prekindergarten through the primary grades. The value of diverse experiences in providing background and purpose for literacy also has been emphasized.

DISCUSSION QUESTIONS

1. The principal walks into your class and observes block play, dramatic play, water play, and various art and manipulative materials activities all happening in a happy clamor. She interrupts your supervision of a cooking activity to ask why you aren't teaching reading according to the day's schedule. How can you help your principal to understand?
2. Describe how some skills traditionally taught through direct instruction could be learned through play.

SUGGESTED FOLLOW-UP ACTIVITIES

1. Observe children engaged in dramatic play. Note their use of props and other examples of symbolic representation. Note how the roles they play affect their vocabulary and otherwise impact their language.
2. Facilitate the use of reading and writing materials and activities as a part of dramatic play. Note how children use reading and writing as part of play.
3. Encourage and/or help children to write the story of their pretend play after it occurs. Note the benefits to literacy and to play.
4. Watch as preschool children build with blocks. Note their processes and type of products they achieve. Arrange to watch older children building with blocks. Compare their levels of manipulative dexterity, symbolic representation, goal-oriented behavior, and quality of products.
5. Plan and implement an activity with a small group to enhance the experience base of young children, following guidelines provided in this chapter. Help children use the experience to enhance their language and literacy.

RECOMMENDED FURTHER READING

Periodicals

Harp, B. (1988). Doesn't play steal time from reading? *The Reading Teacher*, 42(3).

Nourot, P. M., & Van Hoorn, J. I. (1991). Symbolic play in preschool and primary settings. *Young Children*, 46(6), 42–50.

Pellegrini, A. D. (1980). The relationship between kindergartners' play and achievement in prereading, language, and writing. *Psychology in the Schools*, 17(4).

Books

Christie, J. F. (1991). Play and early literacy development. Albany: State University of New York Press.

Jones, E., & Reynolds, G. (1992). The play's the thing: Teacher's roles in children's play. New York: Teachers College Press.

CHAPTER

3

ENCOURAGING EMERGENT LITERACY THROUGH ORAL LANGUAGE AND STORY TIME

Just as speech develops in an environment immensely more rich than the immediate needs of the learner, so the orientation to book language develops.

D. HOLDAWAY, 1991

Knowledge of oral and written language conventions obviously is associated with learning to read and write. Most educators accept that exposure to language and to books is the way to help children to acquire this knowledge. Unfortunately, some adults try to impart this knowledge in ways incompatible with how children learn language. This chapter will present information and examples to help you to teach most effectively in these areas.

ORAL LANGUAGE

Inappropriate language instruction isolates pieces of knowledge about language and teaches youngsters to memorize those pieces. You may have seen an example of this in a DISTAR lesson, in which the teacher pronounces sentences in standard English and children are to repeat them until they get it right. Though DISTAR was abandoned long ago in most schools, the ideas behind this kind of teaching still are in use. Those old ideas viewed learning as memorizing and repeating what someone tells you. The research of Piaget (Piaget & Inhelder, 1969) and Vygotsky (1978) is reflected in the current view that language learning involves much more.

Another problem with the old approaches to language instruction is that they presented material in a predetermined sequence, based on misinterpretation of developmental norm data. Piaget's research often is cited erroneously to support such practices (Harste, 1993). Many people incorrectly believe that Piaget's work was about stages of learning, while it was actually about the process of constructing knowledge. Piaget's descriptions of stages in thinking were merely generalities discovered when exploring the learning process. Like other knowledge, language learning is a process of making sense of things. Learning involves creating personal meaning out of experiences; it is not an accumulation of facts or skills (Piaget, 1985). Each child's meaning-making process is unique, based on a unique set of experiences.

What are some ways teachers can best assist children's oral language learning? Examples from language-rich classrooms help to answer that question. First, let's observe Ms. Reynolds with her preschoolers. She values the language learning that her students have acquired already, so she continues and extends the processes that have proven successful in their past learning. Ms. Reynolds definitely reinforces children's communication efforts in this preschool.

When a child hears good adult language, and when he has the fullest, freest chance to use his own language, he is being taught to read.

(J. Hymes, 1965)

Adult Conversations with Children

Ms. Reynolds knows that the best way for children to become more proficient with language is to use it more. She also knows that having adults to interact with is essential. Therefore, Ms. Reynolds and the parent-helpers put high priority on conversations with youngsters. The give-and-take of conversation gives children feedback about their communication and provides models of language.

Ms. Reynolds pays close attention to children as they talk to her, and she tries to squat or sit at their eye level for the best possible communication. She not only listens respectfully, but also asks questions that encourage the children to think and use additional language. Frequently, she makes comments that extend a child's statement, elaborating on the idea and incorporating new vocabulary words. When Blair tells her that she got a puppy, Ms. Reynolds asks Blair to tell her more about the dog. After Blair's enthusiastic description, she comments, "I think you are going to have a wonderful time playing with that cuddly puppy."

Sometimes teachers have trouble understanding what children are talking about. This may be due to immature language skills, use of a nonstandard dialect, subject matter unfamiliar to the teacher, or cultural differences in

Sometimes it is hard to give individual attention to children when there are many in the group, but it is worth the effort.

narrative styles. Teachers usually lack the familiarity with an individual child's personal and social world that is so critical to effective communication (Cazden, 1988). Ms. Reynolds tries to be sensitive to and accepting of all types of individual communication. Her careful listening and questioning style shows respect for children and their language. If she doesn't follow what a child is saying, she continues to ask questions until she has some sense of the child's meaning. She never asks questions that she knows the answer to, such as "What color is that dress you are wearing?" Instead, her questions are honest inquiries and a means to understand a child. These are the kinds of questions that encourage children to communicate with their teachers.

Much of Ms. Reynolds's individual conversations with children occur incidentally as they arrive at school or while she is assisting them with boots and coats for going outdoors. Other opportunities arise as Ms. Reynolds circulates among her students while they are engrossed in their various chosen activities. She also teaches the parent-helpers how to encourage children's language. Yet she knows that the relationship with the one teacher who is there every day is most important to her students. She makes herself available to more children by keeping herself free to circulate while assigning the parent aides to supervise specific activities such as baking blueberry muffins or creating collages.

When Ms. Reynolds converses with children she herself says little. Instead, she stimulates children's thinking and expression of thoughts. She carefully does not give feedback that turns off conversations. She never makes a judgmental response such as "That wasn't a nice thing to do" when a child confides in her. She rarely gives information or a quick answer to questions, either. Rather, she prolongs the conversation through questions such as "Why do you think that happened?" or simply "What do *you* think?" Her responses indicate acceptance of what is said and frequently seek to verify communication through paraphrasing what she heard. For instance if Marisa says "My baby bad," Ms. Reynolds might use reflective listening and say, "Your baby has been doing something wrong?" Then Marisa knows what message Ms. Reynolds received and can elaborate on it by saying, "Yes, he cry all night. But he just little." This information in turn could be elaborated for further conversation. The information could also result in a topic for a dictated story.

Sometimes teachers experience difficulty in giving individual attention to children when there are so many of them at preschool. Ms. Reynolds believes that two minutes of her undivided attention is worth more to a child than two hours of her attention when that child is part of a group. She strives to build trust and rapport with her students through these one-to-one encounters, knowing that trust and rapport are necessary for effective communication. She makes a point of initiating conversations with those children who make no effort to talk to her. She knows that it is natural to talk most to those youngsters who talk most to her. However, because she realizes that the more verbal children need her interaction the least, she is especially attentive to the quieter children. She has noticed, though, that some quiet children seem to feel overwhelmed by language from very verbal persons. For some children, less talk is a cultural style. Sometimes, Ms. Reynolds makes it possible for a child just to be with her, working on the child's trust before conversation.

Conversations Between Children

Snack time offers an excellent chance for conversation. The parent aides and Ms. Reynolds each sit at a table with about five children. The adults eat with the children, modeling table and mealtime conversation manners. This is a direct contrast with practices is some schools where adults stand around and converse among themselves while children are fed. Such a practice ignores the learning potential of snack time. In Ms. Reynolds's class, the adults talk with youngsters, but take care not to monopolize the conversation at snack time or any time; they encourage children to talk among themselves even more than to the teacher. In this preschool, opportunities abound for children to talk with one another. They talk while they paint, they talk while they build with blocks, they talk while they climb the climbing tower, and they talk while they act out dramas in the playhouse area or pretend to be their favorite television heroes. All the play activities and experiences described in Chapter 2 are also language-learning opportunities.

In addition to informal conversation among children and between teacher and children, teachers plan many activities to enhance language. The changing props in the playhouse—suggesting a store for a while, a doctor's office next, and a fishing boat another time—encourage new vocabulary and different types of verbal exchanges. Additionally, the many stories, songs, poems, and finger plays that children experience daily in this preschool have language development as their primary purpose. Actually, everything children do, from finger painting to playing with the pet gerbil, enhances their language development by providing motivation and content for speech.

In her multiage class with youngsters from five to eight years old, Ms. Montoya provides a rich foundation of play and experiences to assist their language development. She continues the stories, dramatic play, and other language-development activities that most of her students encountered in preschool or child care programs. She plans time for oral discussion about field trips and class events. Ms. Montoya's curriculum builds on what children already know, repeating experiences or extending new challenges as the children's responses indicate. Because children have different experiences and individual responses to them, she must approach their language development in various ways. A flexible curriculum with open-ended activities allows for the necessary variations.

Mrs. Hanna also continues the practice of encouraging children to talk among themselves as they work at learning centers. She knows that talking with others about what they are doing increases children's understanding as well as enhances their oral language proficiency. This type of social interaction is one of the essential ingredients for intellectual development as described by Piaget: When children compare their perceptions with those of their peers, they try to figure out which view is correct. When an adult's perception is different from a child's, the child naturally assumes that the adult is right, whether or not the adult view makes sense to the child. With peers, children assume that their own ideas are of equal value, and they will explain and defend those ideas, which requires their careful analysis. Children do not automatically assume a peer is right; instead, they go through the valuable process of analyzing the other viewpoint, comparing it to personal understandings, and modifying or solidifying their previous views (Kamii & Randazzo, 1985).

Listening and Diagnostic Teaching

Ms. Montoya finds that by being a careful listener she not only encourages more communication from children, but also discovers a great deal about their level of language development. This guides her in planning appropriate educational experiences for each of her students. When she discovers that some children are using more sound substitutions than normal for their age or that some are confusing words that sound somewhat alike, she knows she must make auditory discrimination practice available for those children.

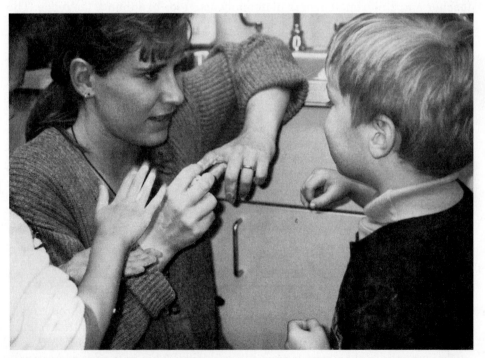

By being a careful listener, a teacher can discover a great deal about a child's level of language development.

She doesn't become concerned when children say, "Is this aw wite?" or when someone asks to hold the "nake." She knows that production of the *l, r,* and *s* sounds will come with maturity. But if children continue to confuse other sounds in kindergarten, perhaps they aren't hearing them properly. Once she has determined that no hearing problems exist, Ms. Montoya engages those children in rhyming word games, introduces a game with a set of sound-matching cans, or helps them to notice various sounds on the playground. Her students also enjoy playing with the sounds and rhymes in songs and poems, which are frequent attractions throughout the day. Careful attention to subtle sound differences is also needed as children begin to figure out which letters are used to represent which speech sounds.

Mrs. Hanna doesn't correct children's speech, either, even though she makes it a point to notice speech problems. She knows that the most effective way to increase language ability is through practice, and she doesn't want to stop anyone from practicing because they fear she will correct them. Children do practice in her classroom. Her kindergarten is not one where the teacher constantly says "shh" to children; instead, children talk to the teacher, to each other, and to themselves.

Children can learn language from talking to their peers, but sometimes they don't know how to start a conversation with another child. Then Mrs. Hanna will help with a comment such as, "Zachary, have you told Maria about your new kitten? I think she has a black kitten, too." Sometimes, Mrs. Hanna will bring a small group together for a discussion. These group discussions have specific purposes, perhaps planning a cooking project or naming the new class rabbit. These situations provide excellent practice in group discussion skills, with Mrs. Hanna guiding the students in taking turns and being sure everyone is heard, but never dominating the conversation.

Occasionally, the whole group is brought together for a discussion of a subject that affects everyone. However, these children are not ready to function for long in a group of twenty-five. They get too squirmy and bored sharing both the limelight and the teacher's attention with so many others. Mrs. Hanna finds it more valuable to divide the group at least in half, with a parent-helper leading one group discussion, or with the rest of the class engaged in independent activities. She keeps in mind James Hymes's (1981) guideline that the right-size group for a child has no more people than that child has had birthdays.

Language Differences

Sometimes a child will come to school who does not speak standard English or any English at all. Although Ms. Montoya knows that this child eventually will need to learn standard English to succeed in American schools, she values whatever language a child speaks. She believes that accepting a child's language is part of accepting that child and that child's background. She has children in her class from Eastern Europe, Southeast Asia, and Mexico. She helps her students value all the languages in the group; and they try to learn something of each new language in the classroom. The children especially enjoyed an activity suggested in a new social studies curriculum guide (Feeney & Moravcek, 1995), learning the action rhyme *Hello Toes* (Barlin & Kalev, 1989) in various languages. Bilingual parents usually enjoy an invitation to teach the rhyme in the language of their heritage.

As they participate in the regular class activities, limited- and non-English-speaking youngsters quickly gain proficiency with English. Interaction with English-speaking peers through play appears to be the best possible English lesson. As those learning English as a second language progress, Ms. Montoya helps them to feel proud of knowing more than one language. When Reid said, "Sergei talks funny," Ms. Montoya pointed out Sergei's bilingual achievements and said that she certainly couldn't learn Russian as quickly as Sergei was learning English. She added that she wished she could speak two languages like he does. The response seemed to make an impression on Reid as well as on Sergei.

Her main concern is that the child uses language to communicate, not what language that child uses. If the child only speaks a language Mrs. Hanna doesn't understand, she works with the school district to bring in an aide who speaks that language. If that isn't possible, sometimes an older child or a par-

As they participate in the regular class activities, limited- and non-English-speaking youngsters quickly gain proficiency with English.

ent can spend time in the classroom to assist as needed. If the difference is merely a dialect of English, she does not feel hampered in teaching. In fact, her method of assisting literacy allows all children to learn to read and write initially in their own dialects. She enjoys the cadences and rhythm brought to English by some African-American youngsters and different ones brought by a Hawaiian child in her class. When she takes dictation, she writes the sentence structures the child uses. This consistency allows the children to read back their words, matching the oral and written language. All of the teachers described here accept the view that language is a personal extension of the child and that to reject a child's language is to reject the child.

Maturation and Speech Development

By the end of first grade, most sound substitutions and overgeneralized grammar rules have disappeared from children's speech. Not due to any specific lessons or drill to correct the problems, this development is a natural process resulting from children's maturation plus their continued analysis of the language around them. As youngsters mature, they become more able to duplicate the sounds of their language. Through continued exposure to the language patterns of their culture, they naturally work to discover the exceptions to grammar rules as well as the rules themselves. Mrs. Thomas listens carefully to students to determine if any of them are still having difficulty and should be considered for speech help.

COMMON MILESTONES IN SPEECH DEVELOPMENT

Years	Accomplishment
3	about 300-word vocabulary
3½	b, m p, v, and h sounds develop
4	about 900-word vocabulary
4½	d, t, n, g, k, ng, and y sounds develop
5½	f sound develops
6½	v, sh, za, and l sounds develop
7½	s, w, r, th, and wh sounds develop
7–8	sentence foundation mastered (pronouns and prepositions)
8	all sounds are developed and speech should be intelligible

Until the end of first grade, or about seven years of age, some immature speech is developmentally normal and requires no remedial intervention. Although alert to children who require special help, Mrs. Thomas does not criticize their speech. She considers the rapport established with her students to be so significant to their language development that she is unwilling to jeopardize that rapport with a critical response to a child's communication.

Meeting the Needs of All

The age or grade level of children learning language isn't what determines appropriate language instruction. Rather, the individual development of each child determines that child's instructional needs. The only way to meet all the various needs in any class is to provide a variety of options for learning activities. Children will generally choose that from which they will most benefit: They like the encouragement of success coupled with the interest that challenge provides. A combination of success and challenge leads to that delicate balance of not being too hard or too easy. Therefore, all developmentally appropriate early childhood programs, whether in preschool or primary grades, tend to provide much the same types of open-ended learning activities. Children themselves may add the complexity and challenge to ensure learning, or the teacher may suggest variations to an activity to enhance the learning value. Certainly the play, language, and literacy of a six-year-old is more sophisticated than that of a three-year-old, but both learn best by interacting and exploring informally in similar kinds of situations.

Mrs. Thomas knows that first graders haven't finished their language development and that they still need practice. She also is aware of the significant role social interaction plays in the intellectual development of her students. Have you guessed by now that Mrs. Thomas also encourages talking in her first-grade classroom? This approach may be quite a change from your experience with first grade. Mrs. Thomas not only makes sure that students get play opportunities that encourage language, but also provides for collaborative discussion while students pursue more academic kinds of learning. Youngsters in this classroom talk together as they compare the stories they have read, plan a puppet show, or discuss proper spelling while they write.

Mrs. Thomas also brings children together in groups for discussions. With first graders, she sometimes feels comfortable working with the total group, but she sees they still function best in smaller units. When she brings the whole group together, she does so for short periods and for specific purposes. As the children begin to gather, she leads the group in conversation, singing, or acting out a finger play. This ensures that those already sitting are involved instead of bored.

Today the topic for discussion is class rules. She creates a language development opportunity as she guides the students in discussing essential, reasonable classroom regulations. Mrs. Thomas records everyone's ideas for rules as they suggest them. Tomorrow, she will assist the children in selecting two or three ideas that will help everyone to live and work together in the classroom harmoniously. After the group disbands, Mrs. Thomas briefly confers with a parent volunteer about the session. The parent tells her about a fascinating informal discussion that had been going on simultaneously with the formal one: Two girls were debating the pros and cons of a rule about interrupting someone who is reading to ask for help with a word. The information helps Mrs. Thomas since she had been wondering whether or not she should have allowed the girls' subdiscussion to continue. This information reinforces her belief that the most important discussions may not be those planned by the teacher.

These teachers believe that children's language reflects their experiences and that a child with meager experience will be a child with meager language. Therefore, the teachers make great efforts to enhance the experience base of all their students as described in Chapter 2. Through these experiences, youngsters in their classes gain subjects to talk about, motivation to talk, and an increased vocabulary.

These teachers also accept as valid for discussion the experiences that children find important from their lives outside of school. They don't limit discussion to certain sterile "school" topics. Additionally, all of these teachers believe that children must talk in order to develop language proficiency as well as increased intellectual growth. None of their classrooms are quiet places. These teachers know that they are dealing with children in their language-acquisition years.

Quiet classrooms are not learning places: Children must talk in order to develop language proficiency and increased intellectual growth.

Oral Language and Written Language

As they help children to develop oral language proficiency, early childhood educators help children to build understanding that assists with mastering written language. However, we must remember the differences between oral and written language and how those differences influence learning. There are many more clues to meaning when we hear oral language than when we read written language. When someone is speaking to us, we gain meaning from voice inflection as well as facial expressions and gestures. Generally, the situation in which the communication is taking place clarifies ambiguities. This assistance is not available for making meaning from the written word. Therefore, written language must provide more complete information to make up for the lack of other clues.

Holdaway (1979) pointed out that oral and written language differ not only in form, but also in function. Ideas are usually written down as a means to record important or memorable matters, whereas conversational oral language may be just to pass the time. Holdaway cites these differences as a problem with the language-experience dictation of many children: They use oral language forms and functions when dictating a written record. Being read to regularly is the best way for children to become familiar with the conventions of written language. We now turn to the subject of selecting and sharing literature for story time.

STORY TIME

When a child has the chance to hear one good story after another, day after day, he is being taught to read. . . .

(J. Hymes, 1965)

Why teach children how to read unless we teach them to *want* to read? Unless they want to read, children won't do enough of it to ever become good at it. When we read stories to young children, we introduce them to the magic of books and awaken their desire to read for themselves. When we share high-quality literature with youngsters, we give them a glimpse of the excitement, the drama, and the beauty that is contained in books. When we share our enthusiasm for a good story with children, we provide a model of interacting with text. When we make the print on a page come to life during a story, we demonstrate the process of reading. As children reenact stories read to them and interact with adults about stories, they gradually and without pressure construct understandings necessary to become readers.

Research repeatedly comes up with the same conclusion: Reading to children is a successful way to teach them to read. Gordon Wells (1986) concluded after a fifteen-year study of children in England that their school success was highly influenced by frequency of listening to stories read to them. Dolores Durkin's (1980) studies showed that the one common factor of children who read early was being read to frequently. Since then, many researchers have determined that children learn ways of constructing meaning for print as adults interpret stories for them (Altwerger, Diehl-Faxon, & Dockstader-Anderson, 1985; Fisher, 1991; Mason, 1989; Teale, 1988). Many emphasized that a combination of reading to children and follow-up activities such as creative dramatics or discussion are particularly important for reading achievement. Story time is a daily staple of teachers attempting to provide literate environments. In many classrooms, story time is the central focus, serving as the basis for other curriculum activities.

As discussed previously in this chapter, exposure to books helps children to understand the kind of language used in writing. Children who have little experience with written language are not skilled at getting meaning from the words alone. They are used to getting language meaning clues from their surroundings and become insecure and disoriented when they can't (Holdaway, 1979). When they get to school, they tend to have difficulty understanding their teacher's oral language as well as written language. Because teachers tend to talk about things that are not physically present, their language has much in common with "book" language (Wells, 1986).

Children not only are able to understand language better as a result of being read to, but also become able to express themselves better. Obviously, their increased vocabulary helps both expressive and receptive language. Additionally, children with a rich background of book experience are able to narrate an event and describe a scene (Wells, 1986). These are useful skills for both oral and written communication and enhance general academic success as well as literacy development.

Ms. Montoya wants to make sure all children get to discover the power of symbolic language "to create possible or imaginary worlds through words" (Wells, 1986, p. 156). Instead of trying to condense several years of missing language enrichment into synthetic substitutions such as flash-card drill, Ms. Montoya attempts to provide what was missing from the previous years of life. She enlists the aid of older students in her multiage class as reading buddies, and invites parents to help provide the one-to-one attention needed by some youngsters. Mrs. Hanna invites volunteers from upper grades: it is common to see a fifth grader in a pillow-softened corner reading to a kindergartner. Upper-grade teachers assure Mrs. Hanna that the older children benefit at least as much as the younger ones from this activity.

First-grade teacher Mrs. Thomas also places a high priority on reading to children. Old approaches to curriculum focused on so many different tasks and skills that it was a challenge to find time for all of them, let alone a story. But new ideas about integrated curriculum and whole language relax the frantic covering of skills and allow children opportunities for more reading and writing. We now know that this approach is a more efficient way for children to make sense of written language and master the skills and concepts they need (Hoffman, Roser, & Battle, 1993). Mrs. Thomas knows that good stories are essential experiences for youngsters as they work at making sense of the written language system.

Starting Early

The research indicates that the earlier adults start to read to youngsters, the greater the benefits. The early childhood years are of the greatest significance in exposure to literature. Even before babies can talk, they enjoy looking at books and being read to. They are able to understand some of what is read to them, just as they are able to understand some of what is said to

Research indicates that the earlier adults start to read to children, the greater the benefits.

them, months before they say their first word. Even before babies understand the content of stories, they enjoy the process of being read to—being held closely and hearing the soothing voice of a loving adult (Fields, 1989).

The intimacy of enjoying a story with a parent or a teacher adds to a child's pleasurable feelings about reading that make children want to read. Attitudes toward reading can begin in infancy and can be enhanced throughout childhood. As with so much of teaching, parents should be the first and foremost influence, with teachers coming to assist and extend what has begun.

Look at Betsy, who at six months of age was developing an interest in books and stories. Already, Betsy wanted to be included when someone read a story in her busy household. She had ample opportunity because her oldest sister read well and was willing to entertain the younger ones, her oldest brother enjoyed sharing his new powers as a beginning reader, and her preschool brother and her toddler sister frequently requested stories. Of course, Betsy's mother and father also read to the children when they have a chance. When asked at what age youngsters should be introduced to books, Betsy's mother says that her theory about that is similar to her theory about when they should be introduced to solid food. Deborah says, "When they grab food off your plate and eat it, they're ready for real food." So whenever her youngsters crawl over to hear a story, they are included.

When Betsy is old enough for preschool, her teacher, Ms. Reynolds, can tell that she has been read to frequently. Not all of the children in Ms. Reynolds's class exhibit Betsy's interest in books and story times. Ms. Reynolds doesn't force stories on these youngsters by insisting that everyone has to come to story time. Instead, she concentrates on making story time as inviting as possible, gradually luring children away from other pursuits to join the story group. As youngsters overhear the exciting plots and observe the interest of other children, they become willing to listen to stories. Until that time, Ms. Reynolds allows them to choose other quiet activities that won't interfere with story time. She also makes a special effort with those youngsters who opt out of group stories; she invites them onto her lap for one-on-one story reading during choice time or else enlists a volunteer helper for lap reading. This process emulates the home literacy model which has proven so effective.

Selecting Appropriate Books for Children

All books are not created equal. When Betsy's mother goes into the grocery store or the toy store, she feels assaulted by the masses of poorly written and unimaginatively illustrated books on the shelves. Just as she is careful in selecting nutritious food instead of junk food, she wants to select books that will fill her children's minds with curiosity and stimulate their thinking instead of books whose story lines and illustrations are based on Saturday morning cartoons. She knows that meaningful connections with books will only occur with meaningful stories (Egawa, 1990).

Even book stores often have a disappointing selection of children's literature. Deborah reads the reviews of children's books in *Parents* magazine, and follows the Caldecott Award winners as ways of keeping up-to-date on high-quality children's literature. She then places special orders at the bookstore when necessary. She also makes requests at the library and encourages the librarian to order books that earned good reviews.

Her children's teachers have similar problems locating current, high-quality literature. They find reviews in professional journals to be helpful. *The Horn Book Magazine, The New Advocate, Young Children* (the journal of the National Association for the Education of Young Children), *The Reading Teacher* (the journal of the International Reading Association), and *Language Arts* (the journal of the National Council of Teachers of English) have reliable book review sections. Mrs. Hanna also likes Bobbi Fisher's list of her favorite children's literature in her book, *Joyful Learning* (1991). Ms. Reynolds uses and recommends to parents *Getting Ready to Read: Creating Readers From Birth Through Six* (Glazer, 1980) and Jim Trelease's *The New Read-Aloud Handbook* (1989) for book suggestions according to children's ages. Ms. Montoya makes an effort to find multicultural literature reflecting the makeup of her classroom. Rudman's *Children's Literature: An Issues Approach* (1984) and *The Interracial Books for Children Bulletin* have been helpful additional sources for that purpose. These teachers also have created their own collection of personal favorites and share them with youngsters year after year. When an adult personally loves a story, sharing it becomes a special experience for both child and adult.

Teachers cannot possibly find an expert opinion on every book, nor should they. You must develop your own criteria for what constitutes a good book and then form an opinion about which books are right for certain children and in which specific situations. One simple guide is to decide whether you like a book yourself. Good children's literature isn't interesting just to children; it is timeless. Have you picked up a child's storybook and found that you couldn't put it down until you finished it? Are there some that you even enjoy reading over and over? Those are definitely signs of a good book.

A good book for any age is one that catches and holds the reader's interest. Suspense or tension of some sort is the classic way of hooking a reader into a story; a book without this has a poorly constructed plot. A good plot is important. For young children, the plot should be simple, without subplots or flashbacks to confuse them. The action should be believable without being predictable, and the problems should not be overcome too quickly. Lenski's *The Little Fire Engine* (1946) has a simple plot suitable for a young child but remains exciting from the beginning, when the fire alarm sounds, to the end, when everyone is safe and the fire is out (see Figure 3–1).

Some books can exist without suspense or plot because they offer something else. The sounds and rhythm of language can be pleasurable in themselves. Readers enjoy books like Wolf's *Peter's Truck* (1992) or Emberley's *Drummer Hoff* (1968) and, of course, there is the fun of nursery rhymes for youngsters. Some books don't even require words to be fascinating. Beauti-

FIGURE 3–1
Lois Lenski's simple, clear illustrations appeal to the youngest book lovers.

Source: From Lenski, L. (1946). *The Little Fire Engine.* New York: Henry Z. Walck. Reprinted by permission from the Lois Lenski Covey Foundation.

fully detailed wordless picture books are appearing more frequently now for children. The books are designed especially for children who are in the stage of reading the pictures. Spier's *Noah's Ark* (1977) and Ormerod's companion books, *Sunshine* (1981) and *Moonlight* (1982), offer delightful opportunities for children to create their own stories to accompany the pictures. The series of wordless storybooks about the dog Carl (*Good Dog Carl,* Day, 1988) are also wonderful examples of this book type.

Whether or not a story relies on words and plot, it should present a main character with whom children can identify. Children easily identify with Flack's little duck, Ping, as he tries to escape punishment. They can relate to the daily routines of the nameless little girl in Ormerod's books, and they can step into Peter's snowsuit and experience the wonder of *The Snowy Day,* created by Keats (1962).

CRITERIA FOR SELECTING AN APPROPRIATE FICTION STORY

Look for the following attributes.

1. A simple, well-developed plot, centered on a sequence of events, with action predominant; a slight surprise element makes the children wonder what will happen next and can add much to a story (*The Little Fire Engine*)
2. A large amount of direct conversation (*Katy No-Pocket,* Payne, 1944)
3. Use of repetition, rhyme, and catch phrases that children memorize quickly and easily (Dr. Seuss books, Geisel, Random House)
4. Use of carefully chosen, colorful language (*The Napping House,* Wood, 1984)
5. Situations involving familiar happenings; the new, unusual, and different may be included, but there must be enough of the familiar with which children can identify (*When Grandma Came,* Walsh, 1992)
6. A simple and satisfying climax (*Miss Rumphius,* Cooney, 1982)
7. One main character with whom children can easily identify, because too many characters can be confusing (*The Story of Jumping Mouse: A Native American Legend,* Steptoe, 1984)
8. A variety of ethnic, cultural, and racial backgrounds; such stories should present realistic pictures, not stereotypes of racial or ethnic groups (*Dumpling Soup,* Rattigan, 1993)
9. Illustrations, because young children "read" pictures; pictures need to accurately portray the content and mood of the story (*Fog,* Fowler, 1992)

We have been discussing fiction books so far, but nonfiction books are significant, also. It is as important that nonfiction books for very young children be as factually accurate as those for adults. They don't need to be complex or detailed, but that does not mean accuracy can be sacrificed. Mrs. Hanna uses Susan Glazer's guidelines (1986) when she evaluates a nonfiction book for her class: She is wary of books that combine fact with fiction or fact with opinion—both of these combinations confuse the young reader who can't tell the difference. She is wary of books that emphasize "cuteness" when they purport to inform. *From Sand to Sea* by Stephanie Feeney and Ann Fielding (1989) provides a model of well-researched factual information at a level appropriate to young children.

Whether the book depicts the mundane or the exotic, fact or fiction, the pictures must accurately portray the book's action, mood, and intent. Emergent readers will pay very close attention to the pictures that tell the story or provide information. Therefore, the pictures need to do that. Youngsters also count on the pictures to give them clues to the print. Therefore, pictures need to do that too.

Donald Crews gives a wealth of picture information to support limited text in his factual books for young children. Beautiful color photographs are essential to Feeney and Fielding's book, *From Sand to Sea*. Jim Fowler's paintings bring to life the stories written by his wife, Susi Gregg Fowler. Action-packed illustrations by Rie Munoz add humor to stories written by Jean Rogers. The detail in Steven Kellogg's and Peter Spier's illustrations delights adults as well as children. The simplicity and color in Ezra Jack Keats's and Gerald McDermott's illustrations also attract all ages. Different children's illustrators have merit for different reasons. However, not all children's book illustrations are art. Teachers and parents need to protect children from too much overly "cute" art. From Disney to coloring books, illustrations without artistic merit surround children; we need to counteract those influences to help youngsters develop taste and to provide worthy models for their own art.

The values represented in the stories and illustrations are another critical issue in selecting books: Sexism, racism, and gratuitous violence are to be avoided. In the appendix to her book *The Whole Child* (1992), Hendrick offers a guide entitled "ten quick ways to analyze children's books for racism and sexism." Other guides are available elsewhere (e.g., Morrow, 1993; Fisher, 1991). As Don Holdaway stated, "Literature at its best, and children's literature in particular, transcends the surface distinctions of cultural difference and embodies universal human concerns" (1979, p. 17). It is worthwhile to search for books that represent the values we wish to pass on to children.

A related issue is the selection of books which authentically reflect a variety of cultures and ethnic groups (Gross & Ortiz, 1994). Simply because a book purports to be about a minority group does not mean it will be accurate or free from stereotypes. It is difficult for those outside the group to judge those features. Mrs. Thomas has been guided in her selection of Native American literature by the eye-opening *Through Indian Eyes* (Slapin & Seale, 1992). She discovered that one of her favorite books, *Annie and the Old One*, (Miska, 1971) was based on a false premise about how a Navajo child would feel about the death of her grandmother. In contrast, Goble's beautiful book, *Star Boy* (1983), is true to the beliefs of the Blackfeet. Mrs. Thomas thinks that the following guidelines for screening a book about Native Americans could be adapted to any group.

■—■—■—■—■—■—■—■—■—■—■—■—■—■—■

QUESTIONS TO ASK IN SELECTING BOOKS ABOUT NATIVE PEOPLES

Does this book tell the truth?
Does the author respect the People?
Is there anything in this book that would embarrass or hurt a Native child?
Is there anything in this book that would foster stereotypic thinking in a non-Indian child?

(Slapin & Seale, 1992)

■—■—■—■—■—■—■—■—■—■—■—■—■—■—■

Ms. Reynolds is concerned that most books about non-European cultures show a historical perspective rather than a contemporary one. Thus, youngsters get the erroneous ideas that their African-American playmates have just escaped from slavery or that their Native American classmates cook over an open fire. However, Munsch and Kusugak do not fall into that trap with *A Promise Is a Promise* (1988). The Inuit family in this book doesn't live in an igloo but in an ordinary house with books and a teddy bear for the little girl. *Through Indian Eyes* also commends *The Goat in the Rug* (Blood & Link, 1976) for presenting a story that "treats Native life as though it were simply a normal part of human existence" (Slapin & Seale, 1992).

Guidelines for Sharing a Story

Ms. Reynolds rarely shares a book with youngsters before she has become familiar with it herself. By reading a book to herself, she discovers whether or not it is of sufficient quality and whether it is appropriate for the age and interests of her preschoolers. Ms. Montoya also wants to know the story well enough to introduce and share it effectively. She wants her lead-in remarks about the book to help children make connections between their own experiences and the story. Another part of getting children involved in a story is helping them to formulate questions about the outcome. Preparing adequately is important for an effective story time.

Mrs. Hanna concentrates on developing proper expression and pacing as she reads so that she can convey the book's full meaning and impact. She also wants to be able to paraphrase or skip any long descriptive passages in case they lose her listeners' interest. Whenever possible, Mrs. Hanna reads a story over several times and practices it before she shares it with children. Children are enthralled by an exciting scene that she reads with breathless haste, they are captivated by the suspenseful moment in which their teacher pauses for effect, and they gain immeasurable meaning from the expressive way she reads direct quotes to bring the characters to life.

GUIDELINES FOR SHARING STORIES WITH CHILDREN

Advance Planning
- Never share a story without being prepared.
- Plan an introduction which will link the story to children's experiences.
- Never share a story just to fill time.

Arranging the Story Environment
- Sit on a low chair or on the floor.
- Share stories in small groups more often than large ones.
- Allow children to choose whether or not to listen to the story.

Effectively Sharing Stories
- Remember to point out book titles and authors.
- Help children formulate questions about the story's outcome.
- Use a conversational tone of voice, and speak slowly and distinctly. Avoid a sing-song or a high-pitched voice.
- Look directly at the children. Include all members of the group, not just those directly in front of you.
- Hold the book steadily and be sure all children can see it.
- Use timing effectively; vary the tempo. As action increases and things begin to happen, hurry the tempo. Before a moment of question, surprise, or awe, a pause can be most effective.
- Model interaction with the story: Predict or wonder about outcomes, express reactions to events, and make other comments as relevant.
- Keep the story or listening period within the limits of the children's attention span.

Ms. Reynolds maintains frequent eye contact with her listeners as part of being responsive to their reactions. She demonstrates an interactive approach to reading with appropriate comments and questions, such as "Oh, what a lot to eat!" when she reads *The Very Hungry Caterpillar* (Carle, 1974), or "Do you think Little Toot is afraid?" when she reads *Little Toot* (Gramatky, 1939). As she nears the end of *The Story Of Ping* (Flack, 1933), she asks the children to remember "What are the ducks supposed to do when they hear the boat master call?" Children gather around Ms. Reynolds as she shares literature with them. She usually sits on a low chair or the floor to enhance interaction and cozy togetherness. The children in Ms. Reynolds's preschool are learning a great deal about reading long before they are able to read on their own.

Mrs. Hanna relies on the intrinsic pleasure of a good book to bring her students together. Like Ms. Reynolds, she doesn't require attendance at story time by all children. If she wants to instill a love of reading, won't forcing stories on children accomplish just the opposite? Instead she merely invites them to hear a story and begins as soon as a small group has gathered. She does not interrupt those who are still too engrossed in a previous activity or those who simply prefer one of the acceptable alternatives to story time. Mrs. Hanna knows these children will be able to overhear the story as they work puzzles or draw pictures. Often one or two will leave what they are doing and join the story groups as the story gets exciting. Sometimes a child still isn't ready to be part of a group and prefers to listen from the side. Some children find it difficult to sit still and listen without doing something else to occupy their hands. Mrs. Hanna's system provides alternatives to meet the varying personalities and maturation levels of her kindergartners.

Big Books help some youngsters to enjoy group stories more because they can see better. More and more children's literature is being published in oversized books. For youngsters who are interested, Big Books provide an opportunity to follow the print as the teacher reads. Opportunity to follow the print extends some of the benefits of lap reading to group reading. As researchers discovered what children were learning by following the print during story time, teachers learned why youngsters get so upset at not being able to see the book being read (Elster, 1994). Big Books were created to address that aspect of learning to read. It is important to remember that just being in a large format doesn't make a book worth reading. Teachers still need to use discretion in selections.

Being able to see the print while the teacher reads is important to a child who is trying to figure out how print works.

Mrs. Hanna knows that children whose past experiences did not provide for optimal language or literacy development can be helped by being read to. Her prescription for counteracting language deprivation is large and frequent doses of story time, on a one-to-one basis if possible since this allows each child to better view the pictures and compare the print to the oral reading. Most of all, an individual story time allows individualized interaction about the story, perhaps as expressions of amazement, sympathy, or outrage (Morrow, 1993). Children continue to benefit from being involved with the kind of comments and questions described in Ms. Reynolds's story time. The comments can also be a way of relating a story to a child's personal background. For instance, when reading *Muddigush* (Knudson, 1992), Mrs. Hanna may ask Natalya if she likes to play in the mud.

QUESTIONS FOR POSSIBLE DISCUSSION

(Do not force discussion of questions.)
For thinking critically:

> Do you agree?
>
> What would you have done?
>
> How do you feel about it?

Follow-up questions (from Egawa, 1990)

> What is this book really about?
>
> Does this story matter to you?
>
> What's on your mind after reading this book?
>
> What are you interested in after this reading?

Because reading critically as well as for comprehension is a necessity in our society, Mrs. Thomas makes sure to incorporate critical reading for comprehension into story time. When she reads *Doctor DeSoto,* by William Steig (1982), she encourages discussion of whether the mouse dentist should have risked treating the fox's toothache and whether it was fair for him to glue the fox's teeth together at the end. *The Story of Ping* by Marjorie Flack presents a topic of personal interest to children as they discuss whether or not Ping should get a swat for being last over the bridge onto the wise-eyed boat. When conflicting opinions are solicited and respected, children learn that they can come to their own opinions about what they read rather than accept whatever is in print. Through such interaction about stories, children can develop a variety of competencies in meaningful text construction before they can read in a conventional sense.

Reconstructing the Story

Each one of these teachers is careful not to ruin a good story with moralizing about the message at the end, but they often plan a follow-up activity or discussion. Ms. Reynolds's students are challenged by the game of retelling the story in sequence either from the pictures in the book or with felt characters on a felt board. At this age, many youngsters also like to reconstruct the story from memory on their own, gaining valuable insights as to what reading is all about.

Children of all ages love to take a book the teacher has just read and go off to the library corner to work at reading it by themselves. "Reading-like behavior" is observed in young children's early reconstruction of stories read to them. We have all seen emergent readers pretend to reach a much-beloved story that has been read to them over and over. They not only remember the plot and sequence, they also change their language style to match book language. This childish activity, once considered merely "cute," is now recognized as the way youngsters practice the language of books. Listen and you will hear the more formal and complete form of written language rather than the ambiguous oral forms that children usually use in speech. By your careful listening, you also will realize that children haven't merely memorized the stories and aren't merely imitating adults. Their story retellings focus on the personal meanings of the story, and use their own immature speech patterns. This is important evidence of how children learn by constructing their own knowledge.

When they practice emergent reading in these ways, youngsters work on the concepts that are appropriate for them maturationally and as individuals seeking understanding. Some are working on the general form of written language as discussed, some are exploring the conventions of direction and position in print, while others are interpreting the written symbols themselves. When they begin the laborious work of decoding symbols, children's past experience with focusing on meaning helps them not to get "trapped into mindlessness by the slow word-by-word visual checking of early reading" (Holdaway, 1979, p. 53). The meaning of the story is both the guide and the impetus to these activities. There would be no purpose and no motivation if the story had no meaning to the child. Additionally, the reading process would become a difficult and mindless decoding task without the guidance of "What makes sense?"

Educators now recognize emergent reading of storybooks as being important enough to observe and record for assessment purposes. Elizabeth Sulzby (1985) developed a classification scheme to guide such assessment, which will be discussed further in Chapter 8. Whatever level a child is working on, teachers assist by applauding the small steps in the direction of literacy. As with oral language, it is important for adults to encourage rather than to focus on errors.

Children have always spontaneously worked at rereading the interesting books that adults read to them. Teaching approaches have finally taken

Readinglike behavior is important in young children's early reconstructions of stories read to them.

their cue from children's own learning approaches and formalized the process. Publishers of reading materials now sell book sets with multiple copies of children's literature in order to facilitate such exploration of books read by the teacher. Big Book versions of stories with accompanying sets of identical little books are currently popular reading instruction materials. Story time is no longer separate from reading instruction periods.

The danger is that formalized shared book experiences (Holdaway, 1979), directed listening/thinking activity (Morrow, 1993), and other instructional activities will take over story time, destroying the pleasure in literature and damaging the learning potential. If this happens, it will not be the first time that descriptions of learning processes have been turned into prescriptions for activities. If teachers begin to "force march" youngsters through activities the children select, it will not be the same activity and will not have the same value. This sort of confused thinking in the 1970s led to curriculum designed to teach the conservation tasks Piaget used in his research to study children's thinking.

Story Follow-Up Activities

For group follow-up activities, Mrs. Hanna enjoys assisting children in dramatizing sections of a story as a way to internalize the meaning (Soundy, 1993). For instance, she follows up a reading of Steven Kellogg's *The Island of the Skog* (1973) with a suggestion that the children show her how the mice must have felt when they saw the monstrous creature lurching toward them on the beach. She encourages the youngsters to show emotion with their whole bodies as well as with their facial expressions. Then she asks what they might say when they feel that way. These creative dramatic experiences often reappear as children later incorporate them into their dramatic play. So the Skog might come to visit the domestic scene in the playhouse the next day, and we might find the playhouse peopled by mice who prepare meals of chocolate waffles and coconut cherry cheese pie.

Murals, individual paintings, clay sculptures, and a variety of artwork may be stimulated by a book and may, in turn, enhance appreciation for the book (Hoyt, 1992). Ms. Montoya suggested that some of her students might enjoy making a mural showing their ideas about the qallupilluits in *A Promise Is a Promise*. As part of this project, she demonstrated to youngsters how to use a water color wash to replicate the subtle background colors in scenes from the book. The children enjoyed learning a new way to paint as well having an opportunity to express their ideas about the scary qallupilluits under the ice. Some youngsters enjoy using music to respond to books and other experiences. The story poem *Real Wild Rice* (Martinson, 1975) inspired some youngsters to put it to music and sing it.

Making their own version of a favorite book is a popular follow-up activity. Pattern books such as *The Important Book* (Brown, 1945) lend themselves well to a class-made adaptation. After enjoying the book, children have an opportunity to contribute their own page for a similar book. They may each offer their own ideas of what's important about something they care about. Children draw their own illustrations and either dictate the written portion for an adult to write or else write it themselves in whatever forms of writing they are currently using. In another version of *The Important Book*, each page is about one child. Thus, a page might read: "The important thing about Katya is. . . ." Katya finishes the statement via dictation or independent writing. Ms. Montoya likes to do this adaptation at the beginning of the school year and use a photograph of each child as the illustration for that child's page. Then, as children read or look at the book, they get introduced to others in the class and learn what their classmates' names looks like. Class-made books are always the most sought-after books in the classroom library.

FOLLOWING THE STORY

Some follow-up activity categories

1. Independent reconstruction of story
2. Group retelling of story in sequence
3. Acting out the climax
4. Adaptation of story into class-made book
5. Responding to the book via art or music expression
6. Responding to the book in writing
7. Experiencing events similar to those in story

A teacher may use many activities relevant to a book as preparation for the story rather than as follow-up. Often a prior personal experience will give meaning to a story otherwise incomprehensible to young children. Playing outside in the snow and making angels gives meaning to Ezra Jack Keats's *The Snowy Day* and picking blueberries adds to a reading of Robert McCloskey's *Blueberries for Sal* (1948) (see Figure 3–2). Children who are familiar with the salmon, eagles, and beaches of western Canada and South-

FIGURE 3–2
After the class picked blueberries and made blueberry muffins, *Blueberries for Sal* was the story of the day.

From *Blueberries for Sal,* by Robert McCloskey. Copyright © 1948 by Robert McCloskey, renewed © by Robert McCloskey, 1976. Reprinted by permission of Viking Penguin, Inc.

east Alaska are more likely to understand Betty Waterton's *A Salmon for Simon* (1978). All of these stories probably would correspond with experiences of children from Juneau, Alaska, but would not be as suitable for children from Phoenix, Arizona. Likewise, Keats's *Clemintina's Cactus* (1982) would have more meaning for youngsters from Phoenix than from Alaska.

Ms. Reynolds's preschool class enjoyed the day when class learning activities centered on the blueberries they had picked. Several children were involved in dyeing yarn in mashed blueberries, and all who were interested took turns making batches of blueberry muffins. Everyone ate the muffins for snack. Naturally, *Blueberries for Sal* was the story of the day.

Some teachers have begun using literature as the base for their entire curriculum. They select excellent fiction and nonfiction books around a specific theme and extend that theme not only into all the language arts, but also into science, social studies, art, and even math. This allows for a project approach (Katz & Chard, 1989) to education that involves children in real activities to assist them in making sense of their experiences. The challenge of integrating curriculum around literature, themes, or any other system is to focus on authentic integration. Many teachers are getting sidetracked into activities that have no meaning and do not extend children's understanding. Activities such as counting gummy bears during a study of bears do not help children learn about bears and therefore represent a correlated rather than an integrated approach to curriculum.

For every activity ask:

> What are children really learning by this experience?
> Does it have a meaningful purpose for children?
> Does it make sense to them?

Another danger to guard against is overdoing the discussion and activities related to a story. Many curriculum and resource guides suggest several days of activities related to one very short story. Though related activities help children to develop meaning for what they read, let's remember that the reading itself is valuable.

CONCLUSION

This chapter presented guidelines to follow and pitfalls to avoid for both oral language activities and children's literature. Opportunities to talk were the main focus of recommended oral language activities and time with high-quality books was emphasized for literature. The important roles of adults and of other children for learning both language and literature were described. This chapter also addressed ways to incorporate language, cultural and racial diversity into both language and literature.

DISCUSSION QUESTIONS

1. A parent is visiting your classroom. Before leaving, he expresses his concern that children aren't learning to sit still and be quiet in this setting. How would you explain why you do not value a quiet classroom?
2. Your school district gets funding to provide special assistance to young children at risk for failure in reading. Describe and defend your plan for the best ways to spend the money.

SUGGESTED FOLLOW-UP ACTIVITIES

1. Practice conversing with young children individually: Use reflective listening and open-ended questions to encourage their language.
2. Observe a master teacher guiding a group discussion. Note ways of encouraging all youngsters to participate and of teaching respectful communication.
3. Find a current list of award-winning books at your local library; examine as many of the books on the list as possible. Note the quality of illustrations that won illustrator awards, and also analyze the stories for their appeal to children.
4. Using the guides in this chapter, select, prepare, and share a book or story with a group of youngsters. Ask a peer to observe and help you critique your presentation and its value for children.

RECOMMENDED FURTHER READING
Periodicals

Hoyt, L. (1992). Many ways of knowing: Using drama, oral interactions, and the visual arts to enhance reading comprehension. *The Reading Teacher,* 45(8), 580–584.

Strickland, D. & Morrow, L. (1989). Interactive experiences with storybook reading. *The Reading Teacher,* 42(4). 240–241.

Books

Fisher, B. (1991). *Joyful learning.* Portsmouth, NH: Heinemann.

Slapin, B., & Seale, D. (1992). *Through Indian eyes.* Philadelphia: New Society Publishers.

CHAPTER

4

ASSISTING EMERGENT READERS

Reading and writing experiences at school should permit children to build upon their already existing knowledge of oral and written language.

INTERNATIONAL READING ASSOCIATION, 1986

This chapter looks at literacy activities which assist emergent readers in their efforts to become independent readers. We continue to emphasize the child's active construction of knowledge in the process of becoming literate. We describe the teacher's role as essential but different from what you are probably used to. Our view is that the teacher is the supporting actor/actress, while the children have the lead roles. We also continue to present literacy as a complex perceptual, linguistic and psychological process rather than a set of rules to be mastered (Ritchie & Wilson, 1993).

We now know that literacy, like other things, is greater than the sum of its parts. Reading is not phonics, word analysis, and sight words any more than a conversation is nouns, verbs, and grammar. Writing is not spelling, punctuation, and penmanship, either. Reading, writing, and oral language are ways in which human beings communicate. They are also the ways in which we record and explore our ideas, feelings, and knowledge. These deeply personal and human motivations give power and significance to both written and oral language. Children want to participate fully in these aspects of their culture, both for the connectedness with other human beings and for the control it gives them in their world. Teachers don't have to work hard at making kids interested in becoming literate if reading and writing maintain purposefulness in school as well as out of school. Who wouldn't work at reading when reading means knowing what is on the lunch menu today or who gets to bring the balls out at recess? Who wouldn't work at writing when writing gets a note back from a friend?

Current teaching approaches acknowledge the need for skills and practice without breaking reading and writing into meaningless little parts. When children work on actual reading and writing, rather than just on the skills involved, the meaning and significance are not lost. This means that fewer children get lost in their quest for learning.

Also, fewer children will get lost in the education process when more teachers also respect the individual nature of the quest for learning. Schools would like it if all youngsters would move from emergent reading to independent reading during first grade. That would be very tidy but totally unrealistic. Some children still will be emergent readers in late elementary school and a few will be independent readers in preschool. Thus, our recommendations for teaching have nothing to do with grade or age, and everything to do with the individual child's current understanding. Recommendations for supporting young independent readers and writers are presented in Chapters 6 and 7. Regardless of what age group you teach, you will have both emergent and independent readers among your students. Multiage classes acknowledge and capitalize on these inescapable differences.

Although this chapter focuses on reading, we are uncomfortable talking about reading and writing separately because they are so intertwined. Please keep this interrelationship constantly in mind as you read these chapters which discuss one or the other. This chapter on emergent reading precedes the next chapter on emergent writing not because reading precedes writing, but because we started talking about reading in the preceding chapter and want to continue building on that discussion.

READING EXPERIENCES

A rich literacy environment offers a multitude of opportunities to read and a wide array of different kinds of things to read (see Figure 4–1). It is through experiences with these reading opportunities and materials that children will come to make sense of the reading process. Therefore, a classroom that best facilitates emergent reading will ensure that children not only experience frequent story times as described in Chapter 3, but they will also participate in shared reading experiences, independent reading, and guided reading on a regular basis. Books will probably be the main focus of reading experiences, but reading includes signs, labels, notes, lists, menus, television guides, and other types of functional print. School reading programs help youngsters best when they reflect the real world.

Story time, which we discussed previously, has some things in common with shared reading. The original idea was that Shared Book Experiences would allow groups of youngsters in school to experience the kinds of interactions that bedtime stories at home can provide (Holdaway, 1979). The emphasis was on allowing children to see and talk about the books' contents. Holdaway's goal was to "build young readers' enthusiasm and confidence" (Holdaway, 1991, p. 86). Unfortunately, as the idea caught on in the United States, many teachers adapted it to their preconceived notions of teaching and changed it substantially. In many classrooms, shared reading looks much like lessons teachers used to teach from basal readers. The differences are in the materials used and perhaps in teaching to the whole group instead of "ability groups." However, we have seen teachers who think they are doing whole language and shared reading, yet still segregate children into ability groups.

Another difference between story time and Shared Book Experiences tends to be in the selection of books. While books offering high-quality artwork and memorable plots are popular for story time, teachers tend to think in terms of "readability" for shared reading. We think it would be a shame if teachers limited read-aloud time to predictable books and other stories that they thought children could learn to read. Much engaging children's literature has more text than is ideal for a shared reading time. The "instant reader" books that beginning readers can use have little content for story time, though they are useful for the children's own practice with reading. We also think it would be a shame if all story times were turned into times of planned instruction. We are convinced that children learn a lot while listening to a story and much of it is not taught directly. One of the most important things to learn from story time is the great pleasure that a good book can bring. When a teacher shares a book that she loves, she demonstrates the joy of reading.

FIGURE 4–1
Literary Basics

Literacy Basics

1. A print-rich environment
   adults who read for their own purposes
   adults who write for their own purposes
   frequent story time experiences
   dictation experiences
   high-quality literature
   contextualized print
   functional print
   answers to questions about print

2. A rich oral language environment
   adult language models
   adults who listen to children
   free exploration of oral language
      peer conversation
      dramatic play roles
   experiences for vocabulary enrichment
   vocabulary information as requested

3. Firsthand experiences of interest
   play
   daily living
   field trips
   nature exploration

4. Symbolic representation experiences
   dramatic play
   drawing and painting
   music and dance

5. Pressure-free experimentation with writing
   drawing
   scribbling
   nonphonetic writing
   invented spelling

6. Pressure-free exploration of reading
   reading from memory
   reading with context clues
   matching print to oral language

Shared Reading

We discussed story time in Chapter 3, but you may be wondering what shared book experiences are. This is an approach to sharing a book that encourages a group of children to participate in the reading, each to the best of his or her ability. The teacher guides the reading but tries to involve youngsters in predicting what will happen next and in following along in choral-reading style.

Big Books assist the shared reading process by making the print visible to groups of youngsters.

Big Books, as described in Chapter 3, assist this process by making the print visible to groups of youngsters. Because of its size, a Big Book needs to be set on an easel instead of held. The teacher's hands are then free to point to the words and help youngsters follow along as they read.

Pattern books and other predictable books assist the process by helping emergent readers to anticipate and guess and remember what the print says. For instance, as Ms. Montoya reads *The Napping House* (Wood, 1984), she doesn't have to read many pages before most of her students are chiming in at the end of each page and saying along with her " . . . in the napping house, where everyone is sleeping." Children and their parents have been enjoying books together this way for a long time, but only fairly recently has the process been recognized as a teaching/learning activity. Don Holdaway (1979) is credited with creating that awareness through his research and writing about more effective beginning reading instruction. Shared reading is now formalized as part of the reading program and has become common practice (Fisher, 1991).

Shared reading is also a good way to model the reading process, simulating parent-child story time. As children are asked to follow along while you read, they experience the directionality of print, the arrangement of print on pages, and the direction in which pages are turned. Children who are tuned in to print want and need to see the page as you read to them. These youngsters follow along carefully as they try to figure out what printed symbols go with what spoken words. The teacher's model provides a scaffold to assist them as they struggle with the question "What is the relationship of print to words?" Shared reading experiences are especially important for youngsters who have not been read to regularly at home. These youngsters often are labeled as "at risk for failure" because they don't have the kinds of knowledge about reading that children bring with them if they have experienced story times all their lives. Holdaway developed his shared reading program with the "at-risk" New Zealand students in mind (1991).

Of course, you can have a shared reading session using something other than a book. Favorite songs and poems written on large chart paper offer excellent opportunity for shared reading. After several repetitions, children will have memorized the oral content, then they will begin matching the written language to the oral language. The teacher has been encouraging this all along by using a pointer and pointing to the words as they say or sing them aloud. Soon youngsters will begin to exclaim over words they have identified. Youngsters love to use the pointers themselves; reading familiar charts with decorated "magic wand" pointers is a popular free choice activity. Many teachers have small cardboard frames in various lengths that they encourage children to use as they identify words and letters. When Felicia announces during shared reading that she sees the word *orange* in the pumpkin poem, Ms. Montoya invites her to hold a frame around the word for all to see. Similarly, Paul is encouraged to frame the first letter in pumpkin after he comments that it starts like his name.

The challenge in this type of activity is to keep the focus on the meaning of what is being read. Schools have such a long history of reductionist approaches to language arts that it is often hard for teachers to visualize more complexity (Ritchie & Wilson, 1993). It is easy for teachers to slip back into skills drills separate from the content that would give them meaning. It is often a fine balance to help youngsters attend to both meaning and to the graphophonemic clues inherent in the print. However, without the meaning, there is no reason to decipher the print. We need to keep that perspective and that priority. Similarly, without the joy of reading, there is little motivation for emergent readers to work at their task. Ms. Montoya makes sure that she offers reading materials that are worth reading and that her reading instruction doesn't get in the way of enjoying the content.

Independent Reading

An inviting library area furnished with soft cushions and an enticing display of children's books can help youngsters to enjoy books. A library area also encourages independent reading during choice times. However, as early as kindergarten, many teachers also set aside a specific time in the daily schedule when everyone is supposed to read. You might well ask, why have a reading time for children who can't yet read? Watch a child and see. Children who have stories read to them will invariably take a beloved book and read it to

An inviting library area furnished with soft cushions and an enticing display of children's books can help youngsters to enjoy reading.

themselves. The youngsters themselves may be the first to tell you that they are not "really" reading, just pretending—or as one child said, "I just 'bemembered' it." But, as explained in Chapter 3, researchers in the field of emergent literacy consider this readinglike behavior a very significant stage in reading development.

Young children will engage in this pretend reading even before they can talk well and before they can speak in sentences (Holdaway, 1979). They will recreate the story as they perceive it, using the language at their command. Adults in the know will encourage any approximations of story reading, just as they encourage any approximations of oral language as the child learns to talk (Elster, 1994). Both constitute important practice in figuring things out.

Sasha, an emergent reader, puts on an important grown-up face and speaks with expression as she turns the pages of *The Very Hungry Caterpillar* (Carle, 1974) and reviews the story. The pictures on the page help her to keep the story in sequence and are the primary source of the story for her now. When she reads *King Bidgood's in the Bathtub* (Wood, 1985), the pictures are also helpful and she is able to recreate the main ideas of the extensive dialogue from memory. At first young children pay little attention to the print on the page, but instead focus on other aspects of book reading.

There is much to learn about reading that is separate from print. First, youngsters discover that books are interesting and enjoyable. Then they quickly learn about how books work: how to turn one page at a time, where to begin, which direction to go, and that book language is different from spoken language. They pick up on the concept of plot: a beginning, a problem to resolve, and an end. They also gradually learn the more formal and complete language structures used in written language. Children who do not have extensive experience with books find it difficult to adjust to the lack of external clues in written language: All of the information is contained in the language of books, whereas nonverbal clues and surrounding context give meaning to oral language.

As youngsters tune in to print, they begin to study the writing in books and to notice print everywhere. Some ask incessantly, "What does that say?" Others want to know "What letter is that?" Individual personalities determine individual approaches to making sense out of what is seen. Children impose their own drill and practice as they work at learning in their own ways. Many work on one-to-one correspondence, at first usually assigning one letter per syllable heard. Eventually it dawns on them that certain letters consistently are correlated with certain words. Then they begin to work on the concept of letters standing for certain sounds. Notice we say that the *children* are working on the concept, not the teacher. We used to think that letter sounds were taught by the teacher or the workbooks; but now we know that children must figure them out for themselves through their own experiences if they are to truly understand. Notice that in reading, like writing as described in Chapter 1, youngsters construct some theories that no adult would teach them. Notice also that phonics is not by any means the starting place for learning to read any more than it is for learning to write.

Typically, most children will be attending primarily to pictures in preschool, and most will be working on sound-symbol relationships in first grade. Realistically, we know that youngsters will be functioning at both levels and everyplace in between during preschool and through the primary grades. Also, we know that youngsters approach the learning process in a variety of ways, depending on their individual styles of work and thought. Some children are extremely methodical and focused, while others are more diverse and broadly observant. (Bussis, Chittenden, Amarel, & Klausner, 1985). Because of this wide span of levels and learning styles, broad choices of activities must be available to children. Teachers who trust their students to choose for themselves can be more certain of the right match between child and educational challenge. The difference between Ms. Reynolds's preschool class and Mrs. Thomas's first-grade class is the proportion of students working at each level rather than the kinds of learning options. Ms. Montoya's multiage classroom was designed with these kinds of differences in mind; she doesn't think of it as teaching several grades, but rather as teaching children at various levels of understanding.

During independent reading time, children may be individually engrossed in a book or share the experience with one or two friends. Blair and Jessica are giggling together about a funny story they are both reading. Tyler is listening to a tape recording of a story and following along carefully in his copy of the book. A parent volunteer is reading to three children in a cozy corner. The teacher is circulating among her students, sharing pleasure in a good book, suggesting another interesting story, and redirecting as needed. Always she is noting children's levels of understanding, their confusions, their breakthroughs, and their interests. Sometimes, she is able to set an example by reading one of her own books for a few minutes.

Materials for Independent Reading

Group story time is an important lead in to independent reading. Youngsters of all ages love to reexperience a story they have enjoyed hearing the teacher read. Therefore, books from story time are important for independent reading. Mrs. Thomas also has several small copies of each Big Book story for her first graders. Youngsters eagerly snatch these up for rereading after experiencing the story with the group. Each child is working to figure out the concepts appropriate to his or her personal way of understanding. Some are perfecting their sight-word vocabulary, some are trying to make sense of the graphophonemic clues, and some are still reading pictures.

Emergent readers, like all learners, are encouraged to persevere when they experience success. Success helps them to gain and keep their momentum for learning. This means that books not only need to be worth reading, but also need to be readable. Fortunately, these are complementary rather than contradictory attributes. Old ideas of readability, based on controlled vocabulary and focused on specific skills, sacrificed meaning in the process. You no doubt remember the boring material you were given to read in first

During independent reading time, children may be individually engrossed in a book or share the experience with friends.

grade. We now know that meaningful content provides important decoding assistance. We also know that interesting content provides the motivation to press on. For instance, if Sukey is stuck on a word, Ms. Montoya would ask her to think about what would make sense there as the start of figuring it out. If the book was put together to give practice in certain words rather than to tell a story, the answer may be that *nothing* makes sense. In addition, Sukey's attitude toward trying to figure out the word may be "who cares?"

As mentioned previously, familiarity with a book makes it more readable. In fact, anything that helps a child predict what comes next helps with reading. Predictability may be a result of knowing a story well, or it may come from having had an experience similar to that in a story. Pictures offer another source of information that helps youngsters predict what the accompanying text will say. Pattern books are another type of predictable book that has recently become popular for reading instruction. Cumulative story patterns such as *The House that Jack Built* or *The Old Woman Who Swallowed a Fly* have been familiar for years. Books such as *The Napping House* or *Drummer Hoff* (Emberley, 1968) adopt that style and assist young readers through repetition of text. Probably the most easily readable pattern books are those such as Bill Martin, Jr.'s famous *Brown Bear, Brown Bear, What Do You See?* (1983) with a repetitive text that changes only slightly from page to page.

These changes are accompanied by picture clues and rhymes that further assist in reading. Patterns, picture clues, and remembered stories offer valuable assistance to beginning readers in much the same way that training wheels help the novice bike rider—providing the support during practice that leads to more independent performance.

TYPES OF PREDICTABLE BOOKS

1. Familiarity
   • Essentially memorized from repeated read-alouds *(The Three Bears)*
   • A known situation or familiar experience portrayed *(The Snowy Day, Keats, 1962)*

2. Patterns
   • Cumulative *(Why Mosquitos Buzz in People's Ears,* Aardema, 1975)
   • Repetitive forms *(The Very Busy Spider,* Carle, 1984)

3. Pictures
   • Picture clues in conjunction with familiarity or patterns can make "instant readers" *(Brown Bear, Brown Bear, What Do You See?)*

It is a challenge to find enough books with which beginning readers can be successful. Good teachers are always on the lookout for more good books for their classrooms. Though Ms. Montoya includes predictable books, she doesn't limit herself to them. She likes Bill Martin, Jr.'s books and the *Berenstain Bear* books. Some of her students enjoy the Dr. Seuss beginning-reader books, while other children complain that the controlled vocabulary doesn't really make sense. They like Eric Carle's other books almost as well as *The Very Hungry Caterpillar,* and the children laugh with glee over Audrey Wood's *The Napping House.* Martha Alexander, Margaret Hillert, Syd Hoff, Arnold Lobel, and Bernard Wiseman are some other authors who cater to beginning readers. In other books for beginners, Shigeo Watanabe writes about a very large bear cub; James Marshall writes about hippos; H. A. Rey writes about a curious monkey; and Cindy Wheeler writes about a cat named Marmalade. Ezra Jack Keats writes about children in ways with which they can identify. James Stevenson's books range from humor and fantasy to realism. Miriam Cohen's *When Will I Read?* (1977) is a favorite that seems to reassure beginning readers.

Some educational publishing companies are attempting to help teachers with the job of finding interesting and readable material for young readers. The Wright Group took the lead in publishing Big Books for the shared reading recommended by Don Holdaway (1979). *Mrs. Wishy Washy* (Rigby Education, 1984) is probably the most popular of their books. All Big Books are accompanied by several smaller copies for independent reading. Most text-book companies now offer Big Books, little books, and pattern books. It is important to remember that these formats do not come with any guarantee of quality or appropriateness. We discuss criteria for selection of materials further in Chapter 9.

Just as different children learn in different ways, they have individual preferences in books. Not only are they interested in different topics, but they also are attracted to different genres. Some like fantasy, while others prefer informative nonfiction. It is important to cater to all tastes. One thing all youngsters seem to have in common, however, is the desire to take books home to share with their parents. They are proud of their ability to read and want to demonstrate their new powers to their families. Mrs. Hanna and Ms. Montoya both have checkout systems that allow youngsters to take books home freely.

Reading Conferences

Brief interactions with youngsters while circulating around the room during independent reading time allow for much teaching and important observations of children's progress. Teachers also notice responses of individual youngsters during shared reading times. However, most teachers find that some one-on-one time with children is also helpful. As she reads the book *Mama, Do You Love Me?* (Joosse, 1991) (see Figure 4–2) with Ivan, Mrs. Thomas assists his understanding of reading as an active process of predicting his way through print (Cutting & Milligan, 1991). Her comments and questions focus his attention on reconstructing meaning rather than just recognizing words.

For instance, when Ivan reads "I love you . . . more than the dog loves his tall, more than the whale loves his spot," Mrs. Thomas asks him if that makes sense to him. She helps him to think about what he knows of dogs and whales and also helps him use the picture clues on the page to figure out the confusing words. She doesn't focus his attention back to the differences between the words *spout* and *spot* because she can tell Ivan is already paying attention to the letters, but perhaps not enough to the meaning.

Mrs. Thomas responds quite differently when Danielle brings her the same book and reads " . . . more than puppies, more than whales." It is clear that Danielle knows the pattern of the book and that she is using the picture clues on the page to remember the content, but it is also clear that she really is not attending to the print. This is appropriate at a certain level of emergent reading, but Mrs. Thomas thinks Danielle can move beyond that now. By pointing to the words on the page, Mrs. Thomas helps Danielle to note the discrepancy between the written word and her oral reading. Then Mrs. Thomas reads the page aloud, encouraging Danielle to read along. They find and talk about the repetition of the words *more than the* on two lines. Mrs. Thomas also asks Danielle to pick out the words *dog* and *whale,* asking her to note the beginning letters. Then they look briefly at the difference between

FIGURE 4–2

The illustrations, story content, and repeat patterns in children's literature such as *Mama, Do You Love Me?* provide readers with a variety of clues for successful reading.

I love you more
than the raven loves
his treasure,

From Joosse, B. M. (1991). *Mama, do you love me?* San Francisco: Chronicle Books. Reprinted by permission.

the words *love* and *loves*. This is a lot for Danielle to think about and she needs time with the book now. She decides to ask her friend Anastasia to read it with her because she knows Anastasia is a good reader.

These conference times provide opportunities to record a child's cur-rent reading strategies as well as offer insights into assisting individual progress. We will postpone discussing the record-keeping and diagnostic/evaluative aspects of conferences until Chapter 8, though we find it difficult to discuss teaching and assessing separately.

Functional Print

Remember, there is much more to read than books. There are name tags, helpers' charts, exit signs, stop signs, cereal boxes, letters from Grandma, and birthday cards. There are McDonald's arches, Baskin-Robbins flavors, and Pepsi cans. There are songs and poems and silly love notes. Reading is all around us just as talk is all around us. Children grow up with it and gradually come to make sense of it and use it. "Reading the room" is a favorite activity in Mrs. Hanna's class. An assortment of decorated pointers that some youngsters refer to as "magic wands" are available to make it more fun for children to wander around the room, alone or with a friend, pointing to and reading the messages on various signs and charts around the room.

Mrs. Hanna's kindergarten classroom is alive with print. Everywhere you look there is a poem that goes with a current classroom theme, a recipe for a recent cooking experience, a group story about a class adventure, or the day's agenda. Mrs. Hanna also entices children to want to read by communicating with them in writing: She writes notes to individual youngsters, she puts riddles on the board, and she posts notices about important events. Just

Children enjoy reading with decorated pointers that some call "magic wands."

because most of them can't read yet doesn't mean they can't be exposed to reading—when they couldn't talk yet they were still exposed to talking. She knows they have been figuring out the print they see on television commercials and billboards for a long time. She values and builds on that knowledge in her classroom.

When her preschoolers go for a walk, Ms. Reynolds talks with them about street signs and advertising signs. When youngsters play at the water table, she provides written labels for sorting items into "float" and "sink" categories. She helps her students to find their own names by their coat hooks and cubbies. Even preschoolers can read these kinds of contextualized print because there are enough external clues or past experiences linked to them. Contextualized print helps children to read environmental print the same way predictable books help them read stories: There is sufficient information in addition to the print to guide children's guesses about the print. A stop sign is an excellent example of contextualized print: Children learn early to read those white letters on a red background, on a hexagonal sign on a corner. Similarly, they can read many advertising logos and product brand names because of how and where they are written. Ms. Reynolds always lets her preschoolers know that they are reading when they can identify contextualized print.

By presenting a print-rich environment in which written language is used and displayed for a variety of purposes, Ms. Reynolds's preschool encourages children's natural interest in reading. As a result, the children themselves initiate much of the inquiry into print. Ms. Reynolds merely needs to be alert and responsive to their interests and questions. Sometimes children ask specific questions about written language; other times their instructional needs show up less directly. Jevon wants to know what the sign by the block center says, so Ms. Reynolds explains that it tells parent-helpers about what children learn when they play there. She also reads the sign to Jevon. When Cassie sees Caleb's name on the helpers' chart and thinks it is her turn to feed the gerbil, her teacher takes the opportunity for an impromptu lesson. Instead of just telling Cassie about the differences between her name and Caleb's, Ms. Reynolds asks Cassie to tell her how they are different. This helps Cassie to be self-reliant and more observant, and helps Ms. Reynolds find out about Cassie's perception.

Many youngsters in Ms. Montoya's class can read the names of their friends on their cubbies and on helpers' charts, too. They can read the recipe for making play dough—a frequent small-group activity. They also work hard at reading the weekly newsletter their teacher sends home to parents. Sometimes child-dictated articles are included in the newsletter. Many youngsters are pretty good at reading their own dictation and some can read what other children have dictated. They love to read the books authored by the class in which each child illustrates one page and dictates the message on it.

Mrs. Thomas's first graders are reading the same kinds of things they read in kindergarten and for the same kinds of purposes. The difference is

Youngsters like to read the class books in which each child illustrates
one page and dictates the message on it.

that more of them rely less on the context clues, such as where and how the
writing appears. Many first graders are developing skills with decontextualized print and can recognize familiar words whenever they occur. They also
do a lot of reading as they write, reading back what they have written as they
plan what to write next.

Whatever their ages, most of these children are excited about reading.
By using reading for real purposes, they discover its importance in their lives.
By experiencing high-quality literature, they know the richness that reading
can bring to them. Because their teachers offer them open-ended literacy
activities, they have felt successful in their efforts to learn. Because they are
constructing their own knowledge about reading, they have a firm foundation
of understanding to build on. These emergent readers are off to a good start.

VALIDATING SKILLS ACQUISITION

The skills issue has polarized the field of reading education. Holistic approaches to literacy have been widely misinterpreted and misrepresented as being anti-skills, while skills-based approaches have been accused of ignoring meaning. We see this polarization as an unfortunate misunderstanding of the holistic approach that recently has been labeled whole language (Church, 1994). The concept of a focus on meaning is intended as a way to teach youngsters reading skills in a more effective way while also teaching a broader range of skills. We see holistic teaching as a more efficient and effective way to help young readers learn everything they need to know in order to become fluent and avid readers.

Our criticism of the skills-based approaches isn't that they teach skills, but rather that they tend to teach them in isolation from meaningful content. This not only makes the skills harder to learn, it also can develop counterproductive reading strategies that create serious reading problems. We have seen many young readers who have learned to focus on individual letters or words and who read by laboriously plodding through a recitation of those items. This slow and painstaking process obliterates both meaning and pleasure in reading. Obviously, the reading skills are not being employed in a useful manner in these cases. We agree that reading skills are essential and we want to be sure they are taught in ways that allow children to make effective use of them in understanding what they read.

Old views of reading instruction were that children learned to read and write as a result of mastering a set of skills. Evidence has been mounting for over thirty years that the reverse is true: Children master skills as a result of reading and writing. Therefore, we no longer talk about skills children must have before they can learn to read. In fact, we don't talk about skills separate from reading and writing at all: We now know that all skills at all levels are learned most efficiently as children participate in authentic reading and writing activities. That doesn't mean that skills are not important, but rather that there is a better way of mastering them.

When children learn to talk, to write, or to read, they are constantly working to refine their understandings of all aspects of the process. They address the entire scope of language arts at all times, with each child delving into more detail as that individual better understands all the concepts involved. Teachers need to assist children with the understandings each is ready for, rather than an arbitrary set of skills mandated for a grade level. Each child progresses at an individual rate, all levels of emergent literacy being evident from preschool through the primary grades.

The children we have described were each working at their own levels to learn strategies that are useful in solving the problem of how to get meaning from a text. That is what most skills are. The purpose of learning phonics, for instance, isn't so you can say the most common sounds of a letter—it is to help you figure out an unknown word in reading.

When you learned your reading skills, they probably had names like phonics, sight words, word analysis, and context clues. Current terminology reflects the whole language philosophy, with a slightly different slant on the traditional skills. For example, phonics is lumped together with word analysis and configuration and placed in the more inclusive category of graphophonemic clues. You may have seen that word and wondered what it meant. Using your word analysis skills, you can break it into two parts: *grapho* meaning written or drawn, and *phonemic* referring to sound. It still has to do with the relationship between what is written and the sounds of the language it represents.

Many people who write and talk about reading strategies refer to cueing systems and graphophonemic cues or semantic cues. In this book we use the word *clue* instead of *cue*. This is a more significant difference than just adding an *l* and it is not an arbitrary difference. The reason for the choice of words is related to the view of learning as constructing knowledge, described in Chapter 1. Construction of knowledge is something that happens inside the learner's brain, not something that happens outside and is then put in. Constance Kamii (1991) helped us to realize that the word *cue* refers to something external and imposed rather than internal and thoughtful. Kamii uses the analogy of an actor following a script to describe why the term *cue* is inappropriate (1991). An actor's cue telling him it is time to say his memorized lines in not at all similar to the complex set of data that must be analyzed in the reading process.

Because *cue* is incompatible with what constructivists and whole language theorists believe about the reading process, we choose to use the term *clue* and the analogy of a detective. We decided that readers are more like detectives than actors. We like the idea that the good reader, like the good detective, must be very clever in putting the clues together. Obviously, the detective is an active thinker, not a passive memorizer.

Sight Words

Now we're ready to talk about reading strategies. Let's start with sight words, because they tend to create a good starting place for youngsters' reading. The term hasn't changed lately, though the way the skill is taught certainly has. When you were young, you may have had to memorize a list of words, possibly the famous Dolch word list (1936). Children used to be drilled in and tested on these sight words with flash cards. We enjoyed seeing reading expert Sam Sebesta demonstrate the best use of Dolch flash cards by tearing them up and throwing them in the air. That doesn't mean we don't think it is important to learn sight words, though.

Sight words, those instantly recognizable words that no longer require effort from a child, stand out as important for beginning reading. They provide youngsters success in their reading efforts, and they provide a starting point for learning graphophonemic strategies. Children learn most words

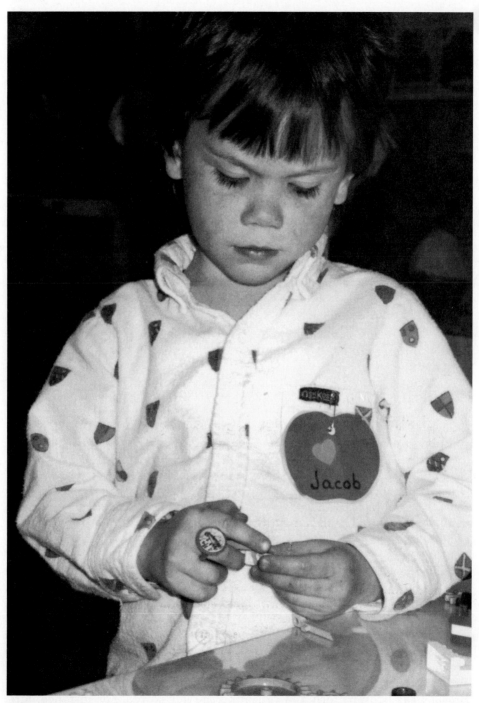

Signs, labels, name tags, and other print in the environment help children to learn words by sight.

through repeated exposure to them while reading various materials. Story time, shared reading, independent reading and reading conferences help youngsters to add to their store of sight words. Repetitious pattern books are especially well suited to assisting the development of a sight word vocabulary. Signs, labels, name tags, and other print in the environment will add to it. As children become aware of and interested in print, they are motivated to memorize some of the words around them that have personal meaning. Most youngsters quickly learn words like *Mom* and *love*, for instance.

You can easily see how helpful it is to instantly recognize the most frequently used words when you realize that just ten words make up almost a quarter of the words in English printed material. When you look at the top twenty-five words, you get up to one-third of all printed material (Fry, Kress, Fountoukidis, & Polk, 1993).

TOP TEN WORDS

the	of
and	a
to	in
is	you
that	it

Almost half of the top fifty words are spelled in ways that make it difficult to figure them out by matching sounds to letters. For example, shouldn't the word *said* rhyme with *aid?* How about *where?* Shouldn't it rhyme with *were* instead of *air?* And *what* surely must rhyme with *at.* Then there is *from* which must rhyme with *Tom,* and *come* which obviously must rhyme with *home.* We could go on and on, but don't worry—we won't. Since youngsters will be constantly frustrated if they try to apply their emerging phonemic understandings to these frequently occurring words, memorizing them is really the only answer.

The fact that these words are so common in print makes it more likely that the more children read, the more they will encounter the words, and the more quickly they will learn them. This process is assisted by frequent and repeated group readings of pattern books that contain many common words, such as Bill Martin's *Brown Bear, Brown Bear, What Do You See?* Follow-up activities can further assist the process for those needing or wanting the extra practice. One such activity is matching teacher-made sentence strips to the story. Another is making and frequently reading a class book adapting the *Brown Bear* book pattern and repeating the key words. For instance, Mrs. Hanna's students love their pattern book about themselves. Each page has a picture of a child and the first few pages read: "Amy, Amy, who do you see? I see Bryce looking at me. Bryce, Bryce, who do you see? I see Ivan looking at me." Research has shown that teaching sight words with pattern books can be three times as effective as using vocabulary-controlled basal readers (Bridge, Winograd, & Haley, 1983).

Games can also help youngsters to learn to quickly recognize common words. Ms. Montoya's students frequently choose the fishing game she made for them. This game involves fishing for paper fish that have a word written on them. Each fish has a paper clip where its mouth should be, and the fishing poles (pointers with string tied to them) each have a magnet at the end of the line. When Tuan hooks a fish, he can't keep it unless he can read the word. If he has trouble landing his fish, his fishing buddies can help him read. The active and interactive nature of this game is an important part of its success. Research has shown that children show a 53 percent greater gain in knowledge than with work sheets when they participate in active games like this. Passive games like concentration are better than work sheets, but they result in only a 30 percent better gain than work sheets (Dickerson, 1982).

Games are useful when, to the children's dismay, many of the words look so much alike. All those words that start with *wh (what, where, when, why,* and *who)* and those other ones that start with *th (then, there, they, those,* and *them)* can slow reading progress. The children have learned these words in a meaningful context, but now they need to develop rapid, rote memory to distinguish among them. Mrs. Thomas is willing for children to work with isolated words for drill under these circumstances. She has created a type of lotto game for practicing quick identification of these words. Sometimes an older reading buddy comes to the first-grade classroom during language arts centers time and plays this game with the first graders who are confusing those abstract *wh* and *th* words.

We must contradict ourselves again. One isolated word does have meaning, and children learn it by itself. That word is the child's name and is generally the first sight word a child learns. Most children also quickly learn to read the names of other children in the classroom if name labels are used frequently for attendance, chore assignments, and identification of work and possessions. This learning of names provides a store of knowledge for comparisons with new words encountered. For instance, when Bryce dictates a story about his beach trip, he can be helped to notice that *shell* begins like his friend Shawn's name. This contributes both to recognizing a new sight word and to an understanding of the nature of graphophonemic systems, better known as phonics.

Graphophonemic Awareness

Yes, emergent readers and writers must learn about letters and the sounds they represent. Mrs. Thomas doesn't take part in any arguments over whether or not to teach phonemic awareness. She thinks it is silly to suggest that children will learn to read by learning the sounds of the letters, but she thinks it is just as silly to suggest not helping them to acquire this useful tool. Ms. Montoya has a clear idea of the role phonics plays in learning to read: It is one of several strategies that may be useful when a child confronts unfamiliar text. Mrs. Hanna agrees and explains to concerned parents that children mainly learn phonics from reading and writing, not reading and writing from phonics. This is consistent with what Ms. Reynolds tells parents who think that their youngsters have to learn the names and sounds of letters before they can begin learning to read.

All of these teachers help their students to increase their phonemic awareness. They provide help at the appropriate levels for each child, and they do it by assisting children to explore their own theories, always within the context of meaningful words and sentences (see Table 4–1). For many of Ms. Reynolds's preschoolers, graphophonemic awareness remains at the stage of discovering that print, not pictures, tell the stories in the books she reads to them. Other children have discovered the print and show their interest through repeated questions of "What does it say?" But remember, literacy development as described in Chapter 1: Children don't instantly start linking letters and sounds when they discover print. For one thing, each letter does not really have its own sound and it isn't even possible to make the sound of a consonant by itself. In addition, youngsters must experience a lot of books

Children learn phonics primarily from reading and writing; they do not learn reading and writing from phonics.

TABLE 4–1
The Best Opportunities to Teach Phonics

Teachers *help children to notice* general phonics principles during the following authentic literacy events:

- As children read and write memorized forms of words
  their own names
  their friends' names
  important words such as "Mom," "Dad," "love," etc.
- As children match oral language to print
  during dictation
  in memorized reading of books, charts and functional print
  as they read along with a tape-recorded story
- As children write with invented spelling
  trying out their theories about phonics
  constantly revising theories as a result of reading experiences

Teachers and other adults *tell* children useful phonics principles during the following authentic literacy events (limiting information to what a youngster appears ready to understand):

- As children dictate ideas and the teacher transcribes them
- As children work at writing independently
- During Shared Reading activities
- As children work at reading independently
- As children observe the teacher writing for adult purposes

---

and stories before figuring out that there is a system for assigning separate letters to the sounds in words. Before that, they have to realize that there are smaller components within words.

Although Ms. Reynolds thinks she would be wasting preschoolers' precious time by drilling on letters and sounds, she always responds to children's questions about letters. She believes that information in response to questions ensures that the child is ready for the information and also ensures that the information will have some personal meaning to that child. She is careful not to tell more than the child really wanted to know.

Ms. Montoya keeps in mind that an attitude of playfulness toward language is the best way to develop phonemic awareness (May, 1994). Rather than use boring work sheets, she plays games, sings songs, and chants rhymes with her students. Children in her class look forward to the silly songs they make up by substituting consonant sounds. For instance, they might change the song "Old MacDonald Had a Farm" so that instead of singing "ee-igh, ee-igh, o," they sing "bee-bigh, bee-bigh, bo" or "dee-digh, dee-digh, do." Youngsters think it is funny to change the birthday song and sing variations such as "Bappy birthday bo boo" (Yopp, 1992). On Ramel's birthday, they sing "Rappy rirthday ro roo" and when they sing to Felicia, the song is "Fappy firthday." On field trip bus rides, children love to sing silly songs such as "Willoughby Wallaby Watya, An elephant sat on Katya. Willoughby Wallaby Waul, An elephant sat on Paul." They are practicing phonics principles as they are having fun.

Rhyming words help youngsters to hear likenesses and differences in words. In addition, knowing a few common word bases can help with reading many words. For instance, knowing how to read *hot* can help in reading *pot, dot, cot, tot, lot, not, got,* and *rot,* as well as *shot, blot, trot,* and so on. Mrs. Thomas makes sure to offer books, poems, songs, and games that focus on rhymes. Of course, many of the predictable books utilize rhymes and Mrs. Thomas often features them during shared reading times. She also helps children who are interested to make rhyming word wheels (see Figure 4–3).

FIGURE 4–3
Rhyming wheel illustration. The outer circle turns and creates different words.

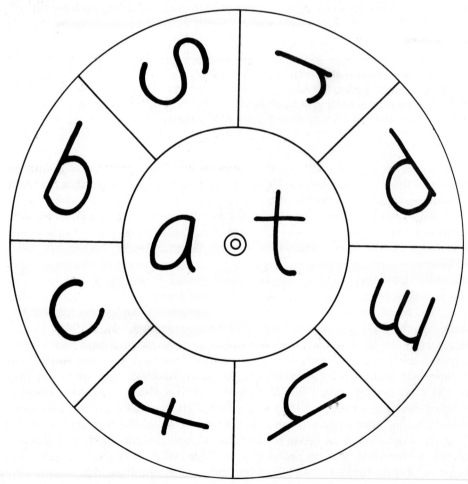

While writing Halloween stories, Heidi has been inspired to see how many different words she can make that rhyme with *bat* and *cat*. Heidi enjoys sharing her rhyming wheel with others in the class, using it like a spinner to play a game of guessing which word it will land on. She and Anastasia decide to work together to find other words that can be similarly made into rhyme wheels.

The next time we visit Mrs. Thomas's room, we find that Heidi and Anastasia have continued their interest in rhyming words. Having composed a rhyming poem, they copy it onto heavy paper to display for the group. Mrs. Thomas encourages further word analysis by beginning another chart. This chart displays compound words that children have recently dictated, written, or discovered in their reading. She encourages children to add to the chart as they discover more words that are made by putting together two shorter words. In a card pocket below the chart are tagboard strips on which youngsters can write the separate words that make up their compound word. Taking these word strips out and putting them together like a puzzle is an attractive activity to many of the first graders. Trevor is amazed at what happens when he recombines just a few common words and discovers the words *nothing, something, somewhere,* and *nowhere.*

Good readers rely on a variety of clues as they read. We generally teach phonics and word analysis clues but sometimes overlook word configuration clues. Mrs. Thomas knows that the general shape of a word, possibly coupled with the initial letter, is often sufficient information to the reader engrossed in the meaning of the material. Although this shortcut to sight word identification is generally intuitive, Mrs. Thomas helps children to notice the general shape of words as she writes and reads with children. She comments on such things as the two tall giraffe neck letters in the word *giraffe*, she points out that the double *o's* in *look* remind her of eyes looking at her, and she mentions when a word is very long or very short. Once children begin noticing the shape of words, they continue to store up this useful information on their own.

Semantic Clues

None of these graphophonemic clues is really useful unless employed in combination with the answer to the question "What would make sense?" The reading strategy involving that question is commonly known as using context clues—*the single most used reading strategy.* Because this semantic reading skill relates directly to the meaning of what is read and therefore reflects the true purpose of reading, Mrs. Hanna, Ms. Montoya, Ms. Reynolds, and Mrs. Thomas are all enthusiastic about helping children learn to use it effectively.

Remember the description of a good reader in Chapter 1—Mandy reading her book without knowing all the words. Because she knows most of the words, the ones she recognizes give her sufficient clues to make a reasonable guess at those she doesn't know. If her guess is wrong enough to affect the sense of what she is reading, she goes back and tries again. Then she might

Good readers figure out an unknown word according to what makes sense in the reading.

apply her graphophonemic knowledge. She could always go to the dictionary, but how much fun would reading be if she had to spend much time with that kind of interruption? After Mandy has encountered a word several times, she will have a good idea of its meaning, whether or not she knows the correct pronunciation. As with most of us, Mandy's reading vocabulary exceeds her speaking vocabulary. Just as our oral vocabulary increases through hearing words used in context, we increase our reading vocabulary through seeing words used in context. Looking up words in dictionaries gives us definitions, but does little for our ability to use words appropriately. Think about reading words you can't define yourself in order to verify the value of meaning clues. (We assume you are using them while reading this text when you come to words like "scaffolding," "semantic," and "graphophonemic.")

Even before children are reading, they can become familiar with the idea of filling in a missing word in a sentence. Oral-context clue games make useful transition time fillers as well as reading skill builders. Mrs. Hanna often plays guessing games with her kindergartners while they wait in line for the bus. She incorporates semantic clues into the games with sentences that have a missing word to be filled in. "We are going _____ now," she says. "We will ride on the _____ bus." Where there are several possible correct answers, she at first accepts all of them. Later, as children develop proficiency with other word-recognition strategies, she will encourage combining them with guesses at what makes sense. She will give clues such as, "It starts with *h*," or "It rhymes with *fellow*."

Guessing games about what a sign might say are also challenging and fun for youngsters trying to make sense of the print in their environment. Here the semantic clues they use have to do with what makes sense from where and how the print is used. It is another way of getting in touch with the meaning of print. When they go for walks, children are full of ideas about the signs they see. They know what the STOP sign says and a few others; they have ideas about many store signs from visits there. Ms. Reynolds encourages their logical thought rather than stopping it all by just telling them the answers. Ms. Reynolds also encourages discussions about signs and labels in the classroom, such as the safety rules in the woodworking center and the labels for where tools belong. She helps children to notice the usefulness of signs in the school, too, such as EXIT, OFFICE, BOYS, and GIRLS.

Ms. Reynolds often uses story time for demonstrating the use of semantic clues. As she reads, she sometimes stops to allow the children to fill in a word. Her preschoolers especially enjoy chiming in on rhyming words in stories or poems. When Ms. Reynolds reads *Mama, Do You Love Me?* (Joosse, 1991), she might read the little girl's question, "What if I stayed away and sang with the wolves and slept in a cave?" Then she would read the Mama's response, "Then, Dear One, I would be very _____." The children like guessing the best word for how Mama would feel if her little girl did things like running away or turning into a walrus. Of course, they all chime in on the repetitive phrase, "But still, I would love you."

Mrs. Thomas demonstrates the value she places on semantic clues when her first graders read aloud to her. When a child stops on a word, Mrs. Thomas first asks, "What word would make sense?" rather than "What are the sounds of the letters?" If the child's guess is close in meaning, but incorrect, Mrs. Thomas continues the flow of the story by telling the child the word rather than stopping to sound it out. However, she often mentions a distinguishing characteristic of the word, such as the beginning consonant, as she tells the child the word. She might say, "Yes, it means *mail* but it starts with an *l* and the word is 'letter.'" Mrs. Thomas is guided by the individual child's needs in what kind of feedback she gives each student. A child confident and excited about reading can profit from more correction than a child who hesitates about the process. For an insecure reader, Mrs. Thomas usually just supplies the missing word to assist fluency and to help the child focus on meaning.

Ms. Montoya keeps in her mind a list of questions she likes to ask youngsters when they run into a reading roadblock (Fisher, 1991). These questions focus on meaning and include the following:

What would make sense?

What other words could make sense?

What does the picture tell you?

Syntactic Clues

Another aspect of meaning in print is reflected in the question teachers ask a child about a reading confusion, "Does it sound right?" In this case, sounding right has to do with the order in which words are written. This relates to the grammatical structure of our language and creates expectations of what kind of word should come next in a sentence. In English, the sequence generally is noun, verb, object. So, if you read "She xxxxxx him," you would expect the unknown word in the middle to be a verb of some sort. If the word starts with the letter *k*, you might use phonics to narrow it down to the following: *kicked*, *kissed*, or *killed*. The previous sentence or else the one following surely would help you to figure out which one it is. But your starting place was the expectation of a verb, and a verb with an object. You knew it wouldn't be "She kitty him," or "She kind him," for instance, because neither would sound right. If context clues from the previous sentence suggested that the next step would be kissing, persons proficient in the English language would know that the word would not be *kissing* because that would require the word *is* to be inserted first. Similarly, it couldn't be just *kiss* without a word like *will* in front of it. That leaves *kissed* as the word that your brain, using your knowledge of English syntax, instantly will sort out from the several options. Of course, if standard English is not your first language, this process may be far from instant or easy.

You may have filled in many a work sheet practicing this sort of thing in school, but really, familiarity with language is gained from using it, not from work sheets. Remember the language development activities described in Chapter 3? Those are critical to children's familiarity with language syntax. The main idea behind all of them is to encourage children to *talk;* the silent classroom is counterproductive to learning of many kinds. Story time, also presented in Chapter 3, is the other main contribution to a child's knowledge of syntax. Hearing the language of literature is especially important for youngsters who do not speak standard English in their home environments: Stories provide a model of language that matches that of the books they will be reading and helps them to develop accurate syntactical expectations.

Personal Schema

Tyler's experiences caring for salamanders create an understanding of salamanders that helps him to read about them. When he reads, his understandings will help him to realize when he misreads something: what he reads won't fit into his personal schema. For instance, if Tyler read "The salamander flew . . . ," he would stop himself and self-correct. His next try might be "The salamander froze until the danger was past." We frequently refer to readers self-correcting as a result of realizing that what they read did not make sense. How do you know when something doesn't make sense? That

Hearing the language of literature is especially helpful to youngsters who do not speak standard English in their homes.

information is not on the page, it is in your head. Your personal experience base, including that gained from prior reading, is an essential component of the reading process. In this case, Tyler knows that salamanders can't fly.

Teachers can assist children's development and conscious use of personal schema for reading. All the meaningful and engaging experiences provided in your classroom add to the knowledge and understanding a child brings to reading. These were discussed in depth in Chapter 2 and include not just field trips and guests, but the entire active, process approach to education. A teacher's comments and questions about what children read can help them to become more aware of how their own experiences relate to what they read. Mrs. Hanna frequently asks children to think about what they already know regarding a topic in a book they have chosen. Ms. Montoya finds that having her students for three years instead of one helps her to know more of their experiences that might relate to their reading. She can remark about Jazzmin's daddy being a dentist when they read *Dr. DeSoto* (Steig, 1982). She can also ask Amber about the dentist that helped her stuck baby tooth come out and how that was different from Dr. DeSoto's method.

Integrating Strategies

All these reading strategies are valuable and good readers use all of them. Good teaching helps children learn how to integrate all strategies at once (see Figure 4–4). For instance, when children have some graphophonemic skill, they combine that information with their idea of what word would make sense and come up with the right one. In determining what would make sense, they use syntactic and semantic clues to select an appropriate word of similar meaning. Thus, reading continues and children gain satisfaction from the process. Having to stop and find the "right" word would destroy the young readers' train of thought and frustrate them. If Mandy misreads a word, changing its meaning, she quickly realizes something is wrong because her word doesn't "fit" with the rest of the story or the sentence. She then checks to find the error and makes sense out of what she is reading. How did she know when a word doesn't fit in with the rest of the story? She relied on her own experiences that formed her personal schema. She was focusing on all necessary clues and using a balanced set of reading strategies.

Comprehension

Comprehension is a result of successfully integrating all of the reading strategies. None of the reading skills has any value unless a person can understand the message in what is read. The bottom line is this communication is what comprehension skills are all about. Traditionally teachers have been directed to test children's comprehension through questions about what they read. Most of these questions tend to be at the literal level—what happened, when, where, who, how many, etc. We now know that we can skip these mundane questions and go on to those that require children to think about, rather

FIGURE 4–4
Integrating Literacy Clues

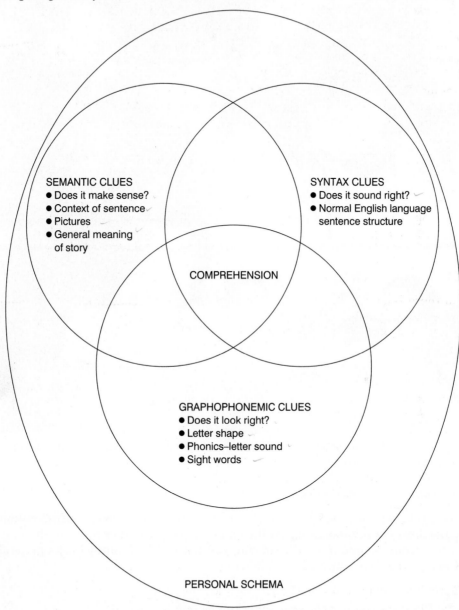

than merely remember, what they read. It is clear that children must use the literal information as a base for their further thinking about a story; therefore, both levels can be covered simultaneously.

Ms. Montoya often asks her students what they think will happen next as they read with her (Fisher, 1991). This question encourages active, predic-

The question "What do you think will happen next?" encourages children's active predictive strategies for reading.

tive strategies for reading while at the same time gives her feedback about the children's understanding. At the end of a book, whether it is one she read to the group or one a child read independently, Ms. Montoya asks general overview questions such as the following:

What is this book about?

What are some of the important things that happened?

What are some things you learned? (Remember, not all books are fiction.)

Does this book remind you of any other books?

Do you know of other books written by this author?

Questions that require critical thinking also require basic understanding of what was read. If a child can participate in discussions about what was right or wrong in a story, you know that child comprehended the story. Chapter 3 described some critical thinking questions in relation to story time. Similar kinds of questions are appropriate in conjunction with shared or independent reading. When Tyler and Mrs. Thomas talk about *The Salamander Room* (Mazer, 1991), their discussion focuses on whether or not Brian, the boy in the story, should be allowed to keep the salamander he found. They also consider the practicality of Brian's ideas for making his bedroom into a salamander room. This approach to checking comprehension does much more than that: Mrs. Thomas is demonstrating how to use active and critical thinking in conjunction with reading. This demonstration contributes to comprehension as well as checks on it; and it helps children to become discerning about what they read. Advertising campaigns increasingly require this kind of thinking in conjunction with reading.

Its never too early to start. The old view was that comprehension skill practice begins when a child begins to read independently. With current understanding of emergent literacy, teachers realize that comprehension skills are developing long before a child can read by conventional standards. The infant's ability to make sense of oral language is the actual beginning of this skill. It is developed and expanded to written language whenever an adult reads to the child.

Story time offers an excellent opportunity for teaching and assessing comprehension skills. Teachers can tell much about a child's understanding and involvement through their nonverbal behavior. Tanya's rapt attention while Ms. Reynolds reads aloud contrasts sharply with Kelly's squirming and fiddling with things. Children's comments and questions during and after a story are also revealing. Scott volunteers an excited guess about what will happen next in the story. Betsy tells of an experience she had which was similar to the one in the story. But Abbey just wants to know what's for snack. Ms. Reynolds was impressed when Tanya made a connection between a fictional story about a train and information from a nonfictional concept book about trains.

The follow-up activities described in conjunction with story time in Chapter 3 relate to comprehension skills. Opportunities for retelling stories while looking at the pictures in the book help children to practice thinking about the meanings in what they read. They also enjoy retelling stories with flannel-board figures, with puppets, and through various art media. Some youngsters are interested in making up new endings or otherwise writing their own version of popular stories. Timmy had fun dictating "Timmy and the Terrible, Horrible, No Good, Very Bad Day." Ms. Reynolds learns a lot about her students' levels of comprehension through observations and discussions with children during these activities.

Many teachers organize their curriculum around themes or projects of interest to children. The classroom library offers a selection of fact and fiction books related to the current topic. As children read in depth about a topic, from a variety of sources, their understanding of what they read increases. For instance, *The Salamander Room* that Tyler was reading is just one of many books about lizards and similar creatures currently in Mrs. Thomas's class library. Tyler and several of his classmates got interested in studying lizards as a result of their questions about dinosaurs and whether anything like them still lived. They are extending their understandings by caring for some salamanders in a classroom terrarium. This experience generates much thought and discussion, which Mrs. Thomas encourages the children to put into writing. The more they experience and think and write, the more understanding they bring to their reading; and the more understanding they *bring* to a book, the more they *get* from it.

Children Who Aren't Getting It

What about those kids who don't seem to get anything from books, despite your best efforts? Are those the ones you start to drill with the work sheets and flash cards trying to get them to catch up? That is precisely what has been done in the past, with dire results. Those children who have difficulty with literacy are the ones who most need the holistic approaches (Salvage & Brazee, 1991). The New Zealand schools adopted whole language approaches in an effort to better meet the needs of the native Maori population, for whom traditional approaches were failing totally (Holdaway, 1991). We hear many teachers in the United States say that the children who surely would have failed using old approaches now have a chance to make sense of reading (Scala, 1993).

There are many different reasons why a child may have difficulty in becoming literate. These include cultural and language differences which make the expectations, explanations, and words of school incomprehensible (Carger, 1993; Pellegrini, 1991; Walker-Dalhouse, 1993). Some cultural differences are not related to ethnicity, but rather to social class and economic status. Sometimes, children experience difficulty in school due to psychological or physical problems. You probably can't do much about these causes, but you can accept each child's efforts and help each child to progress in whatever ways are possible for that child (Flores, Cousin, & Diaz, 1991; Truax & Kretschmer, 1993).

Lumping these children into the "low" group and depriving them of the interesting reading activities is not the answer. Though common, that is precisely the worst possible thing to do. The resulting damage to self-esteem and motivation to learn is often irreversible. These are the two things you need to nurture: children's self-respect and their desire to learn. Without these, educational efforts are wasted (May, 1994).

It may sound radical, but the best teaching for children experiencing difficulty is the same as the best teaching for children who are progressing nicely (Pils, 1993; Fitzgerald, 1993). For instance, children who experience some form of dyslexia especially need a balanced approach to reading strategies in order to utilize the strengths they do have. Drill on letters focuses on their weaknesses, while learning to use syntax and semantic clues allows these youngsters to use what they do know in order to figure out that which is difficult for them. Good teaching is good teaching.

All youngsters benefit from exposure to high-quality literature, models of standard oral and written language, opportunities to explore their theories of literacy, and adults who encourage their efforts (O'Neal, 1991). We have said several times that the children who benefit most from these in school are those who have not experienced them prior to school. For instance, some youngsters know little about reading because they haven't been read to. The obvious solution is massive doses of being read to, accompanied by the kinds of book-talk that literate and doting parents have with their youngsters over bedtime stories. Children who have not been read to deserve the same opportunities to construct their understandings of print as other youngsters.

The highly successful Reading Recovery program (Clay, 1985), imported from New Zealand, approaches remedial reading from a whole language perspective with a special concern for the child's self-esteem. It targets first-grade youngsters who seem to have the least understanding of literacy and gives them special attention to try to catch them up before they feel left behind. Basically, teachers trained in this program do the same things that good whole language teachers do in their classrooms, only they do it with one child at a time for a full thirty minutes every day. The teacher first works to develop good rapport with the child, then they engage in meaningful literacy experiences. They read books together to build fluency and confidence. The teacher and the child focus on meaning rather than mere words or letters, yet do not ignore those components. Children write as well as read in this program—that's what we will be talking about in the next chapter.

Some teachers say that there wouldn't be a need for special Reading Recovery programs if all teachers had such good training in whole language methods and if class sizes allowed that kind of individual attention (Taylor, Short, Frye, & Shearer, 1992; Allington, 1993). Certainly, issues of teacher preparation and class size impact the problem. Youngsters identified as "at risk" in first grade will continue to need high-quality educational experiences (Clements & Warncke, 1994). It would seem that the least we could do is eliminate poor teaching as a cause of reading failure.

Another type of special needs child is the accelerated or gifted learner. We are not going to shortchange that child in the type of program described here: When we encourage children to read and write all they can in response to topics they are truly interested in, there is no limit to the level of literacy that can be attained. Advanced youngsters tend to lose interest in an artificially sequenced program or one that tries to move groups of youngsters through material simultaneously. Flexibility and open-ended teacher expectations are as important to the self-esteem of an above-average learner as to a below-average one. Being *different* can make children feel bad, even if those differences stem from giftedness. Differences are highlighted when teachers expect all youngsters to perform the same tasks in the same way.

Round-robin reading comes to mind here. Do you remember those incredibly boring episodes when everyone in the room had to take turns reading a section from some book? You were supposed to be following along with the reader and know "the place" when the teacher called on you. We don't actually know anyone who ever did know "the place." Kids who were good readers had finished the whole piece by the time the second person had read the second paragraph. Those youngsters were reading something else that looked interesting in another part of the book or else daydreaming. The kids who were not good readers were having trouble following along, mostly because they were paralyzed with fear over having to take their turn. Their minds were busy trying to figure out an escape route. We do not recommend round-robin reading, but will offer some other suggestions for oral reading in Chapter 7.

CONCLUSION

In the classrooms described, the teachers do not define reading as saying words, no matter how accurately or with how much expression. These teachers are so committed to the concept of reading as an active rather than a passive process that they are not satisfied with readers who merely repeat facts from what they read and demonstrate good literal comprehension. These teachers encourage the critical thinking and reading between the lines that result from interaction with print. They want children to question and to criticize, to exclaim and to cry; they want children to be *involved* with reading.

An enriched conception of early literacy expands our ideas of the skills involved (Teal, 1988). We realize now that children must do far more than use the graphophonemic clues on the page and know which way to turn the pages; they must also bring to the printed page their understandings of language, of what they are reading, and of their world. By integrating all these pieces simultaneously, children can experience reading as communication between the author and themselves. New information about learning has given value to the emergent reading processes of pretend reading and reconstructing a text from memory; new views also recognize that children are practicing actual reading strategies in these processes.

DISCUSSION QUESTIONS

1.   A parent says he has heard that you are teaching whole language and he is worried that his child won't learn phonics. How would you answer his concern?

2. A child takes home a pattern book she has memorized and proudly reads it to her parents. She comes back to school crushed, saying that her family said she wasn't really reading. What explanation should have been given to parents before the child took the book home?

SUGGESTED FOLLOW-UP ACTIVITIES

1. Prepare a story from a Big Book and share it with children. Involve them in following the print through use of a pointer.
2. Observe and listen to emergent readers reading familiar predictable books with their friends. Note the clues they attend to and try to determine their current understandings.
3. Familiarize yourself with different types of predictable books. Try to find out by observing various children what makes a book readable for them.
4. Ask a young reader to read aloud to you. As you help the child with unfamiliar words, practice focusing attention on meaning clues first, with graphophonemic clues giving secondary assistance. Note the kinds of errors the child makes and try to determine the strategies he or she is using.
5. Note the current and possible uses of functional print in classrooms you visit.

RECOMMENDED FURTHER READING

Periodicals

Clay, M. (1986). Constructive processes: Talking, reading, writing, art, and craft. *The Reading Teacher, 39*(8), 764–770.

Egawa, K. (1990). Harnessing the power of language: First grader's literature engagement with Owl Moon. *Language Arts, 67,* 582–588.

Flores, B., Cousin, P. T., & Diaz, E. (1991). Transforming deficit myths about learning, language, and culture. *Language Arts, 68,* 369–379.

O'Neal, S. (1991). Leadership in the language arts: Dear principal, please let my special education child read and write. *Language Arts, 68,* 417–423.

Pellegrini, A. D. (1991). A critique of the concept of at risk as applied to emergent literacy. *Language Arts, 68,* 380–385.

Ritchie, J. S. & Wilson, D. E. (1993). Dual apprenticeships: Subverting and supporting critical teaching. *English Education, 25*(2), 67–83.

Salvage, G. J. & Brazee, P. E. (1991). Risk taking, bit by bit. *Language Arts, 68,* 356–366.

Books

Wells, G. (1986). *The meaning makers: Children learning language and using language to learn.* Portsmouth, NH: Heinemann.

CHAPTER

5

RACHEL B.

ASSISTING EMERGENT WRITERS

Perhaps nowhere is the importance of the concept of emergent literacy more evident than with young children's writing.

WILLIAM TEALE, 1986

This chapter focuses on emergent writing and the kinds of writing activities that help youngsters to become better writers and readers. Remember, writing and reading are intertwined: The more people read, the more they know about writing; and the more people write, the more they know about reading. In fact, writing involves reading as you review what you just wrote before writing your next sentence. Of course, we are talking about *real* writing, not copying something off the board for spelling and handwriting practice. In the past, some teachers confused copying with writing, and many thought they were teaching writing when they taught penmanship. Now, however, more teachers are coming to value writing as an important communication tool and to realize that even young children are capable of authorship. These teachers aim toward helping each child to believe in herself or himself as a writer.

What kind of teaching helps youngsters to believe in themselves as writers? It is teaching that helps them to construct their own knowledge. Constructing knowledge about writing means creating and testing theories while working at writing. Just as we said that children learn to read better by reading more, children learn to write better by writing more. The classroom that helps children find reasons to write and that gives them to freedom do so is the classroom that fosters children's understanding and produces proud and capable young writers.

TESTING THEORIES

Writing on their own allows children to explore the information they have accumulated from adult models and other experiences with print. When children write, they are able to use a trial-and-error approach to making sense of written language. They try out their current theories about written language while they practice writing, much as they try out their understanding of oral language as they practice talking. When adults allow children to use this trial-and-error approach, the children build firm understandings of the significant concepts and then are able to transfer these understandings to a variety of related situations.

Constructing Knowledge

When well-meaning adults try to keep children from "wasting time" by making mistakes, they deprive children of significant learning experiences. Telling children the principles involved not only truly wastes the child's time but also may deprive the child of the chance to formulate basic concepts. Understanding may be replaced by rote memory of a few facts. A child cannot easily transfer specific facts to other situations and will have to learn more facts by rote. This approach has the additional danger of discouraging thought through suggesting to children that they cannot figure out things on their own, but must rely on an authority.

Writing on their own allows children to explore the information they have accumulated from experiences with print.

When you consider beginning writing to be an initial experimentation with the written word, your expectations for young students change. Instead of expecting children to form letters correctly and spell words according to custom, you can appreciate each small step toward standard written expression. You can rejoice with a young child over approximations of intent in writing, just as you do with a toddler who makes an imprecise attempt to say a new word.

Initial Explorations

Ms. Reynolds encourages independent writing by both three- and four-year-olds. They have access to blank paper, marking pens, crayons, and pencils. Ms. Reynolds understands the importance of children freely exploring written language to unlock its mysteries. She enjoys watching children "play around" with print in the same way they explore with clay or blocks. These preschoolers are free to squeeze and smash clay, to stack and scatter blocks, and to scribble and scratch with writing utensils. The preschool parent-helpers are used to the idea of process being important whether or not there is any product. Parents are therefore comfortable with the lack of "correct" writing in the writing center.

The adults in the preschool have even learned to read children's attempts to write their own names. They decided that a grown-up who writes a child's name on a painting after the child already has done so is disrespectful of the child's writing. So, as part of empowering children's use of print, they learned the distinctive signature of each child in the school. In the process they decided that children's signatures are as readable as many adults' (see Figure 5–1).

The wide range of writing forms that Ms. Reynolds observes in children's paper-and-pencil work fascinates her. Their writing includes random scribbles and drawing, linear markings, letterlike forms and conventional letters. Most youngsters actually use a combination of forms in their writing. Many children already write their own names with some accuracy, but most tend to turn the letters around randomly. Some children are ambivalent about the difference between drawing and writing: Tabatha says, "I want to draw my name" (see Figure 5–2), while Abbey announces, "I writing a picture" (see Figure 5–3). Some children confidently experiment with letters and letterlike forms, while others limit themselves to tracing or copying correct forms. Some fill pages with rows of squiggles and still others apparently have no interest at all in writing yet.

Some differences are attributable to levels of understanding, but the role of individual personality and style of learning accounts for other differences. Some children don't think at all about what their writing might say; others will decide after they are through that their scribbles look like something specific. Some will ask an adult what their writing says, and some know exactly what they want it to say. Different youngsters attend to different

FIGURE 5–1
Two examples of young children's signatures.

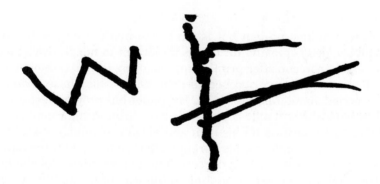

aspects of writing and have different purposes as they write. Some children focus on form, detail, and accuracy, while others are carried away with the stories they have to tell.

Dominic has created a combination of scribbles, drawings, and letter forms that he explains orally in elaborate detail (see Figure 5–4). By listening carefully, Ms. Reynolds discovers that Dominic has a well-developed story in mind, but simply lacks the technical skills to put it into standard readable form. Ms. Reynolds is delighted with Dominic's writing progress. Dominic knows what writing is for, he understands that symbols are used to communicate ideas, and he has the ability to express himself.

FIGURE 5–2
Tabatha said that she drew her name.

Tanya's writing has no plot but is limited to marks that she has designated as symbols for people and for things important to her. Tanya's theories about print lead her to consider print as representing things rather than language. Ms. Reynolds isn't worried because she knows this phase is a natural one. She is worried about Justin, though. His paper has only perfectly spelled words on it because he will only copy words from around the room. He lacks the confidence to try writing on his own and always anxiously asks, "Is this right?" Ms. Reynolds wonders if his parents' effort to teach him the alphabet and sounds at home cause Justin's concern about correctness. All she knows for sure is that Justin's concern is getting in the way of his ability to explore and learn about written language.

Conventional Forms Appear

Betsy's sister, Amy, just started kindergarten and has discovered that spaces appear between segments of writing and that specific kinds of marks make certain letters. Amy has noticed that some writing is made from combinations of straight lines, some from curved lines, and some from both. She has been exploring these observations during the past year, moving from making long rows of circles to creating more letterlike forms.

Amy frequently chooses to work in the writing center. There she alternates between copying words she knows from around the room and creating new ways of putting her own ideas into print. She particularly likes to write

FIGURE 5–3
Abbey said that she wrote this picture.

FIGURE 5–4
A letterlike form of emergent writing.

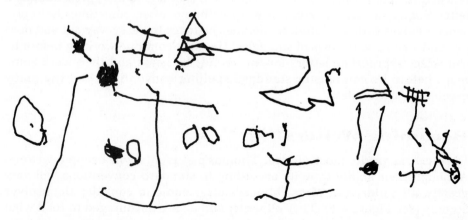

FIGURE 5–5
This child's writing conforms to conventions well enough that we might think we could read it.

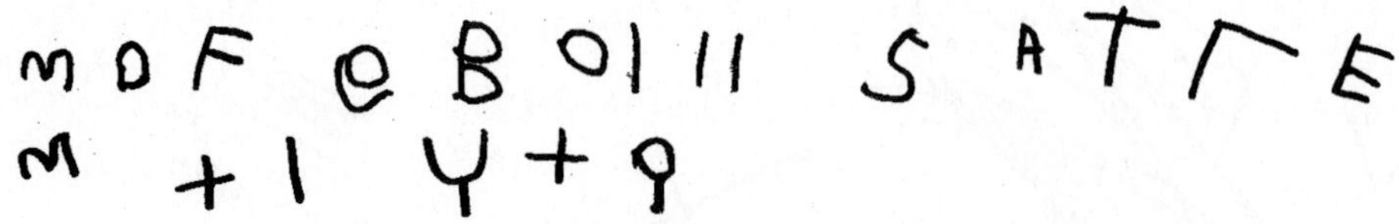

her own name and the names of her friends. She has become skilled at making the letters in her own name and has noticed that these same letters are also in some other names. For a while, she was merely reordering the letters in her own name when she wrote. She used these same letters in some sequence to spell any word she didn't know. She still sometimes uses random assortments of letters bearing no apparent relationship to the sounds of words in the message she may "read" from her paper. Her work and that of her classmates is not just playing around prior to really learning to write; the children's exploration stages of writing are essential elements of learning to write.

Maria has played with print long enough to discover that a relationship exists between sounds and letters. She writes stories in which most of the major sounds are represented by a letter that has a name similar to that sound. Dien has mastered the distinguishing characteristics of letters but has only a vague awareness of a symbol-sound relationship. He has figured out that writing uses a few characters over and over again. His writing conforms to standard writing in that it is a series of letters with not more than two alike adjacent to one another. As we view his work, it looks so much like adult writing that we might think we could read it (see Figure 5–5). However, the groups of letters do not spell words, and we have to rely on the child to read his work to us.

Bryce's concept of the relationship between letters and sounds hasn't reached the point where he knows that each sound is to be represented by a letter. Sometimes he represents a word with one letter; sometimes he represents syllables with one letter. Sometimes he takes the easy way out and does pretend writing with rows of squiggles. He must continue working before he can select appropriate letters for the sounds he hears and then work some more before he can master standard spelling conventions *and* the many exceptions to the rules.

Becoming Writers

During first grade, most of Mrs. Thomas's students will become writers. Although their ability to write according to standard conventions will vary greatly, all children in Mrs. Thomas's class come to consider themselves authors (see Figure 5–6). They all write, and all are encouraged to read what

FIGURE 5–6
Can you read this invented spelling? Put in your own punctuation to discover the plot.

The aly cat   There wus a cat hoo
livd in the aly it wus sckrufy and
sagye and wet it dug in grabij cans
it just found bons and uther shuch
things it slepd on emty grabij cans
won day a gri found it she fed it
melck and gave it a aoft bed to siepe
in it graoo farey piump and fat it
becam to big for its bed it drace
vary litll melck pepl stil kaerd for
it it was not so fat . Ashley

Ashle
By
SThy
Ashley

FIGURE 5–7
This child's writing shows familiarity with the
"once upon a time" story format.

wass	a pon	a tm	ther
woss	som	polpl	

they have written to their classmates. Their desire to have others read their writing becomes a major impetus to learning more about spelling and punctuation.

The content of what children write in this classroom is amazing. Even children who rely on pictures and use few words have wonderful stories to tell. Mrs. Thomas sees a direct relationship between the literature she shares with her students and the type of writing they do (see Figure 5–7). From their knowledge of fairy tales, these children have a useful model of story structure, and many of their stories start with *wuzupnatm*. From other stories they gain favorite characters to write about, such as *Curious George* (Rey, 1941). From still others they learn how to use direct dialogue or a narrative form. Television also serves as an inspiration for children's writing. Mrs. Thomas allows children to write about whatever interests them, even if it is a Saturday morning cartoon character or plot.

Most of her students are trying to match the sounds of their language with letters to write it. Some children are just beginning to explore this concept. Many are working at the letter-naming level, like Maria in the kindergarten class. Some have made the discovery that the names of letters and the sounds aren't always the same. Whatever their level, Mrs. Thomas values and encourages their attempts without criticism of the product. She knows that criticism during their shaky early attempts can discourage further efforts to make sense of writing.

Models of conventional writing are the essential partner to exploration with writing. This partnership provides the framework for all writing instruction.

Instead of criticizing, Mrs. Thomas continues to encourage youngsters to create and test their own theories as they practice writing. She also provides models of conventional writing both through her own demonstrations and through constant exposure to books and other print. She knows that children's own desire to make their writing readable will keep them striving toward those models. She keeps in mind that the more children work at writing, the more they will analyze the writing they see in books and all around them (Smith, 1983). The quote from Eleanor Duckworth at the beginning of

Chapter 1 relates to this process: "If a child has a theory, no matter how primitive, that child will pay attention to instances which confirm or contradict that theory" (1987). Thus, models of conventional writing are the essential partner to exploration with writing. This partnership provides the framework for all writing instruction.

Risk Taking

Felicia's previous feedback about her writing has made her so concerned about spelling and letter formation that she won't explore with print. When Ms. Montoya encourages journal writing, Felicia begs her teacher to tell her how to spell the words she wants to write. Ms. Montoya's sympathy for Felicia's fear of failure makes her want to give in, but her desire that Felicia becomes truly literate, not just a copier of words, makes her hesitate. Ms. Montoya tries to show that she accepts mistakes during various school activities. She calls attention to her own errors such as misplacing a book or miscounting the number of materials. She publicly admires children's writing with invented spelling and pretend writing. Ms. Montoya tells all the children to write however seems right to them and not to worry about adult spelling for now. She explains to youngsters that they don't have to spell correctly when they are just beginning. Gradually, Felicia relaxes and tries to write on her own, and her teacher is relieved.

AUTHENTIC WRITING

At the beginning of the chapter we recommended helping children find reasons to write. You may suspect that we don't have in mind writing to please the teacher when we talk about giving children reasons to write. At least, we hope you suspect that by now. Writers of all ages write best when they have personally meaningful purposes to write (Clyde, 1994). It might be personally meaningful to Omar to write a letter to his grandmother, to Jazzmin to make a phone directory of her friends, to Tyler to write a book about salamanders, and to Betsy to produce a "keep out" sign for her bedroom door. The purpose doesn't matter as long as it is a purpose that the child cares about.

Not all purposes come from the youngsters, however. Teachers are constantly thinking about ways to encourage children to write. Ms. Montoya thinks about the writing as well as the reading and math activities that would be relevant for each topic of study in her classroom. She is also constantly alert to reasons for writing that might come from children's personal interests and play activities. This chapter describes various types of authentic literacy events that help children to find purposes for writing. Notice that we said *authentic* literacy events. Authentic means the kinds of writing done for "real world" purposes rather than for contrived school purposes. We believe kids can tell the difference.

Writers of all ages write best when they have personally meaningful purposes for writing.

Freedom to Write

We also recommended giving children freedom to write. What do we mean by this? You might think we mean giving them enough time to write. Time is essential to good writing and schools rarely allow enough of it. However, the freedom we are most concerned about is the freedom from *fear*. Are you surprised at that statement? If you watch youngsters in a traditional classroom, you will see that many are unable to write due to fear of failure. These children can't express themselves on paper because they feel constrained to use only words they know how to spell correctly; additionally, they can't concentrate on the content of their writing because they are using all their energy on good handwriting. These problems are a result of writing instruction focused on perfection of mechanics—spelling, handwriting, and punctuation. To make matters worse, you get only one chance—no second and third drafts. (We hope you appreciate that we used more than one draft in writing this book.)

Being a risk taker is a conspicuous trait of prolific writers, and risk takers are not fearful. They charge ahead with whatever skills are at their command and they get their ideas down on paper, worrying about details like spelling later. Teachers who honor emergent writing assist children in risk taking and thus assist them as writers. Thus, Ms. Reynolds offers a well-stocked writing center for preschoolers even though most of them are unable to write anything an adult could begin to read. Recognizing the importance of their processes, Ms. Reynolds respectfully discusses their writing and drawing with youngsters in her class. Similarly, children in Ms. Montoya's multiage group feel comfortable writing at whatever level makes sense to them. Their teacher talks with them about the content of what they write rather than just evaluating it for errors. If you have forgotten the many forms of "kid writing," you may need to go back and review Chapter 1.

Journal Writing

Writing in a journal is an excellent way for youngsters to develop that courage and confidence as writers we were talking about. Journals by nature are personal expressions written for personal purposes. This private aspect of journals is critical to their success in building confidence, since such writing is for yourself and is not subject to outside evaluation. Mrs. Hanna has given each child a journal—a small, blank booklet with a sturdy contact paper cover bearing his or her name. Mrs. Hanna encourages the youngsters to write in these journals, even those children for whom writing is drawing or scribbling. What or how they write doesn't matter. What does matter is that they spend energy exploring their theories about writing. She has found that writing in her own journal during daily journal writing time not only provides a model of adults as writers, but also keeps children from asking her how to spell words. She can more easily encourage students to construct their own spelling if they know she is too busy writing to spell for them.

Though most anything is acceptable as a journal entry, there are some rules for journal time: Each child must draw or write something, names are to be written on each day's entry, and the date is to be stamped on each. In Ms. Montoya's class, children individually bring their journals to their teacher to share their work when they are finished writing. She takes notes while they read their writing to her; this information helps her to keep track

Children's backgrounds and progress determine the teacher's expectations for each.

of each child's writing development. Sometimes she thinks a youngster needs a nudge to move from drawing to writing. When Caitlan again brings her the same sort of pictures she has been drawing for a couple of months, Ms. Montoya asks Caitlan to write down a little of what she has said about the picture. This may be a little as the names of the people pictured, but it's a start. The teacher's expectations of children are determined by her knowledge of each child's background and progress (Girling-Butcher, Phillips, & Clay, 1991).

Mrs. Thomas responds in writing to her students' journals. These responses are not evaluative comments like "Good job" or "Great handwriting." Mrs. Thomas responds to what the children have written as she would in a conversation. When Demetrius writes, "I PLD Ol 6 TeTh aWT WaThe Mi haNDS," Mrs. Thomas writes back, "You lost six teeth! Was it hard to pull them out with your hands?" Notice that her comments honor the child's communication and also model the correct form of the words he was writing. This is an effective way of assisting a child's writing development, just as a similar oral response to an oral communication assists language development. As they hear adult speech models, children modify their baby talk to be more adult; similarly they modify their spelling to be more like adult spelling when they have relevant examples.

When asked how she finds time to respond to each child's journal, Mrs. Thomas says that she has time because she doesn't have to correct work sheets. She not only believes that journals are much more educational than work sheets, but also enjoys reading them much more than work sheets.

Making Books

Making books is also a lot more enjoyable than doing work sheets and gives children a purpose for writing. There are so many different kinds of books to make. Some books are whole-class books, some are written entirely by one child. Some are takeoffs on other books, some are accounts of personal experiences. Some are big and some are small, some are rectangles and some are fancy shapes. Some are stapled or bound and some are folded in magical ways. All are fun for children and encourage them to want to write.

We talked about making a class version of *The Important Book* (Brown, 1945) in Chapter 3 and mentioned Timmy's own version of *Alexander and the Terrible, Horrible, No Good, Very Bad Day* (Viorst, 1972) in Chapter 4. Ms. Montoya's class decided to make their own *Snowy Day* book after becoming familiar with Keats's original (1962). All those who were interested contributed a picture and a caption of their favorite thing to do on a snowy day. Some liked to make angels and snowballs like the little boy in the book, and others contributed items like cross-country skiing or helping Mom to shovel the driveway. In writing their captions, children were free to write on their own, to ask a friend, to look in the pictionary, or to find the words in other books. The criteria for acceptability was the child's own satisfaction. The finished book was laminated, bound, and placed in the class library to be enjoyed by all. Of course, Ms. Montoya read it at group time before it went into the library.

Mrs. Hanna's class has just gone on a field trip to the museum. As a follow-up to the experience, she engages the children in conversation about the things they saw there. Then she invites them each to draw and write about their favorite thing for a class book. Many youngsters choose to dictate their narrative and have an adult write for them, but others are happy with their own kid writing. For those who ask an adult to do the writing, the composing experience is still practice with writing. Those who do their own writing actually are interacting with their friends while they are writing. They give and get advice about what to write and how to write it. This peer interaction is an important part of learning to write.

Mrs. Thomas's class has been studying fish recently. She makes blank books with colored construction paper covers in the shape of fish. At choice time she holds one up and mentions that these are available at the writing center for anyone who wants to write their own fish book. Needless to say, many youngsters are attracted by the interesting shape and bright colors; they want to make a fish book and so they write about fish. Dustin's book contains facts he has learned about fish, while Heidi writes about going fishing on her family's boat. Both youngsters signed up to read their books to the class in the author's chair that day. Sharing writing with an audience and getting constructive feedback is an important part of learning to write. Though their audience was appreciative, both Dustin and Heidi found out that they needed to explain parts of their writing better in order for their classmates to understand their ideas.

Research Writing

We started to get into research writing when we talked about the fish books. Writing done in response to information-gathering procedures is what we are calling research writing. This writing can take the form of individual or group books similar to those already mentioned. Tyler's book about salamanders is the result of his experience observing and caring for them, augmented by some fact and fiction reading. His book shows that he knows a lot about both salamanders and writing.

Mrs. Thomas's students enjoy using their research information to make riddle books to share with their classmates. These usually take the form of a "who am I?" sort of riddle. Children write two or three clues on the outside of the book and put the answer and an illustration on the inside. During a study of sea life, Bryce and Ivan worked together looking up information and writing these clues: "1. I hug rocks. 2. I have eyes on the end of my arms." Opening the book, you see a picture of a starfish (see Figure 5–8). At sharing time, these boys and others who have written riddles enjoy sharing them with their classmates, who have fun guessing.

In Mrs. Hanna's class, children make riddle books using their own first-hand observations during science experiences. When they study trees and

FIGURE 5–8
A pop-up riddle book.

seeds, Mrs. Hanna takes her students on walks to collect samples of leaves and seeds from a variety of local trees. The children helped to create a display in which each set of samples is carefully labeled. Then they work in teams to examine the samples and write up their observations in terms of clues for guessing which tree they were describing. One important clue frequently mentioned in various forms is "It hs poky nedls."

Keeping records of experiments and experiences is another form of writing. Ms. Montoya's students have planted beans and are measuring their growth. Each child has a partner and together they record observations of their plant growth in a log book. Part of the log entries are in the form of narrative accounts about how green the plant is or how it is growing toward the light source, while a graph tracking the growth is another aspect of the log. Similarly, recording the change from a caterpillar to a butterfly is an exciting use for a science log book. The amazing experience of seeing a butterfly emerge from a cocoon and then setting it free generates significant drawing and writing in the classroom.

Functional Writing

We talked about reading functional print in Chapter 4; now let's talk about writing it. Lists showing who has had a turn and who wants one are useful in most classrooms. Even preschoolers can write their own names so that they can recognize them and contribute to a wait list. For instance, Dien and Jevon want turns on the minitrampoline, and Jordan is using it now. Ms. Reynolds gets a piece of butcher paper and tapes it to the wall near the trampoline. She encourages Dien and Jevon to sign up for turns, promising that they will be notified as soon as it is their turn. This keeps peace in the classroom as well as helps youngsters to learn about the usefulness of print. They find out that their names on a list can represent their claims just as well as their standing in line does. They also learn that once their names are written on the list, they stay in the order written. These are important discoveries. There are other kinds of lists, too: things to take on the field trip, things to bring for putting on a play, and birthday guest lists. You can even write lists of things you want to write about (see Figure 5–9).

Jazzmin's decision to make a phone directory to help her to call her friends was her idea, but no less valuable than a teacher's plan. A phone directory is a good example of functional print in our society. Much of youngsters' writing during play is pretend uses of functional print. For instance, they write menus when they play restaurant, make tickets when they put on a play, and write checks when they play store. These examples are valuable writing events, helping children to learn just as much as if they were directed by the teacher. Teachers who understand the value of writing in play make sure to offer writing materials along with other dramatic play props.

Personal Communication

Here goes the end to another sacred truth about school. First, we told you children are supposed to talk to each other in school instead of being quiet. Now we're going to tell you to encourage children to write notes to each other. Yes, note writing generates lots of interest in writing. Mrs. Thomas accidentally discovered this when a couple girls in her class started a "love note" fad. It quickly caught on and soon notes were everywhere. From this event, Mrs. Thomas got the idea of encouraging children to write notes by creating a class mailbox for mailing notes. Youngsters take turns with the job of delivering mail to the correct storage cubbies. Mrs. Thomas models this kind of writing when she writes notes to parents and asks children to deliver them.

Letters are important, too. There are more letters to write than just Omar's letter to his grandmother. Many children have loved ones who live far away and who will even write letters back. Getting a letter in response to a letter is motivation to write more. Thank-you letters are another important letter form. These are important to thank hosts for field trips or guests who bring special events into the classroom. Sometimes, Ms. Montoya takes dicta-

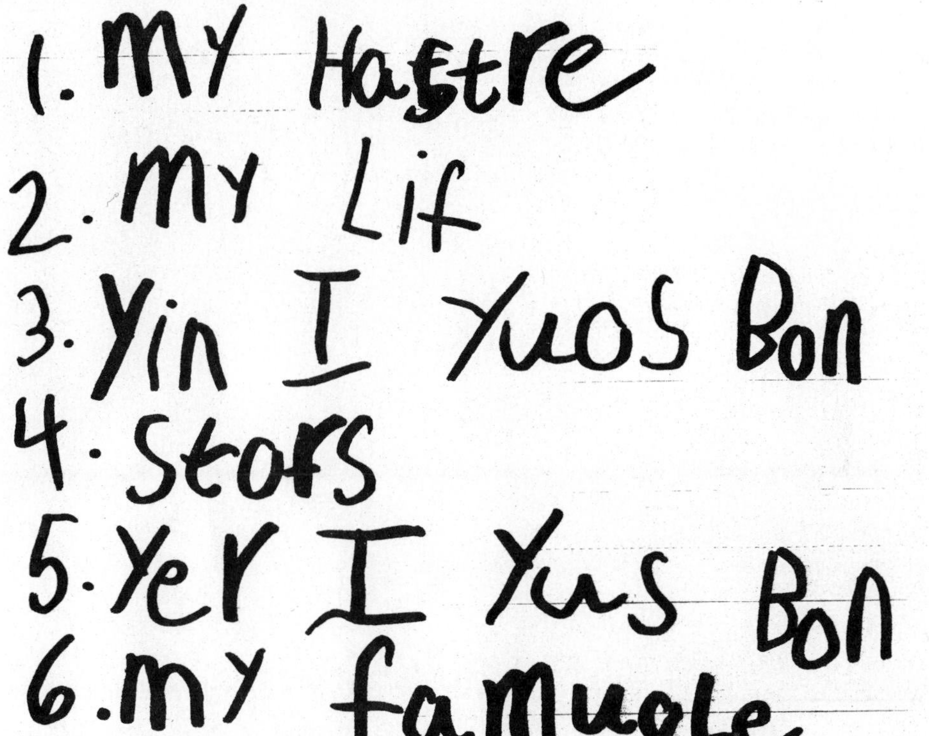

1. my Hastre
2. my Lif
3. yin I yuoS Bon
4. Stors
5. yer I yus Bon
6. my famuole
7. Stors of me
8. riten oBat anmls
9. riten oBat the erth
10. riten oBat me
11. riten ~~oBat me~~

A classroom post office, complete with pretend stamps for sale, encourages youngsters'
letter writing.

tion for a group letter as a way to demonstrate letter writing, and sometimes she encourages each child to write a personal thank-you letter. Mrs. Hanna encourages her students to write to authors of books they especially like, telling what they most like about the book. (Frequently, youngsters will get a response to these, also.) Ms. Reynolds models letter writing for those who are interested when she sits at the writing center and creates the weekly class newsletter for parents. She doesn't write it at home in the evening because she knows that it is valuable for youngsters to see the process and hear her talk about what she is doing. There are many reasons for you and your students to write letters; be alert to possibilities related to any curriculum area or school event.

Writing Centers

Many classrooms have writing centers. Writing centers are places where writing may occur, but mostly they are the place where the writing materials are kept handy. These materials may be used for a variety of purposes and in most any part of the room. If Danielle needs paper to write phone messages in the play house, she gets a notepad from the writing center. If Dominic needs to make a sign to protect his block structure, he can find a piece of tag board and a marker in the writing center. Special-interest items such as Mrs. Thomas's fish book can be placed in the writing center to encourage writing, but they needn't be used only there.

For a sample writing center setup, let's look at Mrs. Hanna's. Unlined paper seems best for most of her students. They are so busy trying to make letter forms that the additional challenge of staying within lines discourages them. Mrs. Hanna's students can select from a variety of sizes, shapes, colors, and textures of paper. She recycles paper that has only been used on one side in order to provide quantities of paper with a clear environmental conscience. Many different kinds of writing utensils are also available. Most of the children prefer to use the water-based marking pens with distinct lines and bright colors. Mrs. Hanna also provides pencils and crayons. The crayons are regular size rather than the fat kind often recommended for small hands, which Mrs. Hanna finds are actually harder for youngsters to hold than the smaller ones. Glue, staplers, tape, and paper clips complete the basic writing center setup.

Besides the basics, there are many other popular writing center materials. As with most kinds of materials, it is best to rotate some of them regularly rather than have everything out all the time. Some possibilities for writing center additions are stamps and stamp pads, business envelopes and order forms from junk mail, cut-and-paste patterns for making envelopes, "stamps" such as those from Greenpeace or Easter Seals, catalogs and order forms, cardboard and wallpaper for making book covers, small notepads, and almost anything else you might find in your desk or in your junk mail.

A computer is also a writing center. Unfortunately, most classrooms have only one computer and it too often is used for workbook-like games.

Word processing is a much better use for a computer. If you think that a computer helps you to write, think how much more helpful it is to a child who has difficulty figuring out which direction a letter faces and who has trouble controlling a pencil. Writing by hand is incredibly labor-intensive for beginners and they can be much more prolific writers with a computer. The printed out results look so grown-up that youngsters feel even more pride in their work. When a child wants to polish a piece of writing by doing another draft, the computer is even more helpful. If the piece was originally written on the computer, the child can easily make revisions. If not, Mrs. Thomas tries to find time to be the child's typist while helping with editing.

Children feel grown-up working at a keyboard, even if it is at an old typewriter. Usually, typewriters that end up in classrooms these days are electric, but, occasionally, youngsters can be found struggling to punch down a key of an old manual typewriter. Mrs. Montoya laughed the day that she saw Katya searching all over the manual typewriter for a place to turn it on. Katya was impressed when she found out it was a machine that ran without electricity.

Painting and Drawing Relate to Writing

Ms. Reynolds provides many opportunities for personal expression in her preschool through drama, music, and art as well as writing. Betsy loves to paint and works at the easel almost every time she comes to school. She is still experimenting with the way the paint drips down the page and what happens when she paints one color over another. But Ms. Reynolds sees that Betsy is beginning to move from exploring this medium to using it for a purpose. One day, Betsy says that her painting is a picture of her mom. Making a symbol for a person with paint is a step toward writing and so is knowing that the letters her teacher wrote say *Mom* (see Figure 5–10).

Although controlling paint is a challenge for Betsy, she is quite confident with a marker. Using the markers at the writing table, she tells complex stories with detailed drawings and symbols. Ms. Reynolds often sits at the table with the children as they work and listens to them talk about their work. Generally, it just looks like a lot of scribbles and mess until the child tells about it. Certainly, no one else could ever decipher Betsy's self-expression efforts, but she has clear ideas about their intent. Ms. Reynolds values Betsy's work and listens respectfully to her explanations. She values her symbolic representations both as drawings and as a step toward writing.

The link between drawing and writing doesn't end with preschool. Ms. Montoya sees how her students of various ages intertwine the two forms of expression. Drawings seem to stimulate writing and writing seems to stimulate drawing. Often, drawing seems to serve as a prewriting process, as a child thinks through an idea by illustrating it first. For youngsters with limited writing ability, drawing can provide the detail and elaboration that they are unable to communicate through writing.

FIGURE 5–10
Making a symbol for a person with paint is a step toward writing, and so is knowing that the letters the teacher wrote say *Mom.*

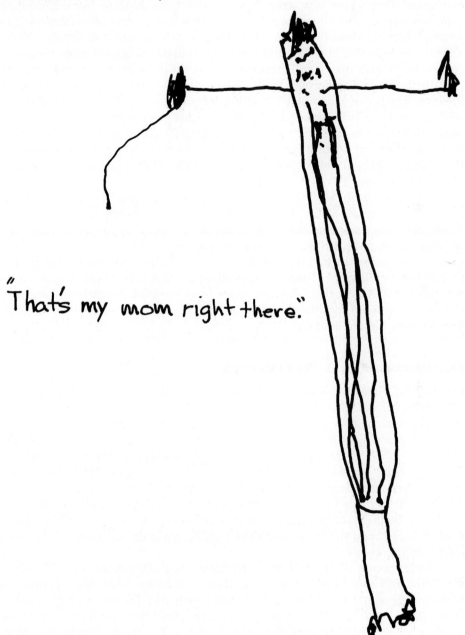

"That's my mom right there."

LEARNING FROM EXAMPLE

There is a lot that children learn about literacy as a result of literate adult examples. They especially need examples to help them to learn the many arbitrary conventions of written language. One way to provide examples is to write children's ideas for them while they watch (Morrow & Sulzby, 1993). You wouldn't do this in a way that suggests youngsters cannot write for themselves, but as an occasional alternative to their doing their own writing (Sulzby, Teale, & Kamberelis, 1989). Taking dictation from children who write for themselves can be compared with continuing to read stories to children who can read for themselves. It merely provides more useful information and some assistance to children's learning. Taking dictation and providing other demonstrations of writing helps children to learn to write in the same way that talking to them helps them to learn to talk. They need models for both kinds of language.

When we write as children dictate their ideas, we are assisting their growth in all areas of the language arts: speaking, writing, and reading. They are using their oral language skills to dictate, they are observing how writing is done, and they are able to read the completed product. This process, common in classrooms for young children for over twenty-five years, historically has been referred to as the Language Experience Approach (LEA). As the LEA has been incorporated into whole language theory, it has been modified somewhat, but the process of writing for children as they dictate is basic.

Kindergarten Activities

Frequently, dictation occurs spontaneously at the children's request, but sometimes Mrs. Hanna suggests it. A shared experience such as a field trip to the grocery store may provide the occasion for group dictation. Mrs. Hanna first engages children in a lively discussion about the trip and then leads them into thinking through the experience sequentially. She asks questions such as "What happened when we first got there?" and "What happened next?" She writes down what the children tell her, using their grammar and vocabulary. Large chart paper allows her to write so that all can see and allows the dictation to be saved for future reference. Youngsters will return to it when they "read the room" with their pointer wands and they will refer to it for spelling words.

A class book about Halloween costumes is a combination of individual dictation and independent writing. Some children want Mrs. Hanna to write for them, while others write in their own way for themselves. Ashley wrote for herself, "Mi Mom mad me a perses drs." Sam prefers to have his teacher write while he dictates an account of his spaceman outfit. Mrs. Hanna writes his exact words as he watches with interest and speaks slowly to allow her time to write. Just as she is ready to write *spaceman,* Sam proudly volunteers the information that it starts with an *s*, like his name. Mrs. Hanna makes a mental note of Sam's progress but doesn't stop the flow of writing. Her main goal is to get Sam's ideas written down. She focuses on the meaning of children's words rather than the specifics of how to write them for now. However, she carefully forms each letter in a consistent manner when she writes because she knows that her students are still sorting out which variations in letter forms are significant.

As with the other children, Mrs. Hanna encourages Sam to watch as she writes. She leaves the paper in front of him and reaches over to write in front of him. Because she is right-handed, she makes sure to reach in from his right so her hand won't be in his way. She wants him to be able to see how she holds the pencil, how she forms the letters, and where on the page she begins writing. As she writes, Mrs. Hanna reads aloud what she is writing.

Mrs. Hanna makes sure that children can see as she writes their dictated ideas.

DICTATION PROCEDURE

1. Encourage discussion to formulate ideas first.
2. Write exactly what the child says.
   • Accept run-on sentences.
   • Accept ungrammatical sentences.
   • Use standard spelling in spite of mispronunciations.
3. Make sure the child can see you write.
   • Be sure your hand is not in the child's way.
   • Be sure the paper is in front of the child.
4. Write legibly and form letters consistently.
5. Read dictation back to the child when finished.
   • Run your hand under words as you read.
6. Encourage child to take the completed transcript to another adult to read.

The Halloween costume book sparks several scary Halloween stories by individual children. Most of the youngsters create several books on their own about various topics. The classroom aide laminates the finished products and binds them into a nice-looking book with plastic binding. It goes into the classroom library along with the many other student-created books. Some of the others are more personal and individual. Some are entirely one child's creation, and other group books contain individual thoughts on a common theme. All are frequently read.

Sometimes, Mrs. Hanna has a hard time finding enough time to complete writing all dictations herself and gets help from parent volunteers and older children she has trained to take dictation. As much as she values long and involved stories, Mrs. Hanna cannot give each child unlimited attention; volunteer assistants are especially helpful for finishing long dictation processes when the teacher's attention is called elsewhere. If the topic allows, Mrs. Hanna sometimes asks a child to limit dictation to one or two main points. This helps children to practice organizing ideas as well as to limit their dictation to the time available.

Preschool Authors

Ms. Reynolds also places great value on dictation as part of the print-rich environment in her preschool program. As we walk into her classroom, we see her engrossed in conversation with Tanya in the art area. Apparently, Tanya spent a great deal of energy creating a collage this morning and wants Ms. Reynolds to make a sign describing it. Ms. Reynolds writes on a piece of tagboard as Tanya tells her about the different items Tanya glued onto her collage. As Ms. Reynolds writes, Tanya watches, stopping her narrative occasionally to allow the writing to catch up. Although the result is a giant run-on sentence with minor grammatical errors, Tanya grins proudly when she hears her words read back from the paper.

After Ms. Reynolds moves on to assist other children, Tanya reads the sign from memory several times to herself. Then she goes to get her friend, Justin, so she can read it to him. Still intrigued with the written form of her own speech, she gets several color crayons and traces over the letter forms that Ms. Reynolds wrote. Colorful wavy lines now cover the original writing. The dictation is difficult to read, but Tanya thinks it's beautiful.

While Tanya makes her sign colorful, Ms. Reynolds responds to a request to get the bunny out of his cage. She stays with the youngsters who are petting him and responds to questions and comments about the rabbit. As the discussion focuses on proper ways to treat the classroom pet, she suggests that the children make a sign by the cage about how to treat bunnies. The four youngsters seem enthusiastic, so Ms. Reynolds quickly gets a portable easel with chart paper already on it. She writes with a marking pen instead of a pencil so that the writing will be visible to the group.

Each child contributes a rule of personal importance. Kelly says, "Don't touch his nose." Betsy says, "Don't squeeze him." Timmy adds, "Just feed him lettuce." Caleb warns, "He might poop on you." All of these are written down just as stated by the children. Then they all read them together as Ms. Reynolds moves her hand under each line of print. The children and Ms. Reynolds carefully hang the new sign on the wall beside the rabbit cage, and all the authors importantly point it out to other children in the class.

When Ms. Reynolds composes her monthly newsletter for parents, she quotes these and several other compositions in describing class activities. She credits the authors, who then experience a wider audience and a different printed form of their thoughts. Although neither the individual collage description nor the small-group rabbit rules were preplanned as language experience lessons, Ms. Reynolds is receptive to the opportunity for children to translate their experiences into oral and then written language. A classroom environment that encourages this type of activity results in frequent spontaneous requests by children for adults to take their dictation.

The four-year-olds as a group are more interested in art project captions and story dictation than the three-year-olds. However, three-year-old Seth got excited about spiders after having several fact and fiction spider books read at story time. He spent some time poring over the pictures in the book and then went to the paint easel to work. When he was finished painting lines all over his paper, he asked an adult to label his picture "Seth's spider with spider web. Eats baby spider webs." Some preschool children dictate lengthy descriptions or stories that Ms. Reynolds helps them to make into small books with construction paper covers. These are placed in the reading corner. Ms. Reynolds also places books of children's drawings and emergent writing in the class library.

After children have authored their own books, which are placed in the reading corner, they enjoy inviting friends over and reading their books to

Seth learned about spiders from looking at books in his preschool library. He decided to communicate his ideas through painting and then he dictated what he wanted written on his picture.

them. Generally, the reading consists of a remembered version of the dictation or writing, but some children recognize a few specific words in their stories. Whether reading from memory or from letter clues, they are learning that their ideas can be put into writing and can be read. As children see books dictated by other children, they often discover that some of the same words are in their own and their friends' books. Sometimes, they can then read parts of someone else's book. As we have said, it is hard to separate writing skills from reading skills.

Proficient Writers

Even proficient writers may benefit from dictation procedures. David signs up for an individual conference with Mrs. Thomas because he wants help with a long story he has been writing. Having written two pages using invented spelling, he is growing weary of the effort involved in sounding out each word, figuring out which letters might correspond to those sounds, and then forming all those letters. Still eager to finish getting his ideas down on paper, David asks to dictate the rest to Mrs. Thomas. David's level of sound-symbol understanding guides Mrs. Thomas as she requests David's involvement in spelling the words. However, as always, Mrs. Thomas's main purpose in taking dictation is to get the communication onto paper. As this is David's intent, too, he feels delighted with the finished product. Mrs. Thomas helps him to make a cover for his book with the title and author's name printed boldly on the wallpaper sample he has selected for the covering. After David has practiced reading his story aloud, Mrs. Thomas arranges for him to go to the kindergarten and read it to children there. David feels proud of his work.

Older Emergent Writers

Older emergent writers especially benefit from dictation procedures. Mr. Larson uses it successfully with his late bloomers in second grade. They have exciting stories in their heads and get frustrated by the mismatch between what they want to write and what they can write. An adult "secretary" can keep enthusiasm for authorship alive while demonstrating the important skills these youngsters need to learn. Additionally, reading the stories they author provides valuable emergent reading practice with material of interest to the children. Some older youngsters in the emergent literacy phase speak a nonstandard dialect of English which contributes to their slower rate of progress. Because their dictated material utilizes their natural language pattern, it is easier for them to read. This gives them reading material in their own language, which matches current recommendations for beginning reading instruction.

Now that you have an idea of the kinds of writing activities appropriate to assist emergent writers, it is time to examine them from the skills angle.

WRITING SKILLS

As with reading, it isn't the skills we focus on when we teach writing, but that doesn't mean that youngsters don't learn writing skills. In fact, they learn to actually *use* them to improve their own writing, not just to fill in the proper work sheet blanks or pass a spelling test. Too often, old approaches to skills instruction resulted in just that, but there was little transfer to actual writing (Stipek, Rosenblatt, & DiRocco, 1994). Skills development does require practice, but practice is more useful as part of actual writing rather than as filling in work sheet blanks. Another significant part of skills development involves the demonstrations and models of competent writers. Demonstrations of writing are much more effective ways of teaching writing than lectures about it.

In this section we give examples of how writing skills are most effectively learned. This discussion will focus on both how children learn as they work at writing for themselves and how they learn from adult models. We have been talking about adult models, so let's continue with that aspect of learning to write. Have you noticed all the various skills being demonstrated and encouraged during dictation? Perhaps we should be more specific and

Effective teaching of writing skills helps youngsters to use them in their writing rather than to fill in worksheet blanks or pass spelling tests.

point out when phonics, spelling, punctuation, handwriting and composing skills are taught. Let's look again at some dictation procedures.

When writing with four-year-olds, Ms. Reynolds often mentions details such as the shape of a letter, the fact that a word starts like a child's name, or where on the page she begins writing. Although she points out the spaces left between words, most four-year-olds find the idea of negative space an abstract concept that is difficult to grasp. Ms. Reynolds doesn't expect children to master any of these concepts yet; she merely helps them begin to take notice. She knows that she cannot speed conceptual learning; it has to come from experiences that assist children in the development of hypotheses that they will challenge, discard, and replace through further experience. Writing with adult assistance helps children who cannot yet write something readable to see themselves as writers, causes them to notice more, and, therefore, helps them learn more about how writing is done (Smith, 1993).

Concepts About Print

With the occasional child who shows readiness through interest, Ms. Reynolds will follow the dictation process with a game of finding words in the dictated piece that start with other letters that the youngster knows. However, many preschoolers are not able to distinguish between the letters, have only a general idea of acceptable letter forms, and have just a vague understanding that letters represent language. Ms. Reynolds knows that with continued exposure to reading and writing situations, these children will refine those understandings and become literate. She doesn't try to rush them past their discovery of foundational concepts and into specifics of letter names and sounds. She certainly doesn't use phonics work sheets or flash cards. She wants them to build on firm foundations for a lifetime of rewarding reading.

Ms. Reynolds understands that children need help to develop the concept of separate words as part of learning to decipher phonics principles. Since no spaces exist between spoken words, children tend to lump together phrases such as "once upon a time" and consider them as a single word. When they find out their understanding isn't correct, they often overcorrect and think that each distinct sound in a word makes up a separate word. Having these confusions, children experience difficulty in matching oral and written versions of language (Clay, 1975). Until this confusion clears up, children cannot progress in discovering sound-symbol relationships. Ms. Reynolds carefully says each word as she writes it during dictation, and she leaves distinct spaces between words. Later, when she and the child read back what was written, she runs her hand along under each word as they read it. Through these kinds of experiences, repeated over and over, children gradually formulate the basic concepts upon which to base understandings of phonics and other word-recognition tools.

Mrs. Hanna doesn't expect most of her kindergartners to benefit from instruction focusing on details about print either. Many are still building their personal foundations of understanding about written language. Most have learned the names of the letters and can recognize them in both capital and lowercase form because they have watched television shows having that emphasis. Mrs. Hanna is grateful that parents no longer think they must teach their children only capital letters. What problems that idea caused! She would write a child's name in lowercase except for the first letter and the child would protest, "That's not my name!" Now that most parents realize children need exposure to the most common forms of letters for recognizing them in books and magazines, few children arrive in kindergarten knowing only capital letters.

Phonics

Although most of her students have learned letter names, few have progressed beyond letter names as sounds (see Figure 5–11). Because many letter sounds are the same or similar to their names, this is a good start. When

FIGURE 5–11
Jennifer combined memorized forms with invented spelling and wrote "I was taking my dog for a walk." Note she tried two different versions of "walk"—one using the conventional first letter and the other using the letter's name as a sound.

she takes dictation, Mrs. Hanna often asks children to contribute the starting letter of words that begin with one of these easier sounds. Because children's comments during dictation are not restricted to answering the teacher's questions, Mrs. Hanna learns about children's perceptions of letters and sounds from their comments. She learns even more from analyzing their invented spelling strategies. She sees children applying and refining their knowledge of phonics as they write with invented spelling. As she observes their processes, Mrs. Hanna gains information that guides her in planning follow-up activities appropriate for each youngster.

Amy demonstrates that she is moving beyond letter names as sounds by saying "I know what that word starts with! It starts with *y!*" as Mrs. Hanna prepares to write what Amy is telling her about what she did "yesterday." Now her teacher knows to involve Amy in discussions about letters that do not make their name sounds, but which are nevertheless regular enough in the sounds they represent to be fairly easily learned. Amy progressed to this point through continued exposure to correct spelling in books and on signs, rather than through direct instruction in these letter sounds. When she figures out for herself that the conventions of her language indicate a certain symbol for a certain sound, she truly knows the rule. If she hadn't spontaneously discovered the principle, Mrs. Hanna eventually would have begun calling it to her attention casually during dictation to help her see the pattern. Mrs. Hanna knows that the best way of teaching phonics is through repeated experience with written forms of language meaningful to the child. She knows that isolating the sounds from words and meaning in workbook or flash card drill is counterproductive for most children (Willert & Kamii, 1985).

Apparently, some children thrive on work sheet phonics drill. Doesn't this refute the theory that such teaching procedures are inappropriate? Actually, the fact that some children are able to make sense of those isolated pieces of information about the sound-symbol system testifies to the effectiveness of children's own approaches, not the workbook approach. Those who succeed with the phonics drill are those who have experiences reading and writing as part of their daily environment; they have learned the basic premises of our written language through their own thoughtful exploration of print. The workbook exercise merely allows them to demonstrate what they already have learned. For those children, the specific information about letters and sounds has attained a meaningful context (Dyson, 1984).

Some teachers who wouldn't consider using work sheets nevertheless plan their curriculum around the "letter of the week." Apparently, they haven't considered that this is just another form of meaningless encounters with letters. Finding words and stories that match a letter is backwards from how children learn and contradicts the theory behind whole language practices (Reutzell, 1992). Instead of thinking about all the things that start with a certain letter, teachers should put their energies into helping youngsters to figure out how letters are part of actual written communication. Letter-of-the-week activities take away opportunities for authentic and meaningful activities related to children's interests (Fisher, 1991). Besides, children don't encounter letters one at a time in the outside world, nor do letters do anything interesting by themselves—except dance around on misguided efforts at educational television.

As Mrs. Hanna encourages her class to explore print for themselves, most of her kindergartners progress to the point of recognizing the regular consonant sounds at least at the beginnings and ends of words; some students recognize the more prominent sounds in the middle of words, too. The long-vowel sounds are easy because they follow that helpful rule of having the same name and sound. Short-vowel sounds are another matter, however. Mrs. Hanna thinks confusing kindergartners with this mass of irregularity and indistinct sounds is cruel. Because vowels in unaccented syllables all have basically the same *schwa* sound, knowing which vowel appears in which word is really a matter of memory through familiarity rather than of learning rules. Mrs. Hanna allows children to take their time with this frustrating aspect of phonics and considers it inappropriate for the kindergarten curriculum.

Even most of Mrs. Thomas's first graders aren't ready for short-vowel sounds. Because children use many other word recognition skills as well as phonics, Mrs. Thomas doesn't find it necessary for her students to know every sound in a word in order to be successful readers. Yet, she assists her students in extending their understandings of phonics principles and of other word formation principles. She, too, works on helping children to construct these understandings through repeated reading and writing experiences. Informal comments during dictation, games, and discussion during follow-up activities all provide useful information for children to use in figuring out how to express themselves in writing.

Spelling

Emergent writers are working on the immense complexity of the sound-symbol relationships in the English language. They will have to grapple with the use of silent letters as markers, as in *light* and *bite;* the use of different letters and combinations for the same sounds, as in *just* and *giant;* the use of the same letter for different sounds, as in *cat* and *city;* and a wide variety of confusion over the irregularity in our language's spellings (see Figure 5–12).

FIGURE 5–12

A child's experimentation with spelling irregularities.

```
Jessica    5-3-8

                          I Want too go Ewt too Plaey. Ewt side   And

Plae All Day.

Jessica 5-8-85
```

Although some spelling defies categorization and has to be memorized, much of the English sound-symbol system follows certain principles that children can figure out as they read and write. Because most adults have an intuitive rather than a conscious knowledge of the system, they find explaining the system difficult. If adults are inhibited from attempting such explanations, their hesitancy is for the best, because such explanations may confuse children and deprive them of the ability to figure out spellings for themselves and to truly learn what they need to know.

Tyler is grappling with this confusion in a systematic way. He carefully says each word several times as he listens for the sounds to write down. When Tyler writes that he wants to *jriv* a car, Mrs. Thomas compliments him on hearing the sounds in the word *drive*. If the child asks, Mrs. Thomas may acknowledge that the word isn't really spelled that way, but she will admire Tyler's spelling as a "good" way to spell. Mrs. Thomas frees children to write and to explore writing by not insisting that they spell words correctly at this point. She makes a distinction between the "right" way to spell and a "good" way to spell. When Tyler uses his best knowledge of sounds and the letters that represent them to spell a word, his efforts constitute a "good" way to spell. His teacher congratulates him for his efforts and focuses her attention on the message of the writing rather than the spelling. This is exactly how adults encourage children to learn oral language—adults respond to the content of what children say rather than the errors they may make in saying it. If youngsters had their baby talk and incomplete and ungrammatical sentences corrected every time they spoke, they probably wouldn't talk very often or make much progress in speech.

This teacher knows that invented spelling does not represent mistakes that she should merely tolerate or ignore for fear of discouraging a child's efforts. Invented spelling serves as an important stage in the process of deciphering the sound-symbol system of written language. Mrs. Thomas explains to parents and administrators that this active exploration of the system will enable children to construct a personally meaningful and useful set of encoding/decoding rules. She explains that this is the best way for youngsters to learn phonics and other word recognition skills (Willert & Kamii, 1985; May, 1994; Ferreiro, 1991; Clay, 1993).

The children do make progress in standard spelling through their observation of print, through discussions with peers about how to spell, and through Mrs. Thomas's assistance (see Figure 5–13). Children who write tend naturally to compare their spellings of words with spellings in books and elsewhere, gradually revising their own spelling until it conforms to what they see (see Figure 5–14). For example, Trevor looks critically at what he has written: *scol*. He comments, "I know that's not right because it's not long enough." He then refers to a book in which he knows the word is written. Previously, he hadn't noticed any discrepancy between his spelling of this word and conventional spelling. As long as he was satisfied with his own version, Mrs. Thomas was, too.

FIGURE 5–13

Some ways to teach spelling.

- **Taking dictation**
  Commenting on some of the spelling as you write
- **Responding to children's journals**
  Modeling standard forms of words children wrote
- **Reading with big books**
  Calling attention to how some words are like other words
- **Encouraging children to read independently**
  Allowing opportunity for standard forms to become part of child's visual memory
- **Encouraging children to write independently**
  Allowing opportunity to explore and refine their understanding through invented spelling
- **Helping children polish their written compositions**
  Giving direct feedback about standard spelling of words individual children use frequently in their own writing

---

Children seem to inspire one another in their writing. We can observe this as Heidi and Anastasia discuss their writing, sharing ideas and viewpoints. Mrs. Thomas is confident their writing will be better for the interaction. In this classroom, students make faster progress because their teacher encourages them to collaborate on spelling while they write; several children who are writing at the same table will discuss and compare ideas about how to spell any word in question. The process of explaining their own rationale for spelling a certain way, coupled with the process of considering and accepting or refuting a classmate's differing ideas, greatly enhances children's understandings about spelling (Kamii & Randazzo, 1985).

Additionally, Mrs. Thomas assists her students in focusing on the correct spellings of words they use frequently in their own writing or dictation. She helps each child to create a "word bank"—the children make file boxes out of milk cartons for their word cards. Alphabetical dividers help children to organize their words by beginning letters. Only words that a child can read belong in that child's word bank.

Writing Mechanics

In addition to learning uppercase and lowercase versions of the twenty-six letters and the forty-four sounds represented by those letters, children must learn the mechanics of writing. Ms. Montoya often notes with amazement how perfectly some of her students can write in mirror images. Mirror-image writing would be difficult for her to do, but if a first grader accidentally starts on the right side of the paper, that child may easily write everything exactly

FIGURE 5–14
This child has begun to incorporate some standard spellings into his writing. He also knows a lot about phonics and uses it to compose long, involved stories with invented spelling of words such as *noticed (nwdest or notest), spooky (spooce),* and *skull (scol).*

```
won    day   i   was  camen   hom
 fram   scol  thes  wos   omost   my
frst  dav   et  wos    halown
as  i  wos  wocen  olog  i  sa
a  spooce  haws  i  wet  op  to
the  frot  seps  and  noct  on
the  dor   the  dor  oped  bot
i  ded  not  see  ene  bote
i  nwdest  tat  i  wos  nocen
on  the  hol  wa  dor  i  opend  the
dor  and  i  so  a  ghost
plaen  the  peano  i  slole  wokt
en  i  wos  rele  scard  i  notest
tat  on  tes  brocen  beth  tar
wos  a  scol  i  trnd  dac  and
the  dor  wos  lokt  i  thect
jest  nabe  i  kod  yows  the
scol  to  owpen  the  dor  i
owpend  the  dor  i  ran  and
ran  i  got  awt  and  ievd
hapole  evr  aftr
```

backwards. So Ms. Montoya carefully points out where on the page writing and print begin, and she points out the return to the left side after coming to the end on the right. Most of her older students have internalized this guideline, but many of the younger ones write until they come to the edge of the page and then write down the side.

Some children have more trouble with these mechanics than others. Heidi is tidy and methodical not only in her writing, but also in her play with items such as blocks and other manipulatives. Her writing stays in neat lines like it is supposed to. Anastasia, on the other hand, is exuberant and messy in everything she does. Her writing goes every which direction, rather like her thoughts.

Most older youngsters in Ms. Montoya's class are able to deal with the concept of space between words, but some focus on other aspects of writing and forget that one. These youngsters can benefit from activities similar to the cut-apart sentence exercise that Mrs. Hanna did with Amy, Maria, and Bryce. Some children initially use periods as markers between words. Ms. Montoya must help her students deal with punctuation, too, but although some youngsters incorporate it in their writing (see Figure 5–15), most of them aren't ready to do more than just notice it.

Conveying Meaning

We gave you many examples of how teachers model writing forms during dictation, but there are other purposes for demonstrating writing. Because the composition process involves much more than spelling and proper placement of words on a page, children also benefit from demonstrations of deciding what to write. This is why youngsters need models of adults composing their own writing. Children need to do more than just see the writing, they need to hear the writer share the composing process aloud. Just as children learn by observing their parents writing notes and lists at home, they benefit from the same kinds of models in school. Of course those who *don't* experience it at home especially need it at school.

When composing parent newsletters, Mrs. Thomas thinks aloud to help her students to understand the thought processes behind writing. She often involves youngsters in thinking through questions important to the composi-

FIGURE 5–15
Patrick included punctuation when he wrote the poem, "Thanks for Thanksgiving": Thanks for the harvest./Thanks for the food./Everybody let's celebrate./On the 28, of November./Thanks for all the harvest./Thanks for all the food.

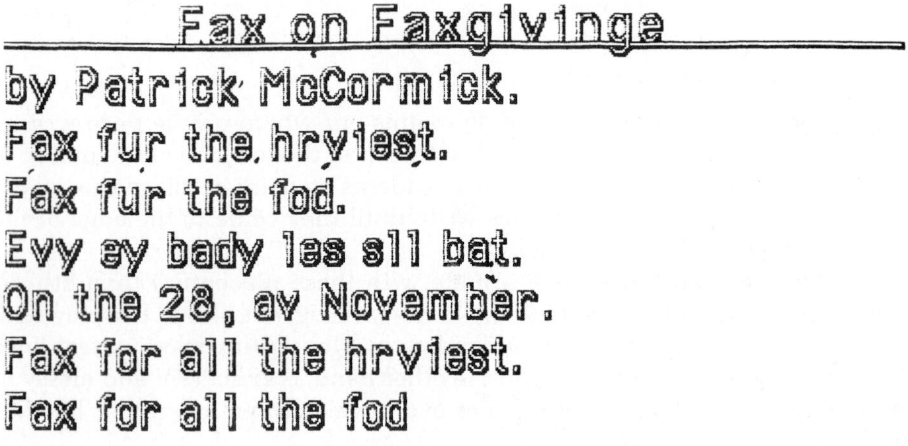
Fax on Faxgivinge
by Patrick McCormick.
Fax fur the. hrviest.
Fax fur the fod.
Evy ey bady les all bat.
On the 28, av November.
Fax for all the hrviest.
Fax for all the fod

tion process. She gets them to think about the events of the week that parents might be interested in and what announcements need to be made. As she composes, she asks herself aloud whether that will make sense to parents. She also talks through some of her spelling and punctuation decisions. She might say, "That sentence is too hard to read unless you know to pause there; I guess I need a comma." Her spelling comments distinguish between those words that look like they sound and those that are impossible to sound out.

Ms. Montoya writes the daily schedule on the board as part of the opening session each morning. She comments about the content as she writes, wondering aloud if visitors to the classroom will understand the day's plan. She involves the youngsters in deciding whether the wording is clear enough. She also asks children to help her to remember when she needs a period or quotation marks. Mrs. Hanna often adds a riddle to her daily schedule and as she writes it, muses aloud about what those reading it might think. "Does this clue tell too much?" she says. "Will anyone be able to make a guess from this clue?"

Even in preschool, Ms. Reynolds makes sure that children see her writing and using that form of communication as she continues the process of socializing youngsters into a literate world. When Justin proudly announces that he succeeded in putting together a certain difficult puzzle, Ms. Reynolds congratulates him and writes a note to his parents about his achievement. Justin watches as she writes and listens as she reads the note back to him. When he hears his mother read it later, he has a greater sense of what writing is about.

What children gain from adult demonstrations depends on the current understanding of each youngster. As youngsters become more sophisticated, they begin to notice the teacher's procedures for adapting writing to a specific audience as well as how to punctuate for meaning. At first, they only notice that writing goes from one side to the other and then starts over again. Different children will get different kinds of information from the same literacy event. Children get only that information which they currently can utilize and they will only observe what they are ready to see. The same writing model will be seen by one child as squiggles and by another as an important composition guide. All learners must fit new data into existing theory systems; this modifies all information significantly.

Editing

Mrs. Thomas knows that children will learn writing skills much more effectively through writing to express their ideas than through drill on isolated sounds. They will learn spelling, handwriting, and even punctuation as they strive to make their writing understandable to others. Therefore, this teacher focuses on the communicative intent, with correctness of form being just one aspect of that. She knows that richer writing and meaning occur in longer "connected discourse" than in isolated words or short phrases (Sulzby, Teal, & Kamberelis, 1989). Therefore, she encourages writing in-depth stories and reports. She also encourages children to read their compositions to others as part of the writing process; she teaches them to edit their work and to keep in mind the question, "Is this what I want to say?" When Kristen reads, "I like to hug her with my bear," she says to herself, "You know this doesn't make sense. I guess I could cross out the *her.*"

When youngsters are tuned in to an audience for their writing, they are motivated to learn standard conventions of print. They have a reason for spelling in ways that others can read and a reason to use punctuation thoughtfully. They also have a reason for making the print legible. Teachers teach skills effectively and efficiently when they assist youngsters in their efforts to edit their work for an audience. The editing process is most appropriate for youngsters who are past their emergent writing stage and have attained more confidence in themselves as writers. Therefore, we will save the description of editing conferences for Chapter 6, in which we talk about more proficient writers. The writing process involves several drafts and a polished product. For emergent writers, the first draft is usually as far as the child can go.

The most important academic idea for children to learn is that writing and reading can be useful communication tools and satisfying activities. Even more important is that each child learns to believe in his or her ability to be successful with these skills.

Slowly Emerging Literacy

Mrs. Thomas has to defend children's need to construct knowledge most vigorously when teaching children whose homes didn't provide the literary knowledge that Betsy and Amy's home did. Children who have not developed basic understandings about print as part of their background experiences often receive "catch-up" teaching efforts that merely provide intensive doses of information to be learned by rote.

Some educators, in their eagerness to help those youngsters catch up, seem to hope that knowledge can somehow be "injected" as a time-saving tactic. Yet, when teachers use this shortcut approach, they doubly deprive the youngsters who previously missed out on important literacy-socialization experiences. These youngsters missed out on literacy at home, and then they miss out again at school when they are not allowed the time and experiences to internalize understandings about written language. Ironically, those children who least need free time to explore print, those who already understand it, are more likely to be allowed the freedom to continue their explorations. Those who most need that opportunity are too often kept busy with remedial drill (Dyson, 1984; O'Neal, 1991). Mrs. Thomas continues to work at counteracting this practice. She strives to allow each child the necessary experiences for building firm foundations of understanding.

Vanessa is flourishing with this approach to literacy. When she reads her long dictated story to the class, she remembers every word. This child had the lowest level of literacy knowledge in the class at the start of the school year; she didn't even know when print was upside down. Yet with the open-ended activities of this classroom, she feels successful and is making good progress and feeling good about herself.

CONCLUSION

We have presented an approach to teaching writing that encourages children to formulate and explore their own hypotheses about the process. Models of writing, both from reading materials and from adult demonstrations play an essential role as children learn to write, with adult demonstrations emphasizing the thinking involved in writing. Spelling, punctuation, and penmanship skills are taught as part of effective communication, rather than as the main focus of writing instruction. Though children's own explorations are the main source of their learning, the teacher's role is to encourage those explorations and to help youngsters improve their own writing through comparison to conventional forms.

DISCUSSION QUESTIONS

1. A fellow teacher questions your kindergarten journal-writing program, saying, "They don't even know their letters and sounds yet. How can they write?" Explain the value of journal writing for emergent writers in a way this teacher could understand.
2. A parent complains because her child is bringing home creative writing papers with misspelled words. How do you explain the approach to writing that you are using?

SUGGESTED FOLLOW-UP ACTIVITIES

1. Provide blank paper and writing materials to preschool, kindergarten, and first-grade children and encourage them to write. Observe to determine their various theories used in their writing. Can you tell by watching what they think writing is, how they think it is done, and what they think it is used for?
2. Ask to borrow (or copy) samples of children's writing, and compare these papers with children's writing samples collected by others. As a group activity, classify the samples of children's writing according to forms described in this chapter and Chapter 1.
3. Encourage a child or a small group of children to tell about an experience or make up a story for you to write down. Follow dictation procedure described in the chapter. What did you learn about the child or children in this activity? What did you learn about the dictation process? What were the children learning?

RECOMMENDED FURTHER READING

Periodicals

Danielson, K. E. (1992, April). Learning about early writing from response to literature. *Language Arts*, *69*, 274–280.

O'Neal, S. (1991, September). Leadership in the language arts: Dear principal, please let my special education child read and write. *Language Arts*, *68*, 417–423.

Reutzell, D. R. (1992). Breaking the letter-a-week tradition. *Childhood Education*, *69*(1), 20–23.

Smith, F. (1983, May). Reading like a writer. *Language Arts*, *60*, 558–567.

Sulzby, E. (1992, April). Research directions: Transitions from emergent to conventional writing. *Language Arts*, *69*, 290–423.

Books

Piaget, J. (1973). *To understand is to invent*. New York: Viking.

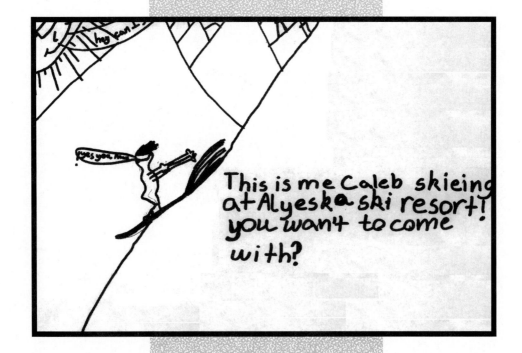

SUPPORTING INDEPENDENT WRITERS

In our classrooms, we can tap the human urge to write if we help students realize that their lives are worth writing about, and if we help them choose their topics, their genre, and their audience. . . . When writing becomes a personal project for children, teachers are freed from cajoling, pushing, pulling, and motivating. The teaching act changes. With a light touch we can guide and extend children's growth in writing. Also, our teaching becomes more personal, and this makes all the difference in the world.

LUCY MCCORMICK CALKINS, 1986

Having watched children get started as readers and writers, let's follow this approach to literacy through the primary grades. If you are a teacher who believes that children learn what is relevant to their own experiences and interests, you will continue emphasizing those experiences and interests in classroom activities at any grade level. If you believe that children learn in an active rather than a passive mode, you will continue the exploration-and-discovery approach to learning beyond first grade. If you believe that children learn best when they have confidence in themselves as learners and experience joy in the learning process, you will nurture successes rather than point out failures for second and third graders, as well as for younger students.

Chapters 2 and 3 showed how children's literacy is nurtured through play, large-muscle activity, and real experience. Chapters 4 and 5 described how children become literate through their experiences with language and print. These experiences should not stop just because a child has become literate. Being talked to, listened to, and read to continue to be important for a blossoming reader and writer. Having opportunities to climb and jump, build block towers, and dam up mud puddles also continues to provide insights, understandings, and enthusiasms for writing, talking, and reading.

This chapter will describe how children learn to read better through additional writing experiences and learn to write better through additional reading experiences.

Remember Betsy's brothers and sisters? Joey, Betsy's big brother, is a second grader. Let's visit his class and observe how his teacher, Mr. Larson, nurtures reading and writing. Later, we'll also visit Mrs. Williams's room across the hall. If Joey gets his wish, this will be his third-grade class next year.

AN ENVIRONMENT FOR WRITING

The first thing you see when you walk into Mr. Larson's class is a chicken wire enclosure in the center of the room. Five tiny chicks hop around under a pair of heat lamps. On the way to his seat, Joey stops to pick up a chick, kisses its beak, and puts it gently back. Joey knows a lot about these chicks: He and the class have been watching a dozen eggs for the past month. In his science folder, Joey has charts he made of the weekly development of the embryos along with a written journal describing each stage of their development. He learned how chicks grow and hatch from observing them, from listening to Mr. Larson, from reading library books, and from daily talk with his friends as they waited for the chicks to hatch. Today, Joey is wondering how long it will take for the chicks to be full-grown, and he plans to bring this question up during this morning's class meeting.

What may first appear to be a classroom steeped in science activities is actually one with reading and writing as its focus. Mr. Larson bases his language arts program on the children's and his own interests. Instead of focusing on what a basal reader or a language textbook say should be studied each week and month, Mr. Larson tunes in to what the children are interested in. He arranges for exciting things to do in the classroom and then bases reading and writing on these topics. For example, last October, after Mr. Larson read *Whale Brother* (Steiner, 1988) to the class, the children decided to study whales. In November, Carolina's family visited relatives in Mexico, so while she was gone the class followed her trip with an in-depth study of Mexico. Because several children in the class have new brothers and sisters, in January the classroom had two "baby weeks" that were highlighted by visits from the babies and a class book of poetry about infants. May is "outdoor education month," and the class will take hikes in different ecosystems each Friday.

Mr. Larson finds that organizing language arts around good books or around science or social studies topics gives the class time to meet more curriculum demands, is never boring, and gives the class a continuing common ground for discussion and learning. He knows that second graders are not interested in reading and writing just to be reading and writing; in fact, neither is he. Instead, they are all interested in what they can learn and enjoy *using* reading and writing. Mr. Larson is interested in plants, animals, art, and hiking. He doesn't have to wait until summer vacation to enjoy the things he loves; instead, he does them all year with the second grade. Although his classroom is small, there is still room for a parakeet and a minigreenhouse. An "art gallery" hangs above the coat hooks. Mr. Larson's enthusiasm for the projects is contagious—he says he gets excited about learning, and that excitement seems to spread through the class. A core experience curriculum (Strickland, 1989), such as Mr. Larson's, uses content as the vehicle to teach reading and writing processes by providing interesting activities for children to do, to talk and think about, and then to read and write about.

This morning, as Joey and his friends come into the room, they cluster around their teacher with information they have to share. Yesterday the children wrote their own questions about chickens which they researched last night, and today they are eager to tell about the rules for keeping chickens in the neighborhood, about how to tell if a chick is male or female, and if handling them too much could make them sick. Mr. Larson is almost overwhelmed with all the answers and asks the children to sit with a friend, tell what they've found out, and then write their discoveries in their journals.

In addition to providing plenty of stimulating content, Mr. Larson allows his second graders to keep the kind of control over their learning that their kindergarten and first-grade teachers allowed. This means that most of his teaching is responding to *what each child is trying to do*. For example, Carlos's reading skills have developed to the point that he wants to learn information from books. So Mr. Larson has steered him toward *A Bird's Body* (Cole, 1982), which Carlos reads himself. Next, Mr. Larson will show him how to use a paragraph frame to report in writing to the rest of the class the new facts he's learned. Thien, on the other hand, is trying to write sentences about the pictures he draws. Mr. Larson ignores the fact that many of his classmates went through this stage in kindergarten and encourages his sentences. Thien's picture of the eggs hatching, captioned "Tdy the chiks pekked ot," hangs proudly from the ceiling above the chicken cage.

Mr. Larson knows that children develop at different rates, and he supports all of his students as they develop. He knows that most children begin to read and write anywhere from ages four to eight, and he does not place any stigma on the late bloomers. He has seen second graders who were already labeled failures by age seven because they were not reading or writing fluently. He recognizes this as lamentable, and never allows the late bloomers to be viewed as remedial or special education students just because their developmental clocks are different from those of other children.

So you can see that Mr. Larson's philosophy for learning is backed by two important ideas: The first is that students learn and practice reading and writing through exploration of meaningful content, and the second is that children must be allowed and encouraged to proceed at their own stage of development.

Their second- and third-grade classrooms are stimulating and safe places for Joey and his friends. Let's take a look at how Mr. Larson and Mrs. Williams have made this happen.

Encouraging Writing

Beginning writers are not proficient writers, but they can quickly become proficient by doing more writing. If you made your students wait until they could spell correctly, write legibly, and use proper punctuation, a long time would pass before they could become writers. By waiting until they became proficient, they would waste valuable time that could be used to gain the benefits of actually writing—understanding the purposes and procedures of communication through print. They would also waste the best opportunities to learn more about spelling and punctuation and to practice handwriting. Probably the biggest waste would be their lost enthusiasm and confidence.

An environment conducive to writing is an accepting one. In this environment, the teacher understands that first drafts, by nature, are messy and contain mechanical errors. The teacher understands that some writing is for personal purposes and needn't be corrected. The class schedule includes time for thinking about a writing topic and getting inspired before having to come up with a product. In fact, the process of writing is valued even more than the products.

Mr. Larson knows how to encourage kids to write. Mr. Larson is willing to fight through 100-word run-on sentences with no punctuation and little recognizable spelling to find out what a child is trying to say. He then responds to the message in the writing rather than to the mistakes. He may comment that he can tell from Joey's story about fishing with his dad that Joey felt scared when they almost capsized in some rapids on the river. What about the twenty-five misspelled words and the twenty missing periods? Are we going to raise a generation of writers whose writing no one can read? No one wants that, of course, but neither do we want people who can pass

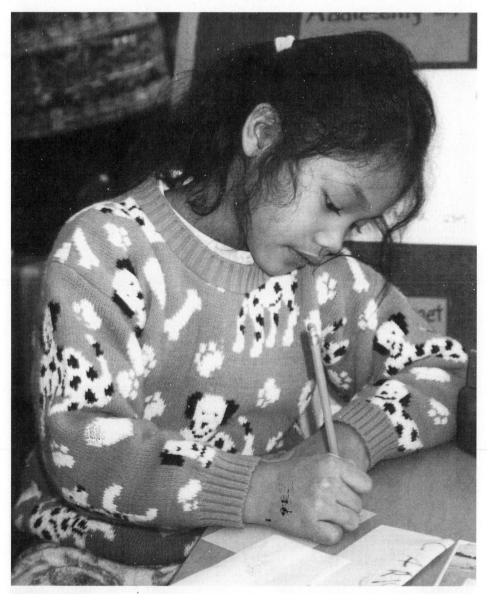

Beginning writers are not proficient writers, but they can quickly become proficient by doing more writing.

spelling and punctuation tests but don't write. How do we get the best of both worlds? We rely on Joey's own desire to communicate through his writing. When he is enthusiastic about his ability to express his feelings and share his experiences through writing, he will want to make sure others can read what he has written. At this point, Mr. Larson responds to the meaning and purpose of the writing. When appropriate, he will help Joey revise and edit his story in preparation for sharing it with others.

Mr. Larson makes his classroom writing workshop time even more safe for young writers by letting them see him write, make mistakes, get frustrated, have to revise, and, perhaps, throw away writing attempts. Sometimes a visitor can walk into his room and see everyone busily writing, including the teacher. Sometimes writing time can get noisy and look like conversation time. That's part of the revision or editing process, when you need feedback from someone else to find out if you said what you meant to say. Mr. Larson will often read something he has written to either one or two students or the class to get their ideas. He finds student input especially helpful when he tries to describe class activities for the parent newsletter. Mr. Larson's writing isn't limited to newsletters, however. He composes funny rhymes about students and class activities for the class to enjoy, and he writes stories to entertain his own three little boys.

Mr. Larson also knows that writers are readers, and readers are writers. He does not separate these two processes, but instead constantly stresses their interconnections. Often, after reading a book to the children, he'll casually point out what the writer did to make the story, poem, or article work. This week, when he read *Whale Brother*, he asked the children to think of other stories in which a boy has to go out alone in the world to prove himself.

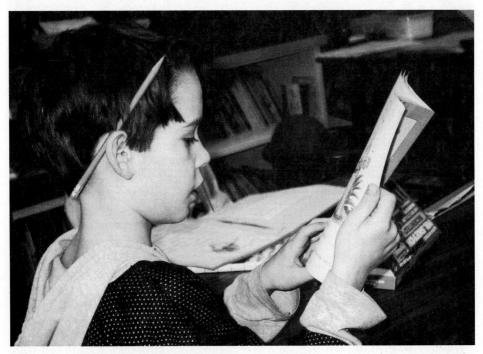

Writers are readers, and readers are writers.

The children thought of *Jack and the Beanstalk,* which some of them had studied in a small group. After they discussed the similarities and differences in the stories, some of the boys began to write their own stories using a similar story structure. Children who read widely and listen to a variety of read-alouds, are exposed to rich vocabulary, beautiful phrasing, and a plethora of types of writing. While their transference from literature may not be as obvious as the example above, it does happen. When a seven-year-old looks at an old-fashioned Christmas card and says, "It's a picture of a parlor," we know he'd probably heard that word in literature, not everyday talk.

Besides emotional safety and a language-rich environment, children need materials for writing. We've described writing centers in the previous chapters. Mr. Larson and Mrs. Williams have their own versions of writing centers in their classrooms, too. In a designated bookshelf, they provide a variety of papers, bookbinding materials, glue, tape, scissors, and an abundance of writing tools—pencils, felt-tipped markers, and colored pencils and pens. No child can ever use the excuse "I don't have a pencil" for not writing! Each classroom has a computer, which is used almost exclusively for revising and publishing the children's writing.

A PROCESS FOR WRITING

Mrs. Williams has been involved in writing-process classes and finds that this open-ended approach supports her view of how young children learn. She

TABLE 6–1
The writing process may include any or all of these stages.

Stage	Activity
Prewrite	Participate in an experience. Talk about the experience. Brainstorm. Think about audience, form, and purpose.
Fastwrite	Put notes and ideas on paper. Prepare "sloppy copy," or first draft.
Respond and Revise (This stage may be repeated more than once.)	Read and share first draft with others. Receive feedback. Change and rewrite draft using feedback.
Edit	Proofread and polish details of final draft.
Publish	Prepare final copy. Share with others.
Evaluate	Assess effectiveness of process and product.

has implemented a daily writing workshop in her third-grade class and is excited about the results. Visiting during a workshop, we observe youngsters working in many of the stages of the writing process (see Table 6–1). Some third graders are mature enough to proceed through all the stages, while others are content simply to write a first draft.

PREWRITING EXPERIENCE

Many students are working on phase one, the *prewrite experience.* Aaron and Ruben are discussing soccer prior to writing about their involvement on a soccer team. (Their actual experience playing soccer also served as an important part of the prewriting experience for this topic.) They review events of the last game, remember interesting plays, and brainstorm together as they

FIGURE 6–1
Michelle's letter to the editor.

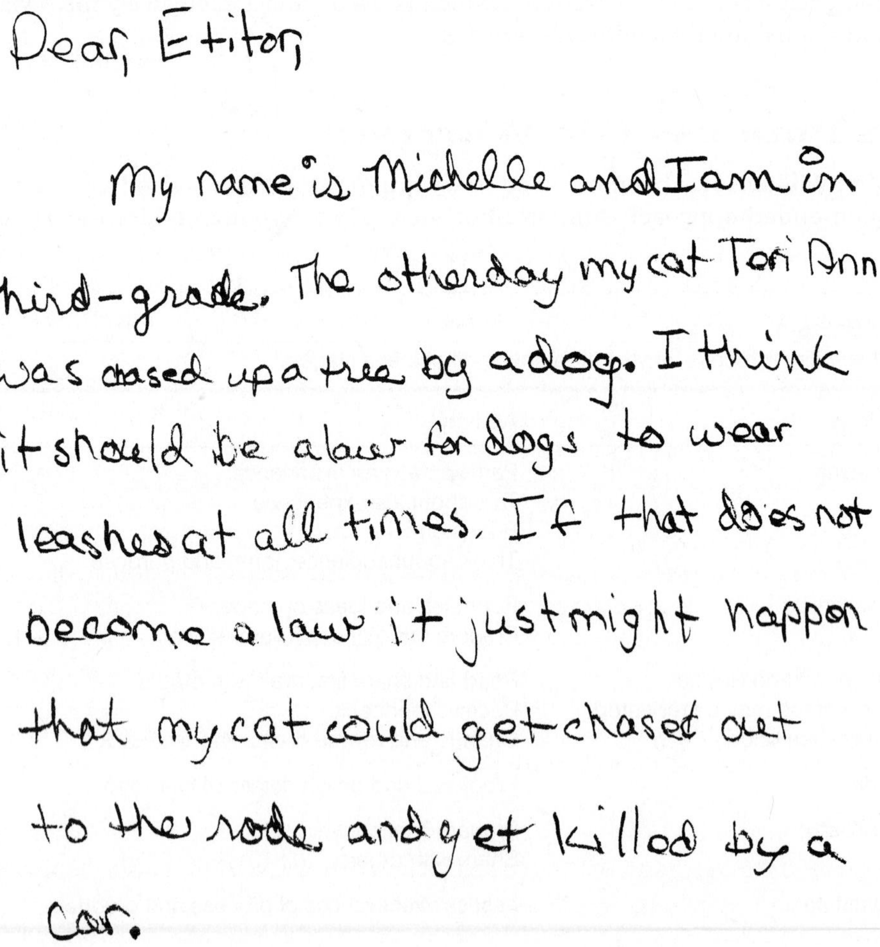

Dear Etitor,

My name is Michelle and I am in third-grade. The otherday my cat Tori Ann was chased up a tree by a dog. I think it should be alaw for dogs to wear leashes at all times. If that does not become a law it just might happen that my cat could get chased out to the rode and get killed by a car.

recall events to include in their stories. They make a list of special words needed for their stories: *referee, goalie, forward, halfback,* and *score.* Prewriting experiences can take many forms: Some, like a field trip, are organized by the teacher, while many other experiences can come from the world outside of school.

FASTWRITE

Michelle works on the next phase, *fastwriting,* which will result in her first draft. Some teachers call this a "sloppy copy" because the important thing is to simply get something down on paper. If she was writing in her personal journal or doing some other writing that she didn't plan to share with anyone and had no desire to polish, this could be her only draft. Sometimes, the writing experience is valuable just for just getting ideas or feelings on paper, so spelling, punctuation, and style are unimportant at this stage. Today, Michelle drafts a letter to the editor for the local newspaper. Her letter requests better enforcement of the leash law for dogs; she is upset about this because a dog chased her cat up a tree yesterday (see Figure 6–1).

RESPOND AND REVISE

In this phase, Michelle wants to write as correctly as possible and to state her case clearly. So she moves into the *response* phase. After rereading what she has written, she reads the letter to her friend, Kenesha, to find out if she has clearly stated her message. Kenesha tells Michelle which parts she understands and points out a sentence that doesn't make sense to her. Together, the girls plan some changes that they think strengthen the letter. Michelle then *revises* the letter and plans to read it again to a group for further feedback tomorrow.

When Michelle meets with a small group the next day to read her letter draft, the others in the group are also in the respond/revise phase of their writing. Each child takes turns sharing a draft and requesting peer response. They have practiced the procedure with Mrs. Williams and now can meet without her. Their comments emphasize the positive, and we hear statements such as "I liked the part about how glad your cat was to get down from the tree" or "You really made me feel how scared your kitty was." Other comments help to focus on clarifications needed, such as "I don't understand how the law will protect your cat." Michelle makes further changes in her letter as she moves through the revision process. She does not hesitate to add or delete sentences or to substitute a word with a better one. At last, Michelle feels satisfied that her letter makes her point. By the end of this year, she will be comfortable with totally reorganizing a paper.

EDIT

Michelle doesn't plan to ask for any further feedback on content, although when she wrote a fairly long play recently, she went through the response/revision process several times before she felt satisfied with her final product. Now she is ready for the next phase, *editing.* This is the time for polishing her paper by proofreading details such as spelling, grammar, punctuation, paragraphing, and handwriting. Mrs. Williams helps with the proofreading and involves Michelle in the process through comments such as "Do any of the words look funny to you?" Mrs. Williams wants her students to learn spelling as a visual image of how a word looks as well as an intuitive, kinesthetic knowledge of which letter to write next. She never uses oral spelling drills or even written practices of writing words over and over. She knows that neither of these approaches will carry over to the actual use of spelling in writing. Later in this chapter, we will look at more details of how these teachers embed spelling instruction into the editing phase.

The amount of proofreading for punctuation varies with different students. Michelle is fairly sophisticated in her understanding of punctuation, but other students may only be ready for some basics. Mrs. Williams encourages all students to read their work aloud to determine where punctuation marks might be needed to direct the reader (long pauses may require periods; small pauses may require commas). The inflection and tone of voice will indicate questions marks and exclamation marks. When children learn punctuation and paragraphing as a means of making their writing more clear to

Children can expect to work in the writing center without interruption.

others, they truly understand concepts of punctuation and are able to use them in future writing. At times, Mrs. Williams sees a punctuation or word choice problem that a number of children are making in their writing, and chooses to do a minilesson with these children. Later in this chapter, we will see a minilesson in action.

PUBLISH

Neatness and handwriting count on the final draft. If Michelle wants the editors of her town's newspaper to take her letter seriously, she knows her work must be legible and clear. Michelle carefully rewrites her letter making it ready for the next-to-last phase, *publishing*. Other types of publishing include making copies of a story or poem for the class or school library, displaying a captioned art project outside the classrooms, sending a factual report of information requested by younger students to their classroom, putting on a play or puppet show, or simply sending a letter to an intended audience.

Mr. Larson's students love the author's chair. A special time is scheduled once a week for children to sign up voluntarily to share their work with the rest of the class. This week LaMarr sits in the special chair, sings a song he has written about his favorite basketball team, and passes out copies of the lyrics that he has written. He then receives special attention and feedback,

Using word processing makes the revision and editing processes much easier.

and leaves school feeling good about his writing and about himself. No child is required to do this, but by the end of the year most of the second graders are eager to be recognized in front of others for their writing accomplishments.

Mrs. Williams encourages students to use the classroom computer for word processing if their written work is lengthy. Some students can type in their own stories, but Mrs. Williams has recruited parent volunteers who type (but not revise or edit) the children's writing. Word processing makes the revision and polishing processes much easier because the entire paper doesn't need to be rewritten each time a child makes a change. Of course, having been done on the computer, the final product looks professional and offers a perfectly typed copy.

EVALUATE

Several weeks later, Michelle's letter and several others for and against a leash law appeared in the newspaper. Mrs. Williams cut out the page from the paper and put it in Michelle's writing folder. Later, when she and Michelle were going through her folder, Mrs. Williams asked her if she thought the letter had done any good. When Michelle explained that the dog who chased her cat was now fenced in the neighbor's backyard, she said she thought that the letter had changed the owner's mind. Mrs. Williams is gently guiding Michelle in the reflective process of self-*evaluation*.

Mrs. Williams also pulled out a copy of a letter Michelle had written at the beginning of the year to her grandparents. In comparing the two, Michelle notes that she now knows how to start a paragraph. Mrs. Williams points out that Michelle is now able to write to a public audience, and that's why the letter was published. Michelle leaves the conference feeling proud of herself, and Mrs. Williams records Michelle's accomplishments in her notebook. She makes a note to herself to share the two letters with Michelle's mother next week at the parent-teacher conferences.

Making the Process Work

Are you impressed at how independently Mrs. Williams's students function while using the writing process? The children's independence didn't happen overnight or by accident: It developed because of their teacher's careful preparation and hard work. Now that Mrs. Williams has taken several writing process classes herself and has taught the process to her students, she feels she has the continuing responsibility for helping her students to function in an independent writing workshop setting. She feels she must constantly work to keep motivation high. She is always looking for ways to refine her class organization for writing time. Let's observe how she manages to do all this.

WARM-UPS

There are several children in the class who bluntly state that they don't like to write and don't know what to write about. Others are still afraid to fast-write and ignore spelling difficulties. With these children in mind, Mrs. Williams takes time each day to lead the class in playing around with words and language. She tries to find as many interesting modes of writing as possible and gives a brief writing warm-up each day. Yesterday, Mrs. Williams was in conference with Shawn, a boy who has little interest in writing, but a great deal of interest in other things. Mrs. Williams wrote down a joke that Shawn told, and they both laughed over the absurdity of it. Mrs. Williams suggested that the other children would love these jokes and encouraged Shawn to make a list of all his favorite jokes and to write some of them down for a joke book. Because each item is a short and manageable writing segment, Shawn felt more comfortable with this task. Today, Shawn shares the joke he wrote down with the class and says he needs more jokes for his book. Mrs. Williams suggests to the class that each child submit a favorite joke to Shawn and appoints him editor of the joke book. It will be Shawn's job to review the jokes for inclusion in his book and later to be in charge of the book's publication.

Short writing such as this often serves as the best starting place. Mr. Larson's class is having fun with bumper sticker messages. The students look for them when they go riding with their families and when they ride on the school bus. They try to remember their favorites to write on the supply of "bumper sticker paper" Mr. Larson keeps on hand. They also make up messages of their own, and reveal some of the unique aspects of second-grade humor. Mr. Larson and Mrs. Williams know that what the children are writing is sometimes silly, but what is important is that they are writing.

Mrs. Williams encourages her students to analyze magazine and television commercials and to write their own. She knows television commercials grab children's interest with their catchy jingles and fast pace. Commercials offer children a high-interest topic for writing. She helps youngsters to think about persuasive techniques used in advertising and asks such questions as "Will you really have as good a time as they show people having if you drink that brand of pop?" Mrs. Williams's students respond by making up their own advertising skits and rhymes with outrageous claims for fictitious products.

PURPOSE

Helping students to establish their purposes for writing is essential. When children have a message and an audience in mind, they want to write. Neither of these teachers assign writing topics or even insist that all children write at a given time. The teachers know that desire to write must come from the children's own interests. They have found that allowing children not to write when they don't feel like it does much more for attitudes about writing than insisting that every child write every day. Of course, their goal remains to have children writing daily.

GUIDELINES FOR TEACHING WRITING

- *Children strive to write so that others understand their meaning.* Always respond to the meaning of a child's message first. Then arrange opportunities for feedback to help children to revise their writing so that others understand it.
- *Children use their natural language when they begin to write their thoughts.* Accept all of the children's writings until they are confident that they can write. Then gradually introduce polishing for more effective communication and standard language usage.
- *Children continue to discover how language works when they write frequently and for various purposes.* Provide opportunities for children to use their writing to explore alternative ways of expressing thoughts.
- *Children write more often, and more effectively, if they are aware of progress and success in writing.* Focus on specific areas of progress in responding to a child's writing; encourage this same focus in feedback from peers.

To help children to establish purposes for writing, these teachers provide a stimulating environment where much happens to write about. Animals in the class, field trips, visitors to the class, science experiments, and new books continuously provide exciting subjects. Books and poetry shared with students have the dual effect of providing ideas for both content and form. Youngsters may try to write in the style of a much-enjoyed author such as Judith Viorst or start to write poems similar to the humorous ones by Shel Silverstein (see Figure 6–2).

JOURNALS

Mr. Larson encourages his students to keep daily journals. He reads these journals only at the invitation of their owners and never corrects any of the

FIGURE 6–2
Poem by Summer Koester.

If they put me in the zoo
what could I do?
I could be a Elafint
or a Sercas trainer
or maby a little scinyor.
I would fly and jump.
Or maby ride on a hump.
And sing with the Birds
and eat erbs
And crackl! crackl! snackl! snackl!
If they put me in the zoo
wat could I do?

journal entries. Most second graders love to share their journals with their teachers, and Mr. Larson's students are no exception. At the end of the school day, they may leave their journals in a special basket by Mr. Larson's desk. Most evenings, Mr. Larson makes time to read and respond to all of the journals.

Reading and responding to journals has become one of Mr. Larson's favorite parts of teaching. He enjoys having a few private moments in each child's world, and feels he comes to know each individual better. He has disciplined himself to respond honestly to what the children are trying to say, not how they say it. Often this simply means echoing their messages. Sometimes children are struggling to understand their lives (see Figure 6–3), and Mr. Larson believes his nonjudgmental replies in the journals can help children to understand their feelings.

FIGURE 6–3
Sometimes, the best response is just letting the child know you understand how he or she feels.

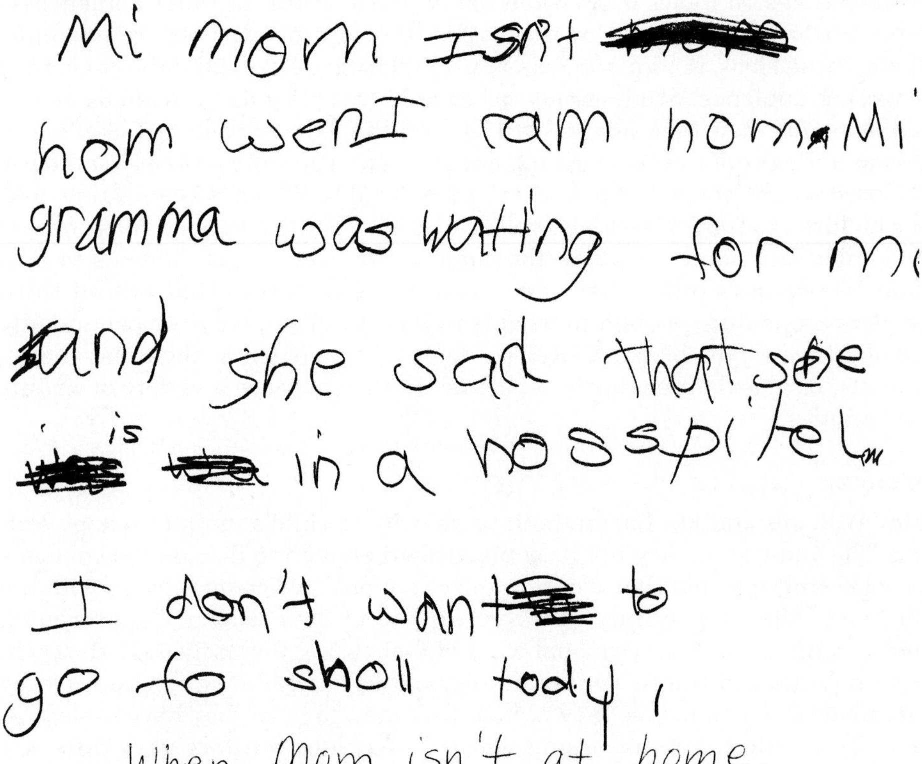

Mi mom isn't ~~home~~
hom wenI cam hom. Mi
gramma was watting for m
and she said that she
is in a hosspitel.

I don't want to
go to shooll tody.

*When Mom isn't at home,
nothing feels right.*

Most of the time, these dialogue journals are plain good fun. The children look forward to reading Mr. Larson's replies when they come into class in the morning and are disappointed if he hasn't had time to read the journals.

Mr. Larson hopes that in time the second graders will expand their dialogue-journal topics, especially to tell him about the books they are reading. He encourages children to pass their journals to each other for responses, a bit like the note passing that was so deliciously fun and strictly forbidden in his elementary school days. This year, Mr. Larson started a home-school journal. Each Friday during workshop, the children are asked to write briefly about the most significant thing that happened at school that week. They take their journals home, their parents are expected to respond, and the children return to school with their journals on Monday. This communication allows parents a view of what is going on in school. The home-school journal also provides parents with a good weekly look at writing development over the school year.

AUDIENCE

Not all journal writing is for others to read. Mr. Larson encourages children to keep notes on topics they would like to write about for other audiences—letters to friends, reports, or poems for the class newspaper, for example. Using these ideas, Mr. Larson helps the children to understand the concept of a writing audience. Students learn not only that they as individuals are an audience for their own private writing and that the teacher and classmates are an audience for public writing, but also that a *specific* or *known audience* differs from the *general* or *unknown audience*. Mrs. Williams spends time asking children to think about who will read their writing and what those people will know and not know about the subject. She tries to get students to consider viewpoints other than their own, but she knows that not all third graders are mature enough to be able to do that. When children can identify broad ideas of possible audiences for their writing (such as their classmates, parents, or a mail order repair department), they may see a variety of writing possibilities.

VOICE

Mrs. Williams and Mr. Larson both prize *voice*, a child's unique style of writing. The youngsters may not be sophisticated enough to discuss the concepts of voice and style, but they can recognize that one's voice might vary with the audience. Most importantly, children respond to their teachers' appreciation and acceptance of their personal ways of expressing themselves. Both teachers know that children's individuality could easily be squelched if they attended too much to how they write rather than to what they have to say.

By reading and discussing works by various authors with different styles, students begin to appreciate differences in writing. When children get a chance to meet the author of a book they have enjoyed, their ideas of a personality behind writing grow. Jean Rogers came to Mrs. Williams's class and told about writing her book *Dinosaurs Are 568* (1988). She made a big impression when she explained how she decided what to write and about throwing away her first efforts. That writing isn't easy even for published authors, but that it is rewarding to them and worth the effort, are important concepts for the children to learn.

ORGANIZING THE WRITING WORKSHOP

Even in such a stimulating, accepting environment, second and third graders may need more help in developing the desire and self-discipline to write every day. Pencils disappear, drafts easily get lost, and a talkative friend easily can distract a child from the task at hand. Mr. Larson and Mrs. Williams believe that an organized room and a few systems can help children to learn to develop their own ability to organize. When you visit Mrs. Williams's room, you'll probably be overwhelmed with all that's going on in there. Mrs. Williams says neither she nor the children could tolerate all this action if it wasn't for some important organizing behind the scenes.

Although reading and writing go on all day in this class, Mrs. Williams has designated a special time after morning recess for writing every day. She often starts this time with sharing something she's written or encouraging one or two children to read their polished projects to the entire group. Once in a while, Mrs. Williams uses this time to give a minilesson to all the children, such as the times she discussed the phases of the writing process. One of the more difficult parts of the writing process for these third graders to learn was working in response groups. Mrs. Williams knew that just telling them to work in these groups would never work, so she first invited a group of fifth graders in to model how their response groups function. After this demonstration, Mrs. Williams and the children brainstormed and then made a poster of a list of questions and comments that were positive and appropriate as responses. Another day, Mrs. Williams asked a small group of children to try to be her response group for a story she wrote about their field trip. As the rest of the class watched and commented, Mrs. Williams coached the children in asking her appropriate questions and giving her encouraging yet honest feedback. Soon, some of the children were asking to form their own response groups. Many third graders still have a very difficult time responding in groups without their teacher, but by now all of the children at least have the idea of how response groups work.

After a short time of listening or sharing, the children are on their own for writing workshop. The writing activities vary, but Mrs. Williams asks the children to try to spend some time each day writing in their journals and some time working on a project. To facilitate this, a huge QUIET sign hangs over one corner table, at which children can expect to work without interruption from other children or the teacher. On the table are large jars of pencils; nearby are shelves with paper and other supplies. The computer is reserved for writing, not games, and many of the children used a self-teaching program to learn to use the Clarisworks software. Talking and sharing with friends, groups, or teachers are encouraged everywhere else in this classroom—but not near this quiet writing center.

In Mr. Larson's room, the children each have a writing folder that is supposed to remain in their cubby at night. In this folder are drafts of current projects, a list of possible topics, and a log in which Mr. Larson asks the children to fill in what they have done each day. Journals can be kept in here too. Beside Mr. Larson's desk is an open file box in which he has a large hanging file for each child. This is where he keeps special finished projects, clipped with their dated drafts, and ready to share with parents during conference time. These files of students' papers help Mr. Larson to communicate the same positive message to parents that he communicates to his students. As he explains the goals of the writing process and invites parents to observe the children in class, he provides examples of the types of writing children do and the progress they have made. He is able to explain the peer editing process and show parents the "student-edited" stamp. Mr. Larson wants to help parents to become involved in what their children are learning and tries to enlist their help, because he knows parents influence their children's attitudes and motivation.

Children can expect to work in the writing center without interruption.

Mr. Larson is always concerned that children view writing as real communication, and therefore finds authentic modes of publication, such as the class newspaper, pen pal activities, and large-scale production of the students' original books. He also looks for ways for the children to share their work with the class. He especially enjoys the weekly author's chair activity that his students so look forward to. During this time, children who have completed the polishing stage of selected works are encouraged to read in front of their friends. The authors are treated with the respect of attentive listening, thoughtful questions and comments, and applause for their efforts.

EMBEDDING SKILLS INSTRUCTION INTO THE WRITING PROCESS

You have seen how Mr. Larson and Mrs. Williams constantly integrate content into their writing programs. After all, without interesting things to write about, why bother? By second or third grade, teachers must also begin purposefully to help children to pay attention to spelling, punctuation, grammar, and the mechanics of writing. Knowing that teaching such concepts in isolation is inefficient and developmentally inappropriate, teachers still must help children to approximate their writing to conventional standards. Second and third graders have enough experience with print to recognize and demand that their work be "right." Therefore their teachers must teach conventions in the context of children's writing. Textbooks, work sheets, and curricula don't work—they provide no relevant context and children do not make the transfer to their own writing. What does work is embedding appropriate instruction, on an individual or small-group basis, into the writing process. Let's look at how Mr. Larson teaches spelling in the second grade.

Encouraging Standard Spelling

One area that Mr. Larson has given a lot of thought to is spelling. Mr. Larson understands the concept of developmental spelling and delights in observing the process. Extensive reading and daily writing in his classroom have helped children to refine their notions about spelling. Many of the second graders are recognizing and experimenting with transitional and conventional spellings in their writing, and demanding the "correct" way to spell words for pieces they wish to share with others. Parents, while informed and supportive of invented spelling, begin to get anxious and to ask when "correct" spelling will be required. Mr. Larson knows that he must take an active role in guiding children's attention to understandings of generalizations about mature spelling. As a constructivist, he knows that the traditional format for spelling instruction (word lists, weekly tests) is unrelated to improved spelling in context, so he has worked to develop a spelling program that is embedded into individual children's writing and reading.

Since Mr. Larson has rejected word lists and spelling textbooks, he has chosen to focus word study only on words that occur in his children's writing (see Figure 6–4). He knows that only words that the children can read and attempt to write are appropriate for consideration. Occasionally, he focuses on words that appear in many of the children's writing for group instruction, but more frequently, he works with children individually during conferences.

When working with one child, Mr. Larson often encounters many misspelled words in one piece. Knowing that trying to correct all the words would be overwhelming and confusing to the child, Mr. Larson refers to four conditions for choosing spelling words suggested by O'Flahavan and Blassberg (1992):

1.　The child's invented spelling pattern is an approximation of the conventional spelling.
2.　All phonemes are represented in the child's spelling.
3.　The student recognizes that the spelling is unconventional.
4.　The student plays a role in choosing words or patterns for further study.

FIGURE 6–4

Justin and his teacher derived a spelling list from this paper: *liked, fight,* and *fire.* Justin made his corrections himself. Other misspellings will be saved for another time.

With these guidelines in mind, Mr. Larson is able to use valuable one-on-one instructional time wisely.

Carlos wants to do some building in the classroom, and Mr. Larson has asked him to make a list of what he will need so a parent volunteer can gather the tools. Carlos wrote, "All I need for the airpinen I's two peeses of wood. A hamr. Sum nells. A so."

How would you embed some spelling instruction into this journal entry? Here are the decisions Mr. Larson makes. First, because Carlos is communicating with someone, Mr. Larson knows he wants his list to make sense, so the motivation to spell conventionally is in place. Carlos recognizes that his spelling of *airplane* is not conventional so he asks Mr. Larson for the adult spelling. Mr. Larson shows Carlos the spelling, but chooses not to focus on this word at this time because all the phonemes are not represented in Carlos's spelling. Besides, *airplane* is a word that Carlos will probably pick up on his own because he reads and writes about planes constantly. When Mr. Larson asks Carlos to underline any other words that he is unsure of, he responds that he doesn't know how to spell the names of the tools. Mr. Larson writes out *hammer, nails,* and *saw* cards for Carlos's word bank, and asks Carlos to draw pictures beside each word when he leaves the conference. Looking at *hammer,* Mr. Larson reminds Carlos that the *r* sound at the end of a word is usually spelled *er* even though we can't hear the *e*. He then points out that *nail* is part of a family of other words, such as *sail, rail,* and *pail,* and asks Carlos to think of and spell others. As he and Carlos correct the words for the tools' names, he reminds Carlos that English is a funny language, and a lot of adult spelling makes less sense than kids' spelling, but they both want other people to read and understand Carlos's list, so he and Carlos will have to go with the conventions.

All this instruction took place in less than two minutes. Carlos got what he needed—a readable list of his needs. Mr. Larson embedded a spelling lesson into what Carlos was trying to do. The words chosen have meaning and motivation for Carlos. He is not overwhelmed. He has a reference when he needs the words again. He has even received instruction on two spelling conventions.

As Carlos and his classmates continue to learn conventional spelling, they must deal with the idiosyncracies of the English language. They will find that besides relying on their well-developed phonemic knowledge, they must depend on other sources of information about spelling: visual memory; references such as a word bank, dictionary, and thesaurus; and environmental print.

In the future, Mr. Larson will look for conventional spelling in the words he helped Carlos to put in his word bank. He will encourage Carlos's desire to communicate and, in doing so, will provide continuing motivation for Carlos to use many resources in becoming a mature speller.

While Mr. Larson believes that children's conventional spelling will develop in time, parental and curricular pressures have forced him to acknowledge that people unfamiliar with emerging literacy are very concerned about spelling. He uses newsletters and parent conferences to explain how children construct knowledge about spelling. He points out the logic of invented spelling so that parents begin to applaud these strange spellings rather than worry about them. He shows parents how he embeds spelling into meaningful contexts, how he empowers kids to use resources for correct spelling, and how he never impedes the writing process with concern for spelling (see Figure 6–5). He provides individual spelling lists in the form of word banks that children can use for reference or for memorization. He encourages the use of the dictionary and thesaurus as references. He has posted a list of high-frequency words such as *were, what,* and *where* on the bulletin board for quick referral. He does not dwell on a lot of rules, but instead guides children into understandings of standard spellings via word

FIGURE 6–5
More ways to teach spelling

- **Modeling correct spelling**
  While writing children's dictated ideas
  When responding to children's journal entries
  Anytime you write anything

- **Continuing to accept invented spelling**
  Thus freeing children to become writers, which makes them more aware of standard spelling

- **Helping children to edit their writing**
  Demonstrating proofreading for errors in your own writing
  Helping children compare their own spelling to standard forms

- **Helping children select spelling words from their own writing**
  Creating personal spelling lists of frequently used words
  Making personal spelling files or books

- **Giving individual mini-lessons relevant to children's own writing**
  Point out common spelling patterns and word families
  Explain spelling rules and conventions applicable

- **Showing how to use spelling resources**
  Demonstrate use of pictionaries or dictionaries
  Allow children to help each other with spelling
  Help youngsters to think of places where they could find a certain word spelled correctly

- **Provide spelling resources**
  Make charts of words from content units and field trips
  Display wall charts of common words that do not follow spelling "rules" (*what, where, the, their,* etc.)

- **Making sure that children love to read**
  The more they read, the more they see standard spelling
  The more they see standard spelling, the more they remember it

families, studies of unique consonant configurations like *kn* and *ph,* and a few consistent rules such as dropping the *e* before adding *-ing.* Parents, who are often unsure spellers themselves, are relieved to learn that invented spelling is a sign of growing phonemic awareness and shows intelligence and creativity in dealing with a tricky language. They are relieved to learn that spelling involves use of references as much as memorization. Best of all, when the papers come home from school, instead of spelling tests with lists of unrelated words checked off as right or wrong, parents get to read letters, stories, songs, poems, and reports that their children have written.

Refining Grammar and Mechanics

When we were children, we were supposed to learn correct grammar by copying sentences and picking the correct verb. Mrs. Williams remembers punctuation exercises that involved copying a paragraph and supplying the correct punctuation marks. We're sure you can see how ludicrous this seems now, and how this kind of exercise must have stifled our ability to write. Today's children who have been encouraged to write are courageous and creative, but they still make mistakes in grammar, and they still need to learn how to punctuate a sentence so it makes sense to the reader. Have you thought about how we can help youngsters to learn these conventions without resorting to the grammar lessons and work sheets that were useless to us as children?

Mr. Larson uses the same approach to grammar and mechanics as he does to spelling. He simply works at individual problems as he conferences with his students. When he sees a grammatical error, he might first ask the child to say the sentence aloud. Does it sound right? Often the error is corrected this way. But other times, the grammatical error is part of the child's oral language, such as "me and my brother," or "my dog, she." If you work with students whose first language is not English, you've probably heard a number of unusual constructions. The first thing to remember about these grammatical constructions is that they are part of a child's best attempt to communicate. If we corrected too many of them, the child would get the message that we are listening to her construction rather than to what she has to say. Mr. Larson feels he often has to make a judgement call on whether or not to correct. His first response is to attend to the meaning of the message, repeating it if possible in standard English. If he decides to suggest a change, he'll preface it with a remark like "In books, it's written this way." Emphasis is always on the purpose, which is communication. Mr. Larson tries to use standard grammar in normal conversation with the child and to point it out in books. He knows that second and third graders are still refining grammar at this age, and that, with lots of exposure, the correct grammar eventually will be learned.

Mrs. Williams finds mechanics a much easier topic to deal with than grammar. All children are excited about learning how to make their written work understandable by others. Since kindergarten, the children have learned about periods and capital letters as their teachers have taken dictation or gone over written work with them. As the children become more adept writers, we see them attempting to use more punctuation marks, experimenting with capital letters, and imitating special written forms such as business letters. Their teachers routinely show children in conferences how punctuation, capital letters, and paragraphs are used.

The Minilesson

Mrs. Williams's class has been invited to be pen pals with a third grade in Florida. The children have agreed that everyone in the class will write a letter, and Mrs. Williams sees this as a perfect opportunity to do a minilesson on letters. She has written a letter back to the teacher in Florida which she is showing on the overhead projector to her class. In five short minutes, she shows the important parts of a friendly letter—date, greeting, and closing. She shows how she uses a comma in the greeting, and another one after "Sincerely yours," in the closing. The children then begin to work on their letters, referring to the sample letter chart Mrs. Williams has posted. When she conferences with children, she looks specifically for their use of these conventions and points them out to the children.

Another day, Mrs. Williams approaches a much more difficult topic—revision. She knows that revision is the hardest part of writing for many writers, so she plans a minilesson to demonstrate how she revised a newsletter that she prepared to send home. Using an overhead projector, she shows the children first her original notes and then her first draft on the word processor. She shares with the children that, after reading it aloud, it seemed to her that many sentences seemed to repeat themselves. She asks children to help her to identify these sentences. After they find three pairs of sentences that said the same thing, Mrs. Williams models how she crossed out the redundant sentences and rearranged those that remained. She then shows the children her revised copy of the newsletter. In future conferences, she will remind children of her revision process as she helps them to revise their own writing.

In these minilessons, Mrs. Williams uses direct instruction with her third graders. Many people who study the constructivist approach to literacy get the impression that direct instruction is inappropriate in a primary classroom. However, we know that there are many things about writing that cannot be figured out logically by children. Punctuation conventions are an example of this type of social knowledge. The children have a personal purpose in the pen pal project and, in this case, a common purpose. The teacher has limited group instruction to less than five minutes, which is a lot less time than it would take to show each child individually. Her model is a real letter she has written, and the children are aware of its purpose. Motivation is high because the children want their letters to be read and understood by a real audience. The children apply their skills right away, and have references in the classroom to help them. In the end, they know they will have a set of letters that their pen pals will be able to read and that they will receive real feedback.

A minilesson uses direct instruction to show children things about writing that they cannot figure out logically.

Mrs. Williams is conservative with using direct instruction with small and large groups, but when she does, she follows a few simple guidelines. Most importantly, the kind of knowledge involved must be considered. Logico-mathematical knowledge, as discussed in Chapter 1, cannot be learned through instruction, but must be constructed by the individual child. In contrast, social knowledge, such as spelling conventions and punctuation, can be taught within a real context.

GUIDELINES FOR USING GROUP DIRECT INSTRUCTION

1. Use primarily for social knowledge.
2. Provide direct instruction only to those with a common need.
3. Keep minilessons under five minutes.
4. Provide context with real examples and authentic purpose.
5. Apply the information immediately, and check for the children's understanding.
6. Provide written examples for future reference.

The Writing Conference

We hope it is clear to you that group minilessons are only a small part of the writing instruction that Mr. Larson and Mrs. Williams do each day. You have probably noticed that most of the instruction we have described in these last three chapters has occurred in one-on-one situations. This is the heart of instruction in a whole language classroom—the student-teacher conference. Conferences are simply a time with the child meets individually with the teacher. Many conferences are informal—the teacher roams around the room, stops briefly to answer questions or to point out something, and moves on quickly to another child. Other conferences are more formal: The child may meet the teacher at a specified place in the room, and may have signed up days in advance for this time alone with the teacher. As we discuss writing conferences here, keep in mind that all of the teachers described in this book integrate writing and reading so much that it's hard for us to separate writing conferences from reading conferences—often both processes are addressed together.

Mr. Larson has a special conference table set out of the line of traffic in order to be secluded but still provide him a view of everything in the class-room. He posts a sign-up sheet there so children easily can schedule them-selves for an appointment as they feel the need or desire for one. If a child goes a week without signing up for a conference, Mr. Larson seeks out that child and spends time casually discussing his or her reading and writing. Mr. Larson tries to make the discussion nonthreatening and supportive to encourage the child to request a conference. Some children seem to sign up all the time. Do they want additional attention, or are they too dependent on teacher direction or praise? With these youngsters, Mr. Larson tries to figure out the cause of constant requests and then to deal with that cause. Generally, he urges his students to try to work a day without teacher direction between conferences.

Conferences may last for only a minute or two or be as long as fifteen minutes. Usually, they last from five to ten minutes, and Mr. Larson is able to meet with about ten children daily. Are you shocked that he doesn't try to work with each child each day? Mr. Larson has found that giving his undivided attention a few times a week to each child is far more valuable than meeting daily with that child in a group. That way, none of the children's time for reading and writing is wasted. Of course, he circulates among the whole

Teachers find that giving their undivided attention a few times a week to each child is far more valuable than meeting daily with that child in a group.

class between conferences and interacts with students incidentally during those times, too.

Mr. Larson keeps his files and records for conferences in the conference area so that he can pull out an old sample of a child's writing for comparison with today's work. Children can see their progress when they make these comparisons. Mrs. Williams keeps her records of conferences in a notebook with a section for each child, just as Mrs. Thomas does. Mrs. Williams records her notes on the children's feelings about writing and reading as well as their skill. She likes students to see what she is writing down about their progress, so she takes notes during the conference sessions. On occasion, she adds notes after a spontaneous interaction outside the conference session when she didn't have her notebook handy.

Sometimes a child has writing to discuss, sometimes reading, and sometimes both at once. Whichever literary endeavor the teacher and student discuss, the teacher always tries to provide specific, positive feedback. Mrs. Williams cautions that positive feedback must be specific rather than general. With general praise, we run the risk of making children dependent on outside approval rather than help them to learn to rely on their own judgement. So while meeting with Jennifer, Mrs. Williams tells her that the turkey dinner she described makes her mouth water. She tries to refrain from saying such meaningless statements as "What a good story" or, worse yet, "You're a good writer."

Mr. Larson has a reputation for boosting the self-esteem of kids who especially need it, and he is a master at positive feedback. He firmly believes that his purpose during conferences is to be supportive, constructive, and specific as he helps students set their next steps in progress toward their goals. He always notes the progress a child has made rather than the errors. He never tries to improve writing with a red pencil or to improve reading with lists of words missed. Instead of talking about errors, he discusses what needs to be learned by saying "Now I think you are ready for. . . ."

Children usually sign up for a conference with a specific purpose—requesting help in finding more information on a topic, wanting feedback on writing, or sharing a story that was particularly enjoyable. The teacher values the child's purpose and uses it as a starting place to extend the youngster's knowledge and understanding. For instance, when Ruben was trying to find information about comets, Ms. Williams helped him to become more proficient in using the table of contents and the index in books. She also felt that moment was good to send him to the school librarian, who helped Ruben to learn how to locate books on the library shelves. When information or skills are important to children, they will learn them.

As children become more proficient and confident in using written language, their purposes change. Now that Melinda can write most of the words she uses, without laboriously matching the sounds of language to the letters, she is more free to concentrate on the meaning and form of what she writes. She no longer has to think about each word as she writes it, so she thinks about how to communicate more effectively. Mrs. Williams's responses to

Melinda during conferences help her to think through the content and the way Melinda's thoughts are structured. Developing syntax, style, and the choice of words to express her thoughts comes next. Refining word usage to paint pictures that show rather then tell the reader what she is trying to say is an exciting continuation of developing Melinda's skill as a writer. Mrs. Williams doesn't spend time with details such as spelling until after Melinda has finished the important process of getting her ideas on paper (see Figure 6–6).

Writing Conferences in Action

Let's go back into Mr. Larson's room and eavesdrop on one of his conferences today. Sam has volunteered for a conference for the first time, and Mr. Larson looks forward to what he brings—a picture and caption (see Figure 6–7) he made after hearing *The Velveteen Rabbit* (Williams, 1963). After Mr. Larson read this story about a beloved stuffed animal, the children were invited to bring in their favorite toys and write about them. Mr. Larson was surprised at how many children like Sam brought in stuffed animals.

> *Mr. Larson:*   All right, Sam, looks like you have a favorite dog. Would you read your story to me?
>
> *Sam:*   OK. (Reads "My favorite toy is my Sweet Puppy. I like my Sweet Puppy.")
>
> *Mr. Larson:*   Gosh, Sam, my favorite toy was a stuffed dog, too!
>
> *Sam:*   I got Sweet Puppy for Christmas.
>
> *Mr. Larson:*   I can see from your picture he's kind of an alert-looking dog.
>
> *Sam:*   Yeah, he's like a watchdog, but he's kind of worn out.
>
> *Mr. Larson:*   How'd he get so beat up?
>
> *Sam:*   Well, he's old.
>
> *Mr. Larson:*   Is there anything else you'd like to write about him?
>
> *Sam:*   Yeah, he fell in the bathtub once, and when we got him out he was all wet. So my grandma put him in the drier, and then he fell apart and. . . .
>
> *Mr. Larson:*   Whoa, Sam. Could you write that down?
>
> *Sam:*   OK.
>
> *Mr. Larson:*   Look here, Sam, before you go, let's add you to the list with everyone's favorite toys. (Writes in his notebook, as Sam watches, "Favorite Toys, Sam—Sweet Puppy.")

Notice that Mr. Larson was not at all dismayed at Sam's writing. He knew that Sam, a transfer student, had not had a language-rich environment either at home or at school. Sam's writing is well below that of his classmates. But Sam had something to say, and Mr. Larson was ready to listen. Notice how he probed Sam for more information—and Sam had plenty to say. Finally, Mr. Larson accepted Sam's invented spelling, but also modeled the standard spellings of *favorite* and *sweet* when he added Sam to the favorite-

FIGURE 6–6
A student essay published as a result of a student/teacher conference.

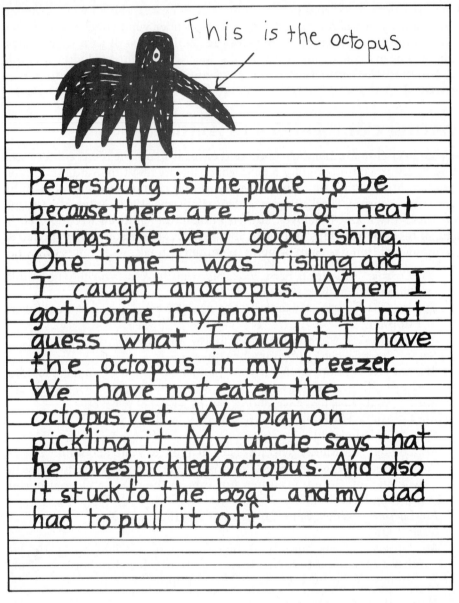

This is the octopus

Petersburg is the place to be because there are Lots of neat things like very good fishing. One time I was fishing and I caught an octopus. When I got home my mom could not guess what I caught. I have the octopus in my freezer. We have not eaten the octopus yet. We plan on pickling it. My uncle says that he loves pickled octopus. And also it stuck to the boat and my dad had to pull it off.

toy list. Sam later added several sentences to his paper, and proudly read it to the class during sharing time. Mr. Larson filed this paper away and will use it as a benchmark to compare with later papers. Notice that Mr. Larson never corrected or suggested changes. As Sam begins to be a writer, Mr. Larson is interested only in encouraging him to write as much as possible.

FIGURE 6–7
This child is making progress toward standard spelling.

My favert toy is my swet puppy.
I like my swet puppy

Across the hall in the third grade, Zachary has been working on a story about his cat all week. He has written several drafts of the story and has even asked his mom to help with correct spellings. Not satisfied yet, Zach has requested a conference so Mrs. Williams can help him type his story on the word processor. Before sitting down at the computer, Mrs. Williams asks Zach to read his story to her. When he is finished, Mrs. Williams tries to find out why he wants help.

Mrs. Williams: What do you like about your story?
Zach: Well, I like it about my cat, and I like the part about Lisa's mother in our garage. But Kelly thinks it's too long, and I do, too.
Mrs. Williams: So you want to make it shorter?
Zach: Yeah.
Mrs. Williams: Well, there are a couple of things you could do: You could just cut some of it out, or you could rewrite some of the sentences. What do you think?
Zach: Could we do it without writing it over?
Mrs. Williams: Let's use the computer here, and see what we come up with. (They sit down at the computer, boot up Zach's disk, and begin.) On the first page here, is there anything that really isn't important to the story?
Zach: Well, it probably doesn't matter about Texas. (Deletes the sentence.) So the title is "The Way I Got Lisa."

Fortunately, Mrs. Williams and Zach had time to work through Zach's story together. At Zach's request, Mrs. Williams previously had typed his story on the computer and had shown Zach how to edit words and paragraphs with the word processor. Zach became so involved that when Mrs. Williams had to take the class out for recess, Zach continued. In Figure 6–8 you can see the result of Zach's revision.

Zach loves to write. He is also a perfectionist. His writing is exceptional for a third grader. Mrs. Williams is glad that his exuberance for writing has not diminished during his four years in school and that she can challenge him to write even better. Zach has profited immensely from the writing process stages that Mrs. Williams taught this year and is the first child in the

FIGURE 6–8

This paper originally was five pages long. Zachary has learned to edit!

The Way I Got Lisa

by Zachary

There was a little cat in our garage. It had fallen out of her mother's nest. So we brought her inside. My mom called the vet, and when we got there we went inside and it got its shots. And they told us she was a girl. I named her Lisa.

Then we went next door to Randall's. We got the special kind of milk for Lisa because she was only about four weeks old.

Then a few days later when we were outside we heard something, it was like a pit pat. Then we found out it was Lisa's mom. A few days later a cat came down in our garage. Everyday we fed her. After about four weeks my grandma called the animal control. They came and took Lisa's mom and her kittens. We didn't see them again.

The End.

class to really be able to edit his own work. Mrs. Williams is also glad that word processing is available for all the children in her class so that the tedious tasks of rewriting can be avoided as much as possible.

In the final copy, Zach corrected a grammatical error on the first page. As he read his story aloud, he noticed *had fell* didn't sound right and made an appropriate correction. Zach's final paper has a real sense of story and extraneous details have been omitted. This is a paper that makes both Zach and Mrs. Williams proud.

In these conferences, Mr. Larson and Mrs. Williams have focused on strategies that Sam and Zach currently are working on and ignored areas that might need attention with other children. Each boy received about five minutes of personalized attention to his own needs and wrote for the rest of his writing time.

GUIDELINES FOR WRITING CONFERENCES

- Let the child take the lead.
- Respond to the child's message.
- Ask questions that teach.
- Work at appropriate stages of the writing process.
- Let the child make the changes.

Mr. Larson and Mrs. Williams find that conference time is the most productive teaching time of the day. They both work hard to do as much as possible within a five- to ten-minute time frame so they can work with each child each week. Each individual writing conference is as unique as each student and each piece of writing. Mr. Larson and Mrs. Williams love the personal contact that conferences allow. In Chapter 7 we will continue our look at conferences when we focus on reading, and in Chapter 8, we'll discuss how conferences are used for both assessment and instruction.

CONCLUSION

Becoming better writers is more than improving spelling, grammar, and punctuation. What is more important is that children write consistently and write a lot, and that we respect and respond to what each child says. As children master the skills of writing, teachers and children become freer to concentrate on improving writing—finding new forms, new topics, and new depth. We can encourage children to find their own unique voices, and to find better ways to say what they have to say by developing catchy beginnings and endings, using all their senses to describe, developing strong plots, and finding unusual metaphors. This chapter described how a classroom writing workshop works for young writers. In Chapter 7, we'll look at reading in the primary grades, and show how a literature program supports the writing process.

DISCUSSION QUESTIONS

1. A third-grade student turns in a poorly written paper done hurriedly. The paper shows no thought or care for spelling, handwriting, punctuation, or even content. What should you do?
2. You are attempting to encourage creative writing in a second-grade classroom. One of the children fears to write any word without knowing the correct spelling. She refuses to make a guess at spelling. Consequently, she writes very little and frequently interrupts the teacher to request correct spelling. How can this child be freed to learn through her own exploration of print?

3.   Can you think of examples in which direct instruction can be used appropriately in primary grades? Explain.
4.   Your second and third graders write widely and often. How can you determine which of their many pieces would be appropriate for revision, editing, and proofreading?

SUGGESTED FOLLOW-UP ACTIVITIES

1.   Help a child or small group find a purpose for writing that involves an intended audience. Assist the writers in analyzing the resulting work in terms of effective communication for that audience. If possible, arrange for the writers to share their work with the intended audience.
2.   Assist a child who wishes to polish something he or she has written. Follow procedures described in the this chapter.
3.   Write something of your own using a word processing program. Use the editing tools to polish your own writing. Contrast this editing process with the process you use for editing on a typewriter.
4.   Learn how to bind books using cloth or contact paper–covered cardboard covers. Use taped or sewn bindings. Help a child to create a book from some special writing.
5.   Engage children of differing writing abilities in private discussions about their writing. Ask what topics they usually write about and how they decide what to write. Ask if they write outside of school and for what reasons. Find out if they use any procedures for polishing when they share their writing with others. Ask what they like about their writing and what more they want to learn in order to write better.
6.   Prepare a letter to parents explaining a constructivist spelling program. Discuss the importance of invented spelling and your alternatives to a traditional spelling program.

RECOMMENDED FURTHER READING

Books

Calkins, L. M. (1983). *Lessons from a child: On the teaching and learning of writing*. Portsmouth, NH: Heinemann.

Calkins, L. M. (1986). *The art of teaching writing*. Portsmouth, NH: Heinemann.

Gentry, J. R., & Gillet, J. W. (1992). *Teaching kids to spell*. Portsmouth, NH: Heinemann.

Graves, D. H. (1983). *Writing: Teachers and children at work*. Portsmouth, NH: Heinemann.

Harste, J. C., Short, K., & Burke, C. (1988). *Creating classrooms for authors*. Portsmouth, NH: Heinemann.

Parry, J. & Hornsby, D. (1988). *Write-on: A conference approach to writing*. Portsmouth, NH: Heinemann.

markim

THE VERY HUNGRY
CATERPILLAr

Once There wase a very hungry caterpiler that
hatched from an egg, and ate threw one
orange and some other food. One day the caterpie
made a cocoen and turnd into a beutiful buterfly
the end.

CREATING A CLASSROOM FOR READERS

- -

"I waited all my life," said Jim. "Now I can read."

MIRIAM COHEN, 1977

Children are eager to "really read." In the beloved book *When Will I Read?* Miriam Cohen (1977) showed us a primary classroom in which the teacher encourages emergent literacy through play, environmental print, and other developmentally appropriate classroom activities. However, children are anxious and eager to "really read." When at last this happens, whether in kindergarten or third grade, a new and exciting world opens for children. They can read independently! In this chapter, we'll look at how our teachers structure a classroom for children who are "really reading."

In Chapter 6, we looked at how Mr. Larson and Mrs. Williams encourage children's writing. We hope it's clear to you that a major factor in their success is that the second and third graders see a clear purpose in their writing. Refinement in form, style, and conventions is much easier to encourage when children are motivated. With reading, too, purpose is paramount to success. Today's children are lucky to have a wealth of children's literature that is richer than ever before. Teachers are lucky, too, because the almost limitless choices of reading materials provide purpose for every child.

At the heart of a developmentally appropriate reading program is individuality. This means children must be free to choose what they read and how they will respond to it. In turn, the teacher must focus individual attention on each child. As with writing, this is done through the reading conference, the core of an individualized reading program. We ended Chapter 6 with some eavesdropping on writing conferences in Mr. Larson's and Mrs. Williams's classes. Let's take a look at a couple of their reading conferences as well.

READING CONFERENCES

It's almost lunchtime, and there's an air of restlessness among our twenty-five second graders. Mr. Larson decides to squeeze in one more conference and sees that Casey's name is next. As Casey gathers his things together, Mr. Larson leafs through his file, reminding himself that Casey only recently began to really read. He is glad he has time to meet with Casey today.

Unlike many of his classmates, Casey was a late starter in reading. Because Mrs. Hanna and Ms. Thomas recognized and accepted his less mature development, Casey arrived in second grade with his self-esteem intact and made great strides this year. For the past month, he has been into Dr. Seuss books. He reads them to his mom, to his sixth grader reading buddy who comes to the room once a week, to the special education teacher, and to anyone else who will listen to him. He sits right down at Mr. Larson's desk and proceeds to read aloud from *The Cat in the Hat* (Geisel, 1957). Mr. Larson was prepared for this and has positioned himself so he can read over Casey's shoulder and mark on his notepad any miscues Casey makes. After Casey reads for a couple of minutes, Mr. Larson notices that Casey read *sold* for the word *should*, hesitated, and looked at Mr. Larson in some confusion.

Mr. Larson: Whoa, Casey, what's the fish telling the cat here?
Casey: I don't know, it doesn't make sense. "He sold not be here."

Mr. Larson: How could you make the sentence make sense?

Casey: "He sold it here"?

Mr. Larson: The *s* and *h* make a sound like *shhhh* here.

Casey: Oh, "He *shol. . . .*" No, "he *should* not be here./Oh, He should not be about./He should not be here./When your mother is out."

And Casey reads on.

Mr. Larson notes here that Casey is not tuning in to the beginning sound of the word *should* and made a nonsensical guess at pronouncing the unknown word. Casey knows that what he reads should make sense, so he paused and waited for Mr. Larson's help. Mr. Larson tried to get Casey to make a reasonable guess at the troublesome word based on the context of the story. Casey usually is pretty good at this, but Mr. Larson noticed that Casey doesn't seem to know the *sh* sound. He briefly demonstrated it to Casey, who quickly picked up where he left off and read on without further help from Mr. Larson.

Imagine if Mr. Larson had stopped to teach a traditional phonics lesson here! He could have spent a half hour on a lesson on the *sh* sound, with lists of words and practice sheets. But, instead, Casey got his fifteen seconds of needed instruction and went on reading, practicing the new sound in the context of real literature.

Mr. Larson is always amazed how children like Casey are so adept at picking out just the books they need. Right now, Dr. Seuss books seem to be perfect for Casey's need to solidify his intrinsic knowledge of phonics because they stress rhyming words, which Mr. Larson calls "word families." Casey may be a less mature reader, but he does know that what he reads should make sense—even silliness like *The Cat in the Hat*. He knew when to ask for help, took the assistance, and continued on his task of reading.

After Casey finishes reading the section he prepared, Mr. Larson suggests he record in his personal dictionary the words from *The Cat in the Hat* that have a *sh*. He might want them so he'll know how to read them and later spell them for something he's writing, or he might want to show them to his mom. Now Casey is eager to get back to his desk to draw a big picture of the mess the Cat made. Later, Casey will write under his artwork, "Her's the Cat in the Hat klening up mie rom."

FORMAT FOR A READING CONFERENCE

1. Discuss the book with the child, ensuring comprehension and helping the child to extend meaning.
2. Have the child read aloud and give help or instruction as needed.
3. Discuss additional activities or readings.

During a reading conference, the teacher can position herself so she can read over the child's shoulder and record miscues.

Notice how Mr. Larson lets Casey take the lead. Casey indicates to Mr. Larson what he needs to learn, not the other way around. Children who are allowed to be in charge of their own learning seem to have a sense of when they need help. Casey leaves his conference, confident and intent on his next project.

It's time for lunch now, and Mr. Larson reminds the class to put their dialogue journals in his basket and to leave their language arts folders in their desks. Mr. Larson had conferences with ten children today and had time to briefly check in with every child. He's tired, too, from such intense teaching and is ready to relax and eat his lunch.

Across the hall, Mrs. Williams is holding her final conferences for the morning, too. She encourages her third graders to make an appointment with her once a week for reading and another for writing. On the calendar now is Jennifer.

Mrs. Williams: So, what did you bring to show me today?

Jennifer: I finished *Sarah, Plain and Tall* [MacLachan, 1985]. I loved Sarah.

Mrs. Williams: Well, tell me about her.

Jennifer: Well, there's this family and they have two kids and the mother died and their father is looking for a new mother and this lady named Sarah comes on the train to live with them. She's tall and she says she's plain.

Mrs. Williams: What does *plain* mean?

Jennifer: Well, it usually means like plain, you know, not pretty. But I liked Sarah. She liked flowers and planted a bunch of them.

Mrs. Williams: What was the problem in the story?

Jennifer: Well, I think the problem is if the kids will like her when she comes to be their mother. They do like her, and she stays.

Mrs. Williams: Is Sarah like your mother?

Jennifer: Well, no. Sarah was really young, I think. Also, my mother goes to work. But I like my mom, and they liked Sarah. Also, I think this story happened a long time ago. Maybe like *Little House on the Prairie* [Wilder, 1953].

Mrs. Williams: So—it sounds like you liked it?

Jennifer: Yeah! I loved it!

Mrs. Williams: Maybe you'd like *Ida Early Comes Over the Mountain* [Burch, 1980]. It's about a girl who is like a nanny to a bunch of little kids. I think Ms. Sanders has it in the library.

Jennifer: OK, can I go to the library now to get it?

And she leaves for the library. Jennifer is a sophisticated reader, and Mrs. Williams enjoys conferencing with her—they talk about children's books as friends talk about their favorite best-sellers or as families talk about movies at home. But this conference was not just idle book-talk. Mrs. Williams was checking that Jennifer is comprehending not only at the literal level, but also at higher levels. She tuned in to Jennifer's inferences when she asked her about the problem in the story and later asked her to evaluate the book in terms of her own life and other books she has read. Jennifer has no problem finding books, but this time Mrs. Williams has responded to her interest in pioneer stories and has suggested another, more difficult book that Jennifer can find in the library. In this way, she is nudging her toward other, more mature books.

Notice, too, the reading strategies that have been touched upon in this conference. Mrs. Williams checked on vocabulary and on finding the main idea. Mrs. Williams had reviewed her conference notebook from Jennifer's section in the moments she was preparing for the conference. In Jennifer's case, Mrs. Williams had noted that they'd been working for over a month on identifying the main idea, problem, or plot of stories. Today, Jennifer was able to tell the problem without a long narrative about all the subplots in the story.

Mrs. Williams finds that reading and writing conferences are the most intense and productive teaching times of the day. She must sit with one eye on the class, but also focus her attention on individual children and their immediate needs. She finds that keeping a notebook helps her to remember what happened in previous conferences and also gives her an overview of the progress each child has made over several months. Mrs. Williams finds the conference approach so much more efficient than the reading groups she previously used. She remembers feeling frustrated and guilty when she would teach the children skill lessons that only some of them needed or when children would have to sit and wait for others to finish reading so that the group could discuss a section of the book.

Like Mr. Larson, Mrs. Williams still has to work hard to keep all conferences within five to ten minutes so she can work with every child each week. Sometimes, when she has a moment, she sneaks a look at the novel she keeps on her desk. This isn't just modeling. Mrs. Williams loves to read both children's and adult books. She knows that occasionally showing her enthusiasm for her own reading adds to the creation of a literate environment. She's made a conscious decision, though, to spend most of language arts time interacting with her children.

Years ago, when Mrs. Williams stopped using a basal reader series to organize her reading program, she worried that the children might not learn reading skills. She also wondered if the activity time spent in response activities and reading aloud each day were good uses of time. After using a literature program for several years, she found that the children do just as well or better than before on the standardized tests they take each year. Mrs. Williams thinks this is because they spend reading time doing authentic reading and responding, and do not waste their time listening to other children in reading groups, answering artificial questions, or doing boring workbook pages. In fact, she marvels at how successful children were at learning to read in spite of the old methods. Mrs. Williams knows that children enjoy reading more now and that this powerful motivation provides momentum from everyone in the class, not just the teacher. And she no longer worries about children missing important skills because she knows that by using reading conferences she can teach skill lessons to any child who needs them.

Conference Processes

Conference sessions generally are a mix of listening to children, talking with them, and listening to them read aloud what they have been reading or writ-

Ultimately, a teacher's goal is for children to determine themsleves what they wish to share in a reading conference.

ing. Mr. Larson often checks reading comprehension by requesting students to tell him about the most interesting (or funny or exciting) part. He also asks questions to encourage critical reading and reading between the lines. Mr. Larson's questions are often the same type of questions you might find in a teacher's manual, but they are aimed at an individual child's own reading selection. Mr. Larson's ultimate goal is for children to determine themselves what they will share with their teacher in the reading conference.

Mr. Larson finds the following type of questions useful during reading conferences.
1. How do you feel about what you are reading?
2. What interesting things did you find out from reading this?
3. What was exciting (or funny) about this story (or article)?
4. What are the main points in the story (or article)?
5. What kind of people are the characters?
6. Do they seem like real people that you might meet or have for friends?
7. How do you think the author felt about the people and the situation?

Mr. Larson tries first to get the student to initiate the discussion or volunteer information. He uses the questions only to probe for something not brought up. Also, he stays alert for insights about how a child is managing the reading process. He knows that many children cannot tell him what bothers them when they read.

Mr. Larson encourages youngsters to come prepared to read a favorite section aloud to him. He doesn't want to ask anyone to read orally without having a chance to prepare first, because oral reading requires more skill than silent reading. This oral reading gives him clues about word identification strategies that the children are using. Mr. Larson takes notes about errors as the child reads, jotting down the type of mistakes made rather than how many. He wants to know whether words substituted make sense in context or whether they are simply similar in appearance. He got worried when Ron read *tree* for *three*, because the substituted word made no sense. But when Sue read *pond* for *lake*, Mr. Larson didn't worry at all. If the sentence and story make sense with the substitution, the reader is reading for meaning, and that is what the reading process is all about. But if Ron says a word that makes no sense and doesn't correct himself, Mr. Larson suspects Ron is only reading letters. In Chapter 8 we will further discuss miscue analysis, the diagnostic process Mr. Larson is using with Ron.

When Aaron read *reptile* in a book about alligators, Mrs. Williams asked him how he figured out that word and made note of his response. When children need help figuring out a word, both Mr. Larson and Mrs. Williams encourage them to use the strategy of making a guess based on what would make sense and then using graphophonemic clues to check their guess. This approach keeps the meaning of the reading, rather than the sounds of letters, in the forefront. These teachers do not encourage vocalizing individual letters in an effort to put sounds together. They know the difficulty of that approach.

Mr. Larson finds that listening to his students read aloud gives him other useful information about their reading progress. While a child reads, Mr. Larson listens for intonation: He notes whether the flow of language sounds similar to natural talking and whether the intonation reflects the meaning of what is read. He also notices pronunciation so that he can help with any mispronounced words after the child is finished reading. Obviously, he doesn't interrupt a reader to correct mispronunciations.

If pronunciation problems stem from dialect or language differences, Mr. Larson ignores them unless the child requests help. Only after a child expresses a desire to develop standard dialect in oral or written language does Mr. Larson consider correction appropriate. When the child requests help, teacher assistance is much more effective during preparation of oral reading than as criticism afterwards. Mr. Larson shares Mrs. Hanna's convictions that children perceive criticism of their language as a personal rejection. He also agrees with her that to keep the child talking and writing best assists language development, whether the speech or writing is standard English or not.

So we see Mr. Larson and Mrs. Williams using conferencing to provide individual instruction in skills, to deepen the children's understanding of text, to plan temporary skills or interest grouping, to encourage continued progress, to provide feedback to children, and to enjoy their reading and writing with them. Conferencing is also a primary mode of assessing student progress, which we'll discuss further in Chapter 8.

AN ENVIRONMENT FOR READING

In the second grade, reading time is much quieter than writing time, when many children were working in groups. Now, during reading, most of the children are intent on their individual books. We see María Elena and two other children working on a poster outside the room and Mr. Larson quietly talking with LaMarr, but otherwise the students are reading on their own.

Melissa is reading *Ramona and Her Father* (Cleary, 1977), a library book about a girl her own age. Because she loves a good story, her purpose is just to enjoy reading and to find out what happens. Lying on the rug in the classroom library corner, she is engrossed in her story. Felipe's purpose in reading today is to find information about comets. He has gone to the school library and checked out several reference books that listed comets in the index. The librarian helped him to find an edition of *Odyssey* magazine that had an article on comets. Now Felipe has spread these materials on a table and is looking up the information in each. These two children are experiencing different but equally valid purposes for their reading. In each case, the purpose is the child's own purpose—something that child wants to do.

Mr. Larson and Mrs. Williams both use a literature approach as the basis for their reading programs. This means that most of the time allotted for reading each day is devoted simply to authentic reading—the reading of real books. Mr. Larson mentions that his philosophy grew from a statement he remembers from his children's literature textbook *Children's Literature in the Elementary School* (Huck, Hepler, & Hickman, 1993) when he was an undergraduate: "Children learn to read by reading." Since then, he has realized that all proponents of a constructivist or a whole language approach to reading support this theory. Therefore, he feels justified in not using basal readers, workbooks, phonics charts, or flash cards as the basis of a reading program. Instead, he uses a simpler, yet vastly richer system—reading books!

An environment conducive to reading provides freedom. Students have the freedom to choose what to read, to decide when and where to read, and even not to read what they've started. Why are these student freedoms important? Let's face it: We never *want* to do what we *have* to do. Adults have to free kids from *having* to read so they can *want* to read, so they *will* read. Surely, we agree that children can never become proficient readers unless they read more than what is required in school. The child who sneaks a book and a flashlight into bed at night will be truly literate.

The second- and third-grade classrooms we are observing provide choices for what to read and offer options within the room of where to read. The children even have some choice of when to read. Mrs. Williams does not use reading a book as a time filler after other work is done. In fact, she allows for at least forty-five minutes of independent reading time a day and does her

Students should have freedom to choose what, when, and where to read.

best not to let assemblies and other interruptions deprive the class of their precious reading time. By never canceling reading and writing times and by modeling reading and writing herself, Mrs. Williams is communicating to her students the importance of literacy.

Mr. Larson has filled his room with books. He doesn't confine books to the class library area because he wants his students to think of books all the time. He makes sure books about chickens are by the chicken cage, he displays books about rockets and planets beside the solar system chart Felipe brought to share, and he puts all kinds of books along the chalkboards. Mr. Larson has noticed that children respond more to books that are displayed showing the front picture rather than shelved so that only the spines show.

Mrs. Williams's classroom has reminders about books and their contents on posters and charts hung around the room. She encourages her students to make posters, book jackets, costumes, and displays in lieu of book reports to let other children know about especially good books. She also copies poetry she thinks they might enjoy onto wall charts for their casual reading. Like Mr. Larson, she features books by displaying them on top of the bookshelves where children easily can find them.

Both classrooms have specially designated library areas where most of the class books are kept. Both Mr. Larson and Mrs. Williams have made their class libraries inviting and pleasant places. Old rugs, cushions, and beanbag chairs provide cozy places for reading and browsing through books. The teachers frequently exchange the books that children have tired of or that they didn't care for in the first place. Also the teachers select books on topics that interest individual children. Decorated book boxes containing a variety of books and interesting materials on a specific topic create special attractions in Mrs. Williams's room.

Today, as Mr. Larson and the children are discussing what to do when the chicks grow up, he pulls out some books on raising poultry and mentions that he found them at the library. Mr. Larson constantly models using libraries and helps the children to be comfortable in the school library. Once a week, they go there for instructions on how to use the library, to hear a story, and to check out books. The librarian has posted a schedule of times when children may go into the library alone or in small groups. Mr. Larson also likes to take at least two field trips a year to the local public library. In the fall, he makes sure that all children have a library card and that they all know how to find the children's section in the local library. A second visit usually is scheduled near the end of the school year so the librarian can give the second graders information about summer reading programs and story times and let them know that someone is always there to help them find a good book.

In both the school and the public library, the librarians have taken special care to teach young children how to select books. They have pointed out sections of the library containing "everybody" books and "easy-to-read" books. The easy fiction, all marked on the spines with yellow tape, is on low shelves in one corner. These books are often just the thing for first and second graders who are practicing their developing reading abilities. Right now, Joey is browsing through the "easy fiction" section and has chosen a favorite of his, *Little Bear* (Minarik, 1957). Joey loves this book because it looks more grown up to him than the picture books his teachers read to him. The short chapters and big print are as inviting to him as the sensitive drawings by Maurice Sendak. Molly picks out *The Stupids Step Out* (Allard, 1974), a hilarious book Mr. Larson has read to the class.

Some of Joey's classmates choose books from the regular fiction section. At school, Mrs. Sanders taught them the rule of thumb: Pick a book that looks good, open it to a middle page, and begin to read. For every word you don't know or can't figure out, put down one finger. If you get to your fifth finger (thumb) before you've finished the page, the book is probably too hard for you. This little rule, devised by Jeanette Veatch (1968), is easy to learn and helps children to feel in charge of their own book selection in the school library.

Mrs. Sanders is also aware that children are attracted to books by their topics and authors. She has shown the children the nonfiction section and how the different topics are organized within this section. These children are probably too young to use the Dewey Decimal System efficiently, but they do know where the animal books, the biographies, and the poetry books are. An avid reader herself, Mrs. Sanders loves to talk to the children and her friends about her favorite children's authors. She also encourages children to select their library books by looking for their favorite authors. Her goal is that all children in the school will be independent, informed, and comfortable using this library.

A LITERATURE PROGRAM

The children in Mr. Larson's class have put away their writing materials and settled in comfortable places around the room with their books. LaMarr sits on the sofa reading *Curious George* (Rey, 1941) for the fifth time. Amy is slouched on pillows in the reading corner, mouthing words as she reads *Maggie's Moon* (Alexander, 1982). Amy only recently began to feel confident enough to read on her own; before, she spent much of her reading time at the listening center. Mason is doing that right now: He is wearing headphones, listening to a tape of *Why Mosquitoes Buzz in People's Ears* (Aardema, 1975) and following along in a paperback copy of the book. Matthew, who doesn't like to wear headphones, reads alone at his desk, absorbed in *The Hardy Boys: The Great Airport Mystery* (Dixon, 1985).

Carlos is reading *Los Músicos de Brema* (Gross, 1979) to Ms. Gonzales, the bilingual tutor. He speaks Spanish as his first language, and although he is learning English from Joey and his friends, Carlos is lucky to have an adult who reads and writes with him in his native language. Children who do not speak English as a first language should begin their reading experiences in their native language if at all possible. When they become independent readers in their first language, and when they can speak English fairly fluently, the transition to reading in English becomes natural.

Molly isn't in the room: She's down the hall reading *Morris Has a Cold* (Wiseman, 1978) to an enthralled kindergartner. Molly has practiced this story and can read it without hesitation. It's hard to tell which child is enjoying the story more, Molly or her kindergarten friend. Multiage reading activities such as this, often called peer tutoring, are academically advantageous

When a young child reads to an older child, they both benefit.

for the younger child, but most likely even better for the older child, who sees a clear purpose for preparing an oral reading.

The children in this class have all kinds of reading styles, interests, backgrounds, and abilities. Mr. Larson finds that an individual reading program helps every child to read what he or she is interested in, at an appropriate ability level. Matthew and Shennelle are good readers; in fact, they hardly ever stop reading. Sometimes Matthew will read three or four books a week. Mr. Larson is delighted to see this enthusiasm and encourages these children to read widely. Amy and Mason, less mature readers, are choosing books with predictable patterns, like *A Dark Dark Tale* (Brown, R., 1981) and *The Napping House* (Wood, 1984), which they've heard the teacher read. They still enjoy a chance to read to any adult who'll listen and display enthusiasm equal to Matthew's. LaMarr has checked out *Curious George* books every week of this school year, and he tells us that he has read *Curious George Rides a Bike* (Rey, 1952) seven times. Mr. Larson doesn't interfere with his choices. He knows that as LaMarr rereads the same book, he's practicing reading, gaining fluency, and developing his concept of a story. Carlos hasn't tried to read in English yet, but listens intently when Mr. Larson reads aloud and has gone through all the Spanish picture books from the public library. What all these children have in common is strong motivation to read, so that's what Mr. Larson encourages them to do.

What if these children were put into three reading groups, in which oral reading was the focus, like you and I were? Matthew and Shennelle probably would be bored with the stories in their readers. They would become adept at keeping the place during the round-robin circle while concentrating on more interesting things. Maybe Matthew would have a paperback hidden inside his book to keep him occupied while he waits for his turn to read. Maybe Shennelle would become vigilant about other children's errors and point them out when they read aloud. These children would probably rush through their work sheets and other assignments so they could get back to their reading. They might cause a teacher to ask why such good readers don't do well in reading assignments. What about Amy? She would probably be placed in a "low" reading group with a small group of children with needs as different as hers and Carlos's. They would plod through oral reading sessions and waste endless time listening to each other stumble through lifeless stories. Amy and Carlos would soon learn that no matter how much they learned and progressed, they'd still be in the bottom reading group. By second grade, they might already have decided that they were "dumb." Amy might withdraw, Carlos might bother other children.

Such a scenario gets very depressing, doesn't it? Mr. Larson, Mrs. Williams, Ms. Montoya, Mrs. Hanna, and Mrs. Thomas are glad that none of the other primary teachers in their school use basal programs anymore. The children in Mr. Larson's room read for about forty-five minutes every day, usually before lunch. Mr. Larson and the children try to arrange each day so that nothing interrupts reading time. Mr. Larson remembers one school where everyone in the entire school would read independently for the first half-hour of the school day, including teachers, the principal, children, secretaries, the nurse, the custodian, and even visitors. He remembers visiting that school and being asked to sit on a bench in the hall until reading time was over; luckily, he had a paperback in his knapsack! A whole-school reading time isn't possible in his school, but Mr. Larson still tries to maintain reading as an inviolate time of the day. It is never replaced with other activities. In fact, on this year's field trip to the beach, the children brought their books for forty-five minutes of rest and reading before lunch.

Flexible Grouping

You might think that these classes have no reading groups. When Mrs. Williams gave up the basal reader, she eliminated fixed reading groups, but many of the class activities still happen in groups. Today, Thu, Aaron, and Melinda are working on a play that Melinda found in one of the old textbooks. They are reading it through in parts and later will make plans for inviting other children to become the minor characters. They will present the play as a radio drama to the other second grades.

Mrs. Williams will meet this afternoon with a literature group of five children who have been reading *Rosie and Michael* (Viorst, 1974), a story about a boy and a girl who are special friends. The group also has read all the *George and Martha* (Marshall, 1974) books and has made their own *George and Martha* book for the class library. Today, they want help in setting up a poster on "how to be a friend." Mrs. Williams then will share a list of some more books about friends that she got from the librarian. After discussing what makes a good friend, the children may choose to write stories about their own friends that focus on the qualities of friendship.

Mrs. Williams and Mr. Larson have dozens of sets of six copies of the same book. These are used by literature groups—teams that are self-selected by youngsters according to interest. Mrs. Williams invites each child to participate in a literature group once a month. The group reads the same book during independent reading time or at home and then meets in class to discuss the book. Sometimes, Mrs. Williams comes to the groups armed with questions, but she prefers the students to come up with their own questions for each other. One way to facilitate this is to start the group discussion with each child taking a turn making an opening statement about his or her thoughts about the book.

Mrs. Williams belongs to a book group herself and notices that the third graders do basically the same thing as the adult group does—they compare notes on a book, discuss what they like and dislike, and comment on how the book relates to their lives. From these discussions often come suggestions for other books that the group would enjoy. Mrs. Williams finds that she enjoys her private reading much more now that she gets ideas from her friends, and she observes that this seems to be happening in the third grade, too. She is especially pleased when children recommend books to each other.

Mr. Larson also uses flexible grouping. Groups form and disband for various purposes. Groups are used for writing response, for help with reading strategies, for art or drama projects, for research, and so on. No child is ever stuck in a "low" group. In fact, Mr. Larson encourages groups of mixed abilities; usually, the children choose their own groups. Mr. Larson encourages everyone to work in writing response groups once a week and in a literature group once a month.

When several children appear ready for a similar concept, Mr. Larson has them form a study group. He can work with several children at once for efficiency, and the children have the benefit of working with peers. Mrs. Williams and Mr. Larson have many small-group activities to help students to learn the major concepts of their grade level. Sometimes children need specific information that simply can be told or shown to them, such as how to use quotation marks or when to use commas. Other times, the understanding needed is more complex and requires that children put together information in ways that are personally meaningful. This kind of understanding includes figuring out how to make writing interesting as well as figuring out the confusion of letter-sound relationships. Group lessons that help youngsters to construct their own knowledge involve peer collaboration as they work on tasks relevant to the concept.

Last week, Mr. Larson worked with Mason, Isaac, and Thu to help them to use context clues. He noticed that these children were hesitant about guessing at unknown words and that they tried too hard to sound them out. In order to help them use picture and sentence context, Mr. Larson supplied comic strips with some missing words, and encouraged them to guess what was in the blanks. Later, during conferences, he reminded the children to use that guessing strategy when they were stuck on words when they were reading aloud to him.

Response to Literature

Do you remember María Elena and her friends who were working on a poster outside the room during reading? Were the girls reading? They were working on an important part of an independent literature program, *response to literature*. When we turn a reading program over to our students, when they choose books they want to read for pleasure or for information, we expect that the children will respond in some way. Often a response to literature is just a thought—a child may wonder what happened to Wilbur after his friend Charlotte died or imagine wild things in his or her own closet. Other children respond by asking questions. Do you remember Ramona asking Miss Binney how Mike Mulligan went to the bathroom in *Ramona the Pest* (Cleary, 1968)? In a literature discussion group, children have a chance to listen to their classmates' responses and to share their own feelings about their readings.

Teachers like Mr. Larson are delighted when children argue over books and recommend good books to each other. Sometimes, during class meetings, a class member will share a book with the whole class. This morning, Amy shared *Crow Boy* (Yashima, 1955). Sometimes, she daydreams and watches the crows hopping around outside the room, and it impressed her that Taro, the hero of the book, did the same thing. Amy shared her impressions of crow calls, and before she was finished with her report, Joey and LaMarr both wanted to see the book.

Mr. Larson never assigns written book reports, but he does encourage the children to write about special books they've read. Sometimes comments on books show up in the dialogue or home-school journals. When this happens, Mr. Larson writes back, both reflecting on what the child has said and asking questions leading to further writing. One month, after the class had been reading folk tales, Mr. Larson noticed that many of the children's stories began to include folkloric elements like "once upon a time," prince and princess, and three wishes. Sometimes, Mr. Larson encourages children to make a poster or some type of advertisement for a book they think others will like. That's what María Elena and her friends are doing. They are writing what reads like a movie advertisement from the newspa-

Response to literature takes many forms. Primary teachers encourage children to express their impressions of stories through art.

per for *The Best Christmas Pageant Ever* (Robinson, 1972). Although it's well past Christmas, the girls giggled over the book as they passed it among themselves, and they decided that Mr. Larson should order lots of copies of it for the class library. Mr. Larson challenged them to prove to him how funny the book was, and their poster is the result. Now, they are decorating their poster with nasty-looking children dressed as angels and laughing as they paint. These girls are responding in writing as well as with art.

Response to literature takes many forms other than thinking, talking, and writing. Mr. Larson, like all the other primary teachers at his school, encourages children to express their impressions of stories through art. Murals, maps, animal cutouts, and all kinds of posters cover the walls and the hallway outside the room. Mr. Larson encourages the children to do all the bulletin boards and room decorations. Inspirations from reading seem to show up everywhere. When Mr. Larson put clay out yesterday, many of the children made chicks and eggs, but Amy made a crow. Children also enjoy making dioramas, shadow boxes, displays, and costumes about their books. Last Halloween, all the children in Mrs. Williams's class dressed up as book characters.

Thu's mother spent a week last October helping the children make puppets out of old light bulbs, pieces of cloth, and paper maché. Most of the children made scary Halloween monsters that they used to act out Jack Prelutsky's *Nightmares: Poems to Trouble Your Sleep* (1976). Another year, Mrs. Williams's class made puppets to act out different folk tales. Puppets seem to open the door for creative dramatics; even the quietest child will act out a part behind a puppet.

Mrs. Williams encourages other dramatic activities such as readers' theater, pantomime, and play reading. Most children in second and third grades love to read aloud. Plays are a natural way to satisfy this desire and to give children practice in reading with expression. When a group asks to do a play for others, a teacher or a parent helps them to stage it so that no child is put on the spot to memorize lines or to be embarrassed in front of others.

Groups usually meet in the afternoon during activity time to work on various projects. Some of these projects involve the whole class; others are initiated by small groups. This can be a noisy part of the day, but Mrs. Williams finds that she enjoys the sounds of children busy at their work. Besides, she knows that an active response will help these children remember, understand, and appreciate the books they've been reading.

Response to literature must involve a creative reaction to the work of literature. The teacher may suggest or determine the medium of response (a radio play, use of pastels on black paper, and so on), but the direction of that response must belong to the children to be authentic. Open-ended activities encourage children to express their own reactions and emotions, not those of the teacher.

GUIDELINES FOR HELPING CHILDREN LEARN TO READ

- *Children work hard at reading whatever is important to them.*
- *Children learn to read by reading.*
- *Learning to read involves construction of knowledge.* Because learning to read is largely constructed understanding, as is most complex learning, explanations, directions, and direct teaching may do more to confuse than to help. After children have established successful reading processes, they can discuss ways to gain greater depth and evaluative ability.
- *Reading involves understanding written thoughts.* To find out how well children read, ask them to tell you about what they have read. Ask follow-up questions in terms of the purpose for which they were reading.
- *Children need to develop self-confidence as readers.* When children select their own reading materials and can talk about what they have read, they experience success. When helping children who have difficulty, emphasize how much they were able to understand on their own.
- *Each child's development and experience with reading is unique.* Because no two children learn at the same rate, listening and responding to them individually and in small groups is more useful than group instruction.
- *When children read effectively, they understand the meaning but may or may not report it in the exact words of the print.* As long as they do not distort meaning seriously, teachers should make no issue of it. If there is distortion, teachers should allow time for children to self-correct. If children do not question the meaning of the distorted sentence, teachers then should raise the question of meaning.
- *Children learn to read most effectively when what they read is important to them.* When children choose their own reading material, it is automatically more important to them than what might be assigned, and they want to find out what their selected books say. They concentrate on getting the meaning.

Related Activities

When you read children's books, you'll see that some books simply must be accompanied by activities that the teacher can organize for the class to do. For example, *Stone Soup* (Brown, M., 1947) and *Blueberries for Sal* (McCloskey, 1948) wouldn't seem complete in a primary classroom if you and your class didn't make a big pot of stone soup or a batch of blueberry muffins. *The Quilt* (Jonas, 1984) is fun to follow by having the children pick out or decorate quilt squares that can be sewn into a huge classroom quilt. *Peter Rabbit* (Potter, 1902) and *Rabbit Hill* (Lawson, 1944) seem to call for planting a garden, or at least some carrot seeds. As you read children's books, always be aware of the art, cooking, sewing, or building ideas that can enrich the meaning of the books for children. Many children's books, such as Peter Spier's *The Fox Went Out on a Chilly Night* (1961), are based on songs and music. Wouldn't it be a shame to miss a chance for a good song, game, or dance that a book like this suggests?

When considering teacher-initiated activities, remember that every activity should have as its purpose a deeper understanding of literature. Activities that precede a reading can help to build a context and provide focus. Activities presented during reading aid understanding and enthusiasm. Follow-up activities help to summarize the meaning of a book and help children to make connections. Remember, though, that teacher-initiated activities do not necessarily allow for individual children's responses and do not replace open-ended response to literature activities.

Reading to Learn

Many primary teachers say that their focus must be developing foundations in literacy and mathematics; therefore, they just don't have time to teach sci-

If science and social studies materials reflect different levels of difficulty, and if their range is varied, every child will be encouraged to read and learn about the topic.

ence, social studies, and critical thinking. Mr. Larson thinks differently. He always makes sure that any area of content study is supported by reading and writing. One way he does this is to stock his room with books on the topics of study and to invite children to read widely in these books. If the books reflect different levels of difficulty and their range is varied, every child will be encouraged to read and learn about the topic. In addition, because content information comes from a variety of sources, the children can function as a learning community, sharing and comparing information.

The classroom science books may lead to collections of shells, insects, or leaves; observation charts of the weather; and experiments with sunlight. When the class decides to study whales, Mr. Larson collects all the whale books he can find, and takes the opportunity to show children how nonfiction books are organized and how to use the table of contents, index, and chapter headings. He assists children in making charts of information they've gleaned from their reading. When the children discovered that some of the whale books discussed orca whales as friendly, intelligent, and sociable, while others labeled them dangerous enemies of people, Mr. Larson helped them compare these different points of view in the different texts and separate facts from opinions.

Trade books on social studies topics lead to maps, charts, and timelines; to comparisons with children in other countries; and to field trips in the community. Health books lead to keeping track of the food the children eat and when they brush their teeth. Do you see how closely related reading and writing are to the other subjects you must cover in the primary grades? There's no need to make content areas separate in a literature program; in fact, they're hard to keep separate. Remember Mr. Larson's hatching chickens? The children learned science and math concepts and processes through observing those chickens while they read and wrote about them. Many teachers who use an integrated or core curriculum like this say that they have more time to do all things they want to, now that their curriculum isn't all chopped up into little sections.

THE TEACHER'S ROLE

We already have discussed the core of a whole language reading program, the conference. We also have described the important role of the teacher in setting the physical and emotional environment conducive to reading. Work on the physical environment involves time before and after school for selecting, sorting, and displaying reading materials. At the beginning of the school year, a teacher arranges a library area so that the children perceive it as semisecluded and comfortable. Maintaining this positive emotional environment and fostering freedom to choose what, when, and where to read becomes a teacher's ongoing job.

If you aren't tied down to meeting with each of three reading groups, you are free for individual reading conferences and for spontaneous interaction with individuals. You can circulate while children work, asking a question here, making a suggestion there. You can spend time guiding children in working independently. For instance, you can help them select books of interest and of appropriate difficulty. You can help children learn to keep their own record sheets of the books they have read. You can help them learn to work in groups and provide guidance so they can learn the limits about where they can work, how noisy they can be, and what materials they can use. You can model the importance of reading by sharing your own favorite books, and reading yourself when you have a spare moment. If you provide guidelines and organization, an individualized, activity-oriented program has a much greater chance of success.

Reading Aloud

One of the teachers' big responsibilities and greatest joys is to read aloud to the children. Even though most second and third graders can read independently, they still love to listen to their teachers read to them. You probably know how satisfying it is to share a good book with a group of rapt listeners. Second and third graders still like picture storybooks, but are also fascinated with chapter books. Beverly Cleary's *Ramona the Pest* is a great way to start young children with chapter books. They will feel smug in their knowledge about the misadventures of Ramona starting kindergarten. Read to your children every day, several times a day. You will be giving your youngsters models of good stories, exciting vocabulary, and beautifully constructed sentences that will not only entertain, but also contribute to the richness of their oral language and their writing. And you will provide a common literary experience for everyone in the class.

Mrs. Williams always starts the day by reading aloud to the whole class. She chooses books that she thinks will "stretch" her listeners, not ones they'll read on their own or that their parents might read to them at home. Right now she's reading *Koko's Kitten,* (Patterson, 1985), a book recommended by the public librarian. As the class hears the story of Koko the chimp who communicates in sign language, many themes emerge to explore and discuss: Can animals really "talk"? Can they "love" another animal? Primary grade children generally enjoy books for their surface stories, but the adept teacher can enrich a story by exploring deeper themes in discussion.

Read-aloud is one of the best times of the day for everyone. Ruben likes to imagine pictures in his head; Molly draws elaborate pictures of the stories she hears. Jennifer just likes to relax and listen. For Mrs. Williams, this is one of the most satisfying parts of the school day—she loves the calm feeling of everyone concentrating on the same thing. With so much going on in class, this is one of the few times of the day when the class has common ground, and Mrs. Williams often will choose a book that represents what the class is studying in science, social studies, or literature. She chose *Koko's Kitten* because the class has been talking about how animals communicate.

ALTERNATIVES TO ROUND-ROBIN READING

There is little evidence that the traditional oral-reading circle is of any educational value. However, many teachers still consider the ability to read orally an important skill. What are some ways to retain oral reading in the program?

Oral Reading for Diagnostic Purposes
- Children can read orally to the teacher in a one-on-one situation.
- Children can read orally to a tape recorder, parent-volunteer, or older child.

Oral Reading for Information Sharing
- Children can read the lunch menu, daily bulletin, and newspaper items.
- Children can confirm an answer by reading it from a book.
- One child (a good reader) can read aloud while others listen with their textbooks closed.
- Children can read passages from reference books or trade books.

Oral Reading for Entertainment
- Two children can share one book, reading to each other.
- Choral reading.
- Reading poems or essays for audience.
- Radio drama, play reading, or readers' theater.

Oral Reading as Part of the Writing Process
- Children can read their own writing in progress to partners or response groups.
- Children can share original creative writing or reports in the author's chair.

Tips About Oral Reading
- Have children prepare in advance anything read for an audience.
- Remember that oral reading decreases comprehension.
- Teach children how to read punctuation and inflection.
- Give children the opportunity to listen to good readers (tapes and records).

Many teachers also enjoy telling stories. When you are not holding a book between yourself and your listeners, you'll have an almost magical connection with them. You all know what it feels like to catch a child's eye while you read aloud. In storytelling, you maintain constant eye contact, and, like an actor or comedian, you respond to your audience—to their giggles and their fears—in a most intimate way. Mr. Larson recently took a storytelling class and learned two folk tales. His children beg him to tell his stories over and over again, so he is learning another story.

Planning a Literature Curriculum

Teachers often organize literature curricula for their classes and sometimes even for their schools. Some, like Mr. Larson, want to be sure that children are reading in a variety of genres so that they are aware of the full range of literary experiences. During this school year, Mr. Larson has highlighted a different genre each month: folk tales, animal stories, mysteries, information books, poetry, fantasy, historical fiction, modern fiction, and biographies. He introduces the genre by reading a good example to the class and then asks Mrs. Sanders, the school librarian, to pull out more books of that genre. Remember Matthew and his *Hardy Boys* mysteries? Maybe he would never have discovered mysteries if it hadn't been for a literature curriculum.

Mrs. Williams prefers to focus on an author of the month. When she read Joanna Cole's *Magic Schoolbus: Inside the Human Body* (1989), many of the third graders were so impressed that they picked up other *Magic Schoolbus* books. Mrs. Williams makes an author display each month and encourages her students to write letters to the featured author. Once in a while, Mrs. Williams is able to coordinate her author of the month with a school visit from the writer. This approach is very useful to the children. They will tell

Constructivist teachers see little carryover to actual reading or writing from the isolated drill provided by workbooks. Instead, they show and model skills and strategies in the context of the children's reading and writing.

you that one of the best ways to find a good book in the library is to look for a favorite author. This year, they'll learn about at least nine authors in great detail.

When you choose challenging literature to read aloud, whether it's by genre, author, or topic or even when it's a list of specific books, you have the opportunity to stretch your listeners by offering them literature they might never have chosen themselves. Many books that teachers read aloud are too difficult for children to read on their own or cover topics that are unfamiliar to them. Mrs. Williams tries not to read books that are popular for independent reading, but instead chooses ones that will give them an enjoyable challenge.

By second and third grade, children have constructed a great deal of knowledge about literature that they probably couldn't verbalize to you. They know about characters and that their changes create a story. They know that certain words create images or feelings and that book language is different from oral language. They know they can find themselves and their own joys and fears in stories, and that myths explain the unexplainable. They know that books can become models for their own writing and that sometimes their own writing sounds like books they've read (see Figure 7–1). Some literature programs and teachers' guides belabor such knowledge and encourage the teacher to "teach" these intangibles. We hope you will help your children to read widely and deeply, and encourage them to take what they learn and apply it to their lives, their writing, and their knowledge of the world. We hope you will not spend time "teaching" such concepts as rhyme in poetry or setting in prose, but instead will simply encourage children to notice them as they read and to use these literary devices as they write.

Teaching Skills and Strategies

If the teacher doesn't have reading groups, doesn't assign required stories, and doesn't teach basal skill lessons, what does the teacher do to help children to learn specific reading skills and strategies? Certainly not assign workbook or ditto pages! Neither Mr. Larson nor Mrs. Williams believes in workbooks. They see little carryover to actual reading or writing from the isolated drill provided in workbooks, except perhaps a negative attitude toward reading and writing. Mrs. Williams says, "If you must use workbooks, just don't call it reading or writing." She has had children in her classes whose past experiences have lead them to equate reading with workbooks.

What can you do to teach children skills and strategies they need? You've probably already figured out that through careful attention to errors in writing and miscues in reading, you can quickly and purposefully see what children's immediate needs are and help them to do what they're trying to do. When you show a child in conference how to indent a paragraph or to look at a long compound word as two parts, you're teaching skills. When you model using context to figure out an unknown word or show a child how to skim a

FIGURE 7–1
Literary models from children's reading are often translated into their own personal writing.

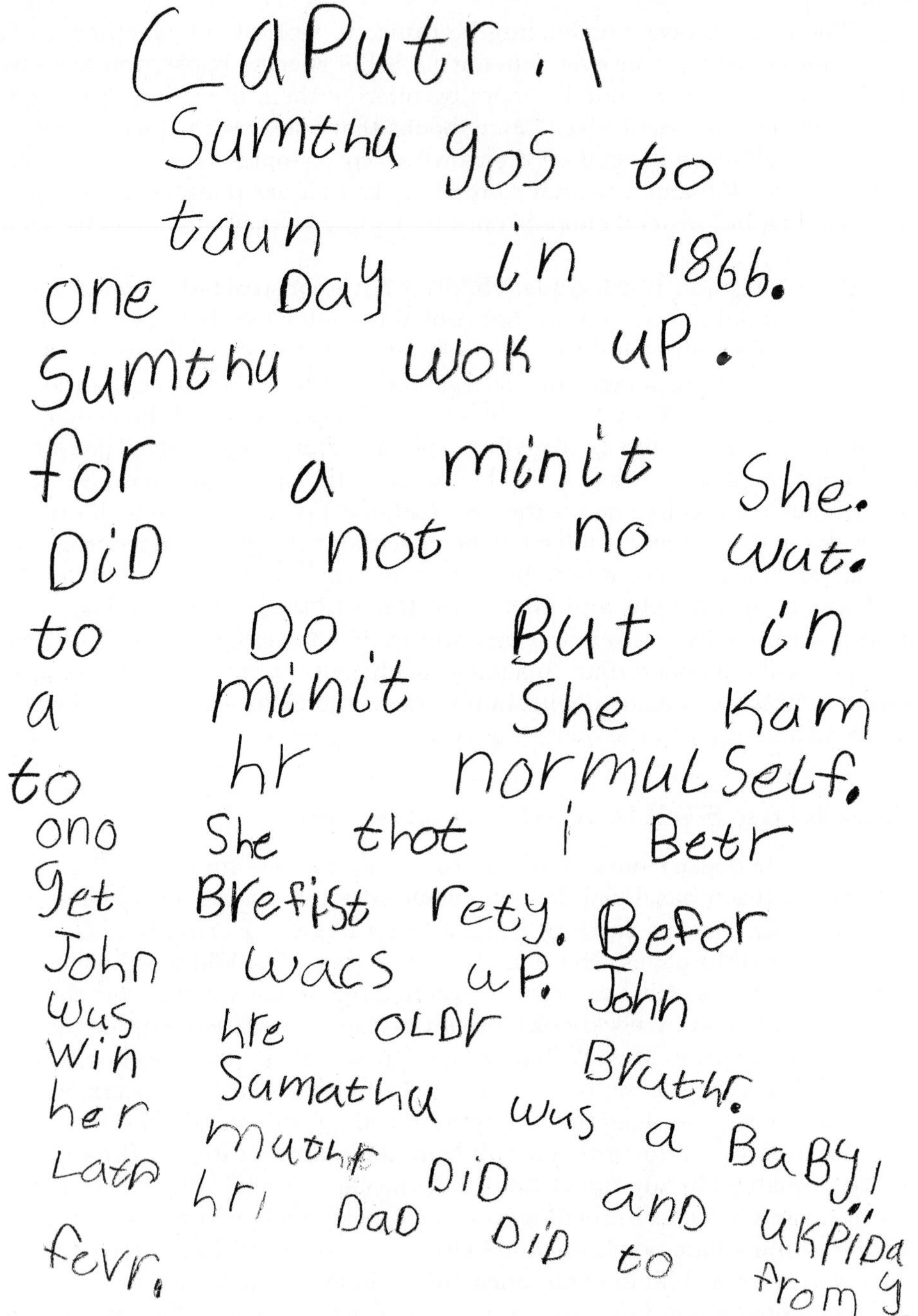

CaPutr. 1
Sumthu gos to
taun
one Day in 1866.
Sumthu wok uP.
for a minit She.
DiD not no wut.
to Do. But in
a minit She Kam
to hr normulSelf.
ono She thot i Betr
get Brefist rety. Befor
John wacs uP. John
wus hre OLDr
win Samathu wus a BaBy!
her muthr DiD and uKPiDa
Latr hri Dao DiD to from y
fevr. s

So that left John and sumthu orfims. Tha wr por so fro ther Dayle mels. tha DID not hav verg much to et. Sumthu and hr Bruthr wr setulrs. John wus 8eighteen, and Samthu wus 8 one morne samthu wok up. fro a cupl of Days Samthu DID not now. That John had urnD Summuny But She found the muny! that he haD urnD!

page for a detail, you are teaching strategies. It is true that a teacher must be vigilant in constantly identifying each child's needs; it also is true that you need never waste a child's time in skill lessons or work sheets that she doesn't need. A child could be reading or writing instead!

Supporting Children with Special Needs

Sometimes a child just doesn't seem to progress. Mr. Larson works hard to determine if the problem is a school-based or a home-based one. Discussions with parents often lead to mutual efforts on behalf of the child. If a situation outside of school is causing learning problems, families can be helped to find counseling and other resources.

If the problem lies with the school situation, then Mr. Larson considers it his job to try to correct it. He has seen some youngsters who had trouble reading because they had a mistaken idea of what reading was. Their previous experience led them to believe it was naming words rather than a thinking process. In these cases, Mr. Larson provided experiences to counteract this previous learning. He has found that going back to taking dictation from a child sometimes helps a youngster to make that missing connection between print and meaning.

Sometimes, a child has not learned procedures for self-help. In such a case, the youngster may become discouraged and stop when encountering an unknown word, not knowing what to do next. If this seems to be the problem, Mr. Larson focuses on helping the student learn to ask questions like "What word would make sense here?" and "What word that starts with that letter would make sense?" Mr. Larson also tells the child not to worry about a word if the story makes sense without knowing what it is. Finally, he reminds the child that there are twenty-four other youngsters in the class who can help if the child asks.

At other times, a child may have a motivation problem. Perhaps a child may have been trying to read material that was of no personal interest. Another youngster may not believe that any reading is worth doing. And still another may be totally turned off by any kind of school work. If a teacher just needs to help a child to find something more interesting to read, the problem is simple. But if the problem stems from a negative attitude toward reading or school in general, then the problem is serious. Mr. Larson spends time and energy trying to determine why a certain student has negative feelings about learning. He needs to know if these feelings reflect past failures with learning, home attitudes, or emotional problems with authority. Until he has this information, Mr. Larson may have a hard time helping a child.

Mr. Larson tries to keep children "turned on" to learning. He tries to involve them in activities that they have selected, and he attempts to maintain teacher-student relationships that keep them open to his suggestions. He knows that when children like their teachers and think their teachers like them, they are influenced by the teachers' enthusiasm and suggestions. He also thinks that encouraging self-direction and personal responsibility for learning keeps kids involved and interested in school.

Mr. Larson doesn't put children with reading problems in groups in which they aren't expected to do much. He believes this action will just ensure that they will never do anything. Mr. Larson also hesitates to endorse traditional remedial procedures, especially those that pull children out of the classroom to drill on isolated letters, sounds, or words. He fears that this type of instruction will make learning meaningless and more difficult. However, the Reading Recovery (Clay, 1985) approach is a pull-out program that he is comfortable with. It is short-term and focuses on meaning in reading rather than on isolated skills. Mr. Larson has learned much about the roots of reading problems and ways to deal with them from talking with the Reading Recovery teacher. Though the program was designed for first graders, Mr. Larson thinks it is important to provide some of the same kind of assistance to his second graders.

He has known some excellent remedial reading teachers who use other approaches and who work with reading problems within the regular classroom. Mr. Larson welcomes help in his classroom from Mrs. Casati, the Chapter 1 teacher. Sometimes he and the specialist together can discover a gap in a child's understanding and remedy it with special attention. Any extra help can ease the burden of trying to provide for each child's interests, levels of knowledge, and style of learning.

In addition, he must help parents to understand and deal with their children's learning problems. Periodically, parents ask if their child is dyslexic. Then, Mr. Larson explains that the term dyslexia has no meaning other than "does not read." When Tom's parents were convinced that Tom was dyslexic because he sometimes wrote letters backwards, Mr. Larson explained that children just becoming familiar with print often fail to notice which way a letter faces. He assured them that most reversal problems disappear by themselves after more experience with print. Naturally, Mr. Larson knows that some children do have physical and perceptual impairments to learning. These youngsters must be accepted as they are and helped to make adaptations in order to achieve whatever their potential may be.

There are children who are clearly "at risk" for school failure for a variety of reasons. Usually, these children's behavior is fine, but their values, experiences, and expectations about learning don't match those of the school. Flexible, developmentally appropriate approaches to education can help to bridge these differences and remove some of these children from the "at risk" category. Standardized tests have had the most negative impact on these children due to the cultural bias inherent in such tests. Whole language teaching and authentic assessment methods are more able to meet the needs of a diverse population of learners.

Oddly enough, the formula for meeting the needs of bilingual and gifted children is the same as for "at-risk" students. Bilingual children need materials and role models in their home language, but their processes in learning to read and write are the same as those of monolingual children. Flexible, devel-

Reading and writing workshops allow individualization of academic needs and nurturance of self-esteem for bilingual, gifted, and at-risk children.

opmentally appropriate approaches allow gifted or "at-risk" children to advance at their own rates, choose challenging and enriching materials, and then analyze them with the depth and breadth they desire. Reading and writing workshops allow the same individualization of academic needs and nurturance of self-esteem for many different kinds of learning needs.

Encouraging Parental Involvement

Mr. Larson and Mrs. Williams know that they cannot be the only supporters of reading and writing because parents and family members are powerful models and teachers. Parents can be involved on several levels by simply knowing what is going on in the class, by becoming cognizant of how and why teachers do what they do, and by actively participating in instruction (Rasinski & Fredericks, 1989).

Mr. Larson sends home a weekly newsletter. In it, he announces classroom activities, themes, and materials needed. He makes liberal use of short articles written by his students and provides information on community activities, television shows, and books that might be of interest. Parents appreciate this consistent direct communication and always have a reference (often kept on the refrigerator or calendar) of class activities.

Remember the activity in Chapter 6 where we suggested that you write a letter to parents explaining invented spelling? This is a way to inform parents of current thought and practice in education. Often, the only model of education parents have is their own schooling. The primary classroom is very different today from what it was twenty or thirty years ago. Parents need to know about current practices, and not just what happens, but why. It is challenging to a teacher to explain complex concepts like construction of knowledge, but it is necessary if you really want your parents to understand and support your teaching methods. Many teachers plan quarterly parent nights when they address specific topics—the writing process, why we don't use basals anymore, invented spelling—as additional ways to inform parents. Some schools provide newsletters and parent meetings at the schoolwide level as well, but we think personal communication is much more powerful.

We don't believe in homework for young children, but we do believe in shared activities for students and their parents. Many of our teachers make it a practice to send a book home weekly for a child to read to a parent or other adult, or vice versa. Other meaningful "homework" assignments include writing in the home-school journal, investigating and recording information about the home, and writing lists and letters. This week Patrick, with the help of his mom, was asked to find all the things that use energy in his house. He then compiled his list himself, which was later used in class discussion. Another time, during study of cultures, he interviewed his parents to find out about the ethnicity of his grandparents.

If we inform parents and include them in what we're doing, we should be able to enlist them as partners, not adversaries, in the educational process.

The most important thing parents can do is work with their children. This does not mean doing their homework for them; it means modeling and supporting literacy and other academic subjects. It means encouraging library use and buying books, reading aloud to children and having them read to parents, writing notes and participating in home-school journals, and actu-

When we inform parents and include them in what we're doing, we should be able to enlist them as partners, not adversaries, in the educational process.

ally stamping and mailing letters to grandparents. Supporting literacy at home means regulating television, talking with children, and paying attention to what they say. It means not criticizing developmental writing, being accepting of invented spelling, and being patient with slow and stumbling reading.

Parents are an extremely valuable resource within the school; however, many parents are uncomfortable at school. They may remember their own painful experiences, or they may be embarrassed by limited education or by their use of English. Most parents are not available during school hours to come to the building. You, as a teacher and as a member of a school staff, must make school a welcoming place for parents and community members during the school day and in the evening. Activity nights, potlucks, and ball games in the gym or playground are nonthreatening events for parents at the school building. Parent conferences, which we'll discuss in Chapter 8, are essential to building personal rapport between teachers and parents. For those parents who are intimidated by the school, these small steps help in building the kind of trust and confidence that may lead to more substantive direct help in the classroom. Most parents who have helped in the classroom during the school day become a teacher's best allies.

Mr. Larson and Mrs. Williams will both tell you that they put a lot of energy into working with parents. Often, it is harder than working with children, but it's a necessary ingredient of success.

CONCLUSION

We hope you agree with us that nurturing children who have learned to "really read" is an exciting and rich process. It need never be boring, because the choices in reading material are boundless. Open-ended response activities allow for individual and group creativity, and reading conferences allow the teacher to keep close contact with each individual reader and his or her needs. In Chapter 8, we'll explore how assessment is an integral part of the reading and writing processes in the primary grades.

DISCUSSION QUESTIONS

1. Think about your own reading interests. How did they develop? What experiences have affected your choice of reading materials? How do you decide whether you will read a particular book?
2. Families seem to spend all their free time watching television and no longer read for pleasure. How can we motivate youngsters to do what their parents do not?
3. Why is response to literature so important? Is it worth valuable reading time to make dioramas or murals, perform skits, or talk to friends? Think of as many ways as you can in which response to literature can be related to writing.

SUGGESTED FOLLOW-UP ACTIVITIES

1.   Assist a child in selecting and preparing a story to read aloud to others. Remember that the choice of whether or not to read aloud must be the child's. The choice of material to read must also be the child's.

2.   Observe children as they select books from a library. Note how they choose as they sort through collections. Try to determine by what criteria or on what basis they make their selections.

3.   Engage several children one by one in private discussions about reading. The children should differ in reading abilities and levels. Ask if reading is enjoyable and why or why not. Ask what kinds of reading materials they prefer individually. Ask how they deal with unknown words. Ask how they feel if they can't pronounce some words. Analyze your findings.

4.   Begin your exploration of children's literature by compiling a classroom display of books to support a topic of study in a primary classroom. Analyze the books: Which are best to read aloud? Which are appropriate for independent readers? Share some of the books with the class.

5.   Learn a story and tell it to a group of young children. Analyze your own delivery and the reactions of your listeners. How is this form of storytelling different from reading aloud?

6.   Organize or join a book group, and participate in several discussions about books your group reads. What contributes to a good discussion? How is your understanding of a book enhanced by group interaction?

RECOMMENDED FURTHER READING

Books

Clay, M. (1985). *The early detection of reading difficulties.* Portsmouth, NH: Heinemann.

Hart-Hewins, L., & Wells, J. (1990). *Real books for reading: Learning to read with children's literature.* Portsmouth, NH: Heinemann.

Harwayne, S. (1992). *Lasting impressions: Weaving literature into the writing workshop.* Portsmouth, NH: Heinemann.

Hornsby, D., & Sukarna, D. (1988). *Read on: A conference approach to reading.* Portsmouth, NH: Heinemann.

Huck, C., Hepler, S., & Hickman, J. (1993). *Children's literature in the elementary school.* Fort Worth, TX: Harcourt, Brace, Jovanovich.

May, F. B. (1994). *Reading as communication* (4th ed.). New York: Merrill/Macmillan.

CHAPTER

8

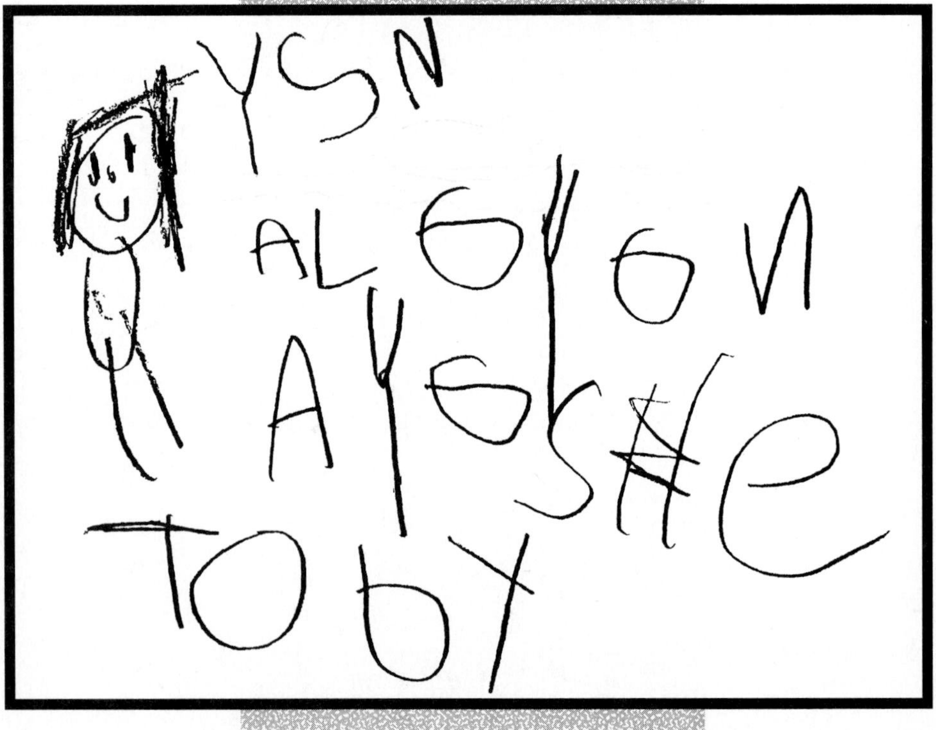

ASSESSING GROWTH IN LITERACY

Teachers will find the information obtained from assessment instruments only as valuable as their interaction with children.

J. M. MASON & J. P. STEWART, 1990

S chools and teachers rapidly are becoming more knowledgeable about
whole language principles and emergent literacy concepts. Teaching
methods and materials are in the process of radical change. Unfortunately,
methods and tools for assessment of instructional outcomes have been slower
to change. Whole language teachers are faced with standardized tests that
are incongruous with their teaching. Many teachers wanting to change to
more holistic approaches are fearful because of this and ask "But what if students don't do well on the test?"

MATCHING ASSESSMENT TO INSTRUCTION

Many teachers have good reason to be fearful because some school districts
still evaluate a teacher's performance on the basis of student test scores. The
old system was a tidy one: Teaching was designed to prepare students to do
well on certain standardized tests, and good test scores made the teaching
look good. Reading textbook companies focused on skills measured in standardized tests; they aimed at teaching skills and provided testing materials
patterned after the standardized tests (Stallman & Pearson, 1990). Too few
educators stopped to consider whether those skills being taught and measured were what created good readers.

Tests for assessing reading ability have had the same flaws as the outmoded approaches to reading (Clay, 1993; Teale, 1990). They emphasize subskills of reading, and they work on these subskills out of the context of real
reading or writing. These tests not only lack validity in content, but they also
lack reliability because of the circumstances under which they are adminis-
tered. They do not provide the context clues and teacher support that are
part of a real reading situation and that assist children in performing at their
best. What's more, the gap between new teaching approaches and old testing
processes makes test results useless as feedback about teaching.

Assessment should promote better teaching and learning, but it cannot
when assessment measures are unrelated to classroom practices. Standardized test scores do not tell the teacher why a child made errors, nor do they
give information useful for helping children to improve. To guide their teaching, teachers actually rely on data they collect as they teach and observe children's learning processes. Marie Clay (1993) likens this to coaching a football
game, saying "You do not improve the play of a team by looking at the outcome score. The coach must look closely at how the team is playing the game
and help them to change the moves or strategies that produce a better final
score" (p. 4). Formal testing processes generally just give the final score.

Nevertheless, the public, school policymakers, and teachers themselves
have shown little faith in alternative measures of progress. Standardized
tests have been revered for their supposed objectivity (Smith, 1990). However,
critical appraisals point out that subjectivity exists in standardized tests via
the selection of what to test and the determination of how to test it. We need

to ask ourselves whether "the fallible human beings who construct the tests" (Stallman & Pearson, 1990, p. 41) are more able to assess a child's learning than that child's own teacher.

Matching Assessment to Young Children

Young children, unsophisticated in the ways of taking tests, are especially disadvantaged by formalized testing. Tests end up testing not reading skills but children's willingness to pay attention to an uninteresting task (Kamii, 1990). They also test the test taking skills: filling in bubbles and circling letters properly and carefully. Many teachers waste days of educational time teaching youngsters how to do these tasks. In spite of teachers' efforts, the resulting scores are totally lacking in reliability. Children may get low scores simply because they weren't in the mood to do what the test required; at another time, the results would be different. This means that standardized tests not only do not measure the things children need to learn, but they also don't give an accurate picture of what they do try to measure (Clay, 1993).

Mrs. Hanna and Mrs. Thomas were among the teachers who dreaded testing days, knowing many children would be in tears. Youngsters felt the pressure as their teachers and parents felt it. Children were admonished to get a good night's sleep, have a good breakfast, and be ready for the big day. The children wanted to do a good job but when they were confronted with questions that were confusing, the adults they usually relied on wouldn't even explain things. The situation was extremely upsetting to many children. Their teachers felt morally compromised when they went along with testing policies that they could see were inappropriate for their students. These feelings gave them and other teachers the courage to question school testing policies and to work for change. Their district no longer gives standardized tests below third grade, accepting that such tests are not developmentally appropriate for young children.

Those working for assessment practices that are developmentally appropriate for young children have been assisted by the publication of guidelines for the assessment of children ages three through eight published jointly by the National Association for the Education of Young Children and the National Association of Early Childhood Specialists in State Departments of Education (1991).

QUESTIONS TO ASK IN EVALUATING A PROGRAM'S ASSESSMENT PROCEDURES

1. Is the assessment procedure based on the goals and objectives of the specific curriculum used in the program?

2. Are the results of the assessment used to benefit children, i.e., to plan for individual children, improve instruction, identify children's interests and needs, and individualize instruction, rather than label, track, or fail children?
3. Does the assessment procedure address all domains of learning and development—social, emotional, physical, and cognitive—as well as children's feelings and dispositions toward learning?
4. Does assessment provide useful information to teachers to help them do a better job?
5. Does the assessment procedure rely on teachers' regular and periodic observations and record keeping of children's everyday activities and performance so that results reflect children's behavior over time?
6. Does the assessment procedure occur as part of the ongoing life of the classroom rather than in an artificial, contrived context?
7. Is the assessment procedure performance-based, rather than only testing skills in isolation?
8. Does the assessment rely on multiple sources of information about children, such as collections of their work, results of teacher interviews and dialogues, as well as observations?
9. Does the assessment procedure reflect individual, cultural, and linguistic diversity? Is it free of cultural, language, and gender biases?
10. Do children appear comfortable and relaxed during assessment rather than tense or anxious?
11. Does the assessment procedure support parents' confidence in their children and their ability as parents rather than threaten or undermine parents' confidence?
12. Does the assessment examine children's strengths and capabilities rather than just their weaknesses or what they do not know?
13. Is the teacher the primary assessor, and are teachers adequately trained for this role?
14. Does the assessment procedure involve collaboration among teachers, children, administrators, and parents? Is information from parents used in planning instruction and evaluating children's learning? Are parents informed about assessment information?
15. Do children have an opportunity to reflect on and evaluate their own learning?
16. Are children assessed in supportive contexts to determine what they are capable of doing with assistance as well as what they can do independently?
17. Is there a systematic procedure for collecting assessment data that facilitates its use in planning instruction and communicating with parents?
18. Is there a regular procedure for communicating the results of assessment to parents in meaningful language, rather than letter or number grades, that reports children's individual progress?

Matching Assessment to Its Purposes

Decisions about assessment need to be made based on the purposes for assessment. Before you can decide how to measure your students' progress, you need to figure out why you are doing it. Are you trying to evaluate your teaching approaches? Are you trying to find out what individual children need to know so that you can teach each child more effectively? Do you want to know how much progress children in your class have made? Do you want to know about progress for individuals or for the group as a whole?

Answers to those questions will guide you in determining what information to collect and selecting the best approach to collecting it. You need current, detailed, descriptive data about individual children when your assessment purpose is to guide your teaching. You need a picture of children's accomplishments over time when you are documenting progress. If your purpose is to assess your teaching or your program, you only need sample data, and you don't need to gather information on every child.

Assessment decisions are also affected by who will receive the information. Are you needing assessment data to share with others or for your own use? Do you need to discuss the children's progress with their parents? What information and in what forms will be most informative for parents? Do you need information to pass along to the child's next teacher? Are you planning to share your observations with children to involve them in self-evaluation? What kinds of information will be useful for each of these audiences?

When you are thinking about communicating with others regarding children's learning, you need to consider whether numerical and statistical data is preferable to descriptive narratives and work samples. In the past, educators and the public have expected numerical comparisons of children in spite of the grave doubts about the usefulness and relevance of such data. Teachers are now learning to communicate with parents, school administrators, and each other in more meaningful terms. Anecdotal records, reading samples, writing samples, checklists, and a variety of observational evidence are now widely used and enthusiastically received. However, sometimes, you do need numbers; then the challenge becomes how to get them to reflect what you know about a child. Problems of accurately quantifying information about a qualitative process are central to the controversies surrounding assessment. Later in this chapter, we will present some suggestions about standardizing and quantifying the direct evidence of a child's learning.

Matching Assessment to Learning Processes

One essential assessment purpose is to gather information that will assist the teacher in providing optimal instruction for each child. A related goal is to increase the match between what is tested and the best information about what should be taught. Unless assessment is based on what children are learning, it is useless. Current recommendations for early literacy assessment (Geneshi, 1992; Hills, 1993; Kamii, 1990; Morrow & Smith, 1990) emphasize *performance assessment*—observing children in the process of learning. Isn't it fairly obvious that we can tell more about how children read by listening to them read than from tests which have little to do with actual reading?

The term *authentic assessment* has become popular for describing approaches that look at skills and knowledge actually in use (Johnston & Harmon, 1992). Kenneth Goodman, a leader in the whole language movement, takes the idea further and insists that in order to be authentic, assessment tasks must be "real ones that can and do occur in the real world outside of school" (Goodman, Bird, & Goodman, 1992, p. 2). Such a level of authenticity surely would eliminate tests of subskills unrecognizable as reading or writing. Marie Clay, originator of the term *emergent literacy*, agrees on the importance of assessing actual reading and writing but cautions that observations of children's literacy behaviors should include "all the behaviors the child produces on the task, including the comments he makes about what he is doing" (1993, p. 22).

Current recommendations for literacy assessment also use terms such as "situated assessment" (Teale, 1990) and "dynamic assessment" (Mason & Stewart, 1990). *Situated assessment* is another term for collecting data about a child's performance while that child actually is engaged in a real literacy activity. The goal is accurate information about what a child can do when pursuing a personally meaningful reading or writing task. Children are to be in a comfortable, familiar, pressure-free environment and therefore are more able to perform at their current normal level. They are also able to use the information normally available to them as they read and write. Whether you use the term performance assessment, authentic assessment, or situated assessment, the idea is that assessment tasks are the same activities used for developmentally appropriate and holistic literacy instruction (Barclay & Breheny, 1994).

The term *dynamic assessment* highlights the contrast between new assessment recommendations and the static approaches of traditional assessment. Static assessment limits the process to certain questions, to specified responses, and to limited tasks. Under static assessment, partially correct answers or unusual approaches to answers are not acceptable. This would rule out acceptance of the hypotheses children work with as they construct their knowledge of a subject. Dynamic assessment is a very different from static assessment. When teachers use information gathered from children's responses "to structure the next step of the assessment as well as to plan the next phase of instruction" (Mason & Stewart, 1990), they are implementing dynamic assessment. This approach frees the teacher to follow a child's line of reasoning during a teaching/assessment conference—the teacher's questions build on the child's responses and allow in-depth communication. Through this communication, teachers come to understand an individual child's learning process and can tailor learning experiences for the child. Clearly, dynamic assessment is most compatible with children's learning process and best assists it.

Ms. Montoya feels freed by these new recommendations. She feels free from having to drill students on test items and from teaching them how to take tests. She also feels free to combine teaching and assessment activities and, therefore, has more time for productive learning. The more she learns about children's processes of learning to read and write, the more confidence she has in her own ability to gather relevant data about children's progress.

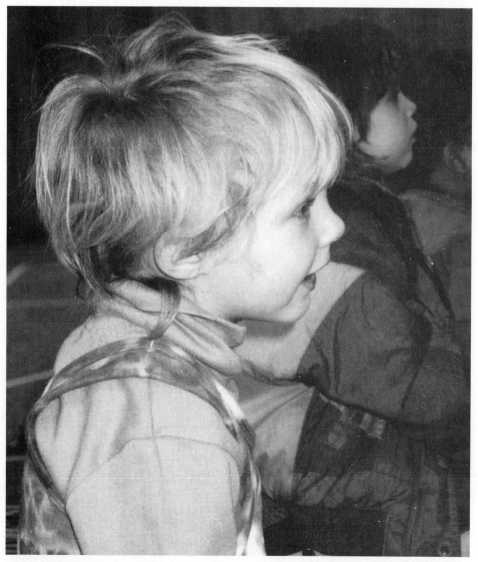

Performance assessment tasks are the same activities used for developmentally appropriate holistic literacy instruction.

Mrs. Thomas greatly values information that helps her to evaluate how well her teaching procedures are working for each child. She also is keenly aware of the importance of accountability in a first-grade class. However, she appreciates not having to put aside her goals for her students and give unrelated tests in order to get a numerical score for each one. Instead, she documents each child's progress through a series of informal assessment and data-collection processes. Using these approaches, Mrs. Thomas is able to simultaneously gather both formative and summative assessment data. *Formative data* gives her information about a child's current instructional needs and helps to form her teaching for that child. *Summative data* shows how far the student has progressed at this point. Both kinds of information are necessary.

ASSESSMENT COMPONENTS

Too often, assessment discussions make no distinction between the collection of data and the methods of recording it. Many people get confused and end up thinking that observation itself is assessment, or that portfolios themselves are assessment. Other times, assessment discussions focus on methods of collecting and recording data, but leave out the question of what it is that should be assessed. We hope that the following analysis helps you sort this out.

Determining Purpose

We see five components in assessment. The first is determining what it is you want to evaluate: Is it how Chantel's writing has progressed this school year, or what kinds of help Felicia needs in order to get past memorized reading, or do you want to know if your literacy program is working for your students in general? Thinking about what or why you are assessing helps you to decide what to look for during assessment.

Once you have decided what you are looking for, there are four further components of the assessment process: collecting data, recording it, organizing it, and analyzing it. In most cases, the assessment process is not complete without all these components.

COMPONENTS OF THE ASSESSMENT PROCESS

Determining purpose

Collecting information

Recording data

Organizing

Analyzing

Collecting Information

Let's look first at collecting information. Probably the most common way to collect data is by simply observing children as they read and write. Observation is highly recommended for assessment, but observation is not in itself an assessment approach. It is a way of collecting data for assessment. You still need to decide what it is you are observing for as well as how to record and organize that information in a useful manner. Work samples are another way of collecting information, especially about a child's progress over time. You still need to decide which samples are useful, what to look for as you analyze the samples, and how to interpret that information to others.

Conferences or interviews with children are also data collection situations. These one-on-one meetings utilize interactive conversations for collecting many different kinds of information. They lend themselves exceptionally well to assessment while teaching. As we describe conferences later in this chapter, you will see how teachers use them to simultaneously teach and assess reading and writing skills. Conference settings are also useful for collecting more structured data such as performance samples.

Tests are yet another method of collecting information. There are formal and informal tests, standard and nonstandard, norm-referenced and criterion-referenced, and published and teacher-made. Tests are just one part of assessment collection, not the entire process, as some believe. Like other data collection, tests must relate to what it is you need to know and why. Test data also requires recording, analysis and organization if it is to be useful to teachers.

Recording

Now let's look at recording assessment data. Keep in mind that recording is the process of putting the information you collect into a form that can be referred to at a later time. Checklists are popular for efficient assessment, but they are only a method of recording information, not an assessment method. You still need to know what you want to record, how you will gather that information, and what it means. The same is true for graphs and charts of progress or accomplishment.

Even collections of work samples require some recording: You at least need the date and the context in which it was produced. Additional comments about whether it was selected by the child or by the teacher and for what reasons are also useful. Photographs as well as audiotapes and videotapes offer some alternative ways to record children's learning, with the capability of recording learning processes rather than just the results.

Narrative reports and commentary about children's processes and behaviors while learning constitute another type of record keeping. These may be short, on-the-spot, anecdotal descriptions or reflective journal entries. The information used for these is collected while observing and interacting with children; like other records, they provide useful guidance only after careful analysis.

Detailed records of children's actual reading can be analyzed for information about specific strengths and weaknesses. Teachers use this information as a guide to teaching individual youngsters just the right things at the right time. *Running Records* (Clay, 1985) and *Miscue Analysis* formats (Goodman & Burke, 1972) are well-known standardized guides for this type of recording; other approaches have also been published (Chittenden & Courtney, 1989); and individual teachers frequently devise their own notation systems.

Test scores are also a record of a data collection process. When teachers grade tests, they are responsible for this recording; commercial tests usually let strangers do the recording. Either way, the teacher needs to analyze the recorded results and put them into perspective with other assessment measures.

Let's not forget children's own record keeping of their progress. These often include reading logs and may utilize the kinds of personal checklists and reflective questions suggested for children's self-evaluation later in this chapter.

Organizing

A portfolio is a common way to organize data. A portfolio can be used to display the information collected about an individual child's learning. Checklists, running records, reading logs, writing samples, test scores, photographs, audiotapes and videotapes, and anecdotal records all may end up in a child's portfolio. The teacher's task is to select those materials that provide the best picture of a child's current level of development as well as demonstrate the progress a child has made.

Typically, teachers collect and record information constantly, and organize it for portfolios periodically. (The impetus to update and organize portfolios usually comes at parent conference or report card time.) Portfolios provide a basis for parent conferences and progress reports. Most of the portfolio material used during the school year to guide teaching and to communicate with children and their parents is not sent on to the next teacher and does not become part of the child's permanent portfolio. Therefore, teachers must also decide what to include in the permanent portfolio.

Considerations involved in portfolio organization relate to sharing it with parents and other teachers, demonstrating progress over time, and putting different aspects of the child's development into proper perspective. Ease of finding or adding information is also relevant. The analysis components of the portfolio are significant. Not only do individual items require analysis, but a systematic review of all materials in relation to one another is necessary for understanding of a child's language.

Portfolio assessment has become a sort of rallying cry for holistic assessment movements. However, portfolios are primarily a means of organizing

Children's own record-keeping of their progress includes reading logs, personal check-lists, and reflective questions.

data and do not in themselves constitute an approach to assessment. You still need to determine what information you need to collect, how to collect it, and how to record it. Portfolios will be discussed in more detail later in the chapter.

Analyzing

"Observing and recording do not, by themselves, constitute assessment. Teachers must reflect on what they have observed and recorded in relation to program goals and objectives for each child" (Hills, 1993, p. 26). We are convinced that teachers' reflection on assessment data is the key to improving teaching.

You may think that teachers can't add anything more to their workloads and therefore cannot possibly analyze assessment data. However, in spite of frequently inhumane workloads, such analysis is already built into narrative progress reports and portfolio procedures. When teachers write reports to parents about children's progress, they are synthesizing all of the data they have collected since the last reporting period. Portfolios generally include a rating scale for placing a child on a continuum of literacy levels. Placing youngsters on this scale requires careful analysis of all relevant data. Often such rating is oral rather than written, and we hear teachers conducting fine analytical discussions with parents about the progress shown in children's work samples. Some teachers use frequent writing in their teaching journal to analyze what is happening in their classrooms. Analysis can and does happen; the quality of analysis depends on the teacher and also on the school district's allotment of time for such activity.

Ms. Montoya keeps in mind the various components of assessment and asks herself the following three questions: 1.) What has the child learned? This question helps focus on the content of assessment and distinguishes it from the processes or activities involved in learning. 2.) How do you know? Answering this question requires her reflective analysis that makes assessment data useful. 3.) How can you document it? This question evokes for the best way to record what she knows about a child's learning.

The idea of documenting that information implies that it will be shared with others and that the recording system must communicate.

THREE QUESTIONS FOR ASSESSMENT

1. What has the child learned?
2. How do you know?
3. How can you document it?

Individual Focus

The new approaches to literacy assessment require more focus on individual children rather than the total group. This might make some educators fearful of spending too much time on assessment. However, the beauty of these approaches is that for the most part, they are part of instruction rather than take time away from instruction. Statistics on the time spent administering formalized group tests versus the time required for informal individual assessment show that the time difference is small (Stallman & Pearson, 1990). Certainly, the time is well spent.

Mr. Larson finds that the individual nature of his assessment processes gives him helpful information about what each child considers important to learn and about personal learning strategies. In spite of the specificity of narrative descriptions of children's progress, Mr. Larson admits and accepts that he can never know exactly where each child is in every area. This is a comfortable position when children, rather than the teacher, direct their own learning.

Now that we have dissected assessment processes in an effort to provide better understanding, we will try to put them back together for you in the rest of this chapter. To understand authentic performance assessment, it must be viewed in context of the classroom and the instructional process. We begin with some examples of observation.

TEACHER OBSERVATION

Observation of children's actions serves as the basis of evaluation for most teachers. Observation checks the teacher's intuitive analysis of a child's needs; observations also can check whether to accept test results as valid or ignore them as inaccurate. Test data can never equal personal knowledge of a child's strengths, motivations, and personality.

Though teachers can hold an amazing amount of information in their heads, most teachers find that documenting their observations is more reliable. Ms. Montoya relies heavily on her anecdotal records to help her remember details of children's behaviors. She uses this format to make note of children's behaviors that she considers significant or that she wants to think about further. In order to make it easier to write down observations on the spur of the moment, she keeps a roll of self-sticking address labels in her pocket. She quickly writes her brief observations on these labels while she is busy with youngsters; at the end of the school day, she takes a few minutes to paste these into the appropriate children's folders. If she notices that a few children don't have many such notes in their folder, she realizes she may need to pay more attention to those youngsters. This system encourages paying attention to each student as an individual.

Mr. Larson acknowledges that his perceptions sometimes can be too subjective; they can be affected by personal feelings and extraneous pressures. Because of this, he too keeps an anecdotal file of his specific observations. He uses a card file with a section for each student. Mr. Larson records children's behaviors and his own comments here as often as he considers necessary. If Mr. Larson is concerned about a child, he might make a concerted effort to record daily behavior over a period to discover patterns or test his perceptions. For instance, he was worrying about Sue recently because she seemed to be asking for help constantly and was unable to work independently. When he kept a tally of her requests, he discovered that the number was decreasing. He then felt reassured.

Ms. Reynolds often observes youngsters interacting with literacy materials during dramatic play to find out what they know about functions and uses of written language (Teale, 1990). She watched them when the dramatic play area was set up as an airport and noticed who wrote pretend tickets on the ticket forms and who pretended to read the arrival charts and travel brochures. When the children play restaurant, she notices who pretends to write down orders on pads provided and who pretends to read the menus. These observations tell her a lot about children's levels of understanding and she makes anecdotal notes about each child's progress.

Ms. Montoya prefers to record her observations on checklists when she is observing with specific objectives in mind. When she wanted to find out about student recognition of letters, she prepared a checklist showing the names of each new student in her program down the side and each letter across the top. Then she set up an alphabet bingo game, invited the youngsters she wanted to assess, and asked an older child in the program to serve as "caller." Ms. Montoya observed the game and was able to record quickly which children had trouble recognizing which letters.

Standardized Recording

Ms. Montoya and her colleagues have been seeking models of checklists and rating scales to extend and validate their own ideas. Fortunately, research has begun to address these needs. The field of emergent literacy recently has spawned several rating scales to validate and regularize teacher observational data. Elizabeth Sulzby has created a classification scheme for describing children's emergent reading of favorite storybooks (see Table 8–1). The categories guide teachers in observing and documenting the extent to which a child can reproduce a story, the extent to which a child can use written language patterns rather than oral language patterns, and the extent to which a child attends to print rather than pictures in recreating a story (Sulzby & Barnhart, 1990).

Though the recording system and the categories of literacy behavior are given in Sulzby's plan, the situations for gathering the data depend on children's activities. Self-selected literacy events offer some of the most useful insights into children's literacy development. Therefore, when she sees Jazzmin in the playhouse reading a favorite story to a doll, Ms. Montoya listens to her story. She makes notes for a checklist derived from Sulzby's storybook reading categories. Ms. Montoya notes that Jazzmin's reading sounds like written language, even though the words she reads are not exactly those on the page. Her sentences are complete and context-free, unlike oral language. Jazzmin still uses picture clues to assist with story sequence, but she has progressed significantly since the start of the school year. In September,

TABLE 8–1
Sulzby's classification scheme for emergent reading

Broad Categories	Brief Explanation
☐ Attending to pictures Not forming stories	The child is "reading" by looking at the storybook's pictures. The child's speech is *just* about the picture in view: the child is not "weaving a story."
☐ Attending to pictures Forming oral stories	The child's speech weaves a story across the pages, but the wording and the intonation are like that of someone telling a story.
☐ Attending to pictures Reading and storytelling Mixed	The child's speech fluctuates between sounding like a storyteller with oral intonation and sounding like a reader, with reading intonation.
☐ Attending to pictures Forming written stories	The child's speech sounds as if the child is reading, both in the wording and intonation.
☐ Attending to print	The child is exploring the print by such strategies as (1) "refusing to read based on print awareness"; (2) "reading aspectually," using only some aspects of print; (3) "reading with strategies-imbalanced"; and (4) "reading independently" or "conventional reading."

From "The Developing Kindergarten: All Our Children Emerge as Writers and Readers" by E. Sulzby & J. Barnhart. In J. S. McKee (Ed.), *The Developing Kindergarten Programs, Children, and Teachers,* © 1990, p. 218. Reproduced by permission of Michigan Association of the Education of Young Children, Ann Arbor, Michigan.

Jazzmin's reading consisted of telling about the pictures on each page. Using Sulzby's classification, Ms. Montoya can document Jazzmin's emergent storybook-reading progress from the first category to the fourth.

The writing center is a good spot for Ms. Montoya to gather information about children's emergent writing progress and current understandings. She wants to watch and listen while children are creating their writing so that she can better interpret the strategies they employ. Not only does she gather data about children's views of composing written language, but she also can find out what they know about letter-sound relationships. She usually has to ask children to read their compositions to her in order to fully understand their intent. This understanding is necessary for analyzing the writing product.

When Ms. Montoya saw that Tuan and Reid were at the science table writing about their jack-o'-lantern's decomposition process, Ms. Montoya went over to watch. Each child was keeping a log recording changes in the pumpkin over time. Tuan wrote "It ss yky" and Reid wrote "Atc SApsg ckunh." Each boy proudly read his log entry to Ms. Montoya. Tuan's message was "It smells yucky," while Reid's was "It smells." Ms. Montoya recorded the

TABLE 8–2
Sulzby's classification scheme for forms of writing

Broad Categories	Brief Explanation
☐ Drawing	Check this form if the child draws one picture for the entire composition.
☐ Scribble/Wavy	Scribble is a continuous (or continuous with breaks) form without the definition of letters.
☐ Scribble/Letterlike	The child is using different forms within the scribble, and these forms have some of the features of letters.
☐ Letterlike Units	The forms may resemble letters, but they appear to be forms the child has created.
☐ Letters: Random	There is no evidence that the child made any letter-sound correspondences.
☐ Letters: Patterns	The child writes with letters that show repeated patterns.
☐ Letters: Name elements	Letters are from the child's first and/or last name.
☐ Copying	Here the child will copy from environmental print in the room.
☐ Invented spelling: Syllabic	The child uses only one letter per syllable (contains phonetic relationships between the sounds in the spoken words and the letters used).
☐ Invented spelling: Intermediate	The invented spelling between *syllabic* and *full.*
☐ Invented spelling: Full	There is a letter for all or almost all of the sounds in the spoken word.
☐ Conventional	The child uses conventional *correct,* or dictionary, spelling.
☐ Other	Mark this box if the child uses a writing system that does not fit the descriptions above.

Adapted from Elizabeth Sulzby, Appendix 2.1: "Forms of Writing and Rereading Example List," in Jana M. Mason (ed.), *Reading and Writing Connections*, Copyright © 1989 by Allyn and Bacon. Used with permission.

information gained from this observation on another checklist derived from Sulzby's research.

Sulzby offers teachers a classification system to guide observation and recording of children's writing strategies and their approaches to rereading what they wrote (see Tables 8–2 and 8–3). The classification system also covers whether the child attended to the print during the rereading. Twice-monthly recording of data is recommended for a continuous view of a child's development (Sulzby, Barnhart, & Hieshima, 1989). Using this system (see Table 8–2), Ms. Montoya recorded that Reid appeared to be using random letters and that Tuan demonstrated intermediate-level invented spelling. Like

TABLE 8–3

Sulzby's classification scheme for forms of rereading from independent writing

Broad Categories	Brief Explanation
☐ Not observed	In some instances, you will not have heard the child reread.
☐ Refusal	Check this if the child says, "I can't," shakes head repeatedly, etc., after you give numerous encouragements.
☐ "I didn't write."	This response is important enough to indicate separately.
☐ Labeling/describing	Check this response if the child labels items or describes items written or drawn.
☐ Dialogue	Check this if the child will respond only if you ask questions.
☐ Oral monologue	Check this if the child gives an orally told story in the intonation and wording of oral language.
☐ Written monologue	Check this if the child recites a story that is worded like written language and sounds like written language in intonation.
☐ Naming letters	This child makes an important move toward attending to print when she/he "reads" by simply naming the letters she/he has written.
☐ Aspectual/strategic reading	The child is attending to print but not yet reading conventionally.
☐ Conventional	The child is reading front print, conventionally.
☐ Other	Check this when the rereading does not fit the other categories.

From "Forms of Writing and Rereading from Writing: A Preliminary Report" (Technical Report No. 20) by E. Sulzby, J. Barnhart, and J. Hieshima. In J. Mason (Ed.), *Reading and Writing Connections,* 1989, Newton, MA: Allyn and Bacon.

most writing samples, Tuan's is difficult to classify because it includes conventional spelling along with examples of both syllabic and full invented spelling. Using a checklist with Sulzby's rereading categories (see Table 8–3), Ms. Montoya recorded that Reid used a written monologue while Tuan was rereading at a conventional level.

Though teachers can create their own categories for observation, communication between teachers will be enhanced if they use the same categories with the same criteria. Such common ground is needed if observational data is to be used and disseminated broadly. For instance, if Paul moves to another city, his new teacher would better understand the records Ms. Montoya sends if both teachers use the Sulzby categories. Establishing a common vocabulary and approach to observational assessment also will help

Observing a child's response during an authentic literacy event such as storytime can give teachers useful information about a child's level of literacy.

administrators and school board members to understand and view these records as reliable assessment data. As long as each teacher is presenting different kinds of records, it will be hard for parents, school administrators, and the public to understand them.

However, we are convinced that teachers must not have standardized observation or recording categories forced on them. Teachers must be able to select assessment formats that reflect their teaching approaches and goals. Without this teacher choice, it is possible that standardized observation could create barriers to learning and authentic assessment similar to those created by standardized tests. With this caution in mind, we present further examples of data collection and recording systems which offer possibilities for standardizing the process.

Marie Clay is the author of several widely used performance samples (1993). The most well-known is called *Concepts about Print* and checks such understandings as directionality and sequence of print. The performance sample is done with one child at a time and consists of discussing and reading specific small books written by Clay. An added feature of these standardized tasks is that Clay has normed them and tested them for reliability and validity. These features allow the observational data resulting from the tasks to be reported in numerical form. Though the numbers don't help you to teach better, the raw data you collect to arrive at the numerical figures is still beneficial. Clay is suggesting a way to appease number crunchers and still use observational assessment.

Clay's running record notation system (1985, 1993) is another standardized documentation system. The running record offers information for a detailed analysis of the reading strategies used and not used by an individual child. Teachers find such analyses rich in useful information about how to guide a young reader. Running record notes are typically recorded during a reading conference and will be discussed further in the conferencing section of this chapter.

Among other contributions to standardized observational assessment are the *Work Sampling System* (Meisels, 1993); the *Measurement and Planning*

Test data can never equal a teacher's personal knowledge of a child's strengths, motivations, and personality.

System (Bergen & Feld, 1993); and the *Child Observation Record* (Schwein-hart, 1993). All focus on a broad spectrum of learning and development, including language and literacy. We believe that each offers significant bene-fits and each has limitations or drawbacks. One major drawback is that none provide in-depth analysis of the processes of learning, but only general indi-cators of progress. Thus, these systems contribute only to reporting progress, but do not give sufficient detail to guide teaching. As Clay (1993) would say, these systems all give us the score at the end of the game, but little guidance on how to improve play during the game.

Each of these assessment systems is based on a developmentally appro-priate view of emerging literacy processes. These views are built into the observations and are explained as part of the assessment materials. An important benefit of adopting these systems would be to focus teacher obser-vation and administrative attention on developmentally appropriate learning processes.

These three systems recommend observation during authentic learning activities, including spontaneous play. They are all designed for data collec-tion during natural teacher interactions with youngsters, either individually or in groups. Each system includes teacher training in observation and recording procedures.

All provide specific categories for systematic observation that result in a progress report summarizing a child's accomplishments. Using any of these assessment systems involves purchasing materials for recording observations and generating progress reports. The Work Sampling System and the Child Observation Record (COR) allow the teacher to analyze and summarize data onto the forms provided. Both of these programs include teacher narrative reports as part of the records. In contrast, the Measurement and Planning System (MAPS) includes optical scanning, database management, statistical analysis, and reporting capabilities. We believe that this is too much "help." These services remove the teacher from the data analysis process and reduce the benefits for improved teaching and learning.

The Work Sampling System is the only one of the three that follows chil-dren into the primary grades. It has components for children ranging from three-year-old preschoolers through fourth grade. However, each level is strictly separate from the others, without provision for differences among youngsters of the same age. The MAPS and COR systems are designed for children in preschool and kindergarten and were originally developed for use in Head Start programs.

Observing Reading

Because we are interested in assessment for improving instruction as well as for reporting progress, let us return to examples of how teachers observe in order to assist children's learning. Once children have begun to read some-what independently, effective teaching requires detailed information about the reading strategies used by each child. Mr. Larson even takes notes about how children spend both their reading time and their time for choosing reading material. He keeps track of which children quickly begin reading and which ones seem continually distracted by other things. He notices if a child idly thumbs through books with no apparent purpose in selecting or reading anything. He also considers reading behaviors outside of class to be significant. He wants to know if his students check books out at the school or local library and if they are reading at home.

All this information guides Mr. Larson in selecting the most appropriate strategy to encourage and assist each child's literacy development. He knows that he cannot force a child to want to read or write, but he must figure out how to help each child find personal meaning and satisfaction in those activities. Mrs. Williams also observes her students during silent reading for clues about their reading processes. She watches and makes note of the behaviors using the following criteria (see Independent Reading Observation Guide).

INDEPENDENT READING OBSERVATION GUIDE

1. Is the child engrossed in the reading?
2. Is the child distracted? If so, by what?
3. How long does the child stay involved?
4. Is involvement time increasing or decreasing?
5. Does the child move his or her lips during silent reading?
6. Does the child ask for assistance?
7. From whom is assistance asked?
8. Does the child ask for help with words only or also about ideas expressed?
9. Are the words that the child can't read difficult to understand in context?
10. Does the child occasionally laugh or otherwise respond while reading silently?
11. How rapidly does the child turn pages?
    - So slowly as to indicate subvocalizing?
    - So rapidly as to indicate skimming?
    - So irregularly as to imply carefully reading selected portions?

Information gained from these observations guides Mrs. Williams as she plans activities for her students. Mrs. Williams also has developed a reading behavior checklist that she distilled from the list of goals shown in the Independent Reading Observation Guide.

Observing Writing

Having kids write is one of Mr. Larson's primary goals. When he observes children writing, he has an additional set of specific goals in mind. He looks for children's progress toward the aims shown in the Writing Goals. Mr. Lar-

Effective teaching requires detailed information about the reading strategies used by each child.

son is convinced that if children can attain the first two goals, they will be successful in reaching the others. When a child shows little progress in writing, Mr. Larson first looks for problems with the child's progress toward the first and second goals—finding satisfaction in writing and recognizing a variety of purposes for writing.

WRITING GOALS

1. Find satisfaction in writing.
2. Recognize a variety of purposes for writing.
3. Select their own topics for writing.
4. Increase fluency and time spent writing.
5. Communicate thoughts, feelings, and information.
6. Expand vocabulary and use of varied sentence patterns.
7. Take into account their audience.
8. Develop their own style.
9. Build plot and characters into story writing.
10. Develop an ability to express themselves poetically.
11. Begin to use writing-process strategies.

Mr. Larson and Mrs. Williams have filled dozens of notebooks with anecdotal records of their students' actions, triumphs, and difficulties. They have found that they can make more sense of the data if they summarize it in some form of checksheet. This year, Mr. Larson experimented with a general checksheet, shown in Figure 8–1, to document writing development. He knows that children do not develop writing strategies in a specific sequence, so he is not concerned with the seemingly haphazard growth that Casey shows between September and December. Mr. Larson will continue to use this checksheet to summarize his observations throughout the year. Casey's mother is interested in Mr. Larson's checksheet because it reflects the changes she noticed in the papers Casey brought home.

In teaching her third graders to use the writing process, Mrs. Williams found that a progress sheet (see Figure 8–2) is useful to both her and the children in demonstrating how youngsters learn to use various parts of the formal writing process. In conference, Mrs. Williams is careful to remind children that revision and editing are necessary only for a few selected writings. When children decide to polish a paper, the checksheet is useful in reminding them of the steps they might follow.

Mr. Larson and Mrs. Williams are both wary of published checklists that seem to dictate what a child is supposed to learn; they choose to make their own lists based on what they see happening in their own class-

FIGURE 8–1
Writing development

Writing Development

	Sept	Oct	Nov	Dec	Jan	Feb	Mar	April	May	June
Writes	barely	+	+	+						
Enjoys writing	no	no	yes!	+						
Chooses topics	no	yes	yes	no						
Time writing	3 min.	10 min.	8 min.	15 min.						
Keeps a journal	begins a journal	no	yes	solicits response						
Expresses ideas or feelings		yes		yes						
Forms used	journal	story report	+ poem letter							
Sees purposes	?	?								
Plays w/ language	–	–	–	yes						

FIGURE 8–2

A checksheet such as this helps both teacher and student to be aware of progress in using the stages of the writing process.

Progress in Using the Writing Process

Mollie can	Sept	Oct	Nov					
Select own topic	✓	✓	✓					
Know purpose	✓	✓	✓					
Consider audience			✓					
Keep a writing folder	✓	✓	✓					
Do prewrite activities								
Talk with others	✓	✓	✓					
Bubble, outline			✓					
Fast-write/draft	✓	✓	✓					
Participate in a response group		✓						
Share own writing								
Respond to others								
Request a conference		✓	✓					
Make revisions								
Add								
Delete								
Change								
Reorganize								
Copyread								
Publish								
Evaluate self								

rooms. However, they are aware that no teacher could document all of the strategies a child uses or all of the goals a child reaches. There are just too many, and besides, these teachers are not interested in breaking down reading and writing into tiny steps like reading and language programs did in the past.

Determined not to get sidetracked by details such as how many phonics rules children know, Mrs. Williams keeps a clear idea of the general literacy goals for her students as she assesses their progress. These long-range goals are generally accepted by all educators, but in the past they often got lost in the crunch of test scores.

LITERACY GOALS IN A WHOLE LANGUAGE PROGRAM

- To enjoy reading and writing
- To frequently choose to read and write
- To read with increasing depth of understanding
- To write with increasing fluency, accuracy, and style

CONFERENCES FOR ASSESSMENT

As you've seen in the preceding chapters, individual conferences with children about their reading and writing provide opportunity for assessment of many literacy concepts and skills. While the primary focus of the conferences is instructional, the performance-based assessment procedures make assessment and instruction complementary parts of the same activity.

Ms. Reynolds and Mrs. Hanna start this process casually in preschool and kindergarten just by answering questions or stopping to talk with individual children about what they are working on. Mrs. Thomas begins scheduling planned official conference sessions with her first graders as they individually arrive at the "Aha, I can read!" stage. By second and third grade, all children should be able to profit from regular one-on-one sessions to discuss their reading and writing with the teacher.

Ms. Montoya meets in individual conferences with all the students in her multiage group class of beginning kindergartners through second graders. The content of these meetings varies with each child's level of literacy. Ms. Montoya uses a variety of record keeping systems to keep track of information gathered during conferences: checklists of skills, running records (see Figure 8–3), and narrative notes . Conferences provide Ms. Montoya opportunities for individualized performance sampling and record keep-

FIGURE 8–3
A teacher's adaptation of a running record reflecting data collected during an instructional conference.

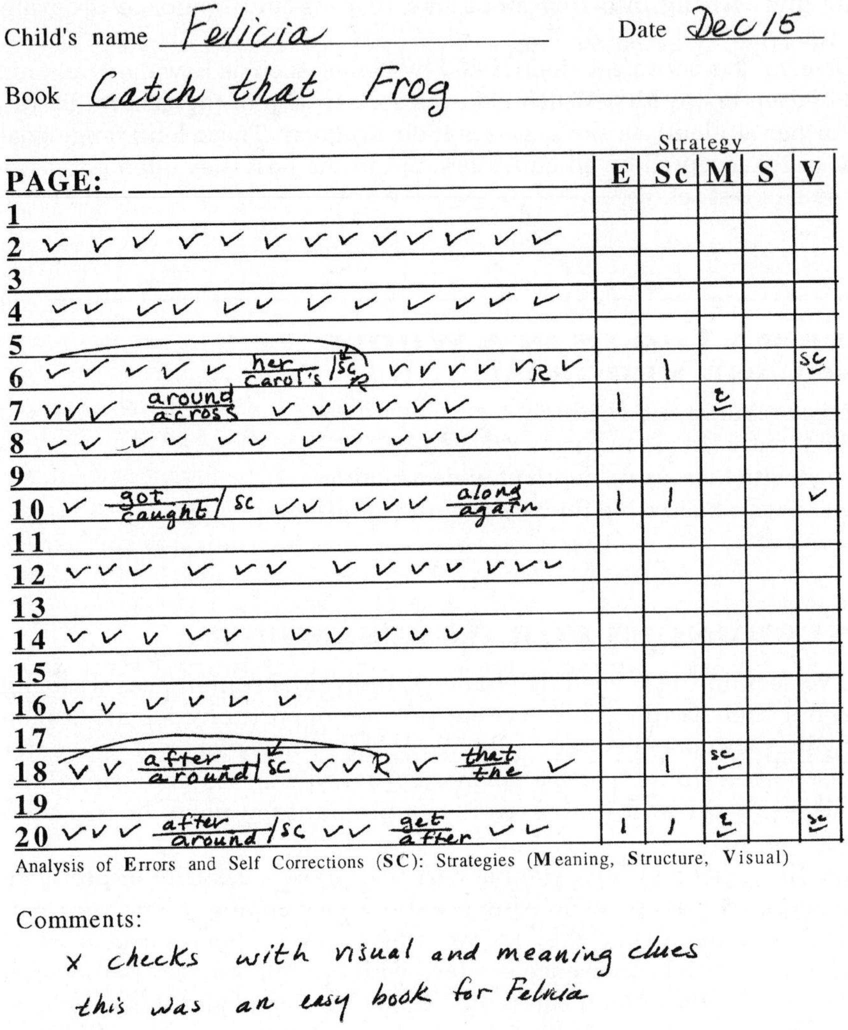

Child's name *Felicia*   Date *Dec 15*

Book *Catch that Frog*

				Strategy	
PAGE:	**E**	**Sc**	**M**	**S**	**V**
1					
2 ✓ ✓ ✓ ✓ ✓ ✓ ✓ ✓ ✓ ✓ ✓ ✓ ✓					
3					
4 ✓ ✓ ✓ ✓ ✓ ✓ ✓ ✓ ✓ ✓ ✓					
5					
6 ✓ ✓ ✓ ✓ her/Carol's sc ✓ ✓ ✓ ✓ R ✓		1			sc
7 ✓✓✓ around/across ✓ ✓ ✓ ✓ ✓	1		1		
8 ✓ ✓ ✓ ✓ ✓ ✓ ✓ ✓ ✓ ✓ ✓					
9					
10 ✓ got/caught/sc ✓ ✓ ✓ ✓ ✓ along/again	1	1			✓
11					
12 ✓✓✓ ✓ ✓✓ ✓ ✓ ✓ ✓ ✓✓✓					
13					
14 ✓ ✓ ✓ ✓ ✓ ✓ ✓ ✓ ✓ ✓					
15					
16 ✓ ✓ ✓ ✓ ✓ ✓					
17					
18 ✓ ✓ after/around/sc ✓ ✓ R ✓ that/the ✓		1			sc
19					
20 ✓ ✓ ✓ after/around/sc ✓ ✓ get/after ✓ ✓	1	1	1		sc

Analysis of Errors and Self Corrections (SC): Strategies (Meaning, Structure, Visual)

Comments:

x checks with visual and meaning clues
this was an easy book for Felicia

Adapted from Marie Clay's work.

ing. With emergent readers, a conference can be a time for listening to and analyzing a child's rereading of a book from story time. With beginning readers, Ms. Montoya listens to them read aloud and frequently keeps a running record of correct and incorrect responses to her questions. She has been trained in recording and analyzing data according to the Reading Recovery system devised by Marie Clay (1985, 1993). With more proficient readers, conferences can be times to discuss the plot of a book in progress. No matter what a child's level of understanding, Ms. Montoya encourages all her students to write and to discuss their writing with her.

At the beginning of the school year, Mr. Larson wanted to find out some baseline information about his students' development in literacy. He had portfolios passed to him from the first grade teacher, but he also had new students coming into his class. Because records did not accompany all the transfer children, and their test scores contained information useless for teaching, Mr. Larson depended on both observation and two informal tests that he easily could give during conferences—the *informal reading inventory* (IRI) and *writing analysis*.

Informal Reading Inventory

The IRI evaluates a child's oral and silent reading of unfamiliar passages at various levels of difficulty. Oral reading gives indications of a child's reading strategies. Answering questions about a silent reading passage demonstrates general levels of reading comprehension. Mr. Larson learned to give and interpret IRIs by studying and applying several different published forms. Over the years, he found that each of these tests varied in its reading passages and instructions, but that the underlying principles of each were the same.

Reading strategies are determined by the teacher's recording and analyzing the deviations from text that a child makes while reading aloud. Comprehension is evaluated through the child's answers to questions following the silent reading. Children are encouraged to read passages of increasing difficulty until the material is clearly too difficult. The teacher then takes the data and makes decisions about the levels of difficulty where the child can understand the text comfortably. The teacher can analyze the words that a child miscalled during oral reading by using a process called *miscue analysis,* which was developed by Yetta Goodman and Carolyn Burke in *Reading Miscue Inventory Manual: Procedure for Diagnosis and Evaluation* (1972). Teachers can categorize a child's errors by whether the misreadings sound or look like the original words (graphophonemic clues), whether the substitutions make sense in the text (semantic clues), and whether changes make sense grammatically (syntactic clues).

Mr. Larson finds that informal reading inventories and error analysis are very useful diagnostic processes. They help him to track the child's thinking and give him some idea why the errors are occurring. This is more useful information than merely knowing that the child made a mistake.

Mr. Larson no longer purchases published informal reading inventories. Many of them have passages that have no relationship to his students' experience, and others rely on inadequate questions. Instead, he just chooses material from books he has in the room—the textbooks that are supposed to represent various grade levels work well. Today it is Ron's turn, and Mr. Larson has chosen passages that he thinks Ron will find easy, challenging, and difficult. After Ron silently reads a selection, Mr. Larson asks him questions about it because he wants to find out whether Ron understands that passage well enough to organize ideas, make inferences, evaluate critically, or apply ideas to other situations.

After experiencing success at one level, Ron is able to face more difficult challenges. Mr. Larson tells him the next reading selections are pretty hard and that he just wants to see if Ron can do them. This preparation prevents Ron from feeling like a failure if he isn't successful with all the material. When Ron's responses indicate that he hasn't understood all that he has read, Mr. Larson asks Ron to read the passage aloud to him so that he can identify the cause of the confusion.

As Ron reads aloud, Mr. Larson records his reading performance on a photocopy of the same passage. Mr. Larson doesn't worry when Ron miscalls a word that makes sense in the story. When Ron confuses the words *the* and *their*, he is so intent on making meaning from the selection that this minor miscue makes no impact on the message of the passages. Later, however, when he consistently misreads *money* for *monster* and *detergent* for *detective*, Mr. Larson is concerned and makes a note that Ron is not paying attention to meaning and contextual clues.

The informal reading inventory gives Mr. Larson more valuable information than any standardized test. He knows not only the approximate level of reading difficulty at which Ron can read independently, but also that sometimes Ron overrelies on phonics. Mr. Larson will use these results as baseline information on Ron's reading ability at the beginning of second grade.

By making a careful record of Ron's oral reading, Mr. Larson can evaluate Ron's reading growth over the school year ahead. He can have Ron reread the same text later in the year and again record miscue information. Ron most likely will show improvement which can be clearly documented on a chart or graph. If Ron does not show improvement, Mr. Larson will have good cause for concern.

Writing Analysis

Just as Mr. Larson takes reading samples from his new second graders, he also takes writing samples. On the first day of school, he asks them to write about anything they wish to. For those who don't know what to write, Mr. Larson provides a brief experience and warm-up and invites them to respond in writing. The resulting papers provide baseline information on each child's writing development. This year, Mr. Larson uses a new check-

FIGURE 8–4

Mr. Larson evaluated a short story that María Elena wrote on the first day of school. Later, he can evaluate other papers María Elena writes and use these checksheets to make comparisons.

Writing: First day of school   Name _María_

Topic _toy_

no Self selects topic

yes Logical development of topic

yes Uses sensory, <u>descriptive</u>, or affective language

no Uses complete sentences

some Shows knowledge of paragraphs

$21/74$ % Invented spelling

/% Standard spelling

sheet that he designed. The checksheet (see Figure 8–4) shows simply how Mr. Larson described María Elena's paper on her favorite toy in terms of the writing content and mechanics. This paper will be filed in María Elena's portfolio for comparison later in the school year. From time to time, Mr. Larson will use his checksheet to evaluate other individual papers. Because he knows he cannot attend to all aspects of writing development, Mr. Larson has chosen to study only a few; as you can see from Figure 8–4, he's particularly interested in the transition from invented to conventional spelling.

Some teachers use a sample of children's writing early in the school year much in the same way that Mr. Larson uses the repeated reading method. Mrs. Thomas keeps copies of children's stories from the beginning of the school year. She is careful to have the children read them aloud to her if she can't understand their writing and then keeps these translations in their portfolios. Later in the year, she or her aide will dictate this transcription to the child, who rewrites the story as she or he hears it. Then the original and dictated versions of the story are compared. It is easy for Mrs. Thomas to point out growth in mechanics and spelling. Mrs. Thomas, along with the children and parents, is amazed at the progress these comparisons show.

IDEAS FOR ASSESSING WRITING
Observe and Gather Data

Teacher
- watches children writing daily
- conferences weekly with each student
- collects writing samples

Children
- seek responses from teacher and peers
- collect writing samples

Keep Records

Teacher
- uses a notebook or file to keep notes on conferences
- assembles portfolios for all children
- utilizes checklists and writing samples to document development

Children
- keep daily logs of writing
- use a writing folder to hold fastwrites and drafts

Analyze and Organize

Teacher
- organizes portfolio materials to document growth
- occasionally analyzes writing pieces in depth
- summarizes development, maintaining a positive attitude

Children
- participate in the evaluation process
- set own goals
- participate in response groups and conferences

Mrs. Williams uses a more complex form of holistic writing assessment with her third graders. During the school year, she often develops class projects that will help children to learn specific types of writing. This year, in conjunction with a yearlong effort to help children to summarize and find main ideas, she and her students wrote movie and television show reviews. After reading and sharing reviews from newspapers and magazines, Mrs. Williams and the children decided that a good review must include a brief outline of the story and an evaluation of how good the story was. Several children also decided that they wanted to learn to write better paragraphs and to use quotation marks correctly. From this input, Mrs. Williams designed an evaluation guide (often called a *primary trait rubric*) that she and the children could use as a guideline for writing and then evaluating television, book, and movie reviews (see Figure 8–5). Over the year, as the children wrote more reviews, they used the evaluation format to see their progress in communicating a message and improving their ability to use paragraphs.

Notice that Mrs. Williams designed the evaluation procedure so that content is more important than the mechanics. Mrs. Williams has designed primary trait rubrics for evaluating business letters and research reports as well. She knows that this type of evaluation takes time to execute and should be used sparingly, and only on polished writings. It is most effective when used with high-quality examples of the writing form the class is learning so that the children can see where they are headed. If the children have input in preparing their own evaluation form, they can better use it as a guideline in their writing.

FIGURE 8–5
A primary trait rubric puts emphasis on content while covering mechanics of writing.

Rubric for_____Lori_____ Date__Feb 26___

"Review"

Story outline
    Brief and clear   20
    Clear, but too long   (15)
    Not clear   10
    Not there   0
Evaluation
    Stated, with good reasons why   20
    Stated, with poor reasons why   15
    Stated, not supported   (10)
    Not stated   0

Paragraphs
    Used, indented, stick to topic   5
    Used, indented   (2)
    Not used correctly   0

Quotation marks used correctly   (5)
Quotation marks needed   0
                    /32

PORTFOLIOS

If you have children, you probably have done as we have: You keep baby books that record significant events in your children's lives. We recorded the eruption of teeth, first words, visits to the doctor, and first steps. When our babies grew into toddlers, we began to collect papers with scribbles they'd made with crayons and to jot down favorite books and playthings. Over the years, these treasures have filled boxes kept on closet shelves. Every once in a while, we bring down the boxes and sort through these treasures, marveling at how our children have grown and changed. Do you remember how you waited to hear the first word or how you worried that your child would never crawl? Later, we look at our children and are amused that we ever worried that they'd grow up!

Teachers who use holistic teaching approaches are now keeping similar records of their students' growth, for similar reasons (Roskos & Neuman, 1994). They find that by collecting and organizing a set of materials over a school year, they easily can document growth in literacy as well as other areas of the curriculum. All the primary teachers at Joey and Amy's school worked together to develop a portfolio system that functions much like those boxes on the closet shelf—only their containers are large folders of documents and examples of each child's work.

Portfolios help parents see exactly what their children have accomplished.

All of the primary teachers at Mrs. Hanna's school keep a portfolio on every child and find it invaluable testament to growth. Teachers, parents, and children can use the materials in a portfolio to document progress. At the end of a school year, parents can take much of the materials home, but enough will be retained in the portfolios to inform the next teachers. Those children who are lucky enough to complete all their primary grades here will leave third grade with portfolios that clearly show their growth in literacy over a four-year span. Teachers in upper grades are considering whether to continue the portfolios when the students reach their classrooms.

Different school districts organize language arts portfolios differently, but most of them include a rating scale that provides a summary of each child's progress (Stewart, Aegerter, Davis, & Wasketh, 1993). The conclusions reflected in the rating scale are supported by the rest of the portfolio contents—narrative observations, samples of writing and responses to literature, examples of books read, audiotapes of oral reading, test results, teacher-made checklists, and student records of reading and writing. We believe that individual teachers need the freedom to select portfolio entries that are meaningful to them and to their students. Otherwise, portfolio assessment can become nearly as impersonal and unrelated to the classroom as standardized tests.

Joey's folder from second grade includes a fastwrite he did the first day of school, as well as a polished report with several drafts stapled to it. Joey's list of favorite books is in there, too, as well as a Polaroid photograph of his chart about chickens. Mr. Larson included a writing behavior checklist that he designed and that has entries for four months. There also is a copy of Joey's scores on the standardized achievement test that the school district requires. Just like the baby book, this portfolio contains information on special events in Joey's development. Joey's writing sample documents the first time he carried the writing process through all of its stages. Joey's book list shows that he has begun to read nonfiction as well as fiction stories. The writing behavior checklist indicates when Joey began to try to write poems, and it also shows his progress in transitional spelling and use of mechanical conventions.

Mr. Larson finds that portfolios are easy to share with Joey's parents. During conferences, parents see exactly what their children have accomplished, rather than try to interpret seemingly meaningless test scores. Children can take ownership of their portfolios, too—Joey enjoys selecting material to add to his. When Joey seems especially proud of something he's done, Mr. Larson invites him to compare it with earlier work. Joey beams with pride as he submits his first poem or when he notices that he has learned to write in paragraphs.

Mrs. Hanna has been recording and storing much of her portfolio data on her computer. This solves some of the storage problems and is efficient for generating reports from her records. For instance, when her checklists are done on spreadsheets, she can merge checklist material from different students to give comparison data when needed. After typing her anecdotal notes into the computer, she can later electronically copy parts of those records for narrative summaries. Her school will get a scanner soon that will allow her to copy photos and artwork as part of the computer record. Mrs. Hanna looks forward to that but has heard that such graphics quickly fill up computer memory. The site-based management team at her school is discussing whether to invest in CD-ROM technology to supplement computer storage capabilities.

She has been using portfolios for several years and it is clear to Mrs. Hanna that they offer an excellent method of demonstrating a child's development regardless of whether she stores the information on a computer or in a box under her desk. Portfolios documenting literacy development have been so successful that her school district now encourages their use for all areas of the curriculum.

SELF-EVALUATION FOR CHILDREN AND TEACHERS

Self-reflection is valuable in both learning and teaching. If you wish children to become autonomous self-motivated learners, you must encourage their reflection on their learning (Crafton & Burke, 1994). As an autonomous self-motivated teacher, you will feel more confident and better able to articulate your teaching approaches as a result of your self-reflection.

Child Self-Evaluation

Children have a responsibility to keep records as part of their self-directed learning and as part of their role in self-evaluation. For example, the cumulative files of sample writings clearly show children how far they have come since the beginning of the school year. Mr. Larson provides a bottom cabinet drawer with a folder for each child to file writing samples. The top file drawer contains his notes from conferences in individual file folders. Children have access to their own files, but not to those of anyone else.

Journal writing samples, with dated entries, are themselves records of children's progress. Youngsters also can use their journals to note relevant information, such as the name of a book just finished or a reaction to a book. Children also can use their journals to record other reading- and writing-related activities, such as reading a story to a kindergarten child, making up a skit and sharing it with the class, completing a mural project about a book, or writing a poem for Mom's birthday. Records kept by both student and teacher are an important guide during teacher-pupil conferences and for parent conferences.

Mrs. Williams encourages her students to keep daily logs of their reading and writing activities at the front of their journals. In this way, both she and the students have a record of how they used their time each day. She also encourages them to keep a list of possible writing topics and books they would like to read. As a guide to self-evaluation of writing, Mr. Larson has developed a set of questions for children to ask themselves. His students can read these questions from a chart in the conference area.

GUIDE TO SELF-EVALUATION OF WRITING

Am I writing more now than I was before?

Do I like most of what I write?

What have I written besides stories?

Can other people understand what I write?

Mr. Larson and Mrs. Williams also encourage all of their students to keep records of the books they have read. In Mrs. Williams's record sheet, shown in Figure 8–6, Kirsten "graded" the books she read. Kirsten keeps this record sheet in her own language arts folder. This year, Mrs. Williams's class participated in the Read-a-thon, and Kirsten found that keeping a book list helped her to estimate how many books she usually reads each month. She was surprised to find that she reads several books each week.

Mr. Larson never makes charts for the classroom that compare numbers of books read by students. He knows this would promote unnecessary comparison between the children. He prefers students to keep their own records of their reading. When Carlos first began "really reading," Mr. Larson helped him to make a chart to keep track of the minutes he read each day at school. Carlos was so impressed with the time he could concentrate that he also kept track of the minutes he read at home and the minutes he watched television.

The culmination of student self-evaluation and record keeping comes at parent conference time. Mr. Larson and Mrs. Williams have student-led parent conferences—the child is in charge when the parents come to school to find out about their child's progress. Each child carefully prepares for the parent conference through discussions with the teacher and by teacher-child collaboration on updating the portfolio.

Juan is very proud and serious when his parents arrive for their conference. He has carefully organized his portfolio materials and has a clear idea of his accomplishments as well as the areas where he needs to work or learn more. Because his parents are more comfortable speaking Spanish, he conducts the conference in Spanish rather than English. Mr. Larson is in the room and available to respond to questions, but he does not sit down with Juan and his parents. At first, he tried to have student-led conferences while he was sitting right beside the child, but they resulted in the child and the parents talking to him instead of to one another. He has learned the wisdom of having several simultaneous parent conferences. This allows him to be

FIGURE 8–6

Children easily can keep track of their own reading.

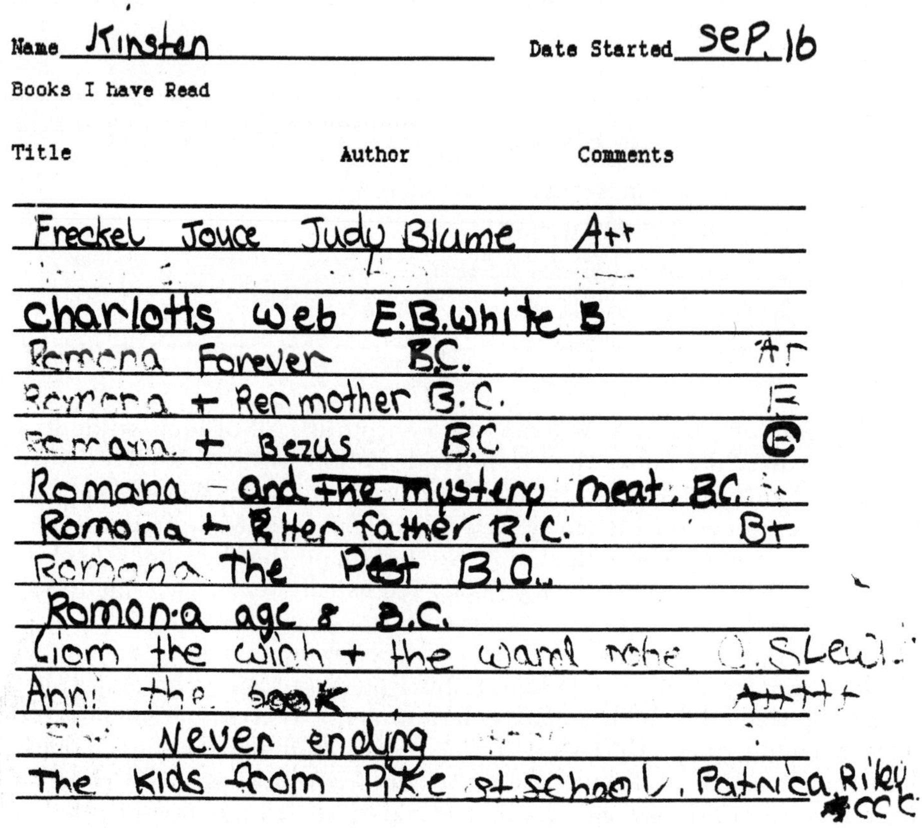

Name _Kirsten_   Date Started _Sep. 16_

Books I have Read

Title	Author	Comments
Freckel Jouce	Judy Blume	A++
charlotts web	E.B.white	B
Remona Forever	B.C.	A+
Remona + Rer mother	B.C.	E
Remana + Bezus	B.C	C
Romana - and the mystery meat	B.C.	
Romona + Her father	B.C.	B+
Romona the Pest	B.C.	
Romona age 8	B.C.	
Liom the wich + the warml rohe	C.S.Lewl.	
Anni the book		A+++++
The Never ending		
The kids from Pike st. school	Patricia Riley	CCC

accessible but not to hover, and makes the conferences truly student-led. Now Mr. Larson schedules four or five parent conferences for up to a full hour at the same time, instead of four fifteen-minute conferences per hour. Parent response to this system has been generally very favorable.

Evaluating Your Program and Your Teaching

Whatever your students' strengths and weaknesses, you will want to continuously evaluate your ongoing program. An ongoing journal can help you record and process day-to-day events. The end of the school year calls for an in-depth look at what really happened to the children in your care—what they accomplished on their way to becoming responsible, contributing citizens.

You will want to analyze your efforts in helping them to move toward confidence in their own thinking, in their ability to identify a problem, and in their approaches to solving it. How much more responsibility are they taking in their own actions, for their learning, for initiating useful suggestions and activities, for providing needed assistance to others? How much more clearly and effectively can they talk to others, write for useful purposes, and write for their own satisfaction? How far have they progressed toward becoming life-long readers?

Input on these and other questions may include comments from parents, any school personnel, and children themselves. The answers to these questions will vary with each individual. A teacher needs to consider each issue for each child to get a complete picture.

For you, other questions arise: How much more able am I to listen to children, to what they really mean? How much more confidence have I developed in children's abilities to learn, to think, to be self-directed, and to be responsible? How much more often do I raise challenging questions rather than make instructional statements? How effectively have I been able to integrate the language arts, thus saving time and making learning more effective? How much more capably have I used language skills as an effective tool in the total school curriculum? In some school districts, this type of self-assessment has led to a "teacher researcher" movement that encourages dialog between teachers. This facilitates self-analysis and ultimately results in better teaching.

Teachers need to be able to evaluate their own ability to listen to children and to hear what they mean.

CONCLUSION

Though there isn't agreement on the format, most recommendations for emergent literacy assessment support the value of recording observations of common classroom activity periods. Early childhood and emergent literacy experts agree that children's abilities are indicated more accurately by their performances in familiar situations than their performances in artificial testing situations. Children's behaviors during literacy events such as story time, independent reading, writing, and choice time tell teachers most of what they need to know about individual children's levels of understanding. Individually focused conferences offer further opportunity for observing, recording, and analyzing a child's learning process and progress. Several published systematic observation and recording systems offer models for standardizing and quantifying observational data.

Portfolios provide a way to keep track of a child's accomplishments by organizing all relevant data collected. When portfolios are carefully planned and skillfully used, the children, teachers, and parents feel a sense of accomplishment. The analysis of information in a portfolio can give teachers useful feedback about a child's learning problems and about the effectiveness of the curriculum.

DISCUSSION QUESTIONS

1. Discuss the pros and cons of teacher-made versus standardized forms of collecting, recording, and communicating information about a child's progress.
2. A parent complains at a parent-teacher conference about being shown a portfolio rather than a graded report card. If you were the teacher, how would you explain?

SUGGESTED FOLLOW-UP ACTIVITIES

1. Use a published informal reading inventory to assess the general reading abilities of several children. When you feel comfortable with this, assemble and administer your own IRI using passages you select yourself from texts or trade books.
2. Analyze errors a child has made during oral reading into categories of those that change meaning and those that do not. If desired, consult Marie Clay's book, *An Observation Survey of Early Literacy Achievement* (1993), or *Reading Miscue Inventory Manual: Procedure for Diagnosis and Evaluation* (Goodman & Burke, 1972) for further information on error analysis.
3. Observe children reading silently. Note behavior and expressions that indicate comprehension and attitude toward the material.

4.   Assist a teacher in assembling a reading or writing portfolio. If possible, sit in on a parent conference where the portfolio is used.

5.   Observe a child's writing behavior, and then fill in a copy of Mr. Larson's checklist of writing development (see Figure 8–1) with your data. Or observe a child's ability to use the writing process, and fill in a copy of Mrs. William's progress sheet (see Figure 8–2) with your data. Or design a checklist of writing development of your own.

6.   Analyze an individual piece of writing to find out percentages of invented spelling compared with standard spelling. Do you see any patterns in the types of words that are spelled the standard way?

7.   Try out the checklists using the Sulzby categories reprinted in this chapter (Tables 8–1, 8–2, and 8–3) to guide and document your observations of a child's emerging literacy. Analyze this experience for convenience and accuracy of information.

RECOMMENDED FURTHER READING

Periodicals

Hills, T. W. (1993). Assessment in context—Teachers and children at work. *Young Children, 48*(5), 20–28.

Roskos, K. A., & Neuman, S. B. (1994). Of scribbles, schemas, and storybooks: Using literacy albums to document young children's literacy growth. *Young Children, 49*(2), 78–85.

Sulzby, E. (1991). Assessment of emergent literacy: Storybook reading. *The Reading Teacher. 44*(7) 498–500.

Teale, W. H. (1988). Developmentally appropriate assessment of reading and writing in the early childhood classroom. *The Elementary School Journal, 89*(2), 173–183.

Books

Clay, M. (1993). *An observation survey of early literacy achievement.* Portsmouth, NH: Heinemann.

Geneshi, C. (Ed.). (1992). *Ways of assessing children and curriculum.* New York: Teacher's College Press.

Goodman, K. S., Bird, L. M., & Goodman, Y. M. (1992). *The whole language catalogue: Supplement on authentic assessment.* Columbus, OH: SRA Macmillan/McGraw-Hill.

Kamii, C. (Ed.) (1990). *Achievement testing in the early grades: The games grownups play.* Washington DC: National Association for the Education of Young Children.

CHAPTER

9

SELECTING EARLY LITERACY MATERIALS

Tell a child WHAT *to think, and you make him a slave to your knowledge. Teach him* HOW *to think, and you make all knowledge his slave.*

HENRY A. TAITT, 1982

In this chapter, we're going to look at materials for young readers. We'll start with libraries and the types of trade books most relevant for beginning readers. Then we'll analyze commercial reading programs and technology products. We recommend that teachers select their materials from many sources and not limit their choices to one program or publishing company.

CHOOSING TRADE BOOKS

We can divide the types of books found in schools that support a literature program into two basic categories: textbooks and trade books. Remember that textbooks are sold as sets of materials and that their basic intent is to instruct. Trade books, on the other hand, generally are purchased and used individually. Laypeople generally know trade books as library books. In this section, we'll look at how library books are made available in school and classroom libraries. We'll also briefly introduce the types of trade books that are essential to a literacy program for young children.

The School Library

Making the library a focal point of the curriculum has been a gradual process at Mr. Larson's school. He remembers when Mrs. Sanders, the school librarian, not only had to run the library, but also had to select and order all the books, teach library skill lessons, and do read-aloud programs by herself. Back in those days, the children went to the library during the teachers' planning time, so that even if he went to the library with his class, Mr. Larson had very little time to talk with the librarian. When the school district adopted the literature-based reading program, a group of teachers and librarians pressed the school board to provide additional support for the school libraries. This included library aides to assist with ordering, checkout, and shelving routines; cataloging; and new book processing. The teachers' planning time was reorganized so they could work more effectively with the librarian and be with the children during library time. Funds that were formerly used for workbooks and other consumable textbook materials were diverted into books for the library. Since the change to reading more library books than basal texts, the library has had to expand and the adjacent classroom was remodeled to accommodate more shelving, an audiovisual area, and work tables for children. Now the library is an inviting place, always open, always busy, and always filled with plenty of reading materials: This is the focal point for the school's literature program. All of the teachers consider Mrs. Sanders as a teacher first and as a resource person, as well as their school librarian.

When a class comes to use the library, Mrs. Sanders and the teacher have had adequate planning time together to prepare the lesson. Mr. Larson now feels that he and Mrs. Sanders team teach much of the second-grade literature program, and he is relieved to have such an accessible resource person. Mrs. Sanders always reads or tells a story when each class comes in, and she was the one who convinced Mr. Larson to learn to tell stories himself.

Every class in the school visits once a week for formal library instruction, and Mrs. Sanders also has an open-door policy for individual children who show that they can use the library responsibly. Teachers find they love having a workplace outside of their classrooms for special projects. This

The school library is the center of a holistic literacy program.

library is far from that old stereotype of the quiet, dusty place where noise was admonished. Instead, the library has become a focal point of the school (Carletti, Girard, & Willing, 1991).

Mrs. Sanders also sees the library as the heart of support for the overall curriculum of the school. She asks teachers to request books or topics that they need to complement their studies. Mrs. Sanders sees herself as a reading teacher and as a school leader in the development of literature-based curriculum. She believes that a well-stocked library is absolutely necessary for a constructivist holistic literacy program, and constantly lobbies for better funding and support. Luckily, her principal is supportive and diverts a large portion of the school's materials budget her way.

Mr. Larson and his colleagues remember trying to set up an independent reading program before the school library was expanded and remodeled. It was difficult at best—a true literature-based independent reading program has to be supported by lots of available books in an environment that invites children.

Children's Literature That Supports Emergent and Beginning Readers

When you think of library books for young readers, do you remember the bins or shelves of picture books in the library? Do you think of Dr. Seuss or Mike Mulligan and his steam shovel? These classic images of trade books are still accurate, but they make up only a fraction of the books that are available today for emergent and beginning readers.

Thousands of trade books are published every year. Among these are expensive hardback illustrated storybooks that truly are works of art, inexpensive paperbacks that are meant to be consumed after a few uses, and everything in between. We cannot give you a course on children's literature here, but instead will discuss several types of books that are essential to a constructivist literacy program for young children. We recommend *Children's Literature in the Elementary Classroom* (1993) by Charlotte Huck et al. for a comprehensive look at the field of children's literature.

"Baby Books"

Today's children *literally* can cut their teeth on children's books. Books for babies, of course, are not designed for them to read, but simply for familiarity with books. Bright, familiar pictures in simple formats capture the interest of very young children, and heavy, nontoxic cardboard, soft plastic, and strong cloth characterize books that hold together even after repeated "tastings." Books for babies obviously are designed for home or child care use, not for school settings. They have an important effect on later schooling, however, in that they familiarize the youngest children with books. Children who have experienced such materials will understand that books carry meaningful and enjoyable messages inside. They also will become familiar with some beginning book handling knowledge—how to turn pages, directionality, and making choices. If you haven't already done so, we recommend a visit to a children's bookstore to look at the baby section. We think you'll be charmed by the works of Eric Hill, Helen Oxenbury, Jose Aruego, and scores of others. Incidentally, the local reading association that Mrs. Thomas and other teachers belong to has an ongoing service project in their community. Each new baby born in the local hospital is presented with a bag containing a baby book and literature for the parents on introducing books to their babies.

Picture Books

Large-format, thin books with both illustrations and text are probably the most familiar for young children. The range of types of picture books is wide, and we will discuss here the types of picture books that Ms. Reynolds, Mrs. Thomas, Mrs. Sanders, and their colleagues choose for young children.

ALPHABET BOOKS

You probably think of alphabet books when you think of young children. Alphabet books are a part of a larger class of picture books, the *concept books*. These books teach simple concepts such as colors, numbers, shapes, and the ABCs. As you know, we are not advocates of "letter-of-the-week" alphabet programs, but we do recognize that children can learn something about letters from alphabet books.

The best alphabet books contain illustrations that relate clearly to each letter of the alphabet, text that makes sense, and sometimes even a story line. We particularly like alphabet books that invite continued inquiry, such as *On Market Street* (Lobel, 1981), which shows market vendors, each hawking items related to a different letter, and *The Caribou Alphabet* (Owens, 1988), which gives both scientific and cultural information about caribou in rhyming, narrative format. Books like these allow children to construct their knowledge about letters within a fascinating context.

WORDLESS PICTURE BOOKS

These unique books have very little or no text. They are often humorous, with piquant illustrations. They can be as simple as Helen Oxenbury's *Good Night, Good Morning* (1982), which shows, in eight simple pictures, a child's nighttime routine. On the other hand, some wordless books are extremely sophisticated, as in *Good Dog, Carl* (Day, 1985). In this book and its sequels, Carl, a large black dog with more than doglike intelligence, cares for a baby while the mother is out. Their improbable adventures in familiar settings, which range from swimming in the fish tank to a ride down the laundry chute, delight both children and adults. Wordless books give children power to "read" on their own and demand that children interact with the story. They also are wonderful to use in school for oral language development.

EVERYBODY BOOKS

Many picture books are not meant for children to read to themselves! This may surprise you until you compare the text and the concepts presented in picture books with the reading abilities of young children. We now call these books *everybody books*, because adults can read them aloud, emergent readers can listen to them, and more proficient readers may enjoy them on their own. Generally, the text presents the story or information without regard to beginning reading ability. As a result, the language is often eloquent and the stories complex. Consider a favorite of ours, *Miss Rumphius* (Cooney, 1982), which traces the life of an unmarried librarian who travels the world trying to live up to her father's advice to "make the world a more beautiful place." In the end, she returns home and sprinkles the countryside with lupin seeds, leaving her legacy behind her. In *Sweet Clara and the Freedom Quilt* (Hopkinson, 1993), a young girl sews the map of the Underground Railroad into a quilt that she leaves behind when she escapes to her freedom. Such books are sophisticated in story, illustrated with works of art, and rich and beautiful in language. Luckily for those of us who often read aloud to our students or our own children, the books are so good that they are a joy to read over and over again.

PREDICTABLE BOOKS

As you browse through the everybody book, or picture book, sections in Mrs. Sanders' library, you also will find picture books that young children can read themselves. *Predictable books* make heavy use of pictures as clues to the story, as well as predictable story patterns, questions, cumulative sequences, and children's songs and rhymes. *Have You Seen My Cat?* by Eric Carle (1987) has only two sentences—the title, and the answer "This is not my cat," but carries a complete story line through pictures showing a child looking for his lost cat, not only at home and in the neighborhood, but also in the jungle, mountains, and zoo. In *Five Little Monkeys Jumping on the Bed* (Christelow, 1989), a predictable pattern and silly illustrations lead the young readers through a mama's tribulations in getting her little ones to bed:

> Then . . . five little monkeys jumped on the bed!
> One fell off and bumped his head.
> The mama called the doctor. The doctor said,
> "No more monkeys jumping on the bed!"
> So four little monkeys . . . jumped on the bed.

Can you tell what will happen next? Can you imagine the fun an emergent reader has with a book like this? Can you see how text like this will aid a youngster in constructing ideas about reading, about the story, and even about phonics?

EASY-TO-READ BOOKS

Traditionally, we think of books with controlled vocabulary, large print, and short sentences when we think of easy-to-read books. The characters in the best of these, such as Dr. Seuss's *The Cat in the Hat*, (Geisel, 1957); Arnold Lobel's *Frog and Toad Are Friends* (1970) and *Frog and Toad Are Together* (1972); Else Minarik's *Little Bear* (1957); and Russell Hoban's *Frances* series (1960–1980) have stood the test of time, in spite of sometimes contrived and unusual language. The worst of the easy-to-read books, fortunately, largely have been replaced in school and classroom libraries with paperback books designed especially for beginning readers. When you visit a children's bookstore or library, look for books from the following series: Parents Magazine Read-Aloud Originals, Scholastic Hello Reading Books, Bank Street Ready-to-Read Books, Random House Picturebook Readers, Dial Easy-to-Read Books, Children's Press New True Books, and Dell Yearling Books. You will find a wide variety of fiction, nonfiction, and folktales with beginning reading levels, good illustrations, and captivating stories and topics. For example, in *Three by the Sea*, Edward Marshall (1981) has three first graders each tell a story while they're digesting their lunches before going swimming. The stories are humorous and short and use normal language patterns—perfect for a young reader to read aloud. Mrs. Sanders, Mrs. Thomas, and Mr. Larson fill their classroom libraries with such books. They are inexpensive, popular, and, while possibly not fine literature, surely good books for youngsters beginning to "really read." For more information on sources and a list of predictable and easy-to-read books, we recommend *Real Books for Reading* by Hart-Hewins and Wells (1990). In addition, journals such as *The Reading Teacher* and *The New Advocate* publish monthly reviews of notable books for young readers.

BIG BOOKS

We have mentioned in previous chapters that many fine children's picture books are published in large format. These are marketed both as trade books and as textbooks. If you've not seen a Big Book, be sure to locate one in a primary classroom. You may be surprised that they are *really* big. Most teachers purchase an easel or use the chalk tray to hold these books, and use a pointer to enhance group reading. Young children also enjoy the large format, whether in groups or reading on their own.

Chapter and Information Books

By the time children are in second or third grade, their tastes usually have graduated to books shelved in the library as juvenile fiction and nonfiction. They may begin their chapter book reading with something their teacher has read aloud to them: maybe *Charlotte's Web* (White, 1952) or a *Ramona* book by Beverly Cleary (1968, 1977). Teachers of the upper primary and middle grades must continue the practice of reading aloud to their classes every day,

Many fine children's books are published as Big Books as well as in regular formats.

not only to share wonderful stories and beautiful language with the whole group, but also to introduce young readers to authors, topics, and genres that they will enjoy in the future.

With so many kinds of books and so many choices, it is essential that every whole language teacher build a classroom library that serves as an addition to the resources of the school and public libraries (Fractor, Woodruff,

Martinez, & Teale, 1993). In the following section, we'll look at how Mr. Larson tackled that task.

Building a Classroom Library

Mr. Larson is always on the lookout for books that will interest each of the children in his class. In fact, one of the first things he does each school year is to find what his students like by giving them an interest inventory to fill out. He keeps these inventories (Figure 9–1) in front of the children's folders to help to remind him of their likes and dislikes. The inventories help Mr. Larson to suggest books or writing topics. Of course, by the end of the school year, Mr. Larson knows the students so well he no longer needs these checksheets.

Any environment that fosters independent reading of literature must be rich with books. Mr. Larson has worked hard to collect an adequate number of books to make up his classroom library. The year he started his library, he aimed for five to eight books per child. Since then he has amassed hundreds of books and has a group of parents and friends who continue to help him gather books.

Mr. Larson subscribes to the Troll Book Club and Scholastic Book Club and encourages the children in his class to order paperbacks each month. For a certain number of books the children buy, Mr. Larson is able to order free books. He has used this system to obtain sets of especially good books that groups of children might enjoy reading together. This year, he received six copies each of *Frog and Toad Are Friends; Amelia Bedelia* (Parish, 1963); *Charlotte's Web; Hailstones and Halibut Bones* (O'Neill, 1961); and *Dr. DeSoto* (Steig, 1982). Seth has requested *Runaway Ralph* (Cleary, 1970) for the next set that Mr. Larson orders.

Mr. Larson and several of his students' mothers are always on the lookout for children's books at garage sales, secondhand stores, and library sales. This year at the school carnival, the librarian had a booth with old books she had weeded from her collection for sale. Mr. Larson bought about 25 books at 50 cents each, including old but serviceable copies of *Stone Soup* (Brown, M., 1947); *Harry the Dirty Dog* (Zion, 1956); and *Curious George* (Rey, 1941, 1952). Later, Linda's mother spent a morning sorting through the books, discarding those with missing pages, and taping and recovering the remaining books.

The bottom shelf of the classroom library is devoted to serial books such as Encyclopedia Brown, Oz, and Nancy Drew. These belonged to Mr. Larson's neighbor's son and daughter when they were in elementary school. These are very popular with second graders because of their predictable characters and plots. Mr. Larson even asks former students when they visit him if they have any donations for his library.

Mr. Larson subscribes to *Ranger Rick* and *Highlights for Children,* children's periodicals that are interesting to second graders. *Ranger Rick* is full of science articles and beautiful photographs; *Highlights* is an excellent source of new short stories. Parents often contribute magazines to the periodicals

FIGURE 9–1
An informal reading inventory gives teachers a general idea of their students' interests.

Name _____

Interest Inventory

Check the 5 things you like best:

___ snowshoeing	___ movie stars	___ airplanes
___ skiing	___ singers	___ cooking
___ sledding	___ drawing	___ animals
___ ice skating	___ jokes	___ dinosaurs
___ roller skating	___ hiking	___ plants
___ soccer	___ ballet	___ birds
___ football	___ dolls	___ cameras
___ hockey	___ stars	___ singing
___ basketball	___ space	___ puzzles
___ baseball	___ video games	___ pioneers
___ swimming	___ computers	___ fishing
___ running	___ TV	___ painting
___ karate	___ radio	___ pets

What was the best book you've ever read?

If you could buy a book, what would you buy?

What book would you like to read?

section, and Mr. Larson brings in the newspaper every day. Materials in the periodicals section change all the time, but when Mr. Larson finds an article or story that he especially likes, he cuts it out, laminates it, and keeps it in a file for future years. His "Chicken and Egg" file has articles from *National Geographic, Scientific American,* and *Farm Journal,* as well as a list of books about chickens and eggs.

Mr. Larson finds that many children want to read the kinds of books found in the grocery store. These books may not be high-quality literature, but the short books printed on inexpensive paper, sticker books, Garfield books, and comic books provide a source of reading entertainment and are acceptable as a type of reading. Mr. Larson knows that his job is to help children to expand their reading taste beyond such books. Many youngsters are fascinated by reference books and encyclopedias. *The Guinness Book of World Records* (McWhirter, 1994) is a standard favorite and is published each year. The Golden Book encyclopedias have entries written at a level most primary-

The classroom library offers books written by children in the class as well as a selection of fiction and nonfiction trade books.

grade children can understand. Some children are interested in using dictionaries; one that seems to be useful for second graders is *The Clear and Simple Thesaurus Dictionary* (Wittles, 1972). A stack of nature guides, including Roger Tory Peterson's *Field Guide to the Birds* (1961), is used constantly.

Another shelf in the class library holds books the class has written themselves. One is about Carolina's trip to Mexico, another includes stories about the class's trip to the zoo, and a group is working right now on their book about the hatching of the chicks. These books, beautifully bound, decorated, and laminated, are very popular with second graders. At the end of the school year, a couple of the best will be donated to the school library, and the rest will go home with individual children.

Because Mr. Larson has focused on inexpensive, homemade, or free reading materials, he still has some money in his book budget for trade books. However, the field of children's literature is overwhelming to him, and he often has difficulty choosing what to buy. So he has narrowed his choices to two type of books for his collection. First, he buys new books that are especially popular with second graders. He can rely on ideas from the "Young Readers' Choice" list that is published each October in *The Reading Teacher,* the journal of the International Reading Association for elementary teachers. He buys about fifteen books a year from this list. For nonfiction books, Mr. Larson focuses on his personal interest in the outdoors and chooses books about camping, nature, weather, and survival. Several other teachers in the building have pet topics: Mr. McCormick likes books about art, Mrs. Williams buys winter sports books, and Ms. Butters has a large collection of books about whales. When Mr. Larson's class expressed interest in learning more about whales, he knew Ms. Butters would lend them her collection of whale books.

When Mr. Larson stopped using sets of basal readers, he couldn't imagine just throwing away books that had some good literature in them. So he kept a few copies of each of the various levels of books from several reading series and shelved them with the storybooks. He also didn't want to give up the plays, poems, and choral readings that were so popular with the second graders, so he marked materials he wanted to save and asked Linda's mother to cut them out from the discarded basals with a razor blade. She then bound the pages in a spiral binder and Mr. Larson invited children to illustrate the cardboard covers after they had read, discussed, and written about the poems or plays. There are now dozens of sets of these materials, and small groups of children love to use them to read plays or to give choral readings or readers' theater presentations.

Rich classroom libraries like these allow every child to have plenty of materials to choose from during reading time. The classroom library often is most useful when a child wants to find something to read right away or needs to look something up quickly. The library nook also serves as a comfortable, relaxed, and quiet place where you can almost always find someone reading contentedly.

Libraries as a source of reading material can dramatically improve the teaching and learning of reading; however, using library books instead of basal readers sometimes is only a superficial change. Some teachers are so programmed from years with basal texts and teachers guides that even when they give them up in favor of library books, they use the library books just as they used the basal readers. They beat the literature to death with the multitude of questions, lessons, and assignments they always have used. They are "basalizing the literature" without the help of a teacher's guide.

Resource Guides and Literature Units

Resource guides and literature units offer sources of inspiration to teachers as they plan a curriculum around trade books. Not surprisingly, the quality of such publications varies greatly, as does the level of whole language understanding demonstrated in them. They can be critiqued through most of the same criteria we set out for analyzing reading programs in the following section.

We have been impressed with the *Bookshelf: Teacher's Resource Book* (Scholastic, 1986), an Australian import. It works from the premise "that literacy develops naturally through meaningful, functional use" (p. 4). Long explanations of why this approach is better than others are not needed in a country that is used to doing it this way. This resource series utilizes oral-language learning as the model for written-language learning. It celebrates approximations of intent rather than expecting beginners to use conventional forms of literacy.

Respect for both teachers and children permeates this guide. Besides respecting children as individuals in the skill acquisition process, it also respects children's choice for reading and writing topics. Even its terminology demonstrates a different attitude: Instead of saying "have" children do something, it suggests that teachers "invite" or "encourage" children. There is no sacred sequence of books to be covered and there is no one way to introduce an activity or read a story. It is assumed that teachers are competent and do not need a script to follow.

The *Whole Language Sourcebook* (Baskwill & Whitman, 1986) comes in a loose-leaf three-ring binder as an invitation to teacher additions and adaptations. The authors demonstrate their respect for teachers by writing "Don't let our catalog of routines stop you from improvising and inventing new ones. Use your imagination and inspiration to devise variations . . . and create new ones to fit your own needs" (p. 39). This approach empowers teachers rather than controls them.

No space is wasted in the *Whole Language Sourcebook* telling teachers how to read a story or how to talk to kids. Instead, it is packed full of helpful hints, such as how to help children to make pop-up books for their writing and how to encourage ideas for readers' theater. Suggestions for teachers represent a wide variety of literacy events and make it clear that there is no way to run out of functional uses for reading and writing. This guide is not selling a collection of books to keep you and children out of the library, nor is it selling blank pages bound into journals. Instead, it helps teachers to empower children with ownership in choosing their own reading and in writing their own ideas.

We hope that many teachers are using *Once Upon a Time . . . An Encyclopedia for Successfully Using Literature with Young Children* (Hurst, 1990). This resource book presents hundreds of worthwhile children's books and organizes them by author, by theme, and by subject. Each book is accompanied by a list of related literature and a short list of relevant activities for children. We think this offers just enough help for the teacher and just enough extension activities for youngsters. There is still room for teacher initiative and still time left for reading. A set of *Literature-Based Thematic Units* by the same author (Hurst, 1992) offers the same set of advantages.

With the current emphasis on literature-based curriculum, there are many books being sold to help teachers plan activities. Many try too hard to be helpful and end up offering enough ideas to beat to death any piece of literature. Many also reach too far in their efforts to come up with activities across the curriculum: A great number of the activities are not worth doing and do not enhance children's understandings in any way. Teachers need to carefully pick and choose among ideas offered from any source.

ANALYZING READING PROGRAMS

We constantly see advertisements for new reading instruction programs that ensure success for all children. Many new or improved reading programs guarantee success by following their "recipes." With all these claims, how does the teacher or curriculum committee decide which approach to choose?

Review reading programs and check whether they do the following:

- Allow construction of knowledge
- Utilize play and experiences
- Encourage oral language
- Incorporate story time
- Utilize high-quality literature
- Include nonfiction reading
- Encourage purposeful writing
- Teach skills in context
- Authentically integrate curriculum
- Utilize performance-based assessment
- Respect teachers
- Respect all children

The Wright Group reading materials from New Zealand can be found in most classrooms for young readers. Similar kinds of beginning reading books are now available from other publishers.

To make this decision more confusing, all programs have the same goal—for children to become proficient readers. Also, most make statements about the importance of helping children to succeed and to enjoy reading. Most offer attractive and colorful formats for children and time-saving, packaged teaching aids for teachers. In practice, the large textbook companies, with their array of readers, workbooks, drill sheets, flash cards, record keeping forms, and tests, have long dictated how reading is taught in the United States.

A look into classrooms suggests that many teachers are rebelling against the old cookbook approach to teaching. More and more are selecting their own eclectic mix of reading materials and children's literature. The Wright Group reading materials from New Zealand have found their way into most classrooms for young children and have significantly influenced U.S. publishers. The move toward authentic literature for reading instruction also has drastically altered reading textbooks. Instead of basals, we now have literature anthologies, Big Books, little books, journals, and trade books. With the widespread move to whole language approaches, most materials now are advertised as being whole language materials. These claims are made with varying degrees of accuracy.

Because the conflicting advertising claims are so confusing, we recommend a systematic analysis of reading programs. Start with the basic principles of sound reading instruction and check each program against those criteria. We caution against just accepting the publisher's claims for the program: The material often doesn't live up to the aspirations. You need to check for yourself. For our analysis, we used the reading instruction principles explained in this text and created a checklist to record our findings.

Allow Construction of Knowledge

Following the organization of this book, we begin our analysis with criteria explained in Chapter 1. Where complex understandings are involved, are children allowed to construct their knowledge in personally meaningful ways? We recognize the existence of social/conventional knowledge that can be told to children, but make a distinction between that kind of information and the intricate web of relationships involved in logico-mathematical kinds of knowledge. As explained previously, the names of letters is social knowledge, but the relationship between letters and meaningful communication through print must be individually constructed.

Creating such relationships is a thoughtful, reflective process requiring unpressured time for thought and experimentation. Teachers' guides that prescribe a rapid-fire series of questions with specific right answers are antithetical to thoughtful reflection. Open-ended questions to provoke thought without expectations for specific or immediate answers are the kind that encourage construction of knowledge. The "answers" may come months later and will be different for each learner. Most questions and discussion topics suggested in teachers' guides focus on immediate answers. However, the Scott, Foresman Kindergarten *Celebrate Reading* Units (Morrow & Sulzby, 1993) frequently suggest that youngsters work together and explain their ideas to one another. This sort of activity encourages the thought processes for constructing knowledge.

The time needed for thought and experimentation is rarely built into any program. In fact, our culture rarely allows for reflective processes and makes it difficult to justify in school. Quick, superficial reactions with immediately observable products generally are valued over deeper thought involving sustained focus. Worksheets and teacher-centered lessons too often get in the way of real learning. New reading programs still suggest multitudes of nonreading and nonwriting busywork. Though the practice of having each child read aloud in turn (round-robin reading) is no longer recommended, teacher guides still assume that youngsters are reading with a group under the teacher's supervision. This requires that everyone moves along at the same pace and discourages personal thought processes. In contrast, reading a self-selected book alone or with a good friend offers opportunity for self-

Adequate time for thought and experimentation is rarely part of a reading program.

paced processing of the reading experience. Most programs acknowledge that this type of reading is useful, but treat it more as something to do if there is time than as an essential learning activity.

Though the specific suggestions in teachers' guides are not generally compatible with construction of knowledge, the introductory materials for new reading programs describe the teaching and learning processes in constructivist terms. Most reading programs recruit respected experts in the field to serve as official authors, and the material written by these persons offers teaching advice that reflects the most current research in the field. However, it usually appears that this advice is not clearly understood by staff writers who prepare the actual teacher guide lesson. Morrow and Sulzby, authors of the Scott, Foresman *Celebrate Reading* kindergarten program (1993), seem to have had more impact on program materials than is usual. Not only is their Instructional Handbook an excellent overview of emergent literacy and developmentally appropriate teaching, but the recommended activities in accompanying kindergarten units are consistent with the overview.

Utilize Play and Experiences

In Chapter 2, we explained the role of play and experiences in emergent literacy. Except for the Sulzby and Morrow materials for Scott, Foresman, play is routinely ignored in reading programs. Even with these two emergent literacy experts explaining the importance of play and showing how to arrange classroom learning centers to accommodate it, Scott, Foresman's program schedule only shows it happening once a week and then only in extended-day kindergartens. However, play is cleverly incorporated into the program through materials that substitute for worksheets. These include a form for making out a shopping list while playing store, a form for taking pretend phone messages while playing house, and a secret code message form for pretend superheroes. Other reading programs seem to misunderstand play and consider the dramatic play center as a place for putting on plays. We thought that activity books might be related to play, but they mostly focus on paper and pencil or cut-and-paste "activities." Frequently, activity books are just fancy workbooks.

Experiences get a little more attention, especially as they relate to integrating the curriculum. Collecting and observing plants or bugs for science-related topics can enhance understanding of what is read, provide ideas for writing and increase understanding of the object studied. This is an example of useful and authentic curriculum integration. On the other hand, making caterpillars out of neckties stuffed with old pantyhose (add eyes and antennae) isn't likely to increase any kind of understanding. Teachers need to exercise professional judgment in choosing from the many ideas now offered for extending literature into theme units.

Encourage Oral Language

We discussed the relationship of oral language and written language development in Chapter 3 and emphasized that children need opportunities to talk. Talking is encouraged in most reading programs through a multitude of discussions and story reenactments. Children are asked to orally predict events and also to retell the plots in stories they encounter. They also are requested to share their favorite parts and to comment on the illustrations. However, child talk is mostly encouraged in structured and teacher-directed situations. Collaborative groups offer potential for more informal discussions, but often the teacher is directed to assign specific and limiting roles such as recorder and reporter to group members.

Recommendations for interpretive oral reading can enhance oral language development; certainly, preparing a reading selection to share with others is an improvement over round-robin reading. Interpretive oral reading offers a reason for reading aloud and an opportunity to practice for a successful performance. Songs, poems, and rhyming games suggested as extensions of reading also assist general language development. There are useful options to select from, but teachers may need to adapt suggestions so that children are free to direct their own involvement in the activities. Most teachers' guides still assume a teacher-centered rather than a child-centered classroom.

Incorporate Story Time

The importance of story time apparently is recognized widely. The programs we reviewed recommended books for teachers to read to children and usually sold them either separately or in read-aloud anthologies as part of the program. Although it is convenient for teachers not to have to search for books in the library, we worry that many wonderful books are overlooked when teachers have no reason to go to the library. We dislike read-aloud anthologies for the same reasons we dislike anthologies of stories for children to read: They dictate a sequence of reading unrelated to reader interest.

Some programs acknowledge the link between emergent reading and story time. Such teacher guides introduce a reading selection to children by having the teacher read it to them first. Often the teacher reads a Big Book version of a story with youngsters, making little-book versions available for emergent reading subsequently. As youngsters ponder the print in these books and relate it to the story their teacher read, they construct their understandings of written language.

Utilize High-Quality Literature

The big change in reading materials for youngsters is that there are a *lot* of good books for them to read. Because schools have been buying more children's books, more have been written. Of course, textbook publishers are concerned about their share of the market. Most publishing companies now offer anthologies of respected children's literature instead of the "made-for-reading-group" material you probably had to read as a child.

Where anthology selections are faithful to the original, they are a big improvement over old basal reader stories. The latest editions advertise that their literature selections are no longer adapted, but you need to compare with the originals to be sure. Until recently, the old monster "controlled vocabulary" reared its ugly head in reader anthologies, "adapting" good literature into predigested, tasteless, boring pap. The problem was the worst in

Preparing a reading selection to share with others provides beneficial oral reading practice.

books for the youngest readers: When editors assume that children know nothing about reading, they give them reading that is nothing.

We noticed that current adaptations tend to cut out illustrations rather than to change words. This cut publishers' costs, but sacrificed meaning where we saw it done. We found the story *Jimmy Lee Did It* (Cummins, 1985) in three different reading programs; two companies condensed the text onto fewer pages and eliminated nearly half the illustrations. Only McGraw-Hill's *A New View* (1993) presented the story with all the original illustrations. The illustrations are integral to the meaning of this story and much was lost in the editions in which they were omitted.

Illustrations are part of the predictability that emergent readers rely on to decipher books. For the most part, new reading materials recognize that predictable stories are required for beginners. The publishers now accept that controlled vocabulary actually made reading more difficult because it created unnatural language. Thus, new beginning reading materials are filled with lively pattern stories and old favorite tales and rhymes, giving youngsters the various kinds of predictability we described in Chapter 4.

Predictability is the basis for the little "instant readers" now common in kindergarten and first-grade classrooms. They rely heavily on picture clues to help youngsters figure out the words; some consist primarily of captions for the pictures. A combination of a repeated word pattern and picture clues allows a beginning reader to experience instant success. Predictable books from the Wright Group have helped young readers to get started since the early 1980s and other companies such as Scott, Foresman now are offering similar kinds of books. We are not suggesting that these are great literature, but they clearly offer children a great sense of achievement. Due to a creative use of illustration, some of them manage to convey a meaningful story or significant information in spite of limited text. Like other kinds of books, they vary in quality. Story time is greatly needed to supplement this kind of reading to ensure that children have models of rich language and high-quality literature.

It is much easier to find high-quality literature for experienced readers because they are able to read "real" books. Reading anthologies for older children offer wider choices and the publishers now are making more attempts to be true to the original books. The importance of the way the text is arranged on the page and how the illustrations interface with the text appears to be better recognized. We also liked how some anthologies featured certain authors: They not only highlighted other stories by the same author, but also gave information about the person and the process of creating the story. When youngsters realize that the authors they read are real people like themselves, they are more likely to see themselves as writers.

Having said that the contents of most literature anthologies are generally good, we need to repeat our concerns about anthologies themselves. The anthology approach is not compatible with a view of each child as a unique person with individual interests and motivations. We acknowledge the useful-

ness of having several copies of a story to encourage interaction and coopera-
tion among those who are interested in reading the same thing at the same
time, but we believe that five or six copies of the original book suffice. Some
reading programs do offer books with this packaging and we prefer the flexibility of separate books over anthologies.

Another concern we have about anthologies is the small number of stories in them. Readers need quantity as well as quality—quantities of books to
choose from and quantities of time to read. If teachers view the anthology
selections as the bulk of what children need to read, there won't be much
reading happening. The teachers' guides that accompany the literature
anthologies further diminish the focus on actual reading. The guides are
crammed with pages and pages of questions, skills lessons, related information, writing assignments, and extension activities. We counted the number of
pages of such suggestions for one story and discovered that there were eigh-
teen pages of teaching ideas for a story that ran two minutes on an audiotape.
The story itself was only about ten sentences long. Do you see why we are
worried about reading getting shortchanged? When you hear people talk
about "basalizing the literature," this is the sort of thing they are referring to.

The teachers' guides say that the anthologies are intended as just the
start of reading and not the total program (McGraw-Hill, 1993; Scott, Foresman, 1993). A small number of trade books are sold with most programs to
supplement the anthologies, and some teachers' guides include coverage of
those additional books, too, which again results in more teaching and less
reading. Children not only need high-quality literature, they need high-quality time to spend with it. The publishers' vision of reading time still seems to
be a group of children reading assigned selections together in front of a
teacher, rather than individual children's relaxed time alone with a book.
With this vision, trade books are not only "taught" rather than read, but they
are also apparently assigned rather than selected by the reader. The idea of
child-selected reading must be foreign to whomever wrote the Scott, Foresman *2nd Grade Assessment Guide* (1993) guidelines for helping teachers to
place their students in the proper trade book.

Include Nonfiction Reading

Of course, literature is only one type of reading: It is important for children to
learn to read for pleasure *and* for information. Reading for information
involves reading in the content areas such as science, social studies and
math. Information can be found in not only books, but also many other
sources such as newspapers, magazines, and pamphlets. Familiarity with all
these sources is part of becoming literate. Many reading programs include
factual sources as well as fiction in the lists of books on topics related to
anthology stories, but magazines, newspapers, and pamphlets seem to be
ignored. It is up to the teacher to include a full selection of reading materials.
We refer you to the children's magazines listed in Chapter 7 and encourage
you to collect relevant current event articles.

Reading for information involves reading in the content areas such as science, social studies, and math.

Encourage Authentic and Purposeful Writing

As explained in Chapters 5 and 6, current views of literacy emphasize the interrelatedness of reading and writing, which makes it imperative that children write in conjunction with reading. Reading program publishers are very aware of this mandate. Teachers' manuals include information about the importance of writing and about emergent writing processes. Programs with authors and consultants who are emergent writing experts, such as Elizabeth Sulzby or William Teale, present the most current and accurate explanations.

Students' journals for children's writing generally are part of the reading program package and most of the newest activity books also encourage narrative writing. Notice that we make a distinction between "narrative writ-ing" and filling in the blanks. Some materials confuse these two and offer youngsters only a chance to copy a word onto a blank line in a sentence. Most programs offer materials for both real writing and for skills drill masquerad-ing as writing. It is up to the teachers and the schools what they purchase. We realize that publishers cater to the market, but we were shocked at the misla-beling of a skills book put out by McGraw-Hill (1993). This *Writers Workshop* book represents the worst of the old workbooks: it consists of drills for copy-ing letters, penmanship practice, spelling drills, and unscrambling sen-tences—all separate from actual writing. We can't imagine why it is called *Writers Workshop* because it violates every principle of an actual writers' workshop.

The best of the journals offer plenty of blank pages with creative ideas for writing topics (see Figure 9–2). The worst are mainly directions for copy-ing the right word onto the correct blank. In the middle are those that seem to offer children freedom to write—as long as they incorporate a given list of vocabulary or spelling words in their stories. Even the best journals are a poor substitute for blank paper, yet cost considerably more. Besides the cost, the problem with the better journals is that the blank pages are not *entirely* blank: They have a title to indicate what the child is to write about, and the pages are usually framed or decorated to make an important-looking finished product. These may sound like nice touches, until you think about some prin-ciples for writing.

The title, combined with teacher directions, eliminates personal pur-pose in writing. What if Felena doesn't want to write about that topic and has another idea? What if she makes a mistake as she writes or changes her mind about how to write something? Then the beautifully framed page is ruined, and Felena feels like a failure. A polished writing product fit for such a fancy page always requires more than one draft, yet the teachers' manual just says to assign that page with no mention of rough drafts. Thus, the writing process is circumvented and children lose the opportunity to learn spelling and punc-tuation rules in a meaningful context. Though blank paper is preferable, no one pays much for it. Publishers sell what people will pay for—whether it is what young writers need or not. Thus, we get a product that on the surface seems responsive to current research, yet misses the essence.

Not only is writing process frequently misinterpreted in reading materi-als, but understanding and respect for emergent writing is varied. The Houghton Mifflin kindergarten journal gives a clear message that kindergart-ners can't write. This journal invites youngsters to draw pictures or copy let-ters; sometimes they can fill in one word. In contrast, the Scott, Foresman kindergarten journal encourages actual writing and guides teachers to remind children that they can write "the kindergarten way."

Obviously, teachers need to be knowledgeable about how children learn to read and write in order to select the best from the huge array of both good and bad materials. You also need to know how much of a good thing is enough. For instance, the Houghton Mifflin journal accompanying its *Book-*

FIGURE 9–2

The best of the commercial journals offer plenty of empty pages with ideas for writing topics. Morgan wrote: I see a starfish. I see a whale. I see people.

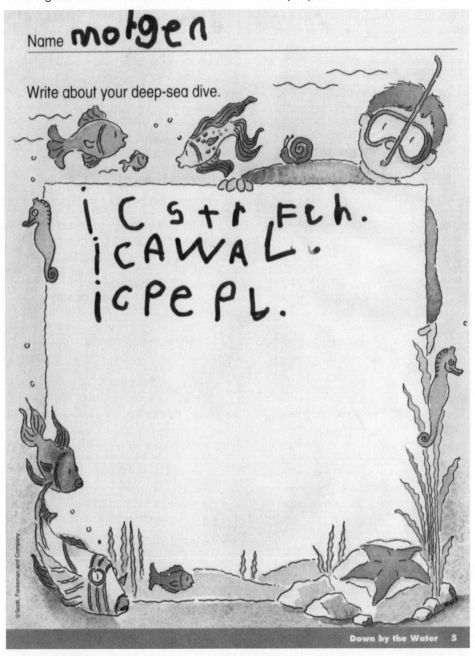

worm anthology has twelve pages for the twelve-sentence story *Jimmy Lee Did It*. Of these twelve pages, two offer ideas for actual writing but limit the space to just a few lines. Three pages ask children merely to list words from the story, and another page asks them to complete words by filling in the vowel pairs *oa* or *ow*. The rest of the pages ask for drawings or for short fill-

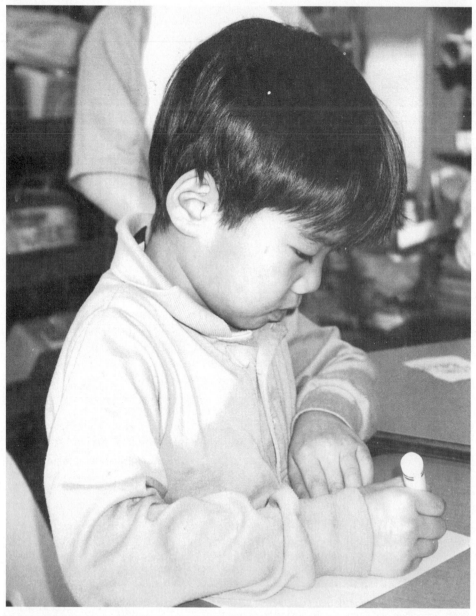

Teachers can share writing ideas with youngsters, but individual child preferences about topics need to be honored.

in-the-blanks answers. Is this a journal or a workbook? It appears that the strategy is to offer some of everything in an effort to please everyone and sell more books.

The publishing companies exist solely to make a profit; therefore, teachers must exercise professional judgement in how best to spend education dollars. In addition, individual preferences of the children need to be considered; teachers can share writing ideas with youngsters and allow them to decide which sound interesting. There are many fine ideas offered, but they become undesirable if forced on unwilling writers.

Teach Skills in Context

Virtually all the reading programs offer materials that explain why skills should not be taught out of context and yet offer materials for doing so. Those respected reading experts hired by the major publishers write valuable descriptions of how to teach necessary skills as part of the reading and writing process and give admirable justifications for abandoning old skills drills; however, the skills drill materials still are part of the program and available to those who want them. As we said, the job of textbook companies is to make money. Publishers' sales representatives apologize for the discrepancies and explain that many teachers won't buy a program unless it has all the familiar workbooks for phonics, handwriting, punctuation, and spelling. How ironic to purchase a new whole language program and then use it as if it were the old, outdated one.

The Scott, Foresman materials offer an example of the whole language rhetoric: "All skills flow naturally from the literature. They are taught in context of making meaning rather than in isolation" (Celebrate Reading, Grade 1 Guide 1993, p. 14). Nevertheless, they offer phonics and spelling practice books, a phonics manipulative kit, a teachers' guide to spelling and phonics, and other trappings of skills drills in isolation. These are available at all but the kindergarten level. (It appears that kindergarten curriculum authors Sulzby and Morrow prevailed in this, because other companies offer such skills materials at all levels—even the kindergarten level.)

Apart from the separate skills materials, the teachers' guides attempt to help teachers demonstrate reading strategies as part of actual reading. The focus now is more on meaning and fluency than on "barking at print." There are frequent directions telling youngsters to read to the end of the sentence to figure out an unknown word. Sometimes, the strategy lessons are done effectively but often they interrupt the story too much. Just for fun, we counted and found that the Houghton Mifflin version of the story *Jimmy Lee Did It* had forty-one skills and information items for that two-minute story. The main problem is that there is too much emphasis on decoding strategies during reading. Because the system is set up for group instruction, it is inevitable that such instruction will not be a good match for the needs of all—if any. As the Scott, Foresman materials say, skills and strategies are not prescribable or standardized (Celebrate Reading, Professional Handbook, 1993) but vary from individual to individual and from context to context.

In the Houghton Mifflin grade 1 Student Resource Book: Support Activities for Reading and Writing (*Bookworm*, 1991), two pages are labeled "Jimmy Lee Did It." Children are to circle the words that complete each sentence and then copy the words. The words are used in the story, but we could find no real relationship to the story at all. This clearly is totally isolated vocabulary skills practice and is common among many publishers. McGraw-Hill has first graders copying words with specific graphophonemic patterns, such as those with a specific vowel sound, nouns ending with *s*, or verbs with an *es* ending. These look like the same materials that have turned off student brains for decades.

Yet, this is comfortingly familiar material to many. As a result, teachers who have learned more effective methods of teaching reading and writing skills often find themselves on the defensive. Parents as well as teachers who don't understand the new approaches criticize the lack of separate, visible drill sheets. Many parents hear the incessant radio and television advertisements for the Hooked on Phonics program and think they need to spend their own money to ensure that their children get this background. Because the idea of learning reading and writing skills while reading and writing is new to most parents, schools or individual teachers find that explanatory presentations at parents night meetings are helpful. Once they understand and observe the new approaches, parents generally become strong advocates and begin to demand that their children continue with whole language approaches. This puts pressure on principals, who then put pressure on teachers to get new training. Obviously, some teachers are not pleased about this; fortunately, others are excited about new ideas.

Teachers and textbook publishers clearly are in transition. Publishing companies are trying to cater to both those demanding the most up-to-date materials and those wanting only the familiar. In almost every school you will find teachers on both ends of the spectrum as well as in between. Many teachers gradually are making changes in their classrooms as they work out their own transitions; others are leaders in helping colleagues to understand and implement emergent literacy instruction along whole language lines. Some teachers are fresh out of college eager to try new ideas, and others are resisting them with all their might. How does a reading program fit all these different teachers?

Utilize Performance-based Assessment

Next we look at how assessment is treated in reading programs. We see that publishers of reading materials know the latest research and recommendations. Most offer excellent explanations of performance-based assessment, but offer materials for both the old and the new assessment approaches. When these are in separate packages, the knowledgeable educator easily can choose to purchase only the desirable materials. When a contradictory mix of approaches is combined into one assessment document, it is difficult for *any* teacher to sift through for the preferred materials.

Once they understand and observe new teaching approaches, parents generally become strong advocates and begin to demand that their children continue to have holistic language teaching.

McGraw-Hill materials say "Because assessment should be continuous and closely integrated with instruction, assessment information for each student should be derived from the student's portfolio materials, including: performance assessment tasks, writing samples, self-assessments, unit 2 progress assessment results" (*You're Invited.* Grade 1/Level 5/Unit 2 Sample, p. 269B). The Unit 2 progress assessment features the old multiple-choice format, but teachers are reminded elsewhere to record observations of children during book-talks or to collect and have children self-select their writings for portfolios.

Like other companies, Houghton Mifflin now has longer reading passages before the multiple-choice questions, apparently in response to criticisms of reading materials that lacked sufficient context. However, the following example from the kindergarten-level theme 2 *Let's Be Friends* uses such unnatural language that it is probably not helpful to young readers.

> "The baby is not in the Fun Run," said Fox.
> "The bear is not in the Fun Run," said Turtle.
> "The baby and I can not run," said Bear.
> "We will not have fun."

Houghton Mifflin theme tests basically are workbook sheets with the old patterns, but the same company also shows how to organize a portfolio and encourages children to keep independent reading logs. Houghton Mifflin also provides forms for anecdotal observations; but, just in case you want a different emphasis, they include checklists for keeping track of decoding skills. This rather split-personality approach is typical of other publishers too.

Scott, Foresman's distinguished group of reading experts provide a wonderful overview of assessment in the 1993 Assessment Handbook (*Celebrate Reading,* 1993). Robert Tierney says, "I think it's very important not to separate assessment from teaching and learning, and that's where assessment goes beyond feedback." Richard Allington offers this view of performance-based assessment: "Authentic assessment simply involves new ways of looking at children as they proceed through the day, doing the kinds of things that children typically do."

But then turn to page 37 of *Celebrate Reading* and find the following assessment item on a familiar-looking worksheet: After reading a short selection children are to circle the right answer.

    I. How is *Three Up a Tree* different than most stories?
       A. It is a story about three kids.
       B. It has stories inside the story.
       C. It shows kids making something together.

Then this assessment handbook switches back and asks children to write a narrative response to some questions. Scott, Foresman also provides a useful overview of holistic scoring of child writing, and the kindergarten materials show the Sulzby categories for emergent reading and writing checklists that we referred to in Chapter 8. In addition, this company shows teachers how to keep running records, to record miscues, and to administer an Informal Reading Inventory. Program materials also explain the value of child self-assessment, anecdotal records, observation, and portfolios. They even provide forms to facilitate all this.

Obviously, there is much valuable assistance for performance-based assessment in the new reading program materials. Teachers have to be very careful in selecting what they use, however. Even the otherwise excellent Scott, Foresman kindergarten program offers a skills assessment test of auditory discrimination and phonics workbook tasks of the type used over thirty years ago.

Integrate Curriculum

Efforts at integrating curriculum are very evident in new reading materials we have seen. These efforts take different approaches and demonstrate different levels of success. Most just focus on the language arts, use the fine arts as an extension, and make token forays into content areas such as science or social studies. A few actually present a model of a fully integrated curriculum that adds purpose and depth to language arts activities.

You will see an amazing number of art and craft suggestions accompanying each story. Children constantly are asked to draw their favorite character or a picture of a similar event in their own lives. We see value in this when the drawing assignment is self-selected or accompanied by an opportunity to write; drawing tends to help youngsters to think about what they want to write and serves a planning, or prewrite, function. However, most young children can't draw realistic or recognizable figures and many are intimidated by directions such as "Think of one thing you would like to be able to do, but can't. Draw a picture of it" (Bookworm Journal, Houghton Mifflin, 1993, p. 94). Perhaps the thing they can't do is draw! Yet, here is a small space all framed and waiting for a masterpiece.

The crafts activities are endless and often incredibly silly and worthless. As with the caterpillars made of old ties and pantyhose, teachers have to ask "What are children *learning* from this activity?" Too often, we found that these craft ideas perpetuated the school tradition of substituting paper activities for the real ones. Do youngsters really learn science from making construction paper replicas of things they read about? Another problem with the recommended craft ideas is that they aren't the children's ideas. If youngsters have free access to a variety of craft materials and freedom to create in response to their experiences with literature or real bugs, babies, bunnies, etc., the children themselves will invent personally meaningful craft activities.

Songs and poems frequently accompany reading selections. These often are used for repeated shared readings and help youngsters to extend their sight-word vocabulary as they memorize the verses. Creating new versions of songs and poems also is suggested often, and generally is described as a group activity although such activity could be done by children individually or in pairs. Such approaches to authorship can help children to learn about writing. Recommendations for writing new versions of pattern stories or new endings for other stories can serve the same purpose for developing writers. But, once again, the value can be destroyed for the child who isn't interested in that particular activity. In order to ensure that children will benefit from activities, teachers need to make suggestions rather than assignments. Giving children options and letting them choose their own approaches will provide the personal meaning and involvement essential to learning.

We also mentioned "token forays" into content areas. Too often, a vaguely related item of information or activity will be added in and called curriculum integration. Counting plastic teddy bears after reading a book about bears is not integrating math and literature; it is tokenism. Making a graph of who likes what kind of bear (or ice cream or . . .) does not integrate curriculum, either—we consider those examples to be correlated curriculum. We make a distinction between correlated curriculum and authentically integrated curriculum. Authentic integration demands that children use the activities to add to their understanding of a topic. For instance, figuring out how high a bear can reach in order to plan safe food storage while camping would provide math measurement problem-solving practice and also enhance understanding of bears. This understanding would help children to bring more meaning to future reading about bears.

Authentic curriculum integration involves literacy with various content areas as children add to their understanding of a topic.

Project approaches (Katz & Chard, 1989) to curriculum planning assist authentic integration by focusing on what children want to learn about a topic. Various content areas are included in the process of gathering relevant information for the project (Trapanier-Street, 1993). This is a natural integration and quite different from artificially adding activities from different content areas for the purpose of integration. The Scott, Foresman kindergarten units suggest authentic integration across the curriculum, also. For instance, the Creeping Crawling Creatures unit suggests that children keep track of the insects they see each day by recording their observations on the class insect graph (see Figure 9–3); later, they will discuss which insects were seen most and least frequently. Other suggestions include observing an ant colony and a spider spinning a web, with follow-up discussions and activities. Many excellent fiction and nonfiction books are recommended as part of the unit. Unfortunately, the Scott, Foresman kindergarten units are not typical examples of approaches to curriculum integration. They are not even typical quality for that publisher: Materials for other grades take very different approaches, with themes of limited usefulness for across-the-curriculum integration.

Respect All Children

When we ask whether teaching materials respect all children, we are looking at respect for various kinds of differences. For instance, are children who learn more slowly still treated as people who are capable of learning and who want to learn? Additionally, are children from all cultures and language backgrounds other than English fully included in the learning process?

Children who experience reading difficulty traditionally have been deprived of important reading experiences. Those who most need exposure to high-quality books and who most need to experience joy in reading are the least likely to get either in a traditional reading program. Children who have trouble reading often are given more work in the resource booklets and less chance to read. The very students who should be reading one good story after another are doing one worksheet after another, instead. Those who are doing well in reading are allowed to enjoy the additional literature selections. The Report Card on Basal Readers (Goodman et al, 1988) calls this phenomenon "The poor get poorer" (p. 93).

Newer reading materials make some progress in changing this picture. Houghton Mifflin suggests opportunities to read books together with you or others for the child who does poorly on a concepts about print test. Unfortunately, they also offer directed instruction lessons on concepts about print, a complex set of understandings best constructed by the child through repeated meaningful interactions with books and print.

Scott, Foresman materials offer tips on modifying instruction so that everyone can experience the same literature at the same time. This demonstrates some movement in allowing all children access to good literature, but makes the unfounded assumption that everyone would want to read the same thing at the same time. Further, the recommendations seem based on an ability group model, though a model in which all groups read the same thing in different ways. Close examination suggests that the group that requires more help, called the Bridge group, seems to spend more time talking about read-

FIGURE 9–3
This insect graph shows that a worksheet can be part of a relevant and thoughtful learning experience rather than a meaningless task all too common in worksheets.

Name

Insect Graph

Make a • when you see an insect.

		Mon.	Tues.	Wed.	Thurs.	Fri.	Total
ant 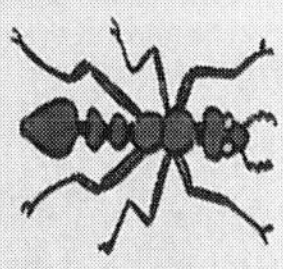							
bee 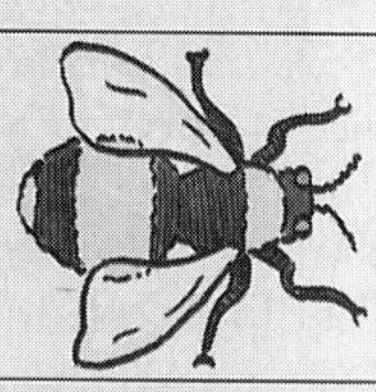							
mosquito 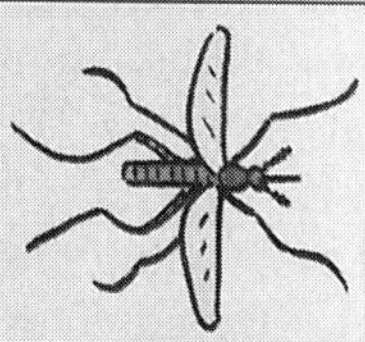							
butterfly 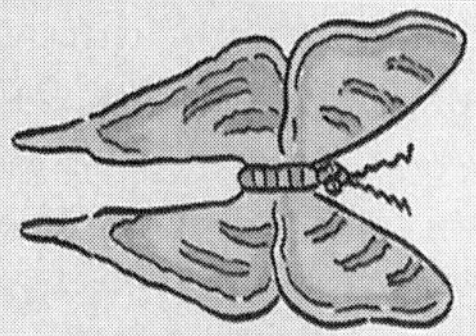							
fly 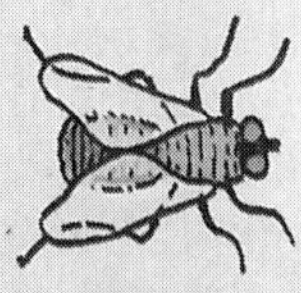							

© Scott, Foresman and Company

Creeping, Crawling Creatures   3

ing and less time actually reading than others. It looks as if they are likely to be cut off from higher-level thinking, too: Teachers are told that some children might not be ready to benefit from a discussion of previewing and predicting before reading.

One crucial difference between traditional reading programs and whole language approaches is ability grouping. In a whole language program, children choose their own reading partners or become part of a group based on common interest in a topic or a book. Shared reading is done in heterogeneous groups so that hesitant readers can benefit from the models of their more confident peers. When you do away with ability groups, you help poor readers to learn more quickly and you keep them from being labeled "dumb."

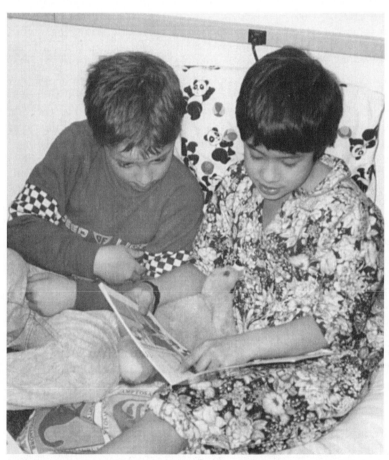

Children choose their own reading partners or become part of a group based on common interest in a topic or a book. They are not grouped by ability.

This is acknowledged in what publishing companies say in the reading materials, but not carried through in their teaching recommendations.

Apart from the fact that many children who end up in the "low" reading group are those from cultures and languages which differ from that of the school, new reading materials do attempt to address multicultural and bilingual issues. All present stories about children of various colors and from many different lands. The McGraw-Hill materials offer tips with each story to assist ESL (English as a second language) students. They provide practice in context and language models for children who have trouble pronouncing certain sounds. They also utilize tape recordings of stories and songs, which allow youngsters to hear unlimited repetitions in standard English. Children who are working at learning English do seem to gravitate to tapes of familiar songs and stories.

Respecting children includes giving them some decision-making opportunities. We see children thrive as learners when they are allowed personal responsibility for their learning. This responsibility includes having a say in what they want to achieve and being involved in self-evaluation of their progress. Most reading materials we looked at included some opportunity for student involvement in the assessment progress, but little chance to set personal goals. The Wright Group materials, in contrast, recommend that students decide what they want to achieve, under the guidance of the teacher. The Wright Group approach emphasizes the importance of giving children as much responsibility for planning and running their learning projects as possible.

Respect Teachers

We found that the Wright Group approach not only respected children as learners, but also respected teachers' ability to teach. Wright Group teacher guides give one detailed example of conducting an effective shared reading session and then assume teachers can figure out how to conduct similar sessions with other stories. Rather than several dozen pages of directions to guide the teacher through each story, the Wright Group offers only two pages of related-activity extension ideas per story.

It is clear that textbooks are changing, but they themselves are antithetical to the new vision of teaching and learning. Effective learning is a "result of the learner's own activity" (Ferreiro & Teberosky, 1982, p. 15), and effective teaching "responds to what the child is trying to do" (Smith, 1976, p. 298). This means that children must be free to direct their own learning and that teachers must be free to respond to children's efforts. This cannot happen when textbook companies dictate what children are to read and to think. It cannot happen as long as teachers are reduced to "scripted technicians" (Goodman et al., 1988) in following the teachers' manuals.

The good news is that some teachers are taking control. They are picking and choosing among their options and creating rich, meaningful learning environments for their students. They are using pieces from various reading programs, selecting from literature programs, and trying ideas from resource books. As a result, not only are children enjoying learning more, the teachers are enjoying teaching more.

INCORPORATING TECHNOLOGY

Today's teachers grew up with television: Today's children are growing up with computers as well. An estimated one-third of all U.S. homes now have computers and they are used by children as well as adults (Lohr, 1993). Children now are playing computer games and using educational software both at home and at school. Using CD-ROMs, the new multimedia platforms integrate computer technology with audio input, videotapes, and graphics, offering ever increasing media possibilities. Many reading programs offer a computer package (e.g., Houghton Mifflin, 1993); and computer companies are offering reading programs (e.g., Apple Early Language Connections, 1993).

Teachers and parents are bombarded with advertisements for increasingly sophisticated types of computer software and hardware that manufacturers guarantee will enhance children's learning. The dilemma for decisions about educational technology is the same as for any other kind of instructional materials: Teachers need well-defined theories about appropriate instruction and must evaluate materials with criteria based on those theories. We find that the same criteria used for selecting written materials can be used to evaluate media materials. Therefore, we recommend adapting the checklist we used for critiquing reading programs and applying it to selecting computer software for the language arts.

As with other kinds of instructional materials, you cannot merely rely on publisher descriptions—you must examine software programs yourself. Ms. Montoya complains that the advertisements always sound so wonderful, but some programs wind up being terrible when she actually tries them. She finds that even award-winning programs aren't necessarily winners on her terms: The awards may have been for the technological aspects and have nothing to do with the educational value. Once again, it boils down to the criteria used to make judgments.

If you want children to construct their own understanding of reading and writing, you will not select programs that just replicate workbook formats. Too many instructional computer "games" are merely animated worksheets. Notice that the "interactive" aspects advertised for most programs often are limited to the child giving an answer and finding out if it is the correct one or not. If you are committed to teaching skills in actual reading and writing contexts, you will not select programs that focus on isolated skills drill. If you want children to engage in purposeful writing, you will not select programs that dictate writing topics.

Computer software has been steadily improving and it is possible to find a few excellent programs that support and extend children's explorations of reading and writing. *Storybook Weaver* (Minnesota Educational Computing

Consortium, 1992) is an example of a writing tool that enhances word processing with options to include graphics, music, and other sound effects. Where hardware allows, children can even use color in the illustrations they create for their writing. Any word processing program, with or without fancy frills, is an asset for writing. Word processing encourages risk taking with writing because it is easy to fix mistakes; word processing also takes the pain out of revising, editing and polishing a finished product. In addition, finding a letter on a keyboard is easier for some beginning writers than forming a letter correctly with a pencil.

Kid Pix (Broderbund, 1992), designed for children as young as preschool age, allows them to draw in color with a variety of "brushes" as in the Macintosh paint program. It also offers a variety of pictures as choices to zap onto the screen for telling or illustrating a story. Using the alphabet letter option, children can even label or name their creations. Six-year-old Patrick demonstrated the program capabilities by combining several functions into one project: He selected pictures of palm trees and an airplane, put them on the screen, and began his oral narrative about a trip to Hawaii. Then he "painted" in a big mountain, which he said was an active volcano. Patrick illustrated the volcanic eruption with a paintbrush stroke that resembled clouds of smoke and soon covered the whole screen. An action narrative such as this can provide an effective prewrite experience and enhance language development (see Figure 9–4).

FIGURE 9–4
Since the volcanic eruption obliterated his Hawaii trip illustration, Patrick made this picture about dinosaurs to show what he can do with the Kid Pix program.

Living Books (Broderbund, 1993) is an example of how multimedia technology can enhance storybook reading by adding animation, voices, music and other sound effects. These programs are built around children's literature and use the original illustrations (Wepner, 1993), making them much more worth reading than some computer story-reading options. In addition, they offer Spanish and some Japanese versions of the stories to assist second language learners. For an example of software that does not utilize high-quality literature and resembles workbook fare, see *Mickey's Magic Reader* (Larimer & Hermann, 1988).

Teachers and parents must beware of software that electronically extends poor educational practices. They "must look beyond the compelling graphics, intriguing sound, and technical wizardry to the core — values and beliefs about writing and about children that are housed in the software environment" (Sharp, 1993). What teachers know about teaching and learning must determine the role of computers in the classroom. Computers themselves are neither good nor bad, they either add or detract from the educational experience depending upon how they are used.

The same is true of television: It, too, is good or bad depending on what is watched and how it is used. Too much television or too many videos appear harmful (Healy, 1990); however, television has much to offer if used wisely. Of course, there are many valuable informational programs and videos, but even poor television programming can be put to advantage. For instance, children can participate in discussions that evaluate violence in cartoons or honesty in advertising. They can become more thoughtful consumers and critics of media and more skillful writers as they create their own commercials, newscasts, and even soap operas. Parents have more influence than teachers on children's television viewing; teachers can only suggest that television viewing be monitored and that it not be used as a baby-sitter. Obviously, when children are watching television they are not reading, and that affects their education.

Conclusion

We strongly recommend authentic literature and purposeful writing for literacy instruction. Though many instructional materials advertise that they are literature-based, we encourage you to evaluate this claim for yourself. Though many programs claim to encourage writing, we suggest that you examine what they mean by "writing."

If educators select computer software or commercially prepared reading and writing materials on the basis of their best understanding about how children learn and about what is worth teaching, then using these materials is both educationally sound and efficient. However, if educators choose materials on the basis of whether the format is attractive, or how easy the materials are to implement, or how well the materials align with standardized tests, then educators are making decisions based on nonprofessional criteria.

A sound research-based theoretical stance must guide judgment in selecting language arts education approaches and materials. Educators first must have a clear idea of what literacy is and how students develop reading and writing competence, then find materials that fit that understanding. Materials should not determine the teaching approach; the approach must determine the materials.

DISCUSSION QUESTIONS

1. Compare your analysis of a reading program with evaluations of other programs done by your colleagues or classmates.
2. What criteria would you change or add to the Reading Program Analysis offered in this chapter?

SUGGESTED FOLLOW-UP ACTIVITIES

1. Observe a reading program from a major publishing company in action. Use the Reading Program Analysis criteria from this chapter to critique what you observe.
2. Interview a teacher about the use of officially adopted texts. Does this teacher feel obligated to use them? Does he or she use them as directed? If not, how does he or she adapt or extend the materials?
3. Observe children using computer-based learning materials and/or try some computer educational software yourself. Evaluate the material in terms of the Reading Program Analysis criteria from this chapter.
4. Visit a school library or media center. Interview the librarian, and focus on his or her role in the school's language arts program. Be sure to look around the library and decide whether it invites children to come in and to use it.

RECOMMENDED FURTHER READING

Periodicals

Hughes, S. M. (1993). The impact of whole language on four elementary school libraries. *Language Arts*, 70(5) 393–399.

Books

Barrett, F. L. (1982). *A teacher's guide to shared reading*. Ontario, Canada: Scholastic.
Goodman, K. (1986). *What's whole in whole language*. Ontario, Canada: Scholastic.

Huck, C., Hepler, S., & Hickman, J. (1993). *Children's literature in the elementary school*. Fort Worth: Harcourt Brace Jovanovich.

Katz, L., & Chard, S. (1989). *Engaging children's minds: The project approach*. Norwood, NJ: Ablex.

TEACHERS' GUIDES AND READING PROGRAMS

Baskwill, J., & Whitman, P. (1986). *Whole language sourcebook*. Ontario, Canada: Scholastic-TAB Publications Ltd.

Bolton, F., Green, R., Pollack, J., Scarfee, B., & Snowball, D. (1986). *Bookshelf stage 1: Teacher's resource book*. New York: Multimedia International (U.K.) Ltd.

Celebrate Reading. (1993). Glenview, IL: Scott, Foresman.

Hurst, C. O. (1990). *Once upon a time . . . An encyclopedia for successfully using literature with young children*. Allen, TX: DLM Publishing.

CONSTRUCTING YOUR UNDERSTANDING

There is a significant difference between being irresponsible and letting go of the need to be in control.

ELIZABETH JONES, 1986

We wanted to conclude this book with something profound for you to carry with you into your teaching. We sat down together to talk about what the most important ideas actually are and we ended up talking about our own learning and growing process. We realized that the most interesting and profound issues for us are in the form of unresolved questions rather than answers.

Marjorie: There are so many topics I'd like to discuss in this chapter, but most of them are problems that we don't have answers for.

Katy: We don't have to sit here like two goddesses telling other people the correct solutions to very difficult educational issues.

Then we realized that we didn't have to provide answers in order to give you something important to take with you: It gradually became clear that our questions would be more valuable. Here we have been telling you that your role as a teacher is to ask thought-provoking questions more than to give information; now it is our turn to take that advice. Following are some questions and our thoughts about them. We hope this will be the start of a conversation which you will pick up and continue with your colleagues.

Passing Fads?

Are whole language and constructivism just passing fads in education? Some teachers think so, having become cynical about new recommendations after seeing so many come and go. We do applaud healthy skepticism and careful consideration before jumping on any new bandwagons. However, these two complementary theories about learning each have a long and well-documented research base and we don't see how either can be dismissed as just another fad.

Let's look briefly at the history behind constructivism as background to this issue. Constructivist theory results from sixty years of detailed, scientific research by Piaget and his associates from around the world. The number of publications by Piaget alone is staggering, and his associates continue to publish their results as they persist in studies of the learning process. Most of these publications were not translated into English until the 1960s, thus delaying recognition in the United States. Constance Kamii, Piagetian scholar, makes the point that constructivism is not just a set of beliefs or another philosophy of education: it is a proven scientific theory (1991).

Whole language, as we have said before, is not a new idea either. It is the result of extensive psycholinguistic and developmental research over several decades. Early work on language experience and individualized reading approaches paved the way for further research and understanding in the United States. Simultaneous research efforts in several countries came to similar conclusions, and international collaboration by a large number of researchers contributed to the current major movement for holistic literacy education. The resulting theory, now named whole language, is based on observations of how children construct their knowledge of reading and writing.

In the folklore of education, there is a saying that there is at least a twenty-year lag between educational research and practice. Are constructivism and whole language now theories whose time has come? Will they be given a real test in the schools, or will they be implemented without adequate staff development and be so poorly done as to ensure failure (Church, 1994)? Will resistance to change doom these theories to oblivion?

Why Does This Seem So Radical?

Because we have been studying these theories for a long time, it is hard for us to understand why they are still viewed as radical changes. Further thoughts about the different origins of new and old practices seem relevant to this question. All teaching practices are based on some concept of the learner and the learning process. In the past, a behaviorist view was assumed and perpetuated as the basis for research comparing teaching approaches. This focus is logical if the learner is considered to be a passive recipient of knowledge rather than an active constructor of knowledge. The simplistic explanation of learning as receiving knowledge from teachers long has dominated public opinion in the United States. Similar naive understandings about learning to read and write have hindered progress in those areas of education.

Both whole language and constructivist research focuses on children's views and actions in the learning process, while behaviorist research focused on teacher interventions. Piagetian scholar and emergent literacy expert Emilia Ferreiro states the constructivist approach when she says, "It is fundamental that we understand the problems as children pose them and the sequence of solutions they find acceptable before we can even imagine the kind of pedagogical intervention that should be designed to meet the real needs of the learning process" (1991, p. 45).

Ferreiro also states that it is difficult to transform educational practices from behaviorist to constructivist because "both the teacher's role and the social dynamics within and without the classroom have to be redefined" (1991, p. 51). The teacher's redefined role is facilitator of learning rather than dispenser of information. Society's view of teaching and learning must

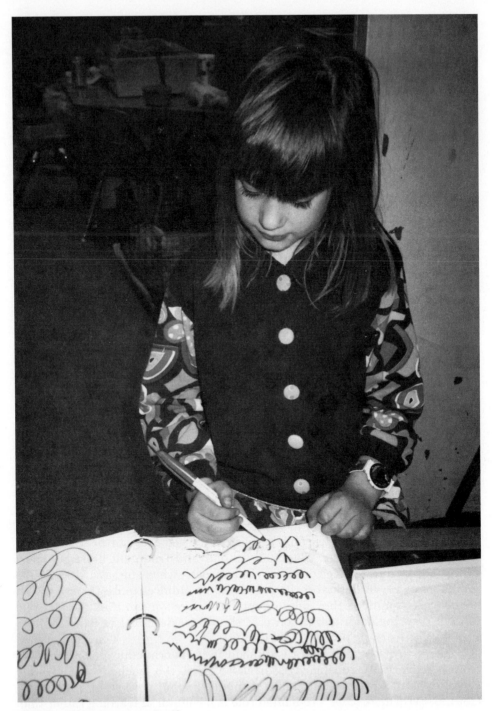

Why does this seem so radical?

change concurrently to allow change in the classroom (NCTE, 1994). If you think of it this way, change of such magnitude *does* sound radical. Ferreiro, who now teaches in Mexico City and has conducted research in several countries, is speaking globally when she refers to "society." Do you think her statements are accurate for the United States?

How Will Ethnographic Research Impact Teaching?

New research approaches have resulted in different kinds of information about learning. When only the experimental design approach was recognized as legitimate for research, educational research often was in a moral bind: There are obvious limitations on using children as experimental subjects. Now that ethnographic research is recognized as being the most relevant for the field of education, the resulting stories of real learning in real classrooms have transformed the knowledge base. With research focused on the processes of learning rather than on setting up teaching experiments and measuring the products, we have different research data on which to build. Whole language and constructivist education lend themselves to the new research methods and are validated by them.

Ethnographic research has been the inspiration for many significant books in the field of education and is the basis for most current articles in professional journals such as *Language Arts* and *Reading Teacher.* Some relevant books include Lucy Calkins's *Lessons from a Child,* Vivian Paley's *Wally's Stories* (1981), and Marilyn Cochran-Smith's *The Making of a Reader* (1984). We see teachers responding to these stories of other classrooms and being motivated to implement similar processes themselves. We also find that teachers are empowered to conduct their own research when they read other teachers' stories. Observing, analyzing and explaining what happens in their classrooms obviously makes much more sense to them and appears more useful than statistical analyses of teaching outcomes.

Research that looks closely at individual learning processes also is uniquely suited to studying children who do not fit the standard mold and who cannot benefit from comparison to national norms. One such example is a third grader with cerebral palsy who has difficulty communicating her thoughts, and whose teacher is recording and analyzing her learning. Another ethnographic study is comparing the grammatical constructions of a three-year-old with that of an older child learning English as a second language. Studies of deaf youngsters include some fascinating examples of invented spelling used in early sign language. Though such research focuses on a single child or just a small sample, the results have broad implications for other children in similar circumstances. Whether ethnographic research focuses on children with special needs or on children in general, the results are offered only as information that *may* be useful in understanding the learning of other children rather than as a formula for others to use. Appreciation for the individual nature of learners is inherent in this type of research and the teaching it fosters.

What Happens When Conflicting Theories Are Combined?

We see teachers who are so confused by new research and past beliefs that they decide to "compromise" and teach with both constructivist and behaviorist approaches. They don't perceive a conflict involved in simultaneously trying to 1) encourage youngsters to think for themselves as they risk errors in the process of constructing knowledge and 2) give children the right answers and ensure that they remember them correctly. As explained in Chapter 1, there are some situations for giving children answers and others for encouraging construction of knowledge. The decision about which kind of teaching is indicated needs to be based on whether the knowledge is social/conventional knowledge or whether it is complex knowledge involving multifaceted interrelationships. We fear that confused children will be the result of teaching decisions based merely on an effort to do a little of everything.

Are Adult and Child Learning Processes Similar?

When we see teachers and parents struggling with whole language teaching ideas, it seems to us that they are going through obvious stages of constructing their knowledge. In playing around with this idea, we contrasted examples of teacher growth in understanding whole language with examples of child hypotheses at different stages of cognitive development. What do you think of the parallels we found?

Initially, adult views of literacy development tend to focus on observable surface features such as identifying letters and attaching sounds to them. This reminds us of Andrew who sees smoke going up into the sky and is convinced that clouds are formed from that smoke. It also reminds us of emergent writing: Children pick up the observable features of what writing is, make rows of squiggles or letterlike forms, and think that you can read it.

Then, as teachers get new information about learning to read that is not consistent with old views, we see them holding on to old, familiar ideas and trying to adapt them to new situations. Literature anthologies that replicate familiar basal reader programs meet these teachers' needs at this stage. This reminds us of Tanya's explanation that "The sea drained like the shower" when the tide went out on the tidal flats; her approach to making sense of a new phenomenon was to view it from the perspective of a known one.

Further growth in understanding does not lead immediately to actual whole language teaching. Many incomplete understandings and "wrong" ideas pave the way to fuller understanding for teachers as well as for chil-

Do children and adults construct knowledge in the same ways?

dren. Sometimes, a wrong idea leads a teacher to temporarily abandon skills instruction altogether when isolated skills instruction is abandoned (Church, 1994). We have also seen old-style reading group lessons taught to whole classes when a teacher was trying to break free of ability grouping. Another classroom had trade books labeled and filed according to level and assigned

Will you feel guilty when it doesn't "feel" like "teaching?"

to children as if they were proceeding through a basal reader. These examples remind us of the interesting errors in children's invented spelling: The errors demonstrate what the learner has learned and what has yet to be learned.

It is important that the errors be part of the learning process, however, and not the final point. It is also important that the errors be viewed as evidence of growth and not as examples of failure. Perhaps, as teachers learn to accept children's errors as a natural part of learning, they will more readily accept their own in the same light. Will this free teachers to make changes without considering such change an admission of past failure?

Will You Feel Guilty?

As they make changes in their classrooms we hear teachers expressing feelings of guilt about not "teaching." Yet, when we observe, we see these teachers teaching constantly, during every interaction with every child who comes up to them during the school day. We see a remarkably efficient use of instructional time in these focused exchanges between teacher and child.

The problem is that this doesn't *feel* like "teaching" to many teachers. The image of a teacher as the center of attention is so imbedded in past experience that it is extremely difficult to change. Though these teachers intellectually accept their role as facilitators rather than directors of learning, past images impact emotional responses to the role. What is your own feeling?

Are There "Too Many Cooks"?

There are so many different people telling teachers what to do in our society: parents, principals, textbooks, and school boards. An international comparison of school systems (McAdams, 1993) concluded that U.S. teachers are very vulnerable to parental pressure. Does all this outside input get in the way of teachers listening to children? How can teachers be freed to teach in response to their students?

Because teachers in the United States *are* responsible to a variety of sources, a proactive stance seems needed to keep teachers from being buffeted about by conflicting expectations. A proactive position certainly would involve educating those concerned about new educational practices. Whose job is it to educate the public?

How Can Whole Language Teachers Help Others to Understand?

Not only do constructivist/whole language teachers have to learn to teach in ways they never experienced themselves, but they also have to help others to understand what is happening. Teachers tell us that it is easier to implement new ideas than to articulate them to parents, principals, and other teachers who may be skeptical. That led us to the question of how teachers can help others to understand (though our own question is why they should *have* to). We present the following analysis of past and present educational theory as background information for your explanations. Our hypothesis is that knowing where ideas come from can help in addressing them, whether it is to argue for or against them.

Educators sometimes discuss reading theory as part of broad educational philosophies, such as maturationist, constructivist, or behaviorist theories. You might hear Gesell's maturationist ideas about time being the basic ingredient for learning and compare them with Piaget's constructivist views that action on the environment, social interaction, and equilibration (Almy, 1973) must be coupled with time. Skinner's behaviorist theories contrast with the other two in detailing step-by-step learning through reinforcement. Although a view of the learner is inherent in each of these theories, sometimes teachers have difficulty relating any one of these broad theories to the specifics of literacy.

Nevertheless, reading theory is related to general educational theory: As we have said, skills-based beliefs are compatible with a behaviorist emphasis on directed instruction and the teacher as the center of learning. Whole language beliefs are compatible with an emphasis on construction of knowledge and the child as the center of learning.

When only behaviorist approaches were recognized, disagreements focused on slight differences on how to implement them. Thus, differences between phonics approaches and sight-word approaches once were debated hotly. Although proponents of each became opponents of the other, these two views are not really very different. Both operate on the assumption that after you teach children a subskill of reading, those children can then unlock the mystery of the printed page. Each method teaches specific facts by rote, whether they are the sound-symbol relationships of letters or the appearance of various words. Each assumes that youngsters can put these parts of the puzzle together to determine the whole of the meaning.

Currently, the significant theoretical debate is that characterized by the differences between whole language and skills-based approaches. Both the phonics approach and the sight-word approach are skills-based. Both focus on pieces of the whole, apart from meaningful context. The intent of skills-based approaches is to break down the huge task of learning to read into child-size chunks. The programs emphasize observable behaviors of saying letter sounds and identifying words. Teachers who use skills-based approaches assume that obtaining meaning occurs as a result of learning these skills. Whole language, in contrast, sees skills acquisition resulting from the process of obtaining meaning. Whole language approaches do not break apart the reading process into little pieces—that is part of why it is called *whole*. The holistic theory is that small pieces are more difficult for beginners: The whole context provides essential information to help children make sense of written language. These ideas are difficult for many people because they are the reverse of what has been done in the past.

The whole language approach is actually not new but the term *whole language* is new, and its widespread recognition in the United States is new. However, the idea has been a guiding principle for many U.S. educators for over forty years and was in existence long before that (Lameroux & Lee,

1943; Lee & Allen, 1963). New Zealand, Australia, and Canada—countries with a much higher literacy rate than the United States—have had whole language style–instruction for years. For teachers like Mrs. Thomas, the "new" whole language bandwagon is just a lot of fuss about what she has been doing for twenty years—making education relevant to children. Her model of teaching is an important source of information to others.

Should There Be a National Curriculum?

New Zealand adopted holistic literacy instruction at the national level in the early 1970s in response to the needs of rural Maori children and others who hadn't thrived on old approaches. A national in-service program for teachers and a complementary program for parents provided essential support for this major change in educational practice. Many major whole language theorists are from New Zealand: Sylvia Ashton-Warner, Marie Clay, and Don Holdaway are among the New Zealanders who made major contributions to the field and are now familiar names in the United States as well as New Zealand; they add their voices to those of North Americans Anne Haas-Dyson, Kenneth and Yetta Goodman, Frank Smith, Elizabeth Sulzby, and William Teale, and to those of Mexico's Emilia Ferreiro, Spain's Ana Teberosky, and Israel's Liliana Landsmann.

However, the United States has no uniformity in educational practice, let alone a national in-service program for teachers or a parent information program. Some districts help teachers to keep current (Johnston & Wilder, 1992); some demand that they do but offer no help; some accept any approach; and some actually discourage any change. The United States has been criticized for such a potpourri (McAdams, 1993). This leads to our questions: Would a national curriculum improve education in reading and writing? If so, how could we ensure that it would be the "right" one? Is educational diversity in the United States both a strength and a weakness?

Will Popularity Kill Success?

Whole language proponents are pleased with the idea that others are coming to understand this approach to teaching and that more children will benefit. However, there is danger in all this popularity (NCTE, 1994): Teachers who don't want to try it and do not understand whole language will be pressured into it. Teachers who want to jump on the new bandwagon will do so without adequate background, make superficial changes to their existing programs, and mistakenly think they have switched to the new approach. Under these circumstances, many predict whole language is doomed to failure. Whole language done poorly will get a bad name just as Open Classrooms done poorly gave Open Education a bad name. As Frank May says, the success of any program "depends upon the knowledge, skill and enthusiasm of the teacher" (1994, p. 298).

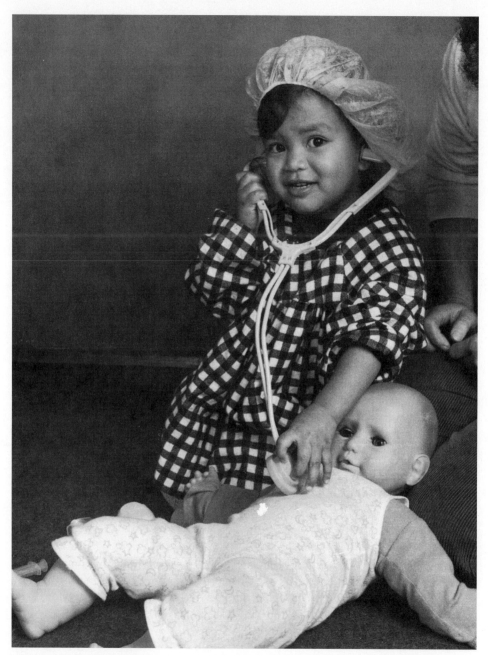

Will popularity kill success?

Are All Instructional Materials Behavioristic?

Emilia Ferreiro says:

> I refuse to conclude my research with the production of new materials, new readiness tests, or new methods. Let me be clear. The tradition of all these "pedagogical gadgets" is behavioristic. These instructional materials are produced, organized, and administered with the idea that adults can control the learning process, that they can decide when it is time to start learning, what is easy to learn and what is difficult to learn, what is "readable," what is "teachable," and what is the right order for presenting stimuli.
>
> *(1990, p. 24)*

The whole language approach is based on the idea that reading and writing are meaningful and purposeful activities. Therefore, literacy practice is embedded in activities that have meaning and purpose for young children. Children can practice literacy skills by writing riddles for a riddle book or reading the daily school lunch menu. Whole language advocates believe that children learn skills as they become necessary for completion of a meaningful literacy task, but that there is no necessary hierarchy or sequence of skills (Goodman, 1986). When children learn phonics, sight words, and other reading skills through whole language approaches, they use written materials that communicate something. Children's dictated account of class events, their invented spelling compositions, or their favorite stories provide the necessary context. Is there a place in this view of literacy instruction for materials other than good books and blank paper, coupled with inspiration?

We also offer a related question: could standardized testing be changed to accommodate whole language? If so, what kind of changes would be necessary?

How Do You Find Support for Continued Growth?

Some changes are easier than others. Most teachers and parents can appreciate better reading material and can accept writing as part of the program, but many cannot conceptualize any other way to teach reading than through directed instruction in isolated skills. Holistic approaches to literacy demand that skills be taught as an integral part of the reading and writing process; this is the part that scares people. Sequential instruction in isolated skills was how they were taught and perhaps how they themselves have taught for years. Some cling to the old ways simply because it is hard to understand the new ones. Others cling because they are afraid that accepting something new means admitting they made a mistake in the past.

We agree that it is hard to understand teaching approaches that you haven't experienced: We believe that observing whole language teachers is essential to becoming one. However, we don't agree that adapting to new information means being ashamed of what we used to do. The learning process for adults as well as children involves letting go of previous ideas to make way for new information. The best anyone can do is the best they know, but what used to be state of the art is now outmoded. The changes in this book from one edition to the next document the changes in the field of emergent literacy as well as new learning by the authors. Keeping current involves knowing both the past and present research as well as nurturing your own personal development (Faucette, 1993/1994).

Teaching in ways consistent with current research sometimes feels uncomfortable. You are making changes, and people often have trouble dealing with change. You may be somewhat insecure about the change, and that feeling makes you vulnerable to criticism. Often, fellow teachers who have taught another way for many years will question new approaches. Parents, having been taught in the old ways, may be concerned that their children aren't bringing home the kind of work they expected. Even principals, who have responsibility for a wide variety of subjects and ages, may not be knowledgeable about new emergent literacy research.

You may have read the research and recommendations from the experts, but still feel shaky about implementing them. It would be easier if you were to teach the same way you were taught as a child. You know what that looks like, even if it is boring and of questionable value. Unfortunately, twelve or thirteen years as a student in public school classrooms often outweighs professional preparation in determining how teachers teach (Ritchie & Wilson, 1993). What can a teacher do to feel more comfortable with current practice? Following are some suggestions you may find useful in answering that question for yourself.

SUPPORT GROUPS

Support groups have proven effective for teachers as well as for other people dealing with change in their lives. A supp rt group may be a couple of fellow teachers who visit and share ideas at lunch or after school, or it may be a formalized national whole language teaching group, complete with newsletter. Some school districts encourage teachers to meet regularly to discuss grade-level issues—another way to form a support group. Professional associations, such as the National Association for the Education of Young Children and the International Reading Association, provide a support group on a larger scale through journal articles and position statements. Some teachers have discovered *The New Advocate*, a journal dedicated to books and the teaching of literature. In addition, there are several whole language support groups around the country; Phoenix-based SMILE (Support and Maintenance for Implementing Language Expression) has been in existence since 1979 and is the prototype for many others (Goodman, Bird, & Goodman, 1991). Computer technology offers another way to communicate with those of like minds: Computer conferences currently facilitate idea exchanges on national and international levels. Though we suspect there are others, we know the computer access for one national whole language computer conference: Ednet@nic.umass.edu.

MENTOR RELATIONSHIPS

A mentor relationship with a teacher you admire may offer a powerful support system for your professional growth. Classes and workshops can get you started, but stalls, breakdowns, and detours along the way are inevitable. If you have someone who is there for "pit stops" and navigation advice along the way, you are more likely to continue to progress successfully. We think a mentor serves a purpose similar to that of an editor—someone who helps you look at your work in order to help you find error and confusion and who then offers suggestions for improvement. Just as children learn the fine points of writing from actually writing and then getting help editing and polishing their efforts, we believe teachers learn the fine points of teaching as they actually teach and then fine-tune their efforts.

EXPLAIN WHAT YOU ARE DOING AND WHY

You can also create support from those around you by explaining what you are doing and why. Ms. Reynolds makes sure that the parents of her students understand her teaching methods and goals. At open house early in the school year, she uses the youngsters in attendance to demonstrate reading of contextualized functional print. She shows off class books made via dictation and encourages children to read them to their parents. She invites parents to a more in-depth presentation in which she reviews the common assumptions explored by youngsters as they experiment with writing. She helps parents to see the connection between the ways children learn to talk and the ways they learn to write. When parents understand why their youngsters are bringing home pages of scribbles instead of phonics worksheets, they become teaching partners instead of critics.

Ms. Montoya makes an effort to communicate with her principal about what she is doing. She invites Mrs. Hanson for special events, such as the grand opening of the class store, which generates much reading and writing as well as mathematics. Occasionally, she arranges for individual children to go to the principal's office to read a story they have written, which makes the child feel very important. Ms. Montoya also shares relevant articles and research with her principal. When she attended a whole language workshop recently, her principal asked Ms. Montoya to make a brief presentation about it in a faculty meeting.

Most teachers find that the very best support comes from their eager students. "Sasha was pointing to the words in the book as she said them out loud, and she did it over and over until she could make her words and the print come out even. It's just like they told us! Children do impose their own study and practice," marvels Ms. Montoya's coworker, who is new to the field of emergent literacy. "I was so worried," admits another new teacher. "For weeks, my kids just scribbled and drew pictures. I thought they would *never* start to write. But, all of a sudden, everyone is writing and everyone wants to share the author's chair."

How About Children with Special Needs?

Sometimes you hear people say that whole language and constructivism are fine for most children, but that they just won't work for children with learning or behavior problems. Children in her classes who surely would have been failures under the old methods have convinced Mrs. Hanna otherwise. She watches Christina, affected by fetal alcohol syndrome, who would be totally confused and frustrated by a workbook page. Christina is rearranging the letters of her own name as she earnestly attempts to put ideas into writing, using the tools she knows. Then she adds more letters, repeatedly writing B O T. Mrs. Hanna wonders where that came from. A conversation with Christina's adopted mother reveals that Christina has been working at writing her brother Robert's name. This child is making progress and feeling good about herself as she learns. The open-ended process approach to emergent literacy is crucial to this child's success.

Christina's story is similar to that of many other children labeled "at risk." These are the ones who most need to have their learning experiences match the ways in which young children learn. Children with everything going for them usually can manage to adapt to less-effective teaching. We are sure that is why developmentally *in*appropriate methods survived for so long: Many children managed to learn in spite of them, while the other children got blamed for having the wrong background and eventually dropped out of school. The amazingly high rate of illiteracy in the United States testifies to past failures of the schools. Even among those who are literate, too few read for pleasure or write as a significant means of self-expression. Clearly, past approaches have not achieved our goals. It is time that we questioned the teaching instead of blaming the children when learning does not occur.

Is Becoming Literate Good for Everyone?

When we try to move out of our ethnocentric views of the world, we do have doubts about whether our values should be imposed on other cultures. It is fairly easy to accept that children from some cultures consider it rude to look at a person to whom they are speaking. It may be harder, but not impossible to accept that children from some cultures consider it bad form to answer a question that a classmate could not. But what about a culture with an oral tradition rather than a literate one? Is it fair to impose our literacy values on a nonliterate culture?

Then we have to think about whether it is fair to expect all children to become literate in *English*. Should the goal be literacy in the child's own lan-

When we try to move out of our ethnocentric views of the world, we do have doubts about whether our literacy values are appropriate for all cultures.

guage? In the United States, parents whose first language is not English generally want their children to speak the dominant language as part of succeeding in the dominant culture. However, children and their parents pay a huge price if this means they cannot communicate comfortably in a common language. Transmission of culture requires intimate conversations in order to include the subtleties.

We ask ourselves about the validity of the current model of an "educated person." Are we still educating for a white, middle-class nation?

Is Professional Theory Linked to World View?

Occasionally, we try to figure out why some people find it so hard to understand and accept an emergent view of literacy. We have a hypothesis that educational views are related to personal life-views. Perhaps people with a generally upbeat and optimistic view of the world tend to perceive children as capable and growth-seeking. They *expect* learners to succeed. Those people would then be more able to accept Piaget's research on children's construction of their own knowledge, more apt to allow youngsters time to learn their own way, and more comfortable with children's trial-and-error approach to learning.

We think that those with a generally pessimistic view of the world tend to see children as having difficulty learning or as not wanting to learn. These people would worry about children failing. Their worry would cause them to try to break down complex concepts into the small pieces they hope will be easy to feed into children's minds. Their worries about failure would make them feel pressured about the pace of a child's learning and cause them to get nervous about incomplete learning or temporary misconceptions.

Those who don't believe in children's innate desire to learn will have trouble accepting that children will work actively to construct their own

Is professional theory linked to world view?

understandings. Such a view of life and learning could leave no alternative but the belief that children won't learn unless adults somehow force knowledge into their minds. This belief is incompatible with accepting that understanding cannot be transmitted to others: Only facts can be given, whereas understanding must be constructed within each child's own mind.

You may find it useful to think about why some people tend to be optimistic and others pessimistic. Which category best describes you? What life experiences might have helped shape you one way or the other? If you yourself experienced learning difficulty, has it given you a more negative view of the learning process? Whether you experienced success or frustration as a student, do you think you might have been a better student with current teaching approaches?

People generally respond as they are treated; therefore trusting that children want to learn encourages them to do so. Trusting children to select the most appropriate learning activities for themselves is part of the package. Teachers need to trust themselves too. They need to trust their own ability to guide children's learning instead of following a recipe book. Administrators and parents need to trust teachers to work without being tied to standardized tests and teaching packages matched with those tests. The whole language approach returns control and responsibility for teaching to teachers. This frees teachers to align their teaching to their students and it frees children to learn in their own best ways. We are sure that one result is greater pleasure in teaching and learning; another result is increased success for all.

CONCLUSION/COMMENCEMENT

Learning is always unfinished: There is never a conclusion, just further steps along the way. We hope the ideas presented and issues raised in this chapter contribute to your thinking and learning process. So, rather than consider this a conclusion to your learning about children's emergent literacy, let's call it a beginning to your further growth as a teacher of young children. We'll be thinking about these ideas, too, and we'd like to hear your thoughts. Exchanges of ideas are essential inspiration to our own continued growth.

DISCUSSION QUESTIONS

1. How can teachers and parents be helped to have faith in children's ability and desire to construct knowledge?
2. How can you learn to view teaching as a process of collaboration with children rather one of directing them?
3. What are the differences between your best and worst memories of early school experiences? Do you find implications for your teaching as you review your own schooling?

RECOMMENDED FURTHER READING

Periodicals

Faucette, R. (1993/94). Sewing my own clothes. *Childhood Education, 70*(2), 97–98.

Mills, H. & Clyde, J. A. (1991). Children's success as readers and writers: It's the teacher's beliefs that make the difference. *Young Children, 46*(2), 54–59.

Ritchie, J. S. & Wilson D. E. (1993, May). Dual apprenticeships: Subverting and supporting critical teaching. *English Education.* 25(2), 67–83.

Books

Ferreiro, E. (1991). Literacy acquisition. In C. Kamii, M. Manning, & G. Manning, *Early literacy: A constructivist foundation for whole language* (pp. 31–56). Washington, DC: National Education Association.

Holdaway, D. (1991). Shared book experience: Teaching reading using favorite books. In C. Kamii, M. Manning, & G. Manning, *Early literacy: A constructivist foundation for whole language* (pp. 91–110). Washington, DC: National Education Association.

Kamii, C. (1991). What is constructivism? In C. Kamii, M. Manning, & G. Manning, *Early literacy: A constructivist foundation for whole language* (pp. 9–16). Washington, DC: National Education Association.

REFERENCES

Books

Allen, J. B., & Mason, J. M. (1989). *Risk makers, risk takers, risk breakers: Reducing the risks for young literacy learners*. Portsmouth, NH: Heinemann.

Almy, M. (1973). *Young children's thinking*. New York: Columbia University Teachers College Press.

Ashton-Warner, S. (1963). *Teacher*. New York: Simon & Schuster.

Baghban, M. (1984). *Our daughter learns to read and write: A case study from birth to three*. Newark, DE: International Reading Association.

Barrett, F. (1982). *A teacher's guide to shared reading*. Richmond Hill, Ontario, Canada: Scholastic-TAB Publications.

Barrs, M. (1989). *The primary language record handbook*. London: Center for Language in Primary Education.

Baskwill, J., & Whitman, P. (1986). *A guide to classroom publishing*. Richmond Hill, Ontario, Canada: Scholastic-TAB Publications.

Baskwill, J., & Whitman, P. (1988). *Evaluation: Whole language, whole child*. Richmond Hill, Ontario, Canada: Scholastic-TAB Publications.

Bloom, B. S. (1956). *Taxonomy of educational objectives*. New York: David McCoy.

Bloome, D. (1986). *Classrooms and literacy*. Norwood, NJ: Ablex.

Boegehold, B. D. (1984). *Getting ready to read*. New York: Ballantine Books.

Bos, B. (1983). *Before the basics*. Sacramento, CA: Cal Central Press.

Bredekamp, S. (1987). *Developmentally appropriate practice in early childhood programs serving children from birth through age 8*. Washington, DC: National Association for the Education of Young Children.

Bredekamp, S., & Rosegrant, T. (Eds.). (1992). *Reaching potentials: Appropriate curriculum and assessment for young children*. (Vol. 1). Washington, DC: National Association for the Education of Young Children.

Bussis, A., Chittenden, E., Amarel, M., & Klausner, E. (1985). *Inquiry into meaning: An investigation of learning to read*. Princeton, NJ: Lawrence Erlbaum Associates.

Butler, D., & Clay, M. (1987). *Reading begins at home: Preparing children for reading before they go to school*. Portsmouth, NH: Heinemann.

Bybee, R., & Sund, R. B. (1982). *Piaget for educators*. Columbus, OH: Merrill.

Calkins, L. M. (1983). *Lessons from a child: On the teaching and learning of writing*. Portsmouth, NH: Heinemann.

Calkins, L. M. (1986). *The art of teaching writing*. Portsmouth, NH: Heinemann.

Carletti, S., Girard, S., & Willing. K. (1991). *The library classroom connection*. Portsmouth, NH: Heinemann.

Cazden, C. (1981). *Language in early childhood education*. Washington, DC: National Association for the Education of Young Children.

Cazden, C. B. (1988). *Classroom discourse: The language of teaching and learning*. Portsmouth, NH: Heinemann.

Chittenden, E., & Courtney, R. (1989). Assessment of young children's reading: Documentation as an alternative to testing. In D. Strickland & L. Morrow (Eds.). *Emerging literacy: Young children learn to read and write* (pp.107–120). Newark, DE: International Reading Association.

Chomsky, C. (1972). *Language and mind*. New York: Harcourt Brace Jovanovich.

Christie, J. F. (1991). *Play and early literacy development*. Albany: State University of New York Press.

Clay, M. M. (1977). *Reading: The patterning of complex behavior*. Exeter, NH: Heinemann.

Clay, M. M. (1975). *What did I write?* Auckland, New Zealand: Heinemann.

Clay, M. (1985). *The early detection of reading difficulties*. Portsmouth, NH: Heinemann.

Clay, M. (1993). *An observation survey of early literacy achievement*. Portsmouth, NH: Heinemann.

Cochran-Smith, M. (1984). *The making of a reader*. Norwood, NJ: Ablex.

Cullinan, B. E. (1987). *Children's literature in the reading program*. Newark, DE: International Reading Association.

Cullinan, B. E. (1989). Literature for young children. In D. Strickland & L. Morrow (Eds.), *Emerging literacy: Young children learn to read and write* (pp. 35–51). Newark, DE: International Reading Association.

Cutting, B., & Milligan, J. (1991). Learning to read in New Zealand. In C. Kamii, M. Manning, & G. Manning (Eds.), *Early literacy: A constructivist foundation for whole language*. Washington, DC: National Education Association.

Davidson, J. (Ed.). (1988). *Counterpoint and beyond: A response to becoming a nation of readers*. Urbana, IL: National Council of Teachers of English.

Duckworth, E. (1987). *The having of wonderful ideas and other essays on teaching and learning*. New York: Teachers College Press.

Durkin, D. (1980). *Teaching young children to read*. Boston: Allyn & Bacon.

Early Childhood and Literacy Development Committee of the International Reading Association. (1986). *A policy statement concerning literacy and pre–first grade*. Newark, DE: International Reading Association.

Educational Testing Service. (1984). *The ETS evaluation of writing to read*. Princeton, NJ: Educational Testing Service.

Feeney, S., & Moravcek, E. (1994). SS Curric: Who am I? AGS.

Feitelson, D. (1988). *Facts and fads in beginning reading: A cross-language perspective*. Norwood, NJ: Ablex.

Ferreiro, E. (1986). *The interplay between information and assimilation in beginning literacy*. In W. H. Teale & E. Sulzby (Eds.), *Emergent literacy: Writing and reading* (pp. 15–49). Norwood, NJ: Ablex.

Ferreiro, E. (1990). Literacy Development: Psychogenesis. In Y. Goodman, *How children construct literacy* (pp. 12–25). Newark, DE: International Reading Association.

Ferreiro, E. (1991). Literacy acquisition. In C. Kamii, M. Manning, & G. Manning, *Early literacy: A constructivist foundation for whole language* (pp. 31–56). Washington, DC: National Education Association.

Ferreiro, E., & Teberosky, A. (1982). *Literacy before schooling.* Exeter, NH: Heinemann.

Fields, M. (1988). Reading in preschool? In E. Jones (Ed.), *Reading, writing and talking with four, five and six year olds* (pp. 15–18). Pasadena, CA: Pacific Oaks College.

Fields, M. (1989). *Literacy begins at birth.* Tucson, AZ: Fisher Books.

Fields, M. V., & Boesser, C. (1994). *Constructive guidance and discipline: Preschool and primary education.* New York: Merrill/Macmillan.

Fisher, B. (1991). *Joyful learning.* Portsmouth NH: Heinemann.

Forman, G. E., & Kuschner, D. S. (1984). *The child's construction of knowledge: Piaget for teaching children.* Washington, DC: National Association for the Education of Young Children.

Frank, M. (1979). *If you're trying to teach kids how to write, you've gotta have this book!* Nashville, TN: Incentive Publications.

Fry, E. B., Kress, J. E., Fountoukidis, D. L., & Polk, J. K. (1993). *The reading teachers' book of lists* (3rd ed.). Englewood Cliffs, NJ: Prentice Hall.

Genishi, C. (Ed.). (1992). *Ways of assessing children and curriculum.* New York: Teacher's College Press.

Genishi, C., & Dyson, A. H. (1984). *Language assessment in the early years.* Norwood, NJ: Ablex.

Gentry, J. R. (1987). *Spel . . . is a four-letter word.* Portsmouth, NH: Heinemann.

Gentry, J. R., & Gillet, J. W. (1992). *Teaching kids to spell.* Portsmouth, NH: Heinemann.

Glazer, J. I. (1991). *Literature for young children* (3rd ed.). New York: Merrill/Macmillan.

Glazer, S. (1989). Oral language and literacy development. In D. Strickland & L. Morrow (Eds.), *Emerging literacy: Young children learn to read and write* (pp. 16–26). Newark, DE: International Reading Association.

Glazer, S. M. (1980). *Getting ready to read: Creating readers from birth through six.* Englewood Cliffs, NJ: Prentice-Hall.

Goodman, K. S. (1968). *The psycholinguistic nature of the reading process.* Detroit: Wayne State University.

Goodman, K. S. (1973). *Miscue analysis: Applications to reading instruction,* Urbana, IL: National Council of Teachers of English.

Goodman, K. S. (1986). *What's whole in whole language?* Richmond Hill, Ontario, Canada: Scholastic-TAB Publications.

Goodman, K. S., Bird, L. M., & Goodman, Y. M. (1992). *The whole language catalogue: Supplement on authentic assessment.* Chicago: SRA, Macmillan/McGraw-Hill.

Goodman, K. S., Goodman, Y., & Hood, W. J. (1989). *The whole language evaluation book.* Portsmouth, NH: Heinemann.

Goodman, K., Shannon, P, Freeman, Y., & Murphy, S. (1988). *Report card on basal readers.* Katonah, NY: Richard C. Owen Publishers.

Goodman, Y. M. (1986). Children coming to know literacy. In W. Teale & E. Sulzby (Eds.), *Emergent literacy: Writing and reading* (pp. 1–14). Norwood NJ: Ablex.

Goodman, Y. M. (1990). *How children construct literacy: Piagetian perspectives.* Newark, DE: International Reading Association.

Goodman, Y. M., & Burke, C. L. (1972). *Reading miscue inventory manual: Procedure for diagnosis and evaluation.* New York: Macmillan.

Gordon, N. (1984). *Classroom experiences: The writing process in action.* Portsmouth, NH: Heinemann.

Graves, D. H. (1983). *Writing: Teachers and children at work.* Exeter, NH: Heinemann.

Graves, D. H. (1991). *Building a literate classroom*. Portsmouth, NH: Heinemann.

Grossi, E. P. (1990). Applying psychogenesis principles to the literacy instruction of lower-class children in Brazil. In Goodman, Y. (Ed.), *How children construct literacy* (pp. 99–111). Newark, DE: International Reading Association.

Hall, N. (1989). *Writing with reason: The emergence of authorship in young children*. Portsmouth, NH: Heinemann.

Halliday, M. A. K. (1982). Three aspects of children's language development: Learning language, learning through language, learning about language. In Y. Goodman, M. Haussler, & D. Strickland (Eds.), *Oral and written language development research: Impact on the schools*. Urbana, IL: National Council of Teachers of English.

Harste, J. C., Short, K. G., & Burke, C. (1988). *Creating classrooms for authors*. Portsmouth, NH: Heinemann.

Harste, J. C., & Woodward, V. (1989). Fostering needed change in early literacy programs. In D. Strickland & L. Morrow (Eds.), *Emerging literacy: Young children learn to read and write* (pp. 147–159). Newark, DE: International Reading Association.

Hart-Hewins, L., & Wells, J. (1990). *Real books for reading: Learning to read with children's literature*. Portsmouth, NH: Heinemann.

Harwayne, S. (1992). *Lasting impressions: Weaving literature into the writing workshop*. Portsmouth, NH: Heinemann.

Healy, J. M. (1990). *Endangered minds*. New York: Touchstone.

Hendrick, J. (1992). *The whole child (5th ed.)*. New York: Merrill/Macmillan.

Hickman, J., & Cullinan, B. (Eds.). (1989). *Children's literature in the classroom: Weaving Charlotte's web.* Needham Heights, MA: Christopher-Gordon.

Hillerich, P. (1985). *Teaching children to write, K–8*. Englewood Cliffs, NJ: Prentice Hall.

Hirsch, E. (1974). *The block book*. Washington, DC: National Association for the Education of Young Children.

Holdaway, D. (1979). *The foundations of literacy*. New York: Ashton Scholastic.

Holdaway, D. (1991). Shared book experience: Teaching reading using favorite books. In C. Kamii, M. Manning, & G. Manning (Eds.), *Early literacy: A constructivist foundation for whole language* (pp. 91–110). Washington, DC: National Education Association.

Hoot, J., & Silvern, S. (1988). *Writing with computers in the early grades*. New York: Teacher's College Press.

Hornsby, D., & Sukarna, D. (1988). *Read on: A conference approach to reading*. Portsmouth, NH: Heinemann.

Huck, C. (1987). *Children's literature in the elementary curriculum*. New York: Holt, Rinehart & Winston.

Huck, C., Hepler, S., & Hickman, J. (1993). *Children's literature in the elementary school*. Fort Worth: Harcourt Brace Jovanovich.

Hymes, J. L. (1981). *Teaching the child under six*. Columbus, OH: Merrill.

Infant Education Committee. (1986). *Beginning reading*. Melbourne, Australia: Curriculum Branch, Ministry of Education.

Infant Education Committee. (1987). *Reading on*. Melbourne, Australia: Curriculum Branch, Ministry of Education.

Johnson, T. D., & Louis, D. R. (1990). Bringing it all together: A program for literacy. Portsmouth, NH: Heinemann.

Jones, E. (1986). *Teaching adults: An active learning approach*. Washington, DC: National Association for the Education of Young Children.

Jones, E., & Reynolds, G. (1992). *The play's the thing: Teacher's roles in children's play.* New York: Teachers College Press.

Kamii, C. (1982). *Number in preschool and kindergarten.* Washington, DC: National Association for the Education of Young Children.

Kamii, C. (1985). *Young children reinvent arithmetic.* New York: Teachers College Press.

Kamii, C. (1990). *Achievement testing in the early grades: The games grownups play.* Washington, DC: National Association for the Education of Young Children.

Kamii, C. (1991). What is constructivism? In C. Kamii, M. Manning, & G. Manning, *Early literacy: A constructivist foundation for whole language* (pp. 17–30). Washington, DC: National Education Association.

Kamii, C., & DeVries, R.. (1980). *Group games in early education: Implications of Piaget's theory.* Washington, DC: National Association for the Education of Young Children.

Kamii, C., Manning, M., & Manning, G. (Eds.). (1991). *Early literacy: A constructivist foundation for whole language.* Washington, DC: National Education Association.

Katz, L. G., & Chard, S. C. (1989). *Engaging children's minds: The project approach.* Norwood, NJ: Ablex.

Lamoreaux, L., & Lee, D. M. (1943). *Learning to read through experience.* New York: Appleton-Century-Crofts.

Landsmann, L. T. (1990). Literacy development and pedagogical implications: Evidence from the Hebrew system of writing. In Y. Goodman (Ed.), *How children construct literacy* (pp. 26–44). Newark, DE: International Reading Association.

Lee, D., & Allen, R. V. (1963). *Learning to read through experience.* Englewood Cliffs, NJ: Prentice-Hall.

Lee, D., & Rubin, J. (1979). *Children and language.* Belmont, CA: Wadsworth Publishing.

Mason, J. (1989). *Reading & writing connections.* Needham Heights, MA: Allyn & Bacon Publishers.

Mason, J., Peterman, C., & Kerr, B. (1989). Reading to kindergarten children. In D. Strickland & L. Morrow (Eds.), *Emerging literacy: Young children learn to read and write* (pp. 52–62). Newark, DE: International Reading Association.

Mason, J. M., & Stewart, J. P. (1990). Emergent literacy assessment for instruction and assessment. In L. Morrow & J. Smith (Eds.). *Assessment for instruction in early literacy* (pp.155–175). Englewood Cliffs, NJ: Prentice Hall.

May, F. B. (1994). *Reading as communication: An interactive approach (4th ed.).* New York: Merrill/Macmillan.

McAdams, R. P. (1993). *Lessons from abroad: How other countries educate their children.* Lancaster, PA: Technomic Publishing Co.

McCracken, J. (1993). *Valuing diversity in the primary years.* Washington, DC: National Association for the Education of Young Children.

Morrow, L. M. (1993). *Literacy development in the early years.* Boston: Allyn & Bacon.

Morrow, L. M., & Smith, J. K. (1990). *Assessment for instruction in early literacy.* Englewood Cliffs, NJ: Prentice-Hall.

Paley, V. (1981). *Wally's stories.* Cambridge, MA: Harvard University Press.

Papert, S. (1980). *Mindstorms.* New York: Basic Books.

Parry, J. & Hornsby, D. (1988). *Write-on: A conference approach to writing.* Portsmouth, NH: Heinemann.

Pearson, D. (1984). *Handbook of reading research.* New York: Longman.

Peetoom, A. (1986). *Shared reading: Safe risks with whole books.* Richmond Hill, Ontario, Canada: Scholastic-TAB Publications.

Pflaum, S. (1986). *The development of language and literacy in young children.* New York: Merrill/Macmillan.

Piaget, J. (1962). *Plays, dreams, and imitation.* New York: W. W. Norton.

Piaget, J. (1963). *The origins of intelligence in children.* New York: W. W. Norton.

Piaget, J. (1964). *Judgment form and reasoning in the child.* Paterson, N.J.: Littlefield, Adams & Co.

Piaget, J. (1973). *To understand is to invent.* New York: Viking.

Piaget, J. (1985). *The equilibration of cognitive structures.* Chicago: University of Chicago Press.

Piaget, J., & Garcia, R. (1989). *Psychogenesis: The history of science.* New York: Columbia University Press.

Piaget, J., & Inhelder, B. (1969). *The psychology of the child.* New York: Basic Books.

Piers, M., & Landau, G. M. (1980). *The gift of play.* New York: Walker & Co.

Pinnell, G. S., & Matlin, M. L. (Eds.). (1989). *Teachers and research.* Newark, DE: International Reading Association.

Pontecorvo, C., & Zucchermaglio, C. (1990). A passage to literacy: Learning in a social context. In Y. Goodman (Ed.), *How children construct literacy* (pp. 59–98). Newark, DE: International Reading Association.

Rhodes, L. K., & Dudley-Marling, K. (1988). *Readers and writers with a difference: A holistic approach to teaching learning disabled and remedial students.* Portsmouth, NH: Heinemann.

Rogers, C., & Sawyers, J. (1988). *Play in the lives of children.* Washington, DC: National Association for the Education of Young Children.

Rudman, M. (1984). *Children's literature: An issues approach.* New York: Longman.

Saunders, R. (1984). *Piagetian perspective for preschools: A thinking book.* Englewood Cliffs, NJ: Prentice-Hall.

Schwartz, J. I. (1988). *Encouraging early literacy: An integrated approach to reading and writing in N–3.* Portsmouth, NH: Heinemann.

Sebesta, S. L. (1987). Enriching the arts and humanities through children's books. In B. E. Cullinan (Ed.), *Children's literature in the reading program.* Newark, DE: International Reading Association.

Siegrist, F., & Sinclair, H. (1991). In C. Kamii, M. Manning, & G. Manning (Eds.), *Early literacy: A constructivist foundation for whole language* (pp. 57–68). Washington, DC: National Education Association.

Silvaroli, N. J. (1982). *Classroom reading inventory.* Dubuque, IA: Wm. C. Brown.

Slapin, B., & Seale, D. (1992). *Through Indian eyes.* Philadelphia: New Society Publishers.

Sloan, P., & Latham, R. (1981). *Teaching reading is. . . .* Melbourne, Australia: Thomas Nelson Australia.

Smith, F. (1975). *Comprehension and learning.* New York: Holt, Rinehart & Winston.

Smith, F. (1982). *Understanding reading.* New York: Holt, Rinehart & Winston.

Smith, F. (1982). *Writing and the writer.* New York: Holt, Rinehart & Winston.

Smith, J. K. (1990). Measurement issues in early literacy assessment. In L. Morrow & J. Smith (Eds.), *Assessment for instruction in early literacy* (pp. 62–73). Englewood Cliffs, NJ: Prentice Hall.

Snow, C., & Ninio, A. (1986). The contracts of literacy: What children learn from learning to read books. W. Teale & E. Sulzby (Eds.), *Emergent literacy: Writing and reading* (pp. 116–138). Norwood NJ: Ablex.

Stallman, A., & Pearson, P. D. (1990). Formal measures of early literacy. In L. Morrow & J. Smith (Eds.). *Assessment for instruction in early literacy* (pp. 7–44). Englewood Cliffs, NJ: Prentice Hall.

Stewig, J. W., & Sebesta, S. L. (1989). *Using literature in the elementary classroom.* Urbana, IL: National Council of Teachers of English.

Stoll, D. R. (1990). *Magazines for children.* Glassboro, NJ: Educational Press Association.

Strickland, D. (1989). A model for change: Framework for an emergent literacy curriculum. In D. Strickland & L. Morrow (Eds.), *Emerging literacy: Young children learn to read and write.* Newark, DE: International Reading Association.

Strickland, D. S., & Morrow, L. M. (Eds.). (1989). *Emerging literacy: Young children learn to read and write.* Newark, DE: International Reading Association.

Strickland, D., & Taylor, D. (1989). Family storybook reading: Implications for children, families and curriculum. In D. Strickland & L. Morrow (Eds.), *Emerging literacy: Young children learn to read and write* (pp. 27–34). Newark, DE: International Reading Association.

Sulzby, E. (1986). Writing and reading: Signs of oral and written language organization in the young child. In W. Teale & E. Sulzby (Eds.), *Emergent literacy: Writing and reading* (pp. 50–89). Norwood, NJ: Ablex.

Sulzby, E. (1990). Assessment of writing and of children's language while writing. In L. Morrow & J. Smith (Eds.), *Assessment for instruction in early literacy* (pp. 83–109). Englewood Cliffs, NJ: Prentice Hall.

Sulzby, E. & Barnhart, J. (1990). The developing kindergarten: All our children emerge as writers and readers. In J. S. McKee (Ed.), *The developing kindergarten programs, children, and teachers* (p. 218). Ann Arbor: Michigan Association of the Education of Young Children.

Sulzby, E., Barnhart, J., & Hieshima, J. (1989). Forms of writing and rereading from writing: A preliminary report. In J. Mason (Ed.), *Reading and writing connections* (pp. 31–63). Needham Heights, MA: Allyn & Bacon.

Sulzby, E., Teale, W., & Kamberelis, G. (1989). Emergent writing in the classroom: Home and school connections. In D. Strickland & L. Morrow (Eds.), *Emerging literacy: Young children learn to read and write* (pp. 63–79). Newark, DE: International Reading Association.

Sutherland, Z., & Arbuthnot, M. H. (1986). *Children and books.* Glenview, IL: Scott, Foresman.

Taitt, H. (1982). *Thinking-learning-creating: TLC for growing minds.* Charleston, IL: Creative Learning Associates.

Taylor, D. (1983). *Family literacy.* Exeter, NH: Heinemann.

Taylor, D. (1986). Creating family story: "Matthew! We're going to have a ride!" In W. Teale & E. Sulzby (Eds.), *Emergent literacy: Writing and reading* (pp. 139–155). Norwood, NJ: Ablex.

Teale, W. H. (1984). Reading to young children: Its significance for literacy development. In H. Goelman, A. Oberg, & F. Smith (Eds.), *Awakening literacy.* Exeter, NH: Heinemann.

Teale, W. (1986). Home background and young children's literacy development. In W. Teale & E. Sulzby (Eds.), *Emergent literacy: Writing and reading* (pp. 173–206). Norwood, NJ: Ablex.

Teale, W. H. (1990). The promise and challenge of informal assessment in early literacy. In L. Morrow & J. Smith (Eds.), *Assessment for instruction in early literacy* (pp. 45–61). Englewood Cliffs, NJ: Prentice Hall.

Teale, W. H., & Sulzby, E. (Eds.). (1986). *Emergent literacy: Writing and reading.* Norwood, NJ: Ablex.

Teale, W., & Sulzby, E. (1989). Emergent literacy. New perspectives. In D. Strickland & L. Morrow (Eds.),

Emerging literacy. Young children learn to read and write (pp. 1–15). Newark, DE: International Reading Association.

Teberosky, A. (1990). The language young children write: Reflections on a learning situation. In Y. M. Goodman, *How children construct literacy: Piagetian perspectives* (pp. 45–58). Newark, DE: International Reading Association.

Temple, C. A., Nathan, R. G., Temple, F., & Burris, N. A. (1993). *The beginnings of writing.* Boston: Allyn & Bacon.

Tierny, R. J., Carter, M. A., & Deaai, L. E. (1991). *Portfolio assessment in the reading-writing classroom.* Norwood, MA: Christopher-Gordon.

Trealease, J. (1989). *The new read-aloud handbook.* New York: Penguin Books.

Tucker, N. (1982). *The child and the book: A psychological and literary exploration.* New York: Cambridge University Press.

Vacca, R., & Vacca, J. (1989). *Content area reading* (3rd ed.). Glenview, IL: Scott, Foresman.

Veatch, J. (1968). *How to teach reading with children's books* (2nd ed.). New York: Citation Press.

Vygotsky, L. A. (1978). *Mind in society: The development of higher psychological processes* (M. Cole et al., Trans. & Ed.). Cambridge, MA: Harvard University Press.

Wells, G. (1986). *The meaning makers: Children learning language and using language to learn.* Portsmouth, NJ: Heinemann.

Wilson, G., & Moss, J. (1988). *Books for children to read alone.* New York: R. R. Bowker.

Wilson, L. (1979). *Write me a sign: About language experience.* Melbourne, Australia: Thomas Nelson.

Wortham, S. C. (1990). *Tests and measurement in early childhood education.* New York: Merrill/Macmillan.

Periodicals

Allington, R. L. (1993). Michael doesn't go down the hall anymore. *The Reading Teacher, 46*(7), 602–604.

Altwerger, B., Diehl-Faxon, J., & Dockstader-Anderson, K. (1985). Read-aloud events as meaning construction. *Language Arts, 62*(5), 476–484.

Anselmo, S., & Zinck, P. (1987). Computers for young children? Perhaps. *Young Children, 42*(3), 22–27.

Barclay, K., & Breheny, C. (1994, summer). Hey, look me over! Assess, evaluate, and conference with confidence. *Chilhood Education, 70*(4), 215–220.

Bergen, J. R., & Feld, J. K. (1993). Developmental assessments: New directions. *Young Children, 48*(5), 41–47.

Bridge, C. A., Winograd, P. M., & Haley, D. (May, 1983). Using predictable materials vs. preprimers to teach beginning sight words. *The Reading Teacher, 36*(9), 884–891.

Bussis, A. M., & Chittenden, E. A. (1987). Research currents: What the reading tests neglect. *Language Arts, 64*(3), 302–308.

Carger, C. L. (1993). Louie comes to life: Pretend reading with second language emergent readers. *Language Arts, 709*(7), 542–547.

Carter, M., & Jones, E. (1990, September/October). The teacher as observer: The director as role model. *Child Care Information Exchange, 75,* 27–30.

Christie, J. F., & Wardle, F. (1992). How much time is needed for play? *Young Children, 47*(3), 28–33.

Church, S. M. (1994). Is whole language really warm and fuzzy? *The Reading Teacher, 47*(5), 362–370.

Clay, M. (1986). Constructive processes: Talking, reading, writing, art, and craft. *The Reading Teacher, 39*(8), 764–770.

Clements, N., and Warncke, E. (1994). Helping literacy emerge at school for less-advantaged children. *Young Children 49*(3), 22–26.

Clyde, J. A. (1991). Lessons from Douglas: Expanding our visions what it means to "know." *Language Arts, 47*(1), 22–23.

Crafton, L., & Burke, C. (1994, April). Inquiry-based evaluation: Teachers and students reflecting together. *Primary Voices K–6, 2*(2), 2–7.

Cunningham, P., & Cunningham, J. (1992). Making words: Enhancing the invented spelling-decoding connection. *The Reading Teacher, 46*(2), 106–114.

Danielson, K. E. (1992, April). Learning about early writing from response to literature. *Language Arts, 69,* 274–280.

Davis, S. J. (1994). Give them a reason to read. *Principal, 73*(4), 37–39.

Degroff, L. J. (1989). Developing writing processes with children's literature. *The New Advocate, 2*(2), 115–123.

Dickerson, D. P. (1982). A study of the use of games to reinforce sight vocabulary. *The Reading Teacher, 36*(1), 46–49.

Dooley, C. (1993). The challenge: Meeting the needs of gifted readers. *The Reading Teacher 46*(7), 546–551.

Duckworth, E. (1973, October). Piaget takes a teacher's look. *Learning Magazine,* pp. 22–27.

Dukes, L. (1982). Dramatic play + symbolic props = reading. *Day Care and Early Education, 10*(3), 11–13.

Dumtschin, J. U. (1988). Recognize language development and delay in early childhood. *Young Children, 43*(3), 16–24.

Dyson, A. (1987). The value of "time off task": Young children's spontaneous talk and deliberate text. *Harvard Educational Review,* 57(4), 396–420.

Dyson, A. H. (1982, Fall). The emergence of visible language: Interrelationships between drawing and early writing. *Visible Language,* pp. 360–381.

Dyson, A. H. (1982, October). Teachers and young children: Missed connections in teaching/learning to write. *Language Arts,* 59, 674–680.

Dyson, A. H. (1982, November/December). Reading, writing, and language: Young children solving the written language puzzle. *Language Arts,* 59, 829–839.

Dyson, A. H. (1984). N spell my grandmama. *The Reading Teacher,* 38(3), 262–271.

Dyson, A. H. (1985). Puzzles, paints, & pencils: Writing emerges. *Educational Horizons,* 64(1), 13–16.

Dyson, A. H. (1985). Writing and the social lives of children. *Language Arts,* 62, 632–639.

Edwards, L. H. (1994). Kid's eye view of reading: Kindergartners talk about leaning how to read. *Childhood Education,* 70(3), 137–141.

Egawa, K. (1990, October). Harnessing the power of language: First graders' literature engagement with Owl Moon. *Language Arts, 67,* 582–588.

Eller, R. (1989). Johnny can't talk, either: The perpetuation of the deficit theory in classrooms. *The Reading Teacher,* 42(9), 670–674.

Elster, C. A. (1994). I guess they do listen: Young children's emergent readings after adult read-alouds. *Young Children,* 49(3), 27-31.

Farris, P. (1989). Story time and story journals: Linking literature and writing. *The New Advocate, 2*(3), 179–185.

Faucette, R. (1993/94). Sewing my own clothes. *Childhood Education, 70*(2), 97–98.

Feeley, J. T. (1984). Print and reading: What do preschoolers know? *Day Care and Early Education, 11*(3), 26–28.

Fein, G. G. (1981). Pretend play in childhood: An integrative review. *Child Development, 52,* 1095–1118.

Fields, M. (1988). Talking and writing: Explaining the whole language approach to parents. *The Reading Teacher, 41*(9), 898–903.

Fields, M. V., & Hillstead, D. V. (1986). Reading begins with scribbling. *Principal, 65*(5), 24–27.

Fitzgerald, J. (1988). Helping children revise: A brief review for teachers. *The Reading Teacher, 42*(2), 124–129.

Fitzgerald, J. (1989). Enhancing two related thought processes: Revision in writing and critical reading. *The Reading Teacher, 42*(1), 42–48.

Fitzgerald, J. (1993, May). Literacy and students who are learning English as a second language. *The Reading Teacher, 46*, 638–647.

Flood, J., Lapp, D., Flood., S, & Nagel, G. (1992). Am I allowed to group? Using flexible patterns for effective reading instruction. *The Reading Teacher, 45*(8), 608–616.

Flores, B., Cousin, P. T., & Diaz, E. (1991, September). Transforming deficit myths about learning, language, and culture. *Language Arts. 68*, 369–379.

Fractor, J. S., Woodruff, M. C., Martinez, M. G., & Teale, W. (1993). Let's not miss opportunities to promote voluntary reading: Classroom libraries in the elementary school. *The Reading Teacher, 46*(6), 476–485.

Franklin, E. (1988). Reading and writing stories: Children creating meaning. *The Reading Teacher, 42*(3), 184–190.

Freebody, P., & Baker, C. (1985). Children's first schoolbooks: Introductions to the culture of literacy. *Harvard Educational Review, 55*(4), 381–398.

Freeman, D. E., & Freeman, Y. S. (1993). Strategies for promoting the primary language of all students. *The Reading Teacher, 46*(7), 552–558.

Freeman, Y., & Whitesell, L. R. (1985). What preschoolers already know about print. *Educational Horizons, 64*(1), 22–24.

Freire, P. (1985, January). Reading the world and reading the word: An interview with Paulo Freire. *Language Arts, 62*, 15–21.

Genishi, C. (1988). Children's language: Learning words from experience. *Young Children, 44*(1), 16–23.

Genishi, C., & Dyson, A. H. (1984, Winter). Ways of talking: Respecting differences. *Beginnings,* pp. 7–10.

Girling-Butcher, W., Phillips, G., & Clay, M. (1991). Emerging readers and writers: Fostering independent learning. *The Reading Teacher, 44*(9), 694–697.

Goldfield, B. (1984, Winter). The fine art of reading aloud. *Beginnings*, pp. 27–29.

Goodman, Y. M. (1985). Developing writing in a literate society. *Educational Horizons, 64*(1), 17–21.

Graham, S. (1993-1994). Are slanted manuscript alphabets superior to the traditional manuscript alphabet? *Childhood Education, 70*(2), 91–96.

Graves, D., & Hansen, J. (1983, February). The author's chair. *Language Arts, 60*, 177–183.

Green, J. O. (1984, March). An interview with Don Graves. *Classroom Computer Learning,* pp. 20–23.

Gross, A. & Ortiz, W. L. (1994). Using children's literature to facilitate inclusion in kindergarten and the primary grades. *Young Children, 49*(3), 32-35.

Hall, N., & Duffy, R. (1987). Every child has a story to tell. *Language Arts, 64*(5), 523–529.

Harp, B. (1988). When the principal asks "When you do whole language instruction, how will you keep track of reading and writing skills?" *The Reading Teacher, 42*(2), 160–161.

Harp, B. (1988). Doesn't play steal time from reading? *The Reading Teacher, 42*(3), 244–245.

Harp, B. (1989). Why aren't you using the phonics workbooks? *The Reading Teacher, 42*(4), 326–327.

Harp, B. (1989). When the principal asks "What do we know about ability grouping?" *The Reading Teacher,* 42(6), 430–431.

Harp, B. (1989). When the principal asks "What do we put in the place of ability groupings?" *The Reading Teacher,* 42(7), 534–535.

Harp, B. (1989). When the principal asks "How are we using what we know about literacy process in the content areas?" *The Reading Teacher,* 42(9), 726–727.

Harste, J. C. (1993, April). Inquiry-based instruction. *Primary Voices,* pp. 2–5.

Hill, L. B., & Hale, M. G. (1991). Reading recovery: Questions classroom teachers ask. *The Reading Teacher,* 44(7), 480–485.

Hills, T. W., (1993). Assessment in context—Teachers and children at work. *Young Children,* 48(5), 20–28.

Hohmann, C., & Buckleitner, W. (1988, September). Six good computer programs for young children. *Exchange,* pp. 15–17.

Hoffman, J. V., Roser, N. L., & Battle, J. (March 1993). Reading aloud in classrooms: From the modal to a "model." *The Reading Teacher,* 46(6), 469–503.

Honig, A. S. (1984, Winter). Why talk to babies? *Beginnings,* p. 306.

The Horn Book Magazine. Boston, MA.

Hoyt, L. (1992). Many ways of knowing: Using drama, oral interactions, and the visual arts to enhance reading comprehension. *The Reading Teacher.* 45(8), 580–584.

Hughes, S. M. (1993). The impact of whole language on four elementary school libraries. *Language Arts,* 70(5), 393–399.

Hymes, J. (1965, March). Being taught to read. *Grade Teacher, 82,* 88–92.

Interracial Books for Children [periodical]. New York: Council on Interracial Books for Children.

Isenberg, J., & Quisenberry, N. (1988). Play: A necessity for all children. *Childhood Education, 64*(3), 138–145.

Johnston, P. H., & Harmon, S. (1992). Snow White and the seven warnings: Threats to authentic evaluation. *The Reading Teacher, 46*(3), 250–252.

Johnston, J. S., & Wilder, S. L. (1992). Changing reading and writing programs through staff development. *The Reading Teacher, 45*(8), 626–631.

Kamii, C. (1985). Leading primary education toward excellence: Beyond worksheets and drill. *Young Children, 40*(6), 3–9.

Kamii, C., & Randazzo, M. (1985). Social interaction and invented spelling. *Language Arts, 62*(2), 124–133.

Komoski, K. (1984). Educational computing: The burden of ensuring quality. *Phi Delta Kappan, 66*(4), 244–248.

Lamme, L. L. (1989). Authorship: A key facet of whole language. *The Reading Teacher, 42*(9), 704–710.

Lohr, S. (1993, December 8). Microsoft aims at 10-and-under set. *In Star-Bulletin,* p. C-6.

Manning, M., Manning, G., & Kamii, C. (1988). Early phonics instruction: Its effect on literacy development. *Young Children, 44*(1), 4–8.

Martinez, M. (1983, February). Exploring young children's comprehension through story time talk. *Language Arts, 60,* 202–209.

Martinez, M., & Teale, W. (1987). The ins and outs of a kindergarten writing program. *The Reading Teacher, 40*(4), 444–451.

Martinez, M., & Teale, W. (1988). Reading in a kindergarten classroom library. *The Reading Teacher, 41*(6), 586–572.

Meisels, S. J., (1993). Remaking classroom assessment with the work sampling system. *Young Children, 48*(5), 34–40.

Mills, H., & Clyde, J. A. (1991). Children's success as readers and writers: It's the teacher's beliefs that make the difference. *Young Children, 46*(2), 54–59.

National Association for the Education of Young Children. (1988, March).

NAEYC position statement on standardized testing of young children 3 through 8 years of age. *Young Children, 42,* 42–47.

National Association for the Education of Young Children & the National Association of Early Childhood Specialist in State Departments of Education (1991). Guidelines for appropriate curriculum content and assessment in programs serving children ages 3 through 8. *Young Children, 41*(3), 47–52.

National Council of Teachers of English (1994, February). The practice and politics of whole language. *The Council Chronicle, 3*(3), 1 & 7.

Nourot, P. M., & Van Hoorn, J. L. (1991). Symbolic play in preschool and primary settings. *Young Children, 46*(6).

O'Flahavan, J., & Blassberg, R. (1992). Toward an embedded model of spelling instruction for emergent literates. *Language Arts, 69*(6), 409–417.

O'Neal, S. (1991, September). Leadership in the language arts: Dear principal, please let my special education child read and write. *Language Arts, 68,* 417–423.

Pellegrini, A. D. (1980). The relationship between kindergartners' play and achievement in prereading, language, and writing. *Psychology in the Schools, 17*(4), 530–535.

Pellegrini, A. D. (1991, September). A critique of the concept of at risk as applied to emergent literacy. *Language Arts, 68,* 380–385.

Pils, L. J. (1993). "I love you, Miss Piss." *The Reading Teacher, 46*(8), 648–653.

Pinnell, G. S., Fried, M. D., & Estice, R. M. (1990). Reading recovery: Learning how to make a difference. *The Reading Teacher, 43*(4), 282–295.

Provenzo, E., & Brett, A. (1984). Creative block play. *Day Care and Early Education, 11*(3), pp. 6–8.

Rasinski, T., & Fredericks, A. (1987). Dimensions of parent involvement. *The Reading Teacher, 43*(2), 180–181.

Reimer, B., & Warshow, L. (1989). Questions we ask of ourselves and our students. *The Reading Teacher, 42*(8), 596–606.

Reutzell, D. R. (1992, Fall). Breaking the letter-a-week tradition. *Childhood Education,* 20–23.

Reutzell, D. R., & Cooter, R. B., Jr., (1991, April). Organizing for effective instruction: The reading workshop. *The Reading Teacher, 44,* 548–554.

Riding, R. J., & Powell, S. D. (1987). The effect on reasoning, reading and number performance of computer-presented critical thinking activities in five-year-old children. *Educational Psychology, 7*(1), 55–65.

Ritchie, J. S., & Wilson, D. E. (1993). Dual apprenticeships: Subverting and supporting critical teaching. *English Education, 25*(2), 67–83.

Roser, N., & Martinez, M. (1985), Roles adults play in preschoolers' response to literature. *Language Arts, 62*(5), 485–490.

Roskos, K. (1988). Literacy at work in play. *The Reading Teacher, 41*(6), 562–567.

Roskos, K. A., & Neuman, S. B. (1994). Of scribbles, schemas, and storybooks: Using literacy albums to document young children's literacy growth. *Young Children, 49*(2), 78–85.

Salvage, G. J., & Brazee, P. E. (1991, September). Risk taking, bit by bit. *Language Arts, 68,* 356–366.

Schacter, F. F., & Strage, A. A. (1982). Adults' talk and children's language development. In S. G. Moore & C. R. Cooper (Eds.), *The young child: Reviews of research* (Vol. 3). Washington, DC: National Association for the Education of Young Children.

Schell, L. M. (1988). Dilemmas in assessing reading comprehension. *The Reading Teacher, 42*(1), 12–16.

Schweinhard, L. J. (1993). Observing young children in action: The key to early childhood assessment. *Young Children, 48*(5), 29–33.

Seefeldt, C. (1984). What's in a name. *Young Children, 39*(5), 24–53.

Shannon, P. (1985, October). Reading instruction and social class. *Language Arts, 62,* 604–613.

Sharp, J. (1993). Selecting or designing software to support children's writing. *The Whole Idea, 4*(1), 6–7.

Slaughter, H. (1988). Indirect and direct teaching in a whole language program. *The Reading Teacher, 42*(1), 30–34.

Smith, C. (1989). Emergent literacy—An environmental concept. *The Reading Teacher, 42*(7), 528.

Smith, F. (1975). The role of prediction in reading. *Elementary English, 54,* 305–311.

Smith, F. (1976). Learning to read by reading. *Language Arts, 53*(3), 297–299, 322.

Smith, F. (1983, May). Reading like a writer. *Language Arts, 60,* 558–567.

Snow, C. E. (1983). Literacy and language: Relationships during the preschool years. *Harvard Educational Review, 53,* 165–189.

Solsken, J. W. (1985, September). Authors of their own learning. *Language Arts, 62,* 491–499.

Soundy, C. S. (1993). Let the story begin! *Childhood Education, 69*(3), 146–149.

Stewart, R. A., Aegerter, J., Davis, D., & Wasketh, B. (1993). Portfolios: Agents of change. *The Reading Teacher, 46*(6), 522–524.

Stipek, D., Rosenblatt, L., & DiRocco, L. Making parents your allies. *Young Children, 49* (3), 4–9.

Strickland, D., & Morrow, L. (1988). Creating a print-rich environment: Emerging readers and writers. *The Reading Teacher, 42*(2), 156–157.

Strickland, D., & Morrow, L. (1988). Reading, writing, and oral language. *The Reading Teacher, 42*(3), 240–241.

Strickland, D., & Morrow, L. (1989). Interactive experiences with story-book reading. *The Reading Teacher, 42*(4), 322–323.

Strickland, D., & Morrow, L. (1989). Young children's early writing development. *The Reading Teacher, 42*(6), 426–427.

Strickland, D., & Morrow, L. (1989). Family literacy and young children. *The Reading Teacher, 42*(7), 530–531.

Strickland, D., & Morrow, L. (1989). Assessment and early literacy. *The Reading Teacher, 42*(8), 634–635.

Strickland, D., & Morrow, L. (1989). Creating curriculum: An emergent literacy perspective. *The Reading Teacher, 42*(9), 722–723.

Sulzby, E. (1985). Children's emergent reading of favorite storybooks: A developmental study. *Reading Research Quarterly, 20*(4), 458–481.

Sulzby, E., (1991). Assessment of emergent literacy: Storybook reading. *The Reading Teacher, 44*(7), 498–500.

Sulzby, E. (1992, April). Research directions: Transitions from emergent to conventional writing. *Language Arts, 69,* 290–423.

Sulzby, E., & Teale, W. (1985). Writing development in early childhood. *Educational Horizons, 64*(1), 8–12.

Sutton, C. (1989). Helping the nonnative English speaker with reading. *The Reading Teacher, 42*(9), 684–689.

Swan, A.M. (1993). Helping children who stutter: What teachers need to know. *Childhood Education, 69*(3), 138–141.

Swift, K. (1993). Try reading workshop in your classroom. *The Reading Teacher, 46*(5), 366–371.

Taylor, B., Short, R., Frye, B., & Shearer, B. (1982, April). Classroom teachers prevent reading failure among low-achieving first-grade students. *The Reading Teacher, 45*(8), 592–597.

Teale, W. H. (1988). Developmentally appropriate assessment of reading and writing in the early childhood classroom. *The Elementary School Journal, 89*(2), 173–183.

Teale, W. H., Hiebert, E. H., & Chittenden, E. A. (1987). Assessing young children's literacy development. *The Reading Teacher, 40*(8), 772–777.

Teale, W., & Martinez, M. (1988). Getting on the right road to reading. Bringing books and young children together in the classroom. *Young Children, 44*(1), 10–15.

Thomas, K. F. (1985, September). Early reading as a social interaction process. *Language Arts, 62,* 469–475.

Throne, J. (1988). Becoming a kindergarten of readers? *Young Children, 43*(6), 10–16.

Trachtenburg, P., & Ferruggia, A. (1989). Big books from little voices: Reaching high risk beginning readers. *The Reading Teacher, 42*(5), 284–289.

Trapanier-Street, M. (1993). What's so new about the project approach? *Childhood Education, 70*(1), 25–28.

Truax, R. R., & Kretschmer, R. R. (1993). Finding new voices in the process of meeting the needs of all children. *Language Arts, 70*(7), 592–601.

Tunnell, M., & Jacobs, J. (1989). Using "real" books: Research findings on literature based reading instruction. *The Reading Teacher, 42*(7), 470–477.

Tway, E. (1990). Evaluation of language and learning. *Language Arts, 67*(3), 307–311.

Valencia, S., & Pearson, P. D. (1987). Reading assessment: Time for a change. *The Reading Teacher, 40*(8), 726–733.

Vukelich, C. (1993). Play: A context for exploring the functions, features, and meaning of writing with peers. *Language Arts, 70*(5), 386–392.

Walker-Dalhouse, D. (1993). Beginning reading and the African American child at risk. *Young Children, 49*(1), 24–28.

Wallace, C., & Goodman, Y. (1989). Research currents: Language and literacy development of multi-lingual learners. *Language Arts, 66*(5), 542–551.

Walton, S. (1989). Katy learns to read and write. *Young Children, 44*(5), 52–57.

Weir, B. (1989). A research base for prekindergarten literacy programs. *The Reading Teacher, 42*(7), 456–460.

Wepner, S. B. (1993). Technology and author studies. *The Reading Teacher, 46*(7), 616–619.

Wild, S. (1990). A proposal for a new spelling curriculum. *The Elementary School Journal, 90*(3), 275–289.

Willert, M. K., & Kamii, C. (1985). Reading in kindergarten: Direct vs. indirect teaching. *Young Children, 40*(4), 3–9.

Wolfgang, C., & Sanders, T. (1981). Defending young children's play as the ladder to literacy. *Theory into Practice, 20*(2), 116–120.

Yaden, D. (1988). Understanding stories through repeated readalouds: How many does it take? *The Reading Teacher, 41*(6).

Yopp, H. K. (1992, May). Developing phonemic awareness in young children. *The Reading Teacher, 45,* 696–703.

Children's Books

Aardema, V. (1975). *Why mosquitoes buzz in people's ears.* New York: Dial.

Alexander, M. (1982). *Maggie's moon.* New York: Dial.

Allard, H. (1974). *The stupids step out.* Boston: Houghton Mifflin.

Barlin, A., & Kalev, N. (1989). *Hello toes: Movement games for children.* Pennington, NJ: Dance Horizons Book, Princeton Book Co.

Berenstain, J. (1969). *Bears on wheels.* New York: Random House.

Blood, C., & Link, M. (1976). *The goat in the rug.* New York: Aladdin.

Brown, M. (1945). *The important book.* New York: Harper.

Brown, M. (1947). *Stone soup.* New York: Scribners.

Brown, R. (1981). *A dark dark tale.* New York: Dial.

Burch, R. (1980). *Ida Early comes over the mountain.* New York: Avon.

Carle, E. (1974). *The very hungry caterpillar.* New York: Scholastic.

Carle, E. (1987). *Have you seen my cat?* New York: Scholastic.

Carle, E. (1984). *The very busy spider.* New York: Philomel Books.

Christelow, E. (1989). *Five little monkeys jumping on the bed.* New York: Clarion.

Cleary, B. (1968). *Ramona the pest.* New York: Morrow.

Cleary, B. (1970). *Runaway Ralph.* New York: Morrow.

Cleary, B. (1977). *Ramona and her father.* New York: Morrow.

Cohen, M. (1977). *When will I read?* New York: Greenwillow Books.

Cole, J. (1982). *A bird's body.* New York: Morrow.

Cole, J. (1989). *Magic schoolbus: Inside the human body.* New York: Scholastic.

Cooney, B. (1982). *Miss Rumphius.* New York: Viking Press.

Crews, D. (1991). *Bigmama's.* New York: Greenwillow Books.

Cummins, P. (1985). *Jimmy Lee did it.* New York: Lothrop, Lee & Shepherd Books.

Day, A. (1988). *Good dog Carl.* San Diego: Green Tiger Press.

De Paola, T. (1975). *Strega Nona: An old tale.* Englewood Cliffs, N.J.: Prentice Hall.

Dixon, F. (1985). *The Hardy Boys: The great airport mystery.* New York: Grosset & Dunlap.

Emberly, B. (1968). *Drummer Hoff.* Englewood Cliffs, NJ: Prentice-Hall.

Feeney, S., & Fielding, A. (1989). *From sand to sea.* Honolulu: University of Hawaii Press.

Flack, M. (1933). *The story of Ping.* New York: Viking Press.

Fowler, S. G. (1992). *Fog.* New York: Greenwillow Books.

Goble, P. (1983). *Star boy.* Scarsdale, NY: Bradbury Press.

Gramatky, H. (1939). *Little Toot.* New York: Putnam.

Gross, R. B. (1979). *Los músicos de brema.* New York: Scholastic.

Hillert, Margaret. (1982). *The funny ride.* Chicago: Follett.

Hoff, S. (1985). *Danny and the dinosaur.* New York: Harper & Row.

Hopkinson, D. (1993). *Sweet Clara and the freedom quilt.* New York: Knopf.

Jonas, A. (1984). *The quilt.* New York: Greenwillow.

Joosse, B. M. (1991). *Mama, do you love me?* San Francisco: Chronicle Books.

Keats, E. J. (1962). *The snowy day.* New York: Viking Press.

Keats, E. J. (1982). *Clemintina's cactus.* New York: Viking Press.

Kellogg, S. (1973). *The island of the skog.* New York: Dial.

Knudson, K. (1992). *Muddigush.* New York: Macmillan.

Lawson, R. (1944). *Rabbit hill.* New York: Viking.

Lenski, L. (1946). *The little fire engine.* New York: Henry Z. Walck.

Littledale, H. (1964). *Alexander.* New York: Parents Magazine Press.

Lobel, A. (1970). *Frog and toad are friends.* New York: Harper.

Lobel, A. (1972). *Frog and toad together.* New York: Harper & Row.

Lobel, A. (1981). *On Market Street.* New York: Greenwillow.

MacLachan, P. (1985). *Sarah, plain and tall.* New York: Harper & Row.

Marshall, E. (1981). *Three by the sea.* New York: D.C. Heath.

Marshall, J. (1974). *George and Martha.* Boston: Houghton Mifflin.

Martin, B., Jr. (1983). *Brown bear, brown bear, what do you see?* New York: Holt, Rinehart & Winston.

Martinson, D. (1975). *Real wild rice.* Duluth, MN: Anishinabe Reading Materials.

Mazer, A. (1991). *The salamander room.* New York: Knopf.

McCloskey, R. (1948). *Blueberries for Sal.* New York: Viking Press.

Minarik, E. H. (1957). *Little bear.* New York: Harper & Row.

Miska, M. (1971). *Annie and the old one.* Boston: Little, Brown & Co.

Munsch, R. (1986). *Love you forever.* Scarborough, Ontario, Canada: Firefly Books.

Munsch, R., & Kusugak, M. (1988). *A promise is a promise.* Toronto: Annick Press, Ltd.

O'Neill, M. (1961). *Hailstones and halibut bones.* New York: Doubleday.

Ormerod, J. (1981). *Sunshine.* New York: Lothrop, Lee & Shepard Books.

Ormerod, J. (1982). *Moonlight.* New York: Lothrop, Lee & Shepard Books.

Owens, M. B. (1988). *A caribou alphabet.* Brunswick, ME: The Dog Ear Press.

Oxenbury, H. (1982). *Good night, Good morning.* New York: Dial.

Parents Magazine read-aloud originals. New York: Bantam Books.

Parish, P. (1963). *Amelia Bedelia.* New York: Harper & Row.

Patterson, F. (1985). *Koko's kitten.* New York: Scholastic.

Payne, E. (1944). *Katy No-pocket.* Boston: Houghton Mifflin.

Potter, B. (1902). *Peter Rabbit.* London: Warne.

Prelutsky, J. (1976). *Nightmares: Poems to trouble your sleep.* New York: Greenwillow.

Rattigan, J. K. (1993). *Dumpling soup.* Boston: Little, Brown & Co.

Reading Rainbow Library. (1987). *Gregory, the terrible eater.* New York: Checkerboard Press.

Rey, H. A. (1941). *Curious George.* Boston: Houghton Mifflin.

Rey, H. A. (1952). *Curious George rides a bike.* Boston: Houghton Mifflin.

Robinson, B. (1972). *The best Christmas pageant ever.* New York: Harper & Row.

Rogers, J. (1988). *Dinosaurs are 568.* New York: Greenwillow.

Rogers, J., & Munoz, R. (1988). *The runaway mittens.* New York: Greenwillow.

Seuss, Dr. (Geisel, T. S.). (1947). *McElligot's pool.* New York: Random House.

Seuss, Dr. (Geisel, T. S.). (1957). *The cat in the hat.* New York: Random House.

Seuss, Dr. (Geisel, T. S.). (1974). *Great day for up.* New York: Beginner Books, Random House.

Sharmat, M. W. (1962). *Nate the great.* New York: Coward, McCann & Geoghegan.

Spier, P. (1961). *The fox went out on a chilly night.* Garden City, New York: Doubleday.

Spier, P. (1977). *Noah's ark.* Garden City, New York: Doubleday.

Steig, W. (1982). *Doctor DeSoto.* New York: Farrar, Straus & Giroux.

Steiner, B. (1988). *Whale brother.* New York: Walker & Company.

Steptoe, J. (1984). *The story of Jumping Mouse: A Native American legend.* New York: Lothrop, Lee & Shepard.

Stevenson, James. (1972). *The bear who had no place to go.* New York: Harper & Row.

Viorst, J. (1972). *Alexander and the terrible, horrible, no good, very bad day.* New York: Atheneum.

Viorst, J. (1974). *Rosie and Michael.* New York: Antheneum.

Walsh, J. P. (1992). *When Grandma came.* New York: Penguin.

Watanabe, S. (1980). *What a good lunch!* New York: N. Collins Publishers.

Waterton, B. (1978). *A salmon for Simon.* Hartford, CT: Connecticut Printers.

Wheeler, C. (1982). *Marmalade's snowy day.* New York: Knopf.

White, E. B. (1952). *Charlotte's web*. New York: Harper & Row.

Wilder, L. I. (1953). *Little house on the prairie*. New York: Harper & Row.

Williams, M. (1963). *The velveteen rabbit*. New York: Godine.

Wiseman, B. (1978). *Morris has a cold*. New York: Dodd Mead.

Wolf, S. (1992). *Peter's truck*. Morton Grove, IL: Whitman.

Wood, A. (1984). *The napping house*. New York: Harcourt Brace.

Wood, A. (1985). *King Bidgood's in the bathtub*. San Diego: Harcourt, Brace Jovanovich.

Yashima, T. (1955). *Crow boy*. New York: Viking.

Zion, G. (1956). *Harry the dirty dog*. New York: Harper & Row.

Children's Book Series

Bank Street ready-to-read books. New York: Bantam Books.

Braun, F. L. The Wizard of Oz series. CN Potter, Derrydale Books, Grosset & Dunlap, Random House, Rand McNally, Puffin Books.

Children's Press new true books. Chicago: Children's Press.

Choose your own adventure series. New York: Bantam Books.

Dell yearling books. New York: Dell Publishing.

Dial easy-to-read books. New York: Dial Books for Young Children.

Farley, W. *The black stallion*. New York: Random House. (Sixteen more books in set.)

Hoban, R. Francis series. New York: Harper & Row.

Keene, C. Nancy Drew series. Wanderer books, Pocket Books, Grosset & Dunlap.

Random House picturebook readers. New York: Random House.

Children's Magazines

Highlights for Children, Inc. *Highlights for children*. Columbus, OH.

National Wildlife Federation. *Ranger Rick*. Washington, DC.

Instructional Reading Materials

Clay, M. M. (1972). *Sand—the concepts about print test*. Auckland, New Zealand: Heinemann.

Clay, M. M. (1979). *Stones—the concepts about print test*, Aukland, New Zealand: Heinemann.

Rigby Education. (1984). *Mrs. Wishy Washy*. San Diego, CA: Wright Group.

Scholastic hello reading books. New York: Scholastic.

Reference Materials

Meisels, S. J., Dichtelmeller, M., Dorfman, A., Jablon, J. R., & Marsden, D. B. (1993). *The work sampling system (tm) resource guide*. Ann Arbor, MI: Rebus Planning Associates, Inc.

McWhirter, N. (1994). *Guinness book of world records*. New York: Sterling.

Peterson, R. T. (1961). *Field guide to the birds*. Boston: Houghton Mifflin.

Wittles, H. (1972). *Clear and simple thesaurus dictionary*. New York: Grosset & Dunlap.

Computer Software

Apple early language connections. Cupertino, CA: Apple Computer.

Broderbund's Living Books. (1991). Grandma and me. Broderbund Software, Inc.

Broderbund's Living Books. (1992). Arthur's teacher trouble. Broderbund Software, Inc.

Broderbund's Living Books. (1993). New kid on the block. Broderbund Software, Inc.

Broderbund's Living Books. (1993). Tortoise and hare. Broderbund Software, Inc.

Broderbund's Living Books. (1994). The ruff's bone. Broderbund Software, Inc.

Broderbund's Living Books. (1994). Little monster. Broderbund Software, Inc.

Kid pix. (1991). Broderbund Software, Inc.

Larimer, N., & Hermann, M. A. Mickey's Magic Reader. Cupertino, CA: Apple Computer, Inc.

Literature Enrichment Activities for Paperbacks. (1984). Amelia Bedelia. Sundance Publishers & Distributors.

The media experience, (1991). Boston: Houghton Mifflin.

Millie's math house, Edmark. 800-426-0856.

The playroom, Broderbund, 800-521-6263.

Storybook weaver, MECC. 800-685-6322.

Reading Programs

Bookworm. (1991). Boston: Houghton Mifflin.

Celebrate reading. (1993). Glenview, IL: Scott, Foresman.

A new view. (1993). New York. McGraw-Hill.

The story box. (1990). Bothell, WA.: The Wright Group.

Teachers' Guides

Baskwill, J., & Whitman, P. (1986). *Whole language sourcebook.* Ontario, Canada: Scholastic-TAB Publications.

Bolton, F., Green, R., Pollack, J., Scarfee, B., & Snowball, D. (1986). *Bookshelf stage 1: Teacher's resource book.* New York: Multimedia International (U.K.) Ltd.

Hurst, C. O. (1992). *Literature-based thematic units.* Allen, TX: DLM Publishing.

Hurst, C. O. (1990). *Once upon a time . . . An encyclopedia for successfully using literature with young children.* Allen, TX: DLM Publishing.

Level 1 teacher guide. Bothell, WA: Thomas C. Wright, Inc./The Wright Group.

Morrow, L. M., & Sulzby, E. (1993). *Teacher's workshop: An instructional handbook for kindergarten teachers.* Glenview IL: Scott, Foresman.

Roettger, D. (1987). *"Frog and toad are friends" teacher's guide. Reading beyond the basal.* Logan, IA: Perfection Form.

Scott, Foresman. (1993). *Celebrate Reading, Professional Handbook.* Glenview, IL: Scott, Foresman.

INDEX

ABOUT THE AUTHORS

MARJORIE V. FIELDS   **KATHERINE L. SPANGLER**

MARJORIE V. FIELDS is professor of early childhood education at the University of Alaska Southeast. She coordinates graduate and undergraduate early childhood teacher education programs on campus and offers early childhood endorsement courses throughout the state of Alaska. A former kindergarten and first grade teacher, she teaches courses in beginning literacy, guidance and discipline, and classroom management as well as general early childhood topics. She has published several articles in professional journals and chapters in edited books on the topic of emergent literacy, has also written a book for parents on that topic, and has recently written *Constructive Guidance and Discipline: Preschool and Primary Education* (Macmillan, 1994). She is active in professional associations at the local and national levels, having just completed a term as vice-president of the National Association of Early Childhood Teacher Educators. Marjorie has also served on the Governing Board of the National Association for the Education of Young Children. In her spare time she has raised two sons: Michael, who is currently in law school, and David, who is just completing a degree in engineering.

KATHERINE L. (KATY) SPANGLER is associate professor at the University of Alaska Southeast, where she coordinated and teaches in an elementary teacher certification program for students in small communities in Alaska. A former bilingual elementary teacher, she now teaches courses in child development, reading, writing, and children's literature. As a specialist in children's literature of Alaska and the North, Katy is the Alaska editor of *Exploring Our United States: the Pacific States* (Oryx, 1994). Katy is also an active volunteer in the classroom of her young children, Patrick and Mary McCormick, who are pictured on pages 231, 235, and 261 of this book.